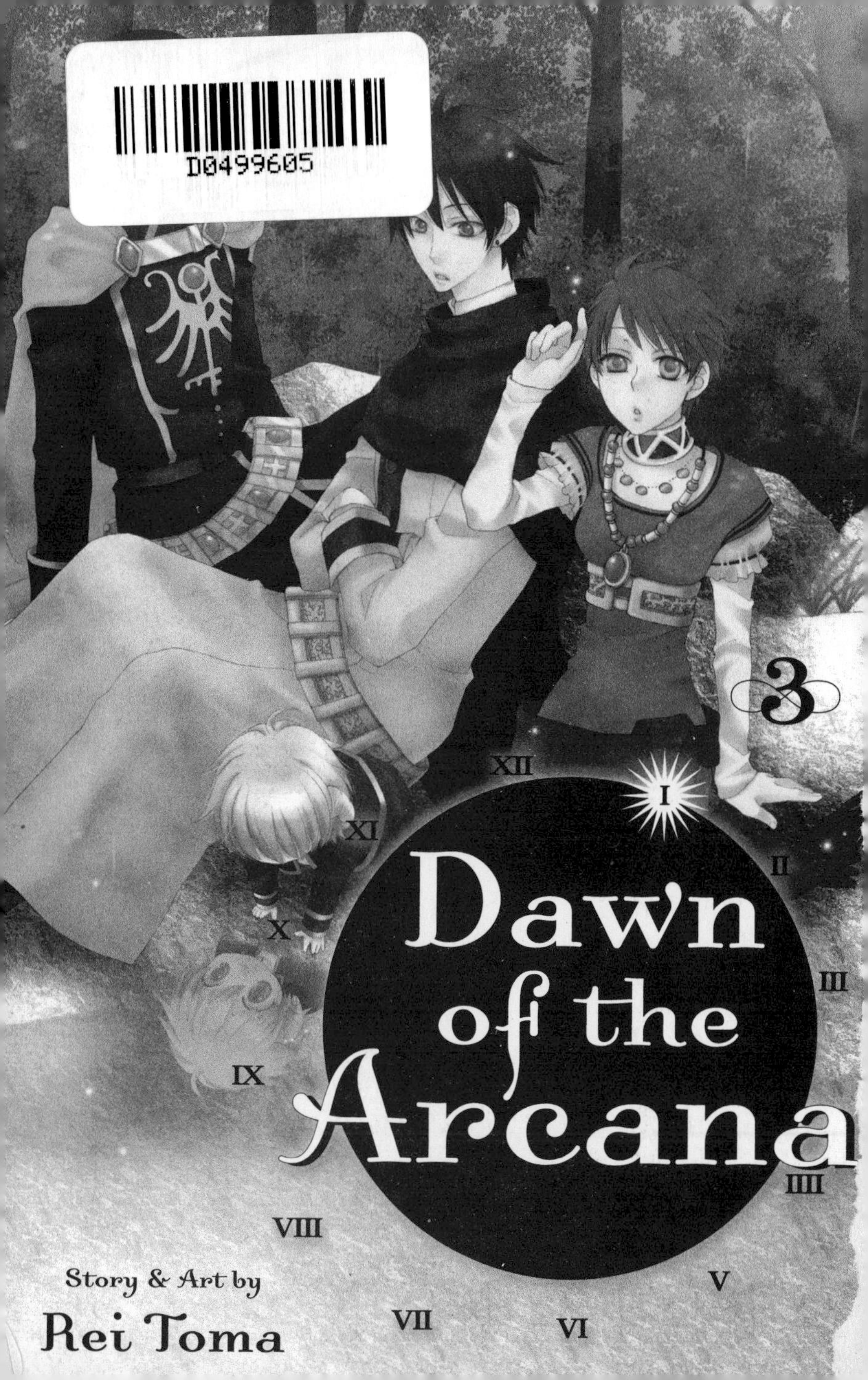
3
XII
I
XI
II
Dawn of the Arcana
X
III
IX
IIII
VIII
V
VII
VI
Story & Art by
Rei Toma

Dawn of the Arcana

Volume 3

XII

XI

X

IX

CONTENTS

VIII

VII

VI

characters

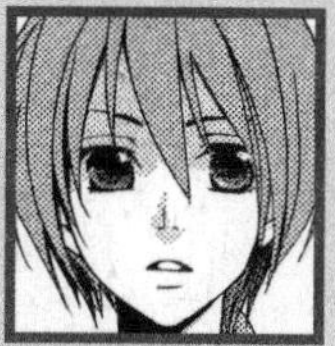

Nakaba
The princess royal of Senan. Strong of will and noble of spirit, she possesses a strange power.

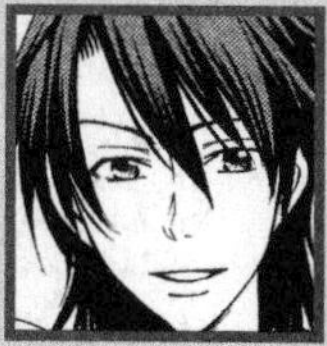

Caesar
The second-born prince of Belquat. Nakaba's husband through a marriage of political convenience. Headstrong and selfish.

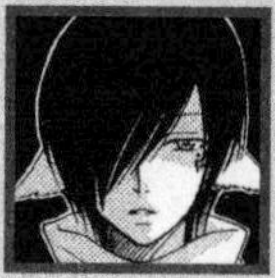

Loki
Nakaba's attendant. His senses of perception are unmatched.

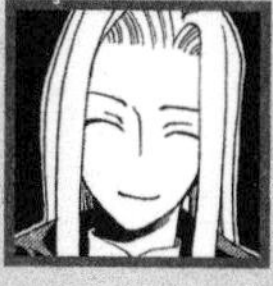

Bellinus
Caesar's attendant. Always cool and collected.

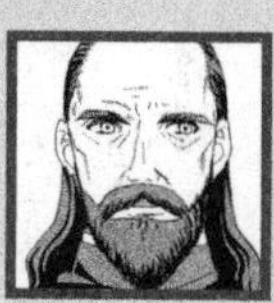

Guran
King of Belquat.

story

• Wed to Prince Caesar as a symbol of peace between their two countries, Nakaba is actually little more than a hostage. Unbeknownst to King Guran, she is a survivor of the race he tried to destroy for fear of their power.

• The political marriage between Nakaba and Caesar got off to a rocky start. As they grew to know each other, the gulf between them began to close, but Loki was quick to warn Nakaba not to let Caesar into her heart. Despite herself, Nakaba finds her feelings for Caesar deepening.

Neighboring Kingdoms

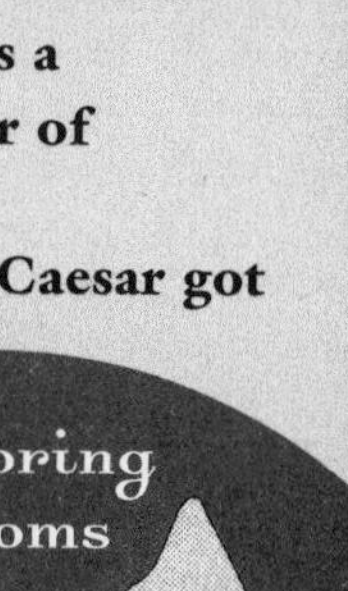
Senan
Belquat

Senan
A poor kingdom in the cold north of the island. Militarily weak.

Belquat
A powerful country that thrives thanks to its temperate climate.

Chapter 8

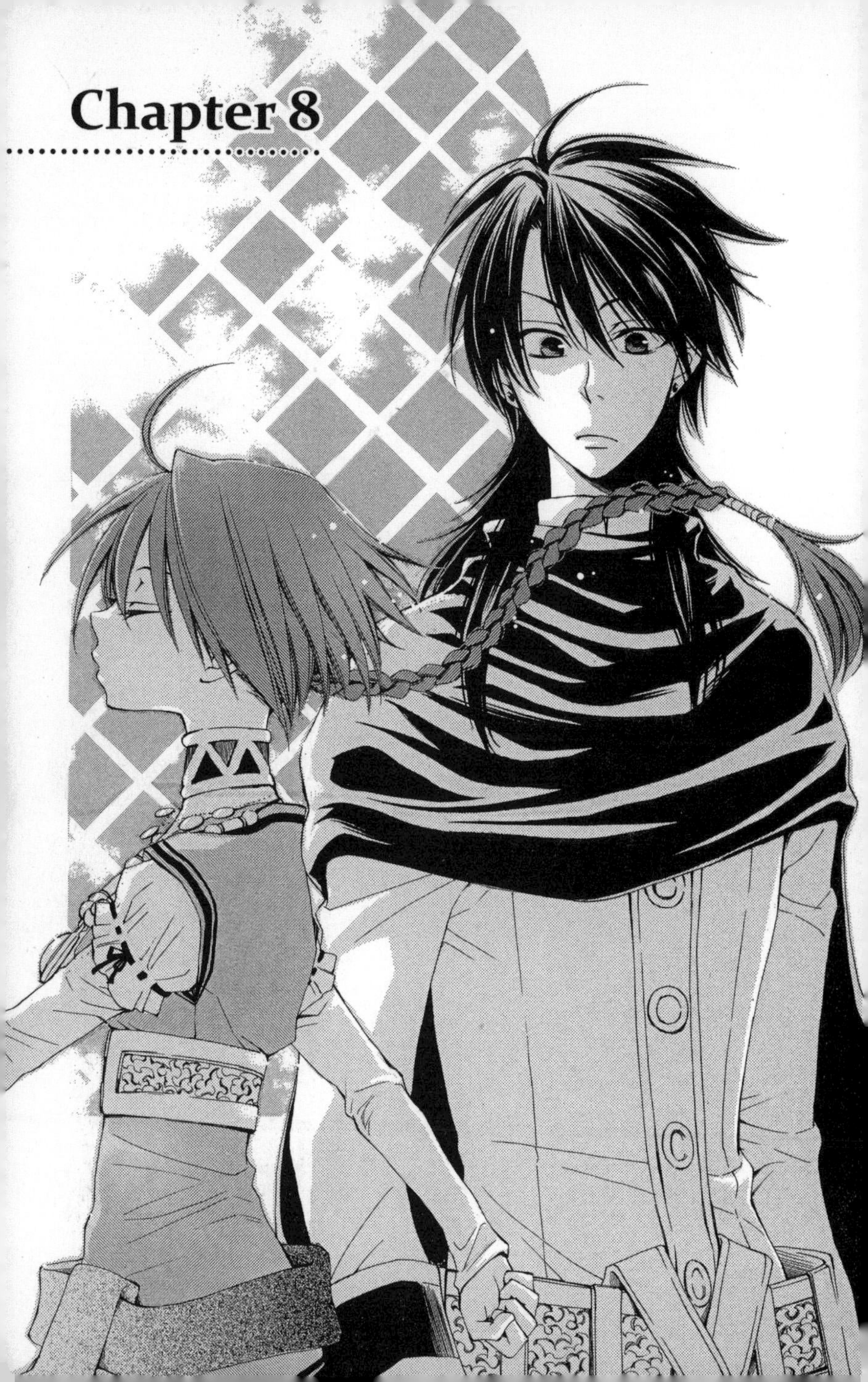

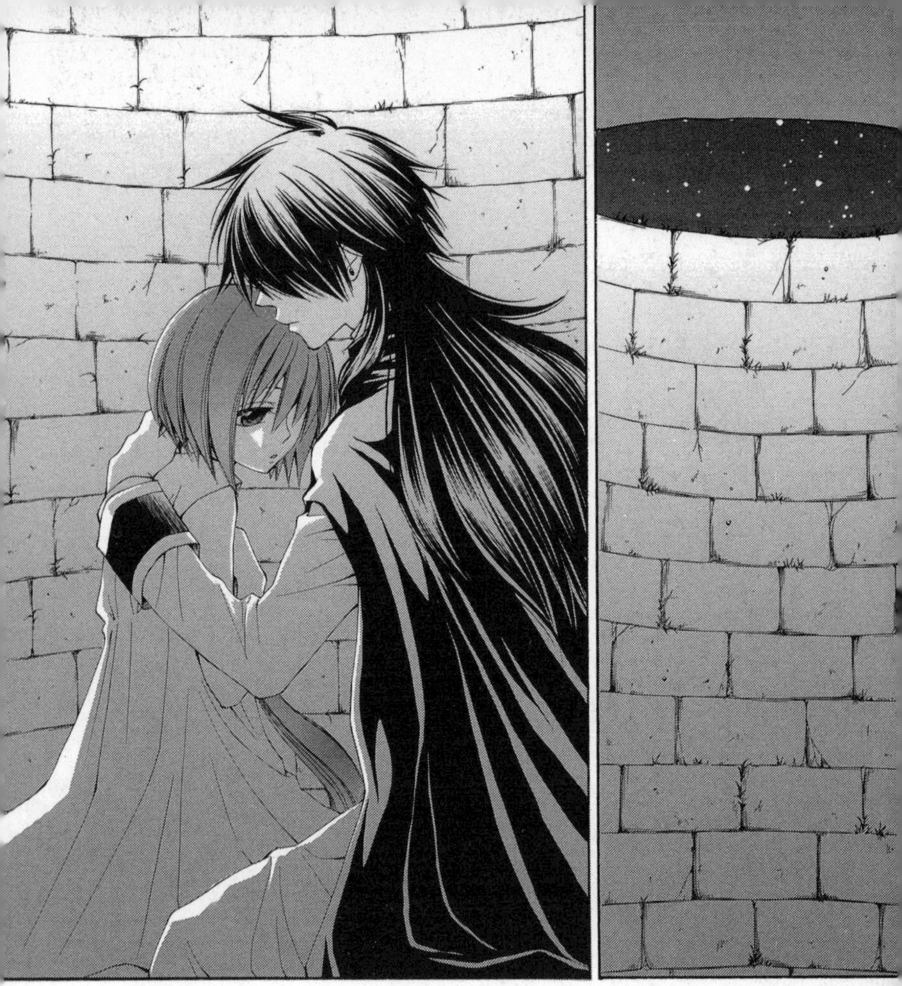

Dawn of the Arcana

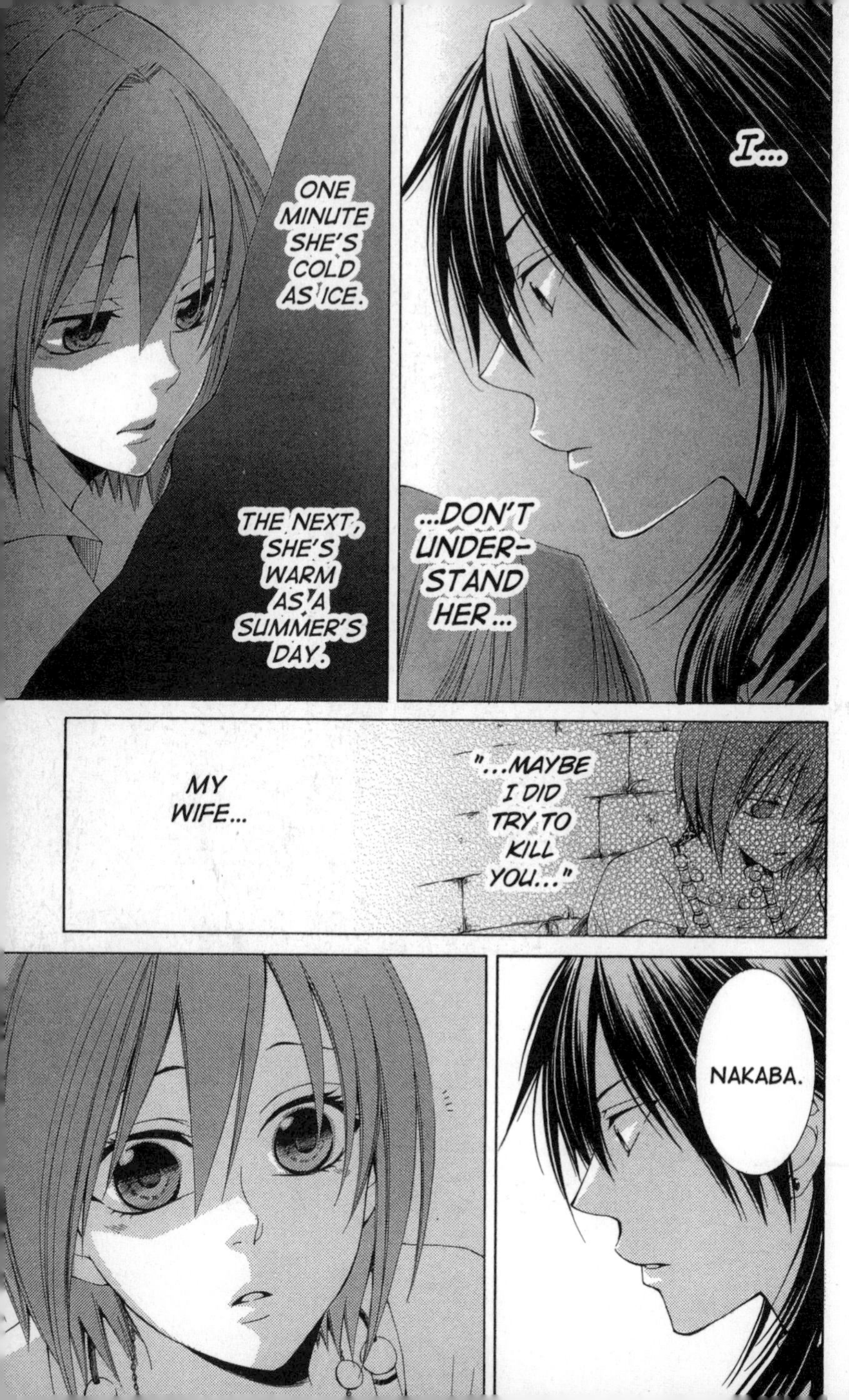
I...
...DON'T UNDERSTAND HER...
ONE MINUTE SHE'S COLD AS ICE.
THE NEXT, SHE'S WARM AS A SUMMER'S DAY.
"...MAYBE I DID TRY TO KILL YOU..."
MY WIFE...
NAKABA.

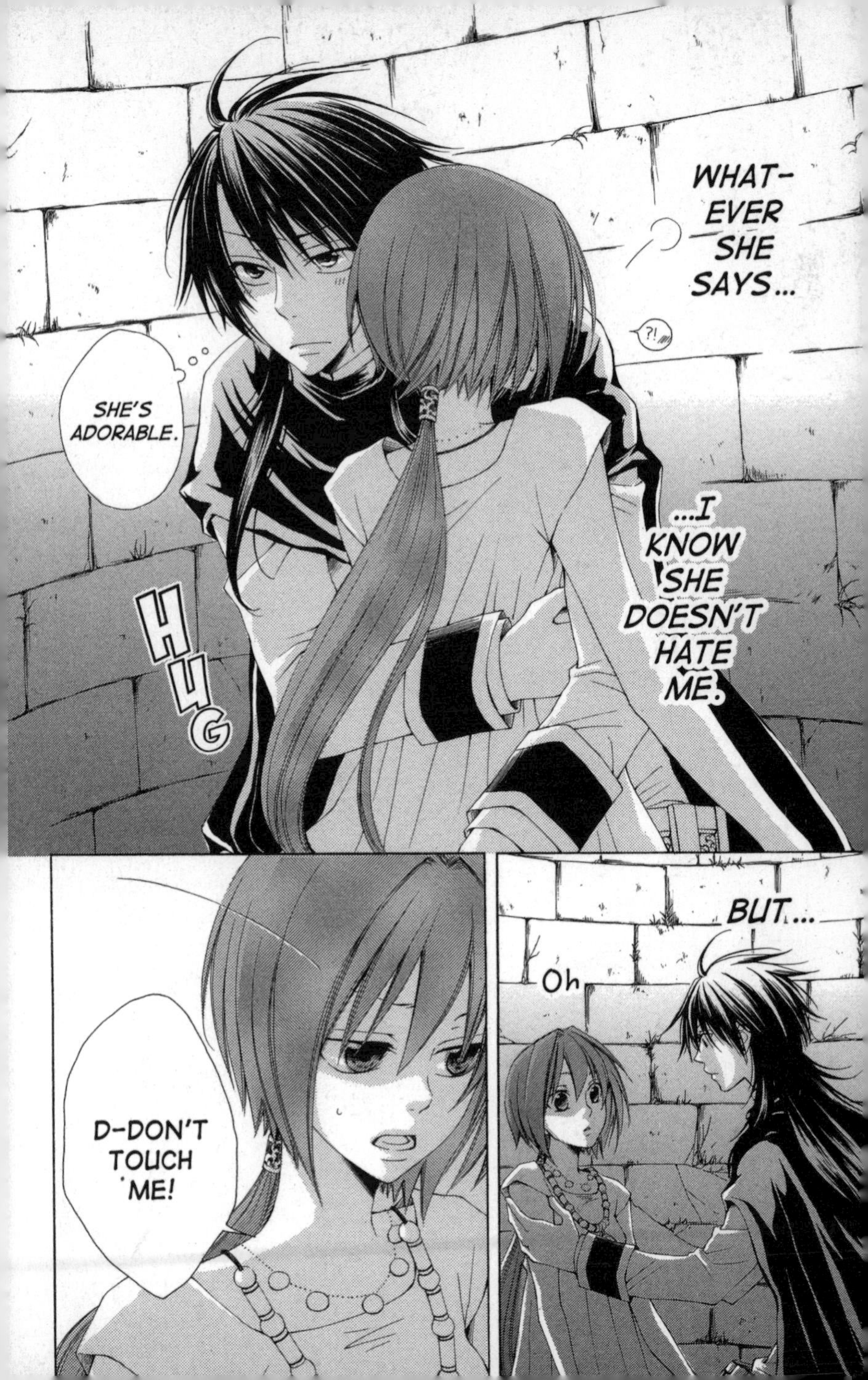
WHAT-EVER SHE SAYS...
?!
SHE'S ADORABLE.
...I KNOW SHE DOESN'T HATE ME.
HUG
BUT...
Oh
D-DON'T TOUCH ME!

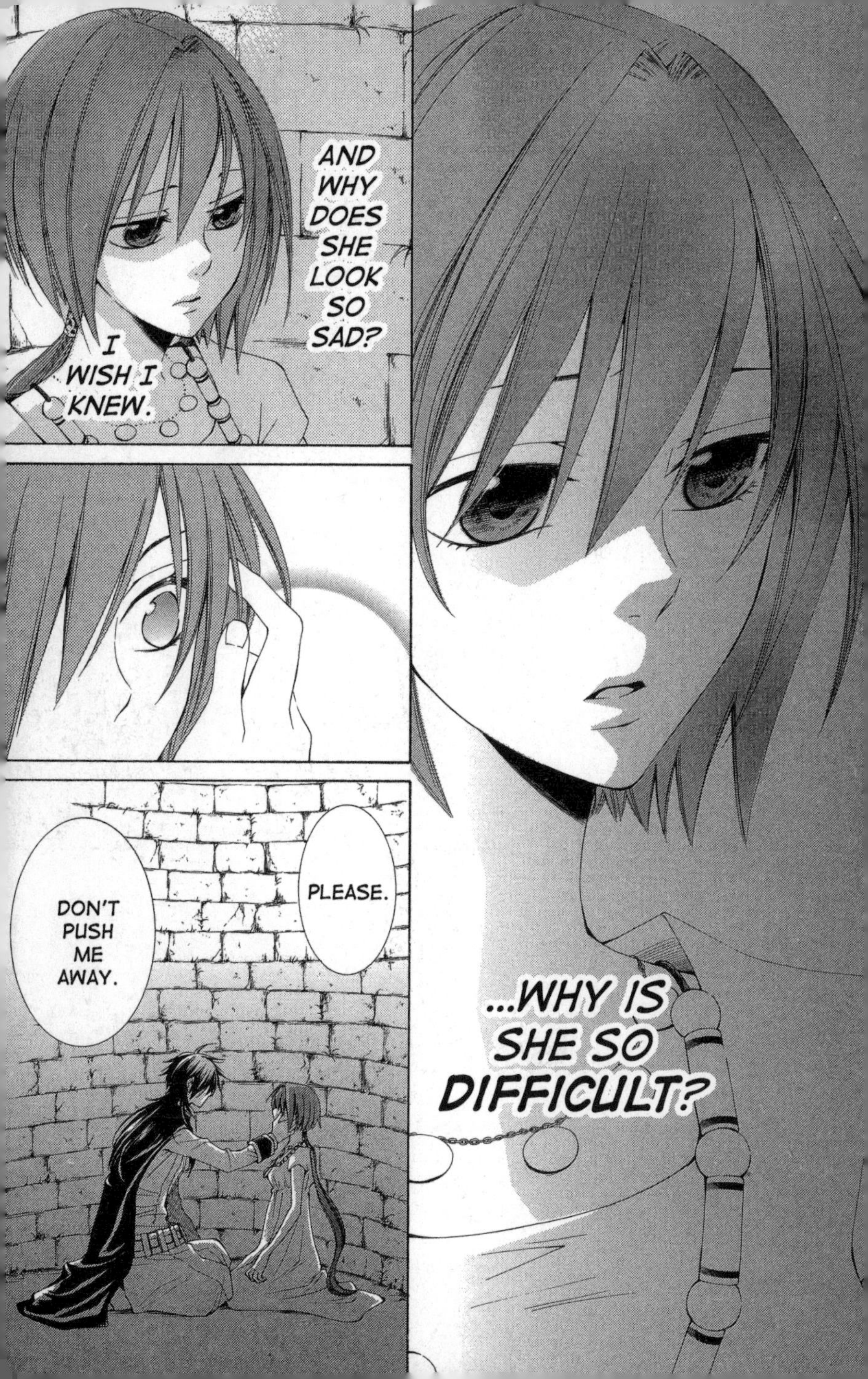
...WHY IS SHE SO DIFFICULT?
AND WHY DOES SHE LOOK SO SAD?
I WISH I KNEW.
PLEASE.
DON'T PUSH ME AWAY.

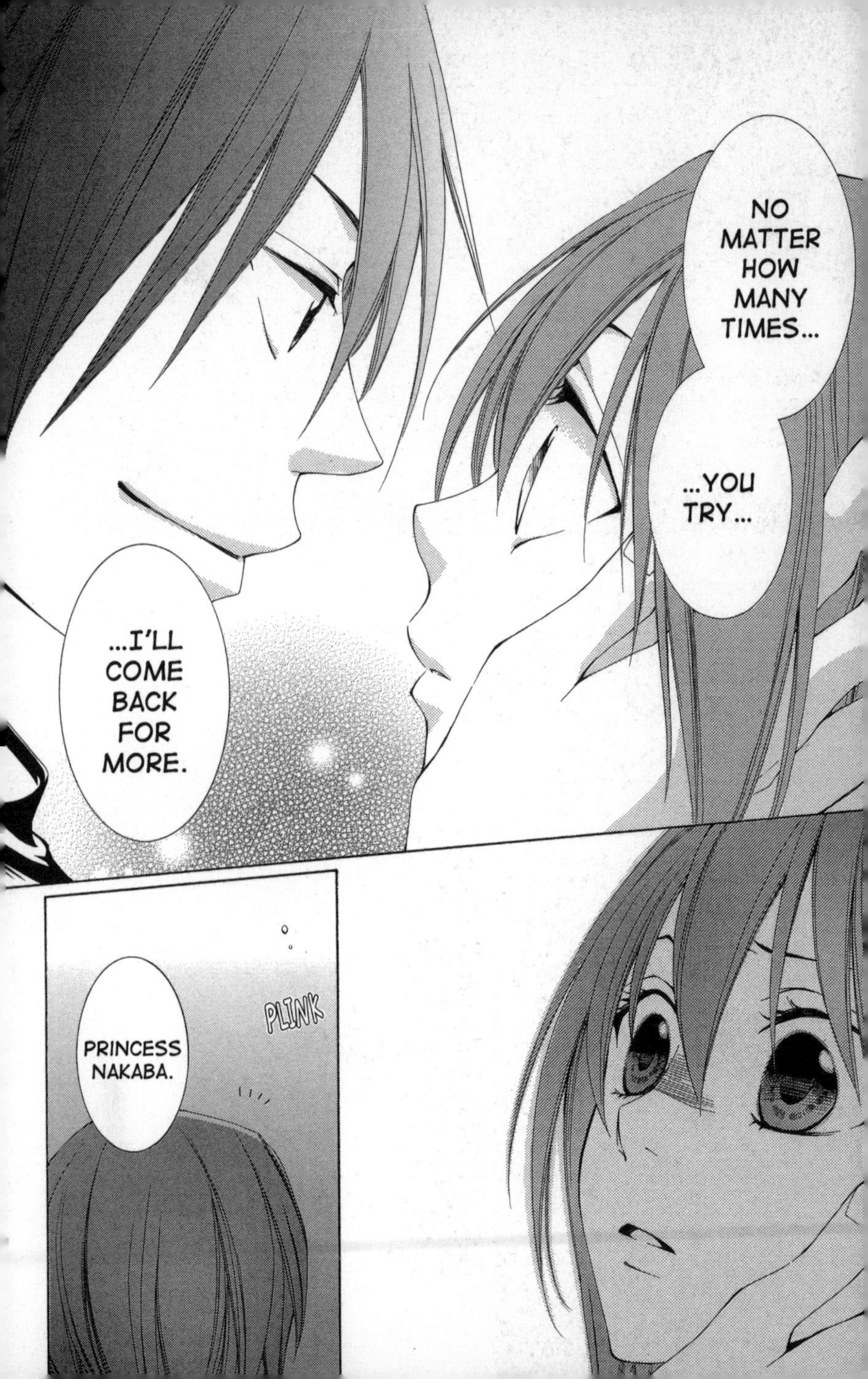
NO MATTER HOW MANY TIMES...
...YOU TRY...
...I'LL COME BACK FOR MORE.
PLINK
PRINCESS NAKABA.

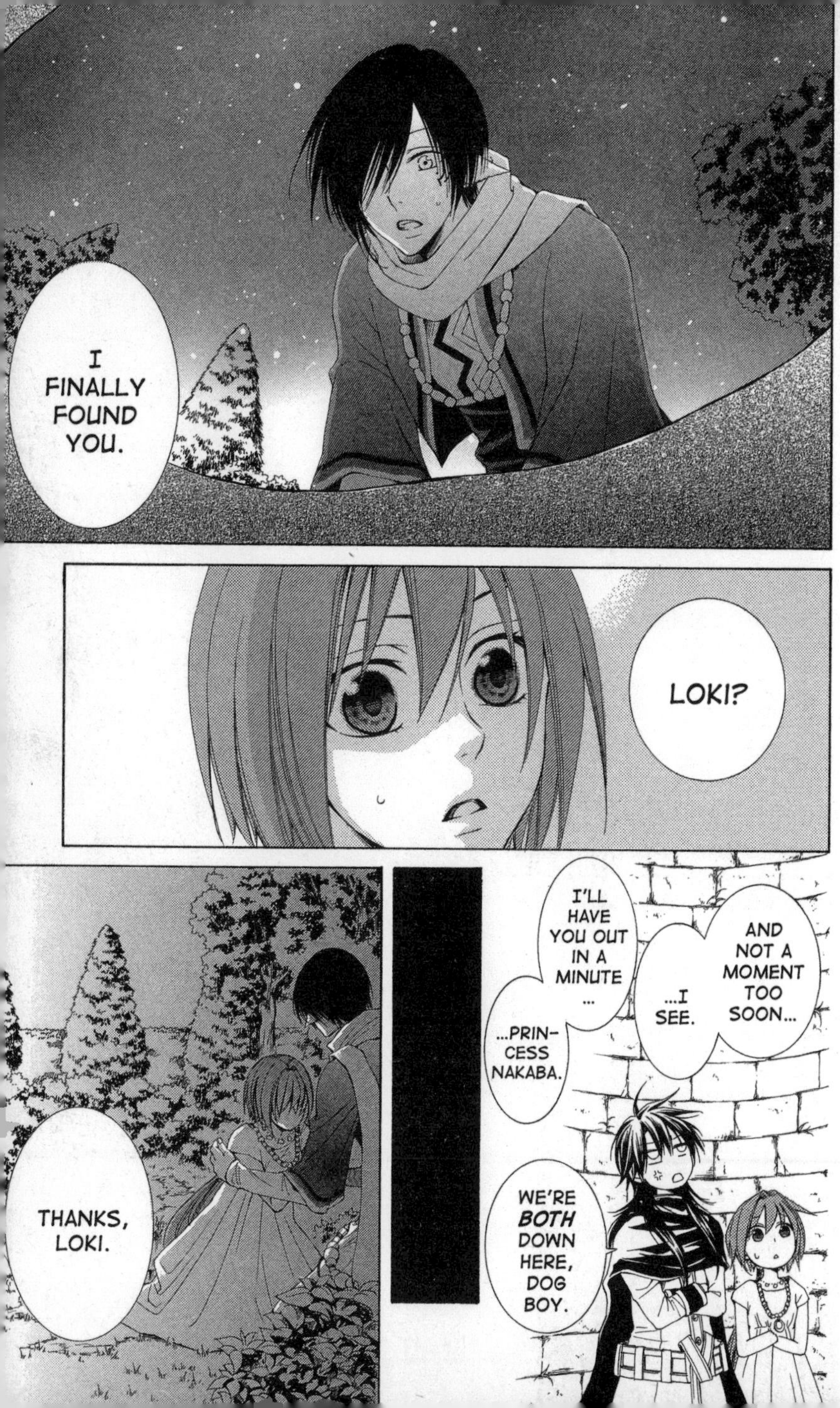
I FINALLY FOUND YOU.
LOKI?
AND NOT A MOMENT TOO SOON...
...I SEE.
I'LL HAVE YOU OUT IN A MINUTE ...
...PRINCESS NAKABA.
WE'RE *BOTH* DOWN HERE, DOG BOY.
THANKS, LOKI.

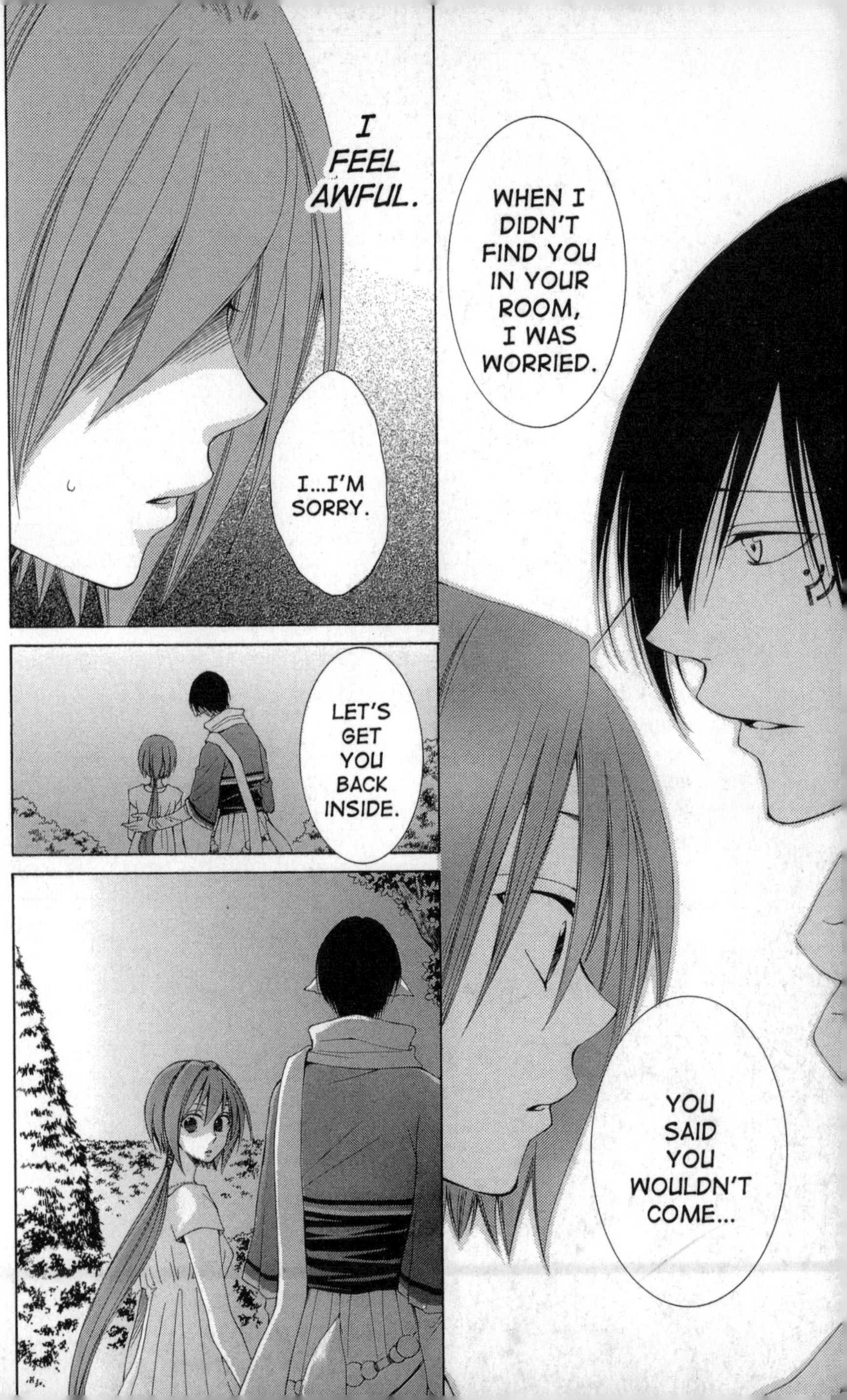
WHEN I DIDN'T FIND YOU IN YOUR ROOM, I WAS WORRIED.
YOU SAID YOU WOULDN'T COME...
I FEEL AWFUL.
I...I'M SORRY.
LET'S GET YOU BACK INSIDE.

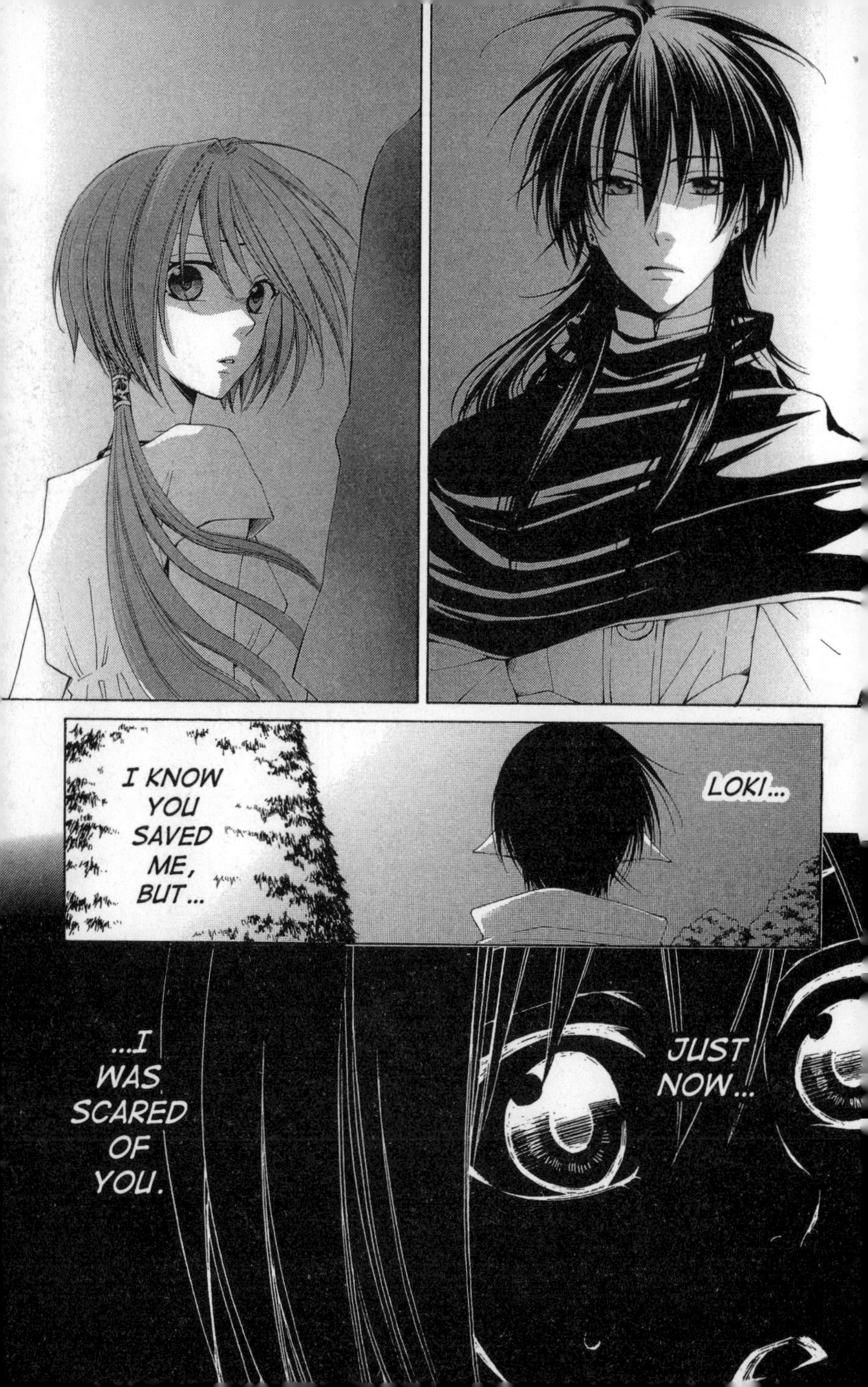
LOKI...
I KNOW YOU SAVED ME, BUT...
JUST NOW...
...I WAS SCARED OF YOU.

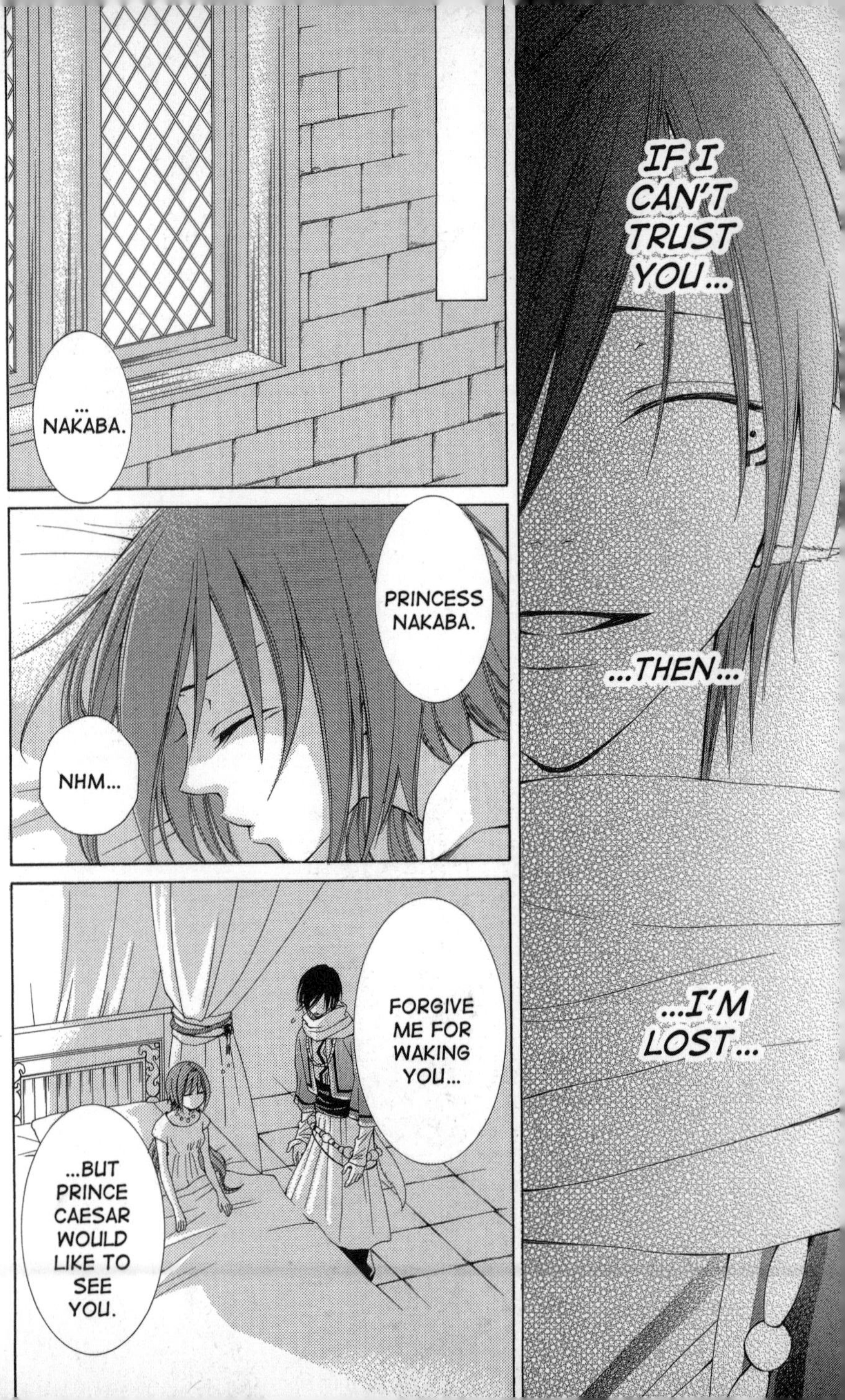
IF I CAN'T TRUST YOU...
...THEN...
...I'M LOST...
... NAKABA.
PRINCESS NAKABA.
NHM...
FORGIVE ME FOR WAKING YOU...
...BUT PRINCE CAESAR WOULD LIKE TO SEE YOU.

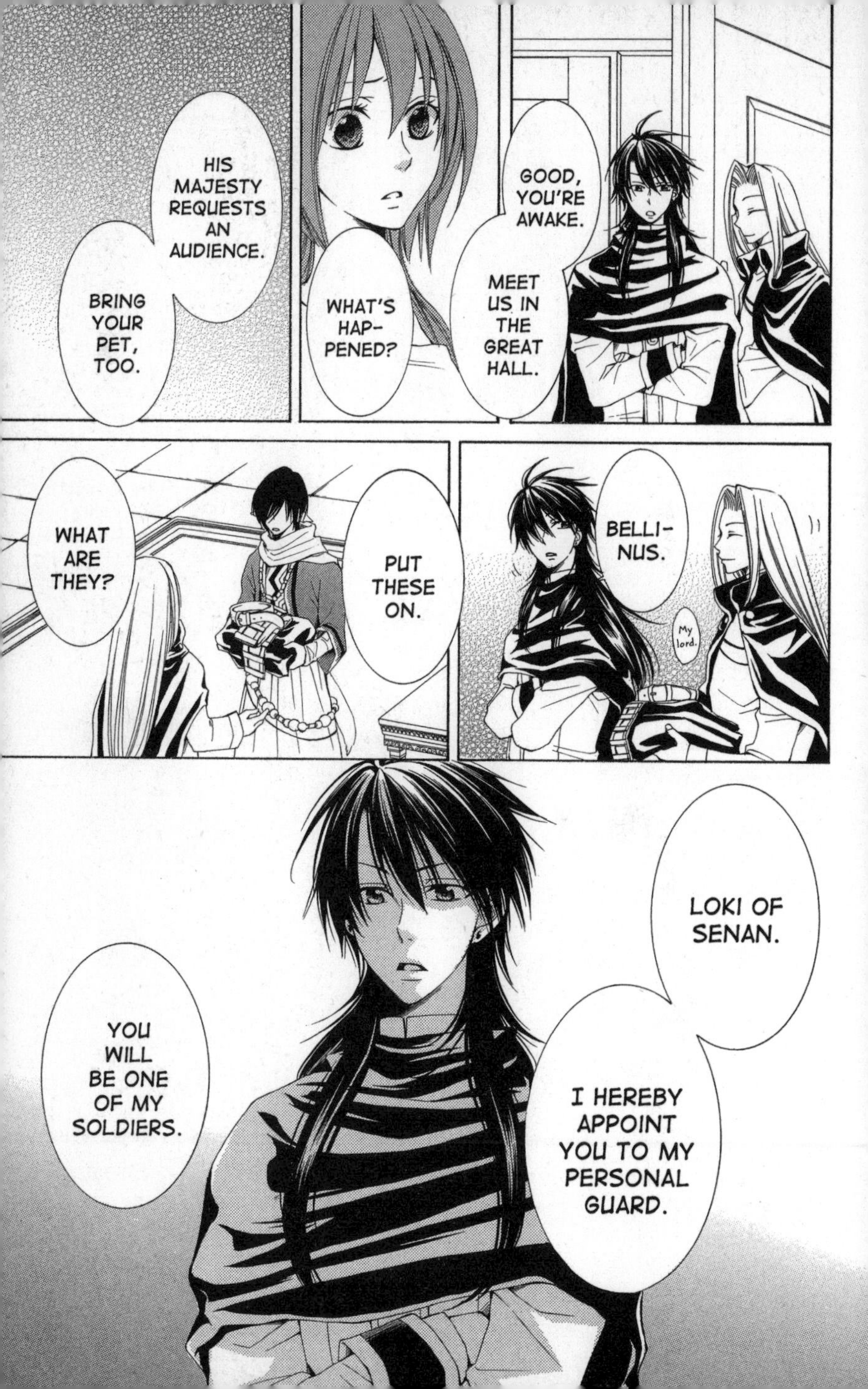
GOOD, YOU'RE AWAKE.
MEET US IN THE GREAT HALL.
WHAT'S HAP-PENED?
HIS MAJESTY REQUESTS AN AUDIENCE.
BRING YOUR PET, TOO.
BELLI-NUS.
My lord.
PUT THESE ON.
WHAT ARE THEY?
LOKI OF SENAN.
I HEREBY APPOINT YOU TO MY PERSONAL GUARD.
YOU WILL BE ONE OF MY SOLDIERS.

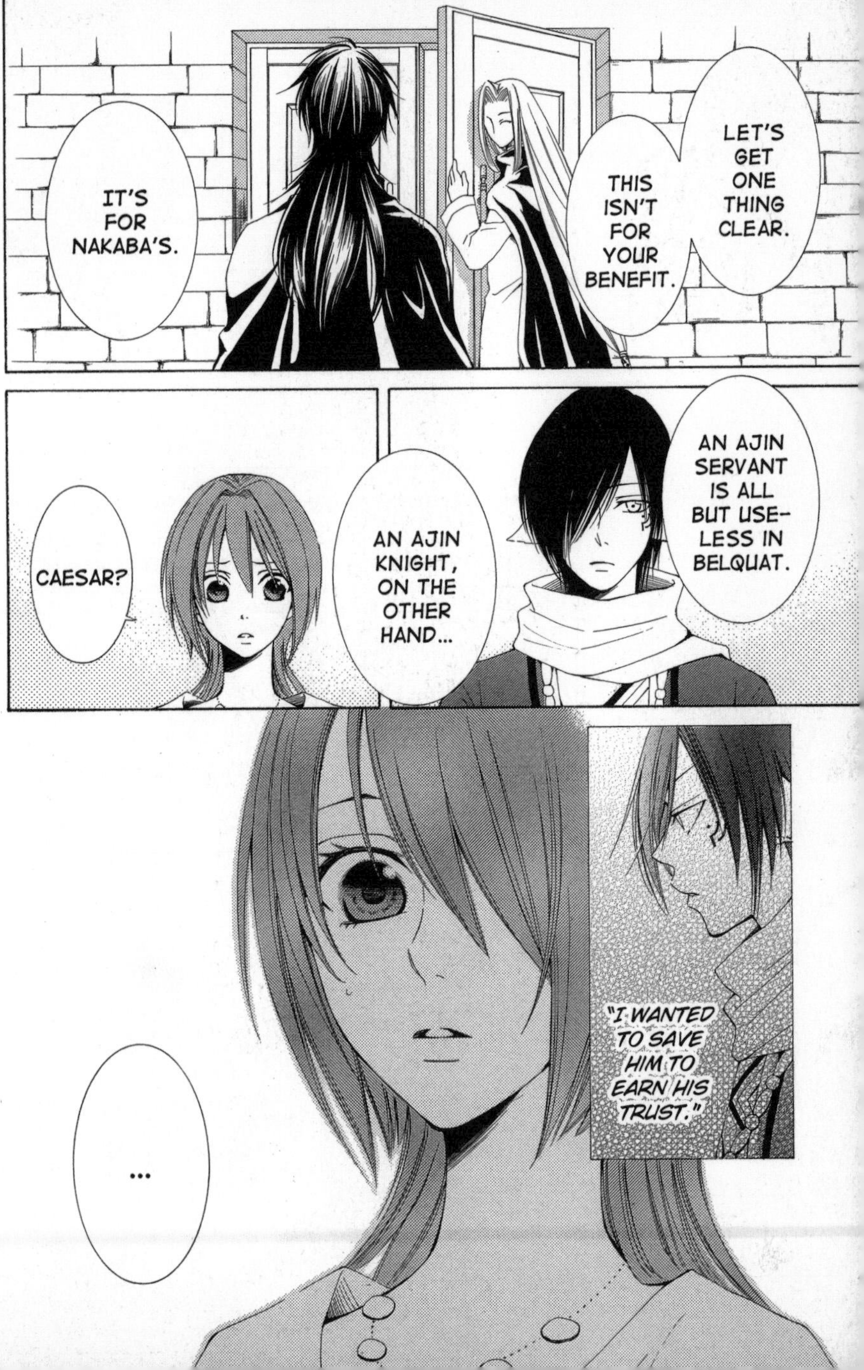
LET'S GET ONE THING CLEAR.
THIS ISN'T FOR YOUR BENEFIT.
IT'S FOR NAKABA'S.
AN AJIN SERVANT IS ALL BUT USE-LESS IN BELQUAT.
AN AJIN KNIGHT, ON THE OTHER HAND...
CAESAR?
"I WANTED TO SAVE HIM TO EARN HIS TRUST."
...

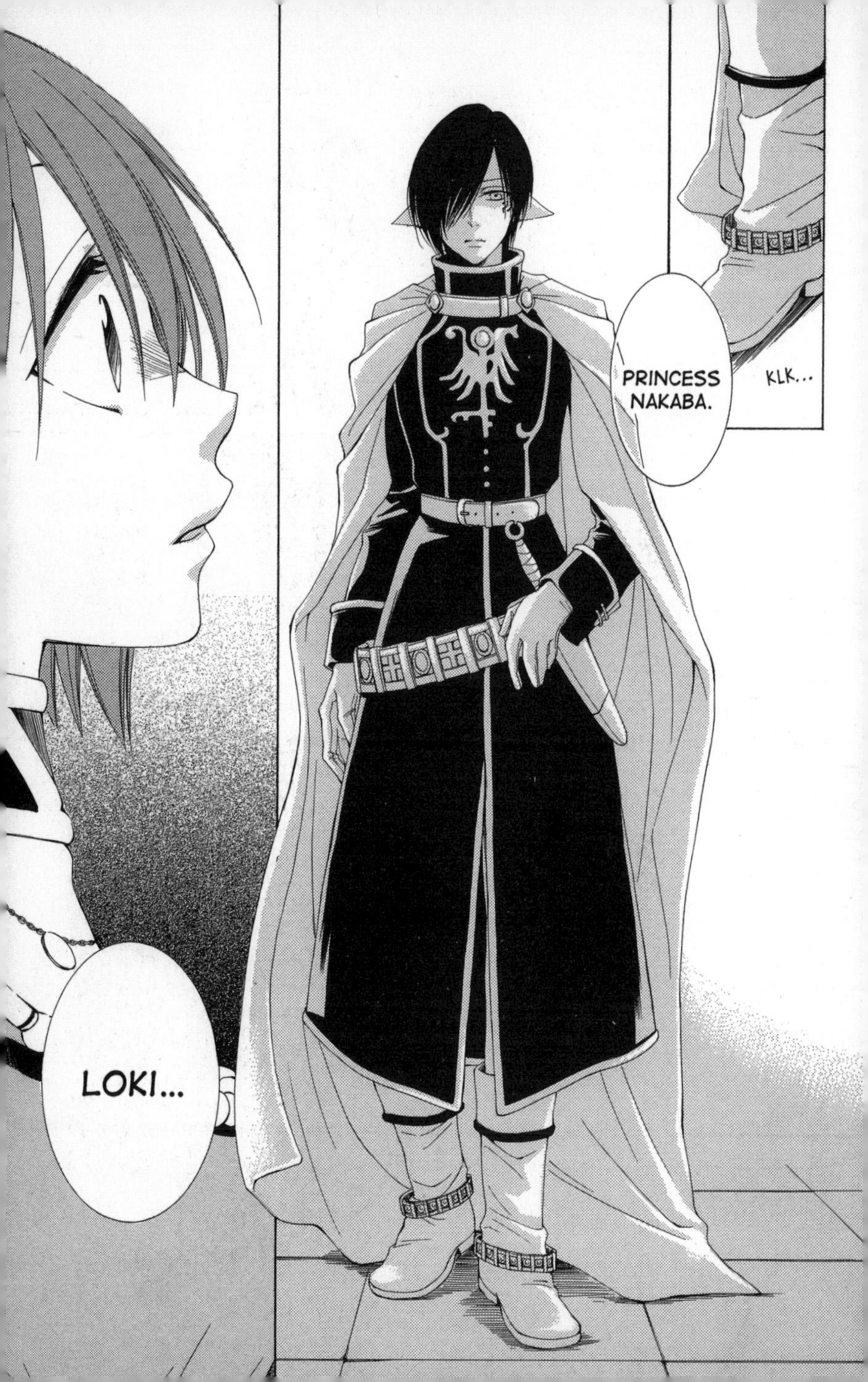
KLK...
PRINCESS NAKABA.
LOKI...

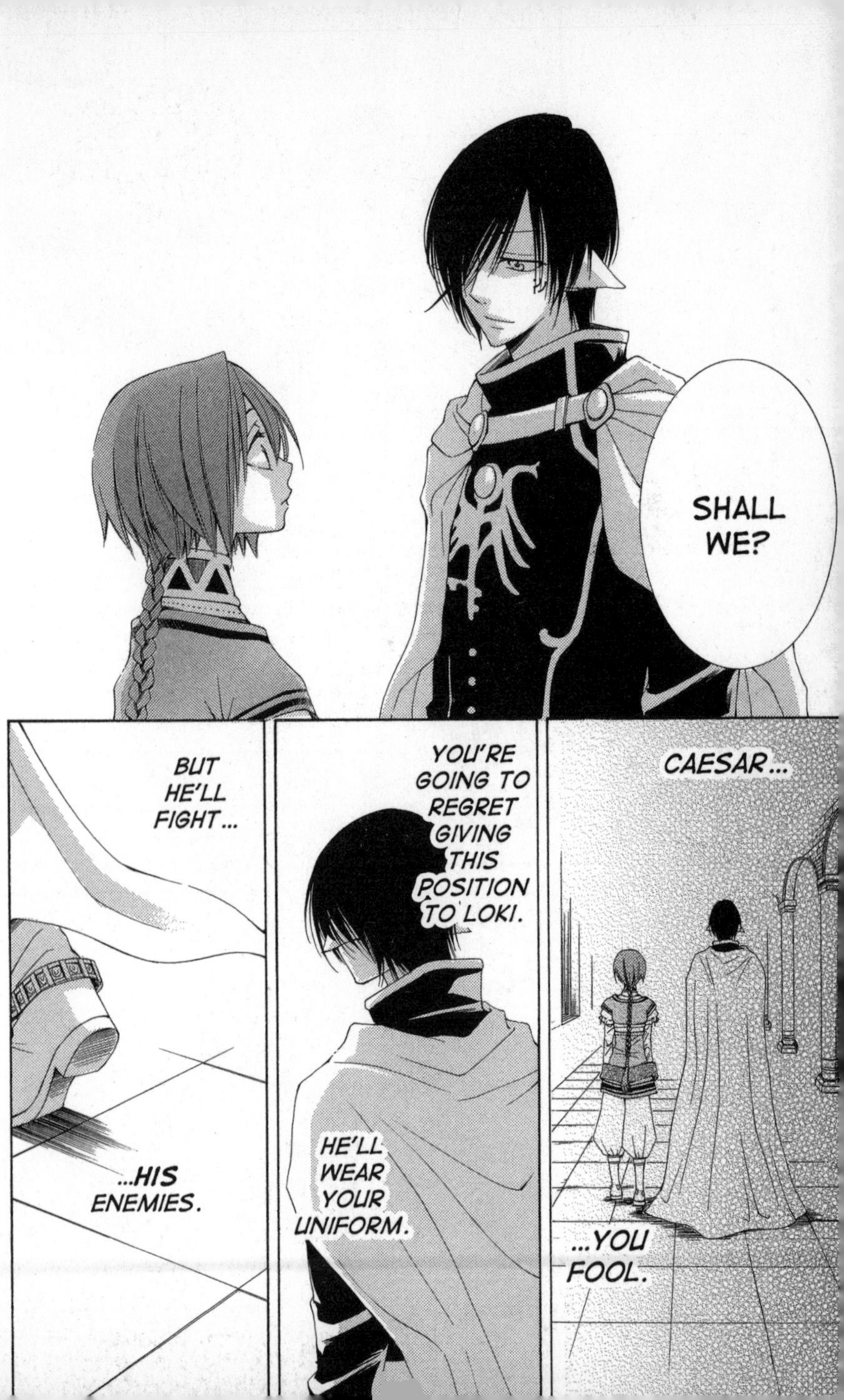
SHALL WE?
CAESAR...
...YOU FOOL.
YOU'RE GOING TO REGRET GIVING THIS POSITION TO LOKI.
HE'LL WEAR YOUR UNIFORM.
BUT HE'LL FIGHT...
...HIS ENEMIES.

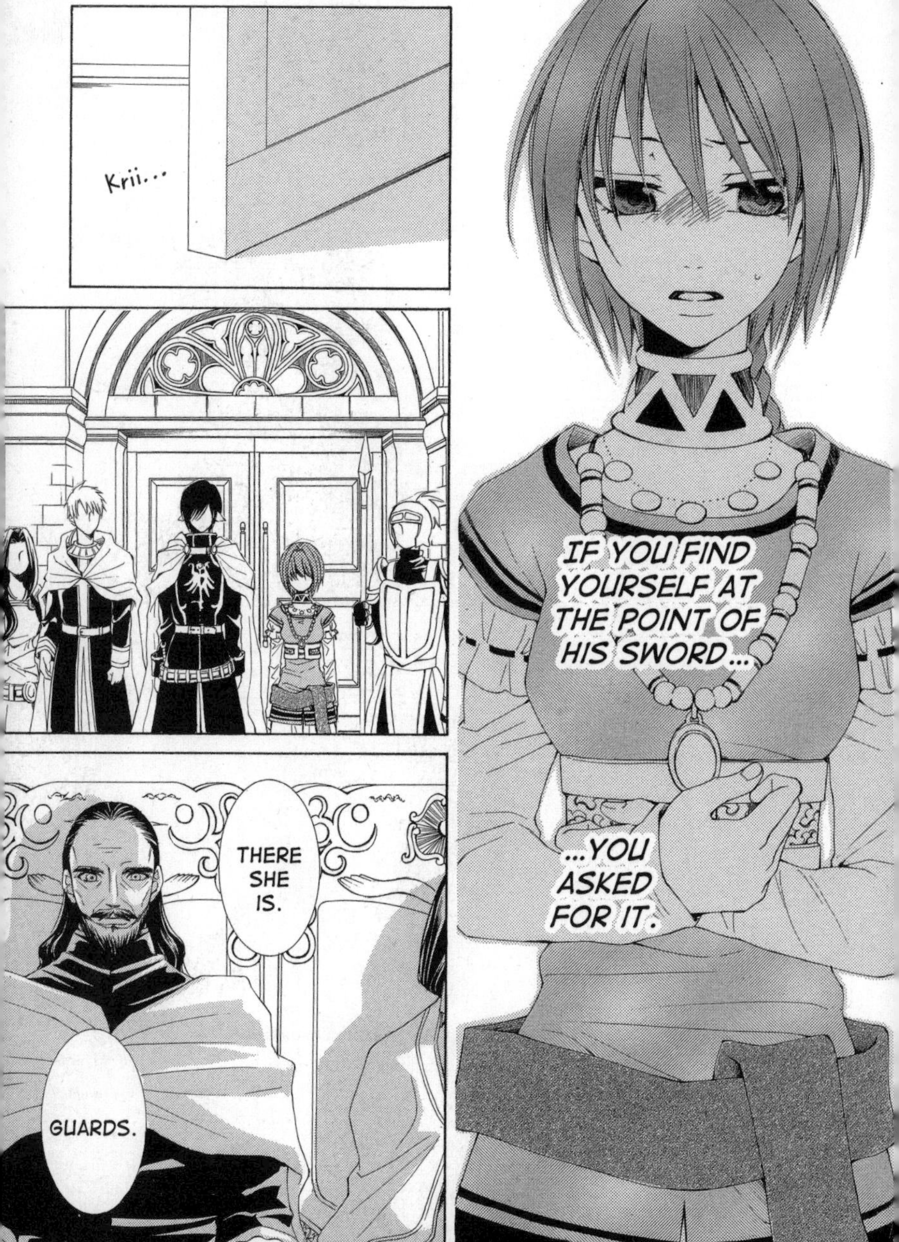
IF YOU FIND YOURSELF AT THE POINT OF HIS SWORD...
...YOU ASKED FOR IT.
Krii...
THERE SHE IS.
GUARDS.

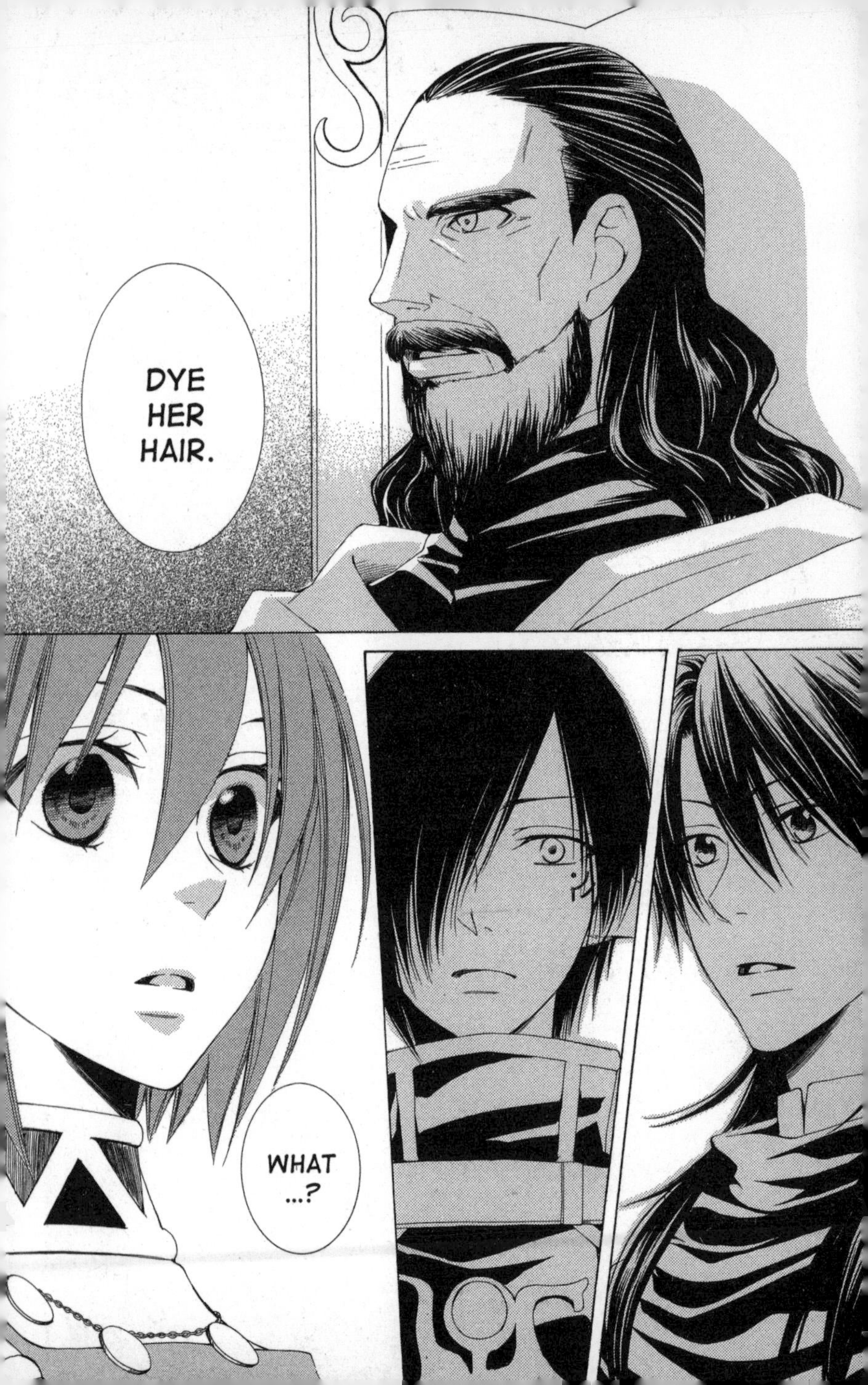
DYE HER HAIR.
WHAT ...?

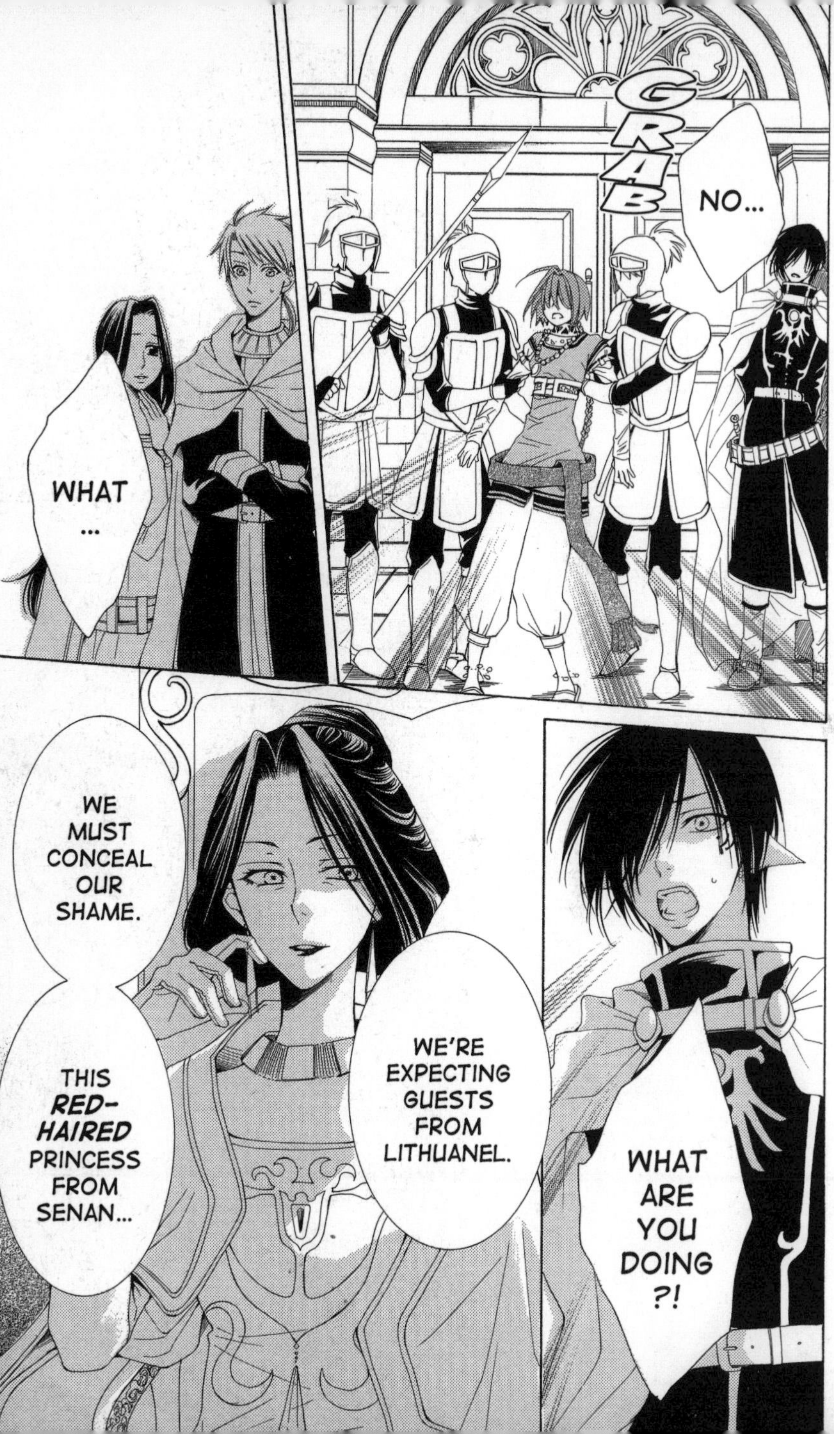
GRAB
NO...
WHAT ...
WHAT ARE YOU DOING ?!
WE MUST CONCEAL OUR SHAME.
THIS *RED-HAIRED* PRINCESS FROM SENAN...
WE'RE EXPECTING GUESTS FROM LITHUANEL.

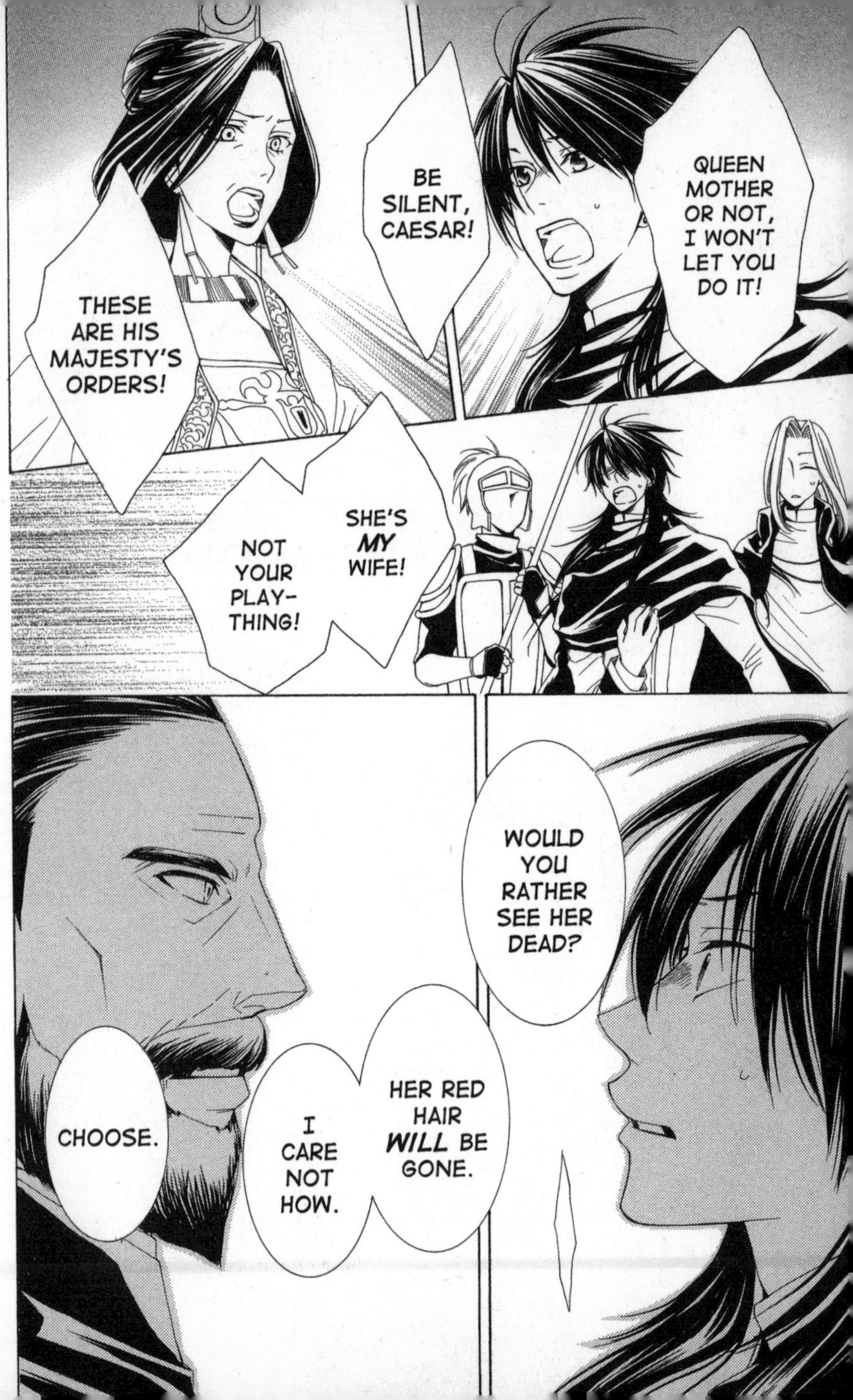
QUEEN MOTHER OR NOT, I WON'T LET YOU DO IT!
BE SILENT, CAESAR!
THESE ARE HIS MAJESTY'S ORDERS!
SHE'S *MY* WIFE!
NOT YOUR PLAYTHING!
WOULD YOU RATHER SEE HER DEAD?
HER RED HAIR *WILL* BE GONE.
I CARE NOT HOW.
CHOOSE.

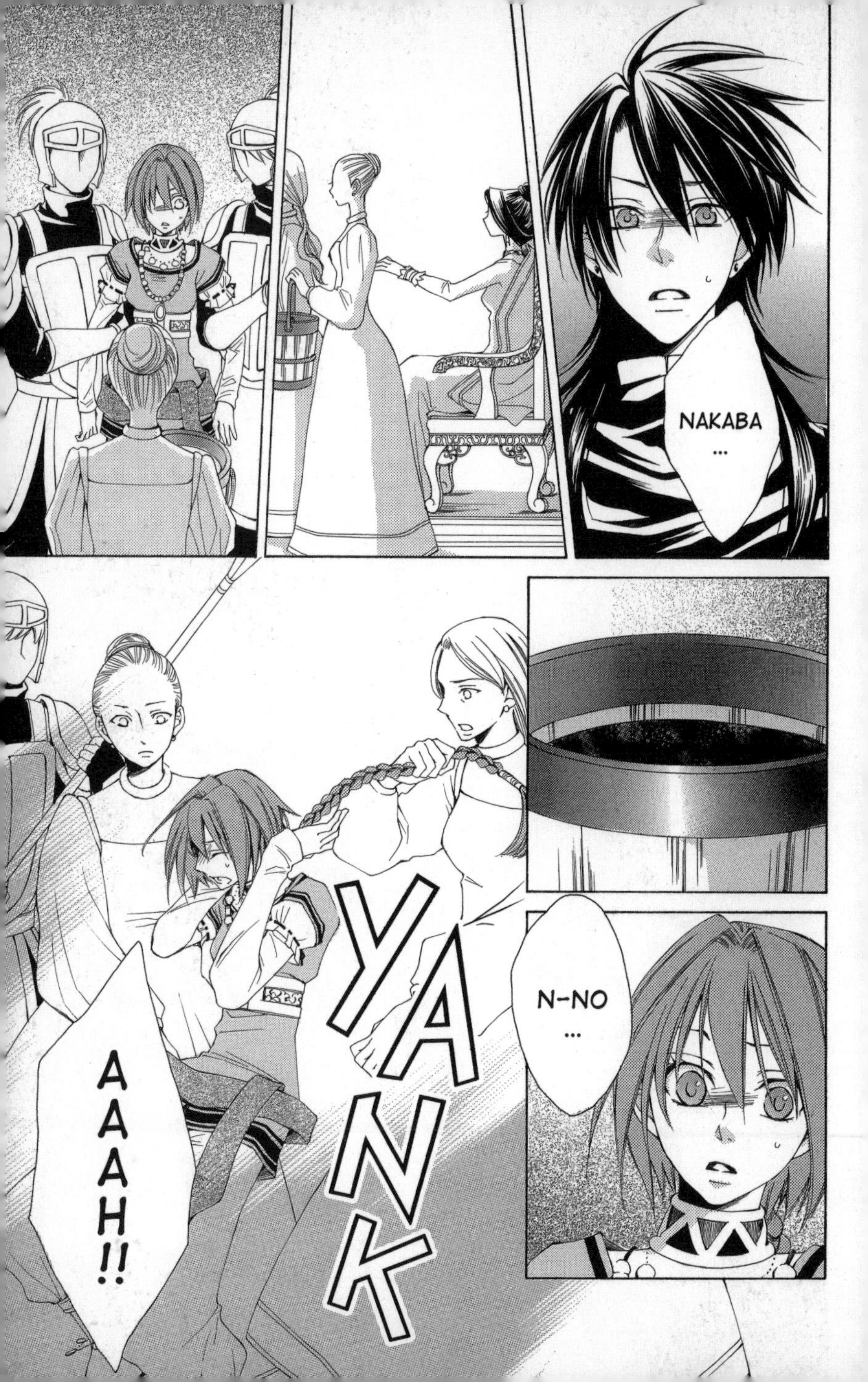
NAKABA ...
N-NO ...
YANK
AAAAH!!

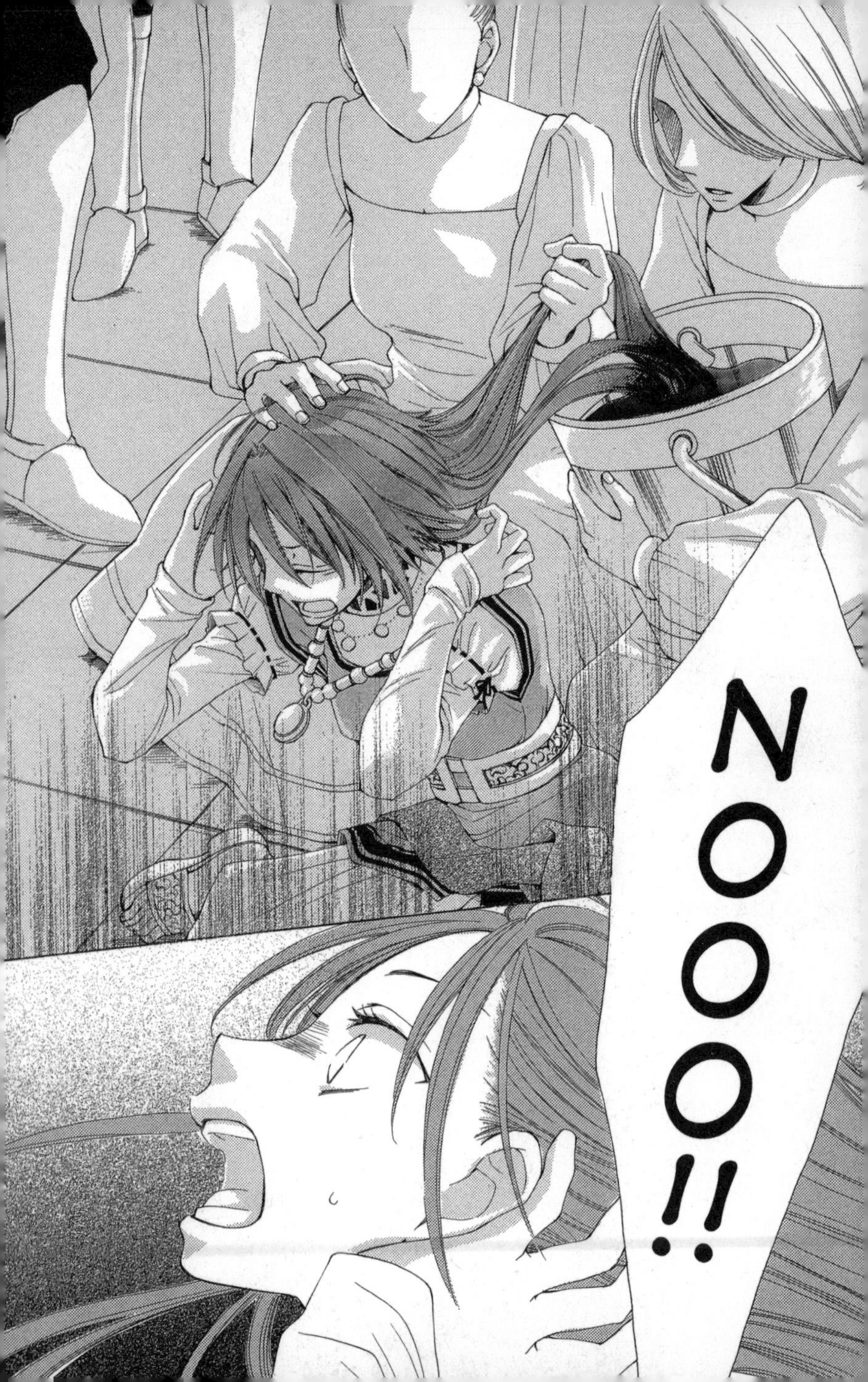
NOOO!!

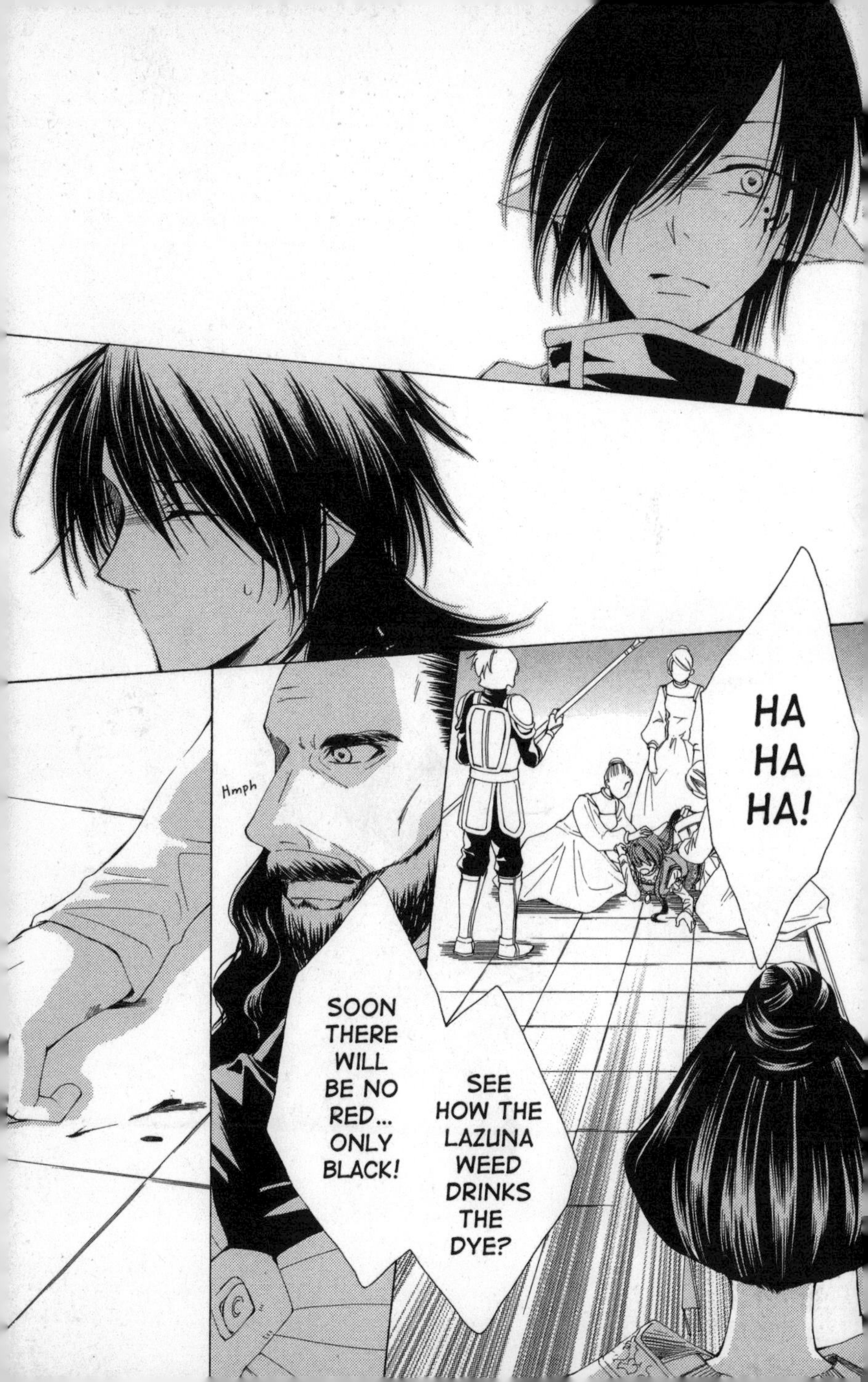
HA HA HA!
Hmph
SEE HOW THE LAZUNA WEED DRINKS THE DYE?
SOON THERE WILL BE NO RED... ONLY BLACK!

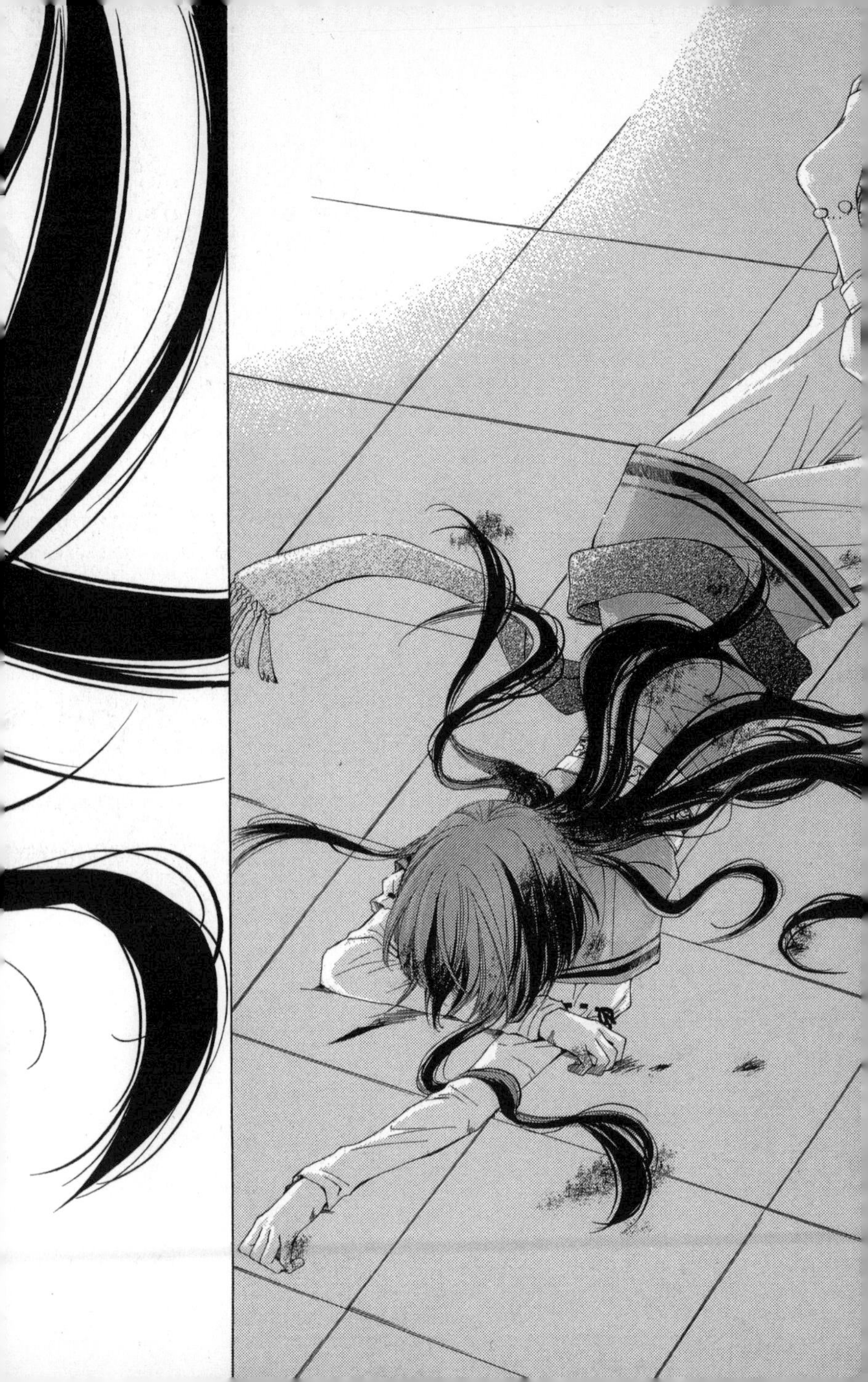

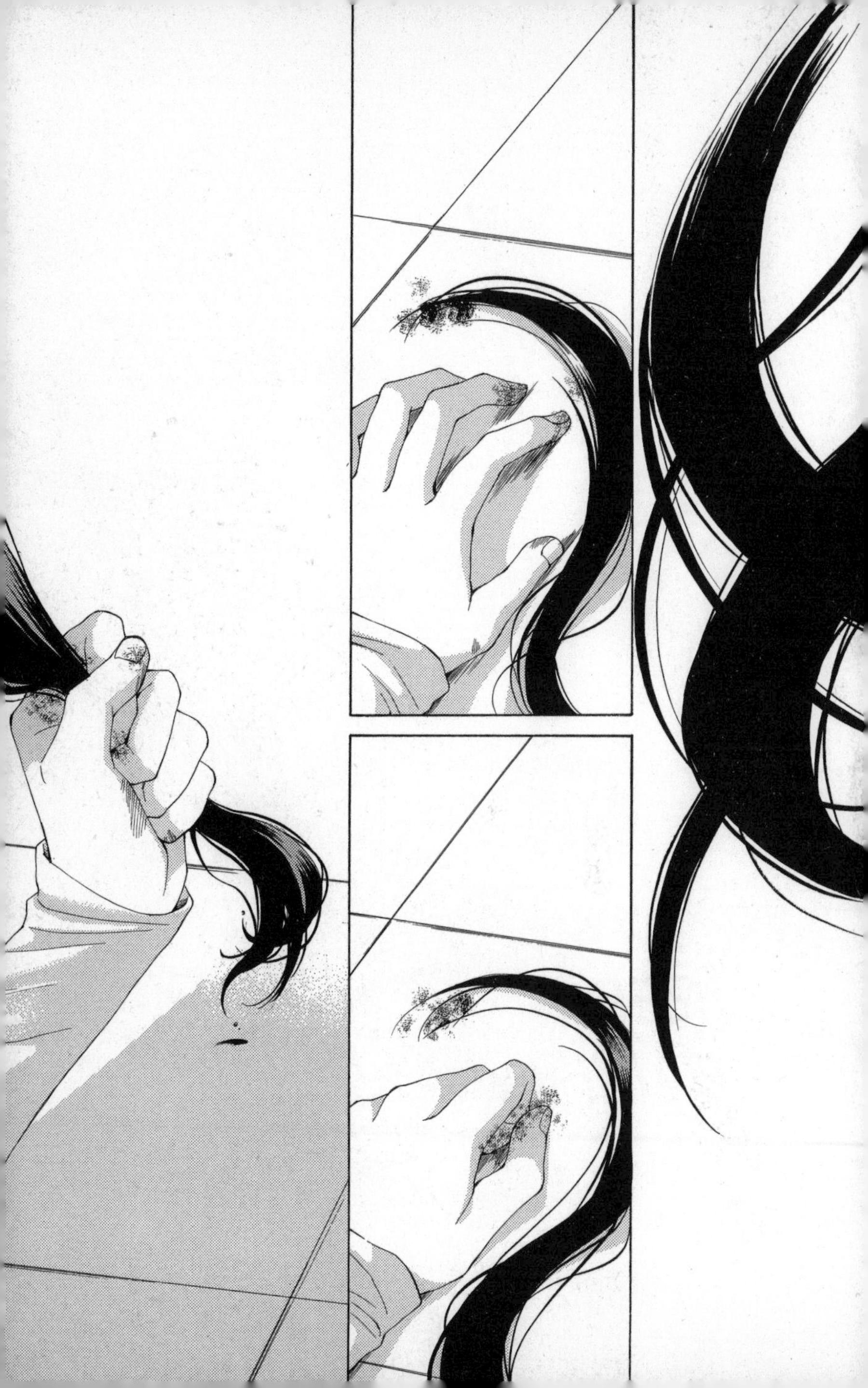

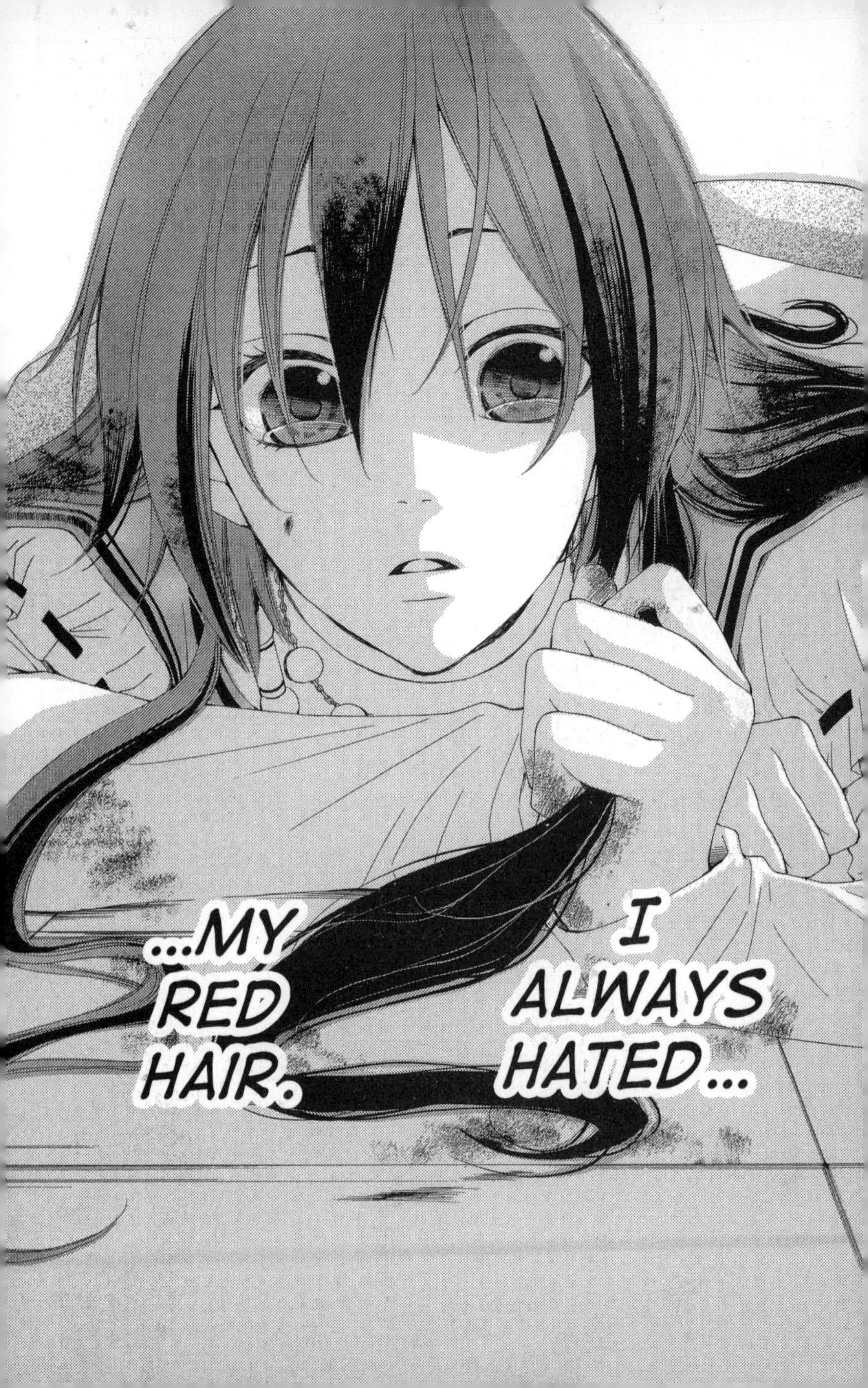
I ALWAYS HATED...
...MY RED HAIR.

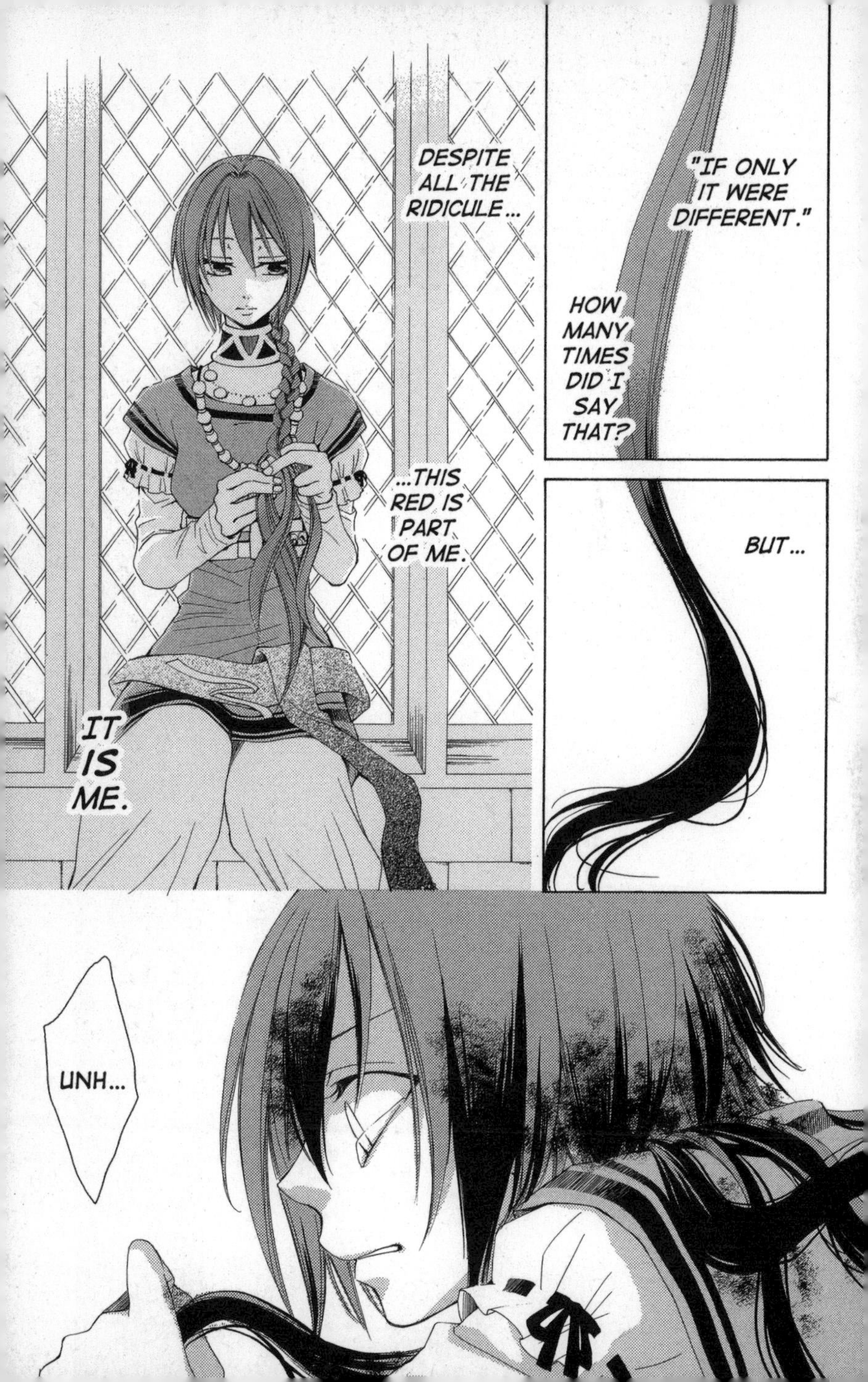
"IF ONLY IT WERE DIFFERENT."
HOW MANY TIMES DID I SAY THAT?
BUT...
DESPITE ALL THE RIDICULE...
...THIS RED IS PART OF ME.
IT IS ME.
UNH...

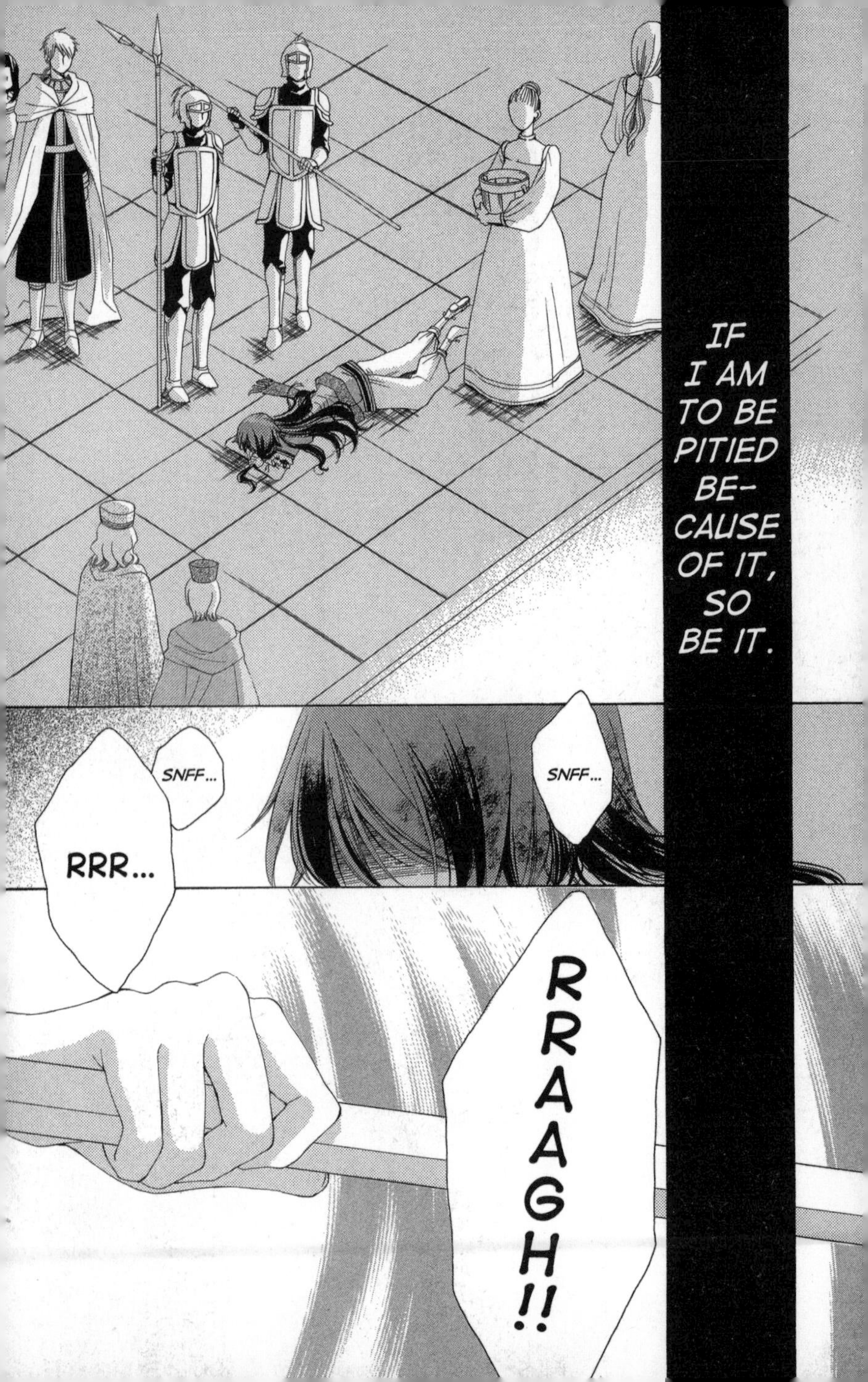
IF I AM TO BE PITIED BE-CAUSE OF IT, SO BE IT.
SNFF...
SNFF...
RRR...
RRAAGH!!

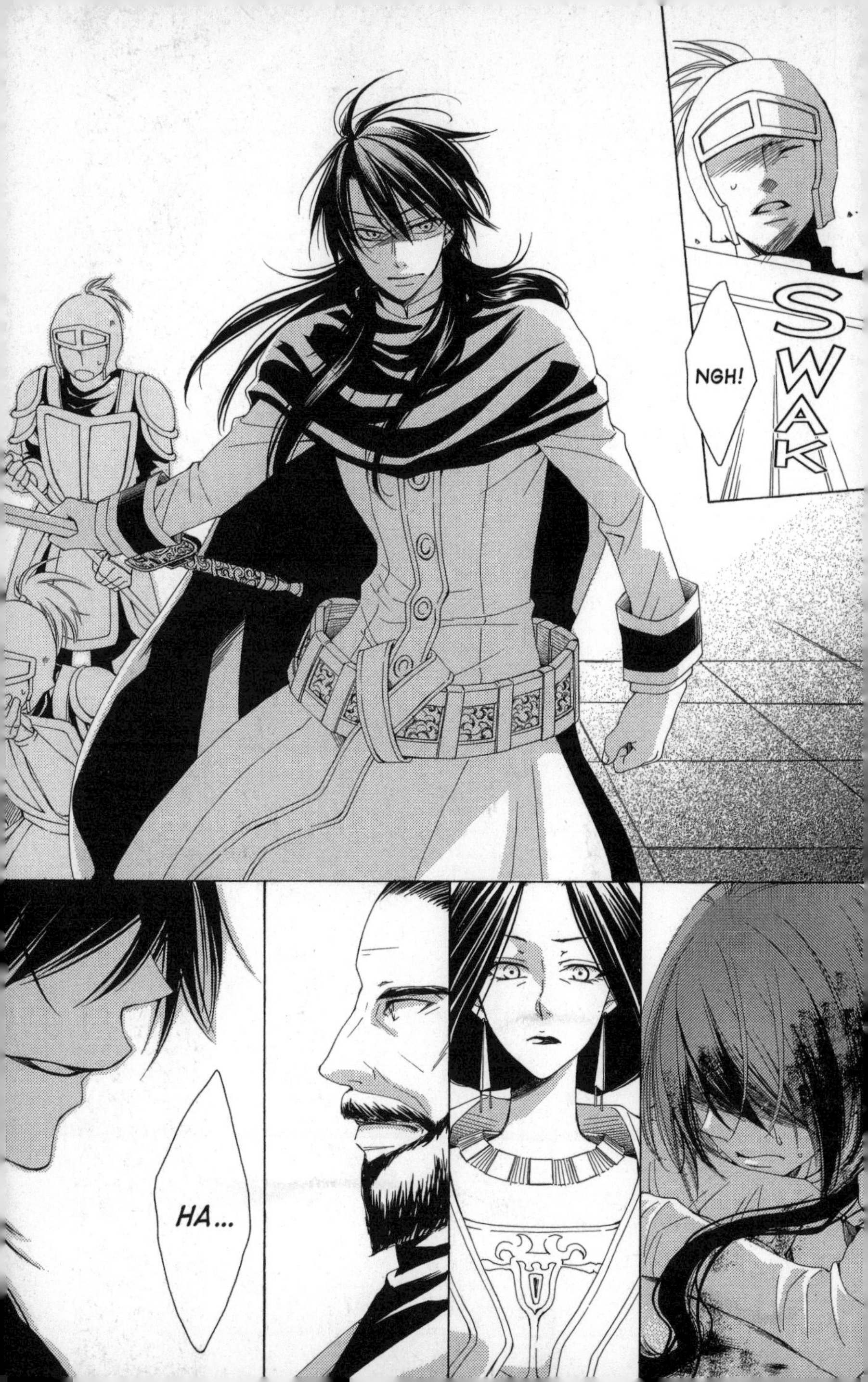
NGH!
SWAK
HA...

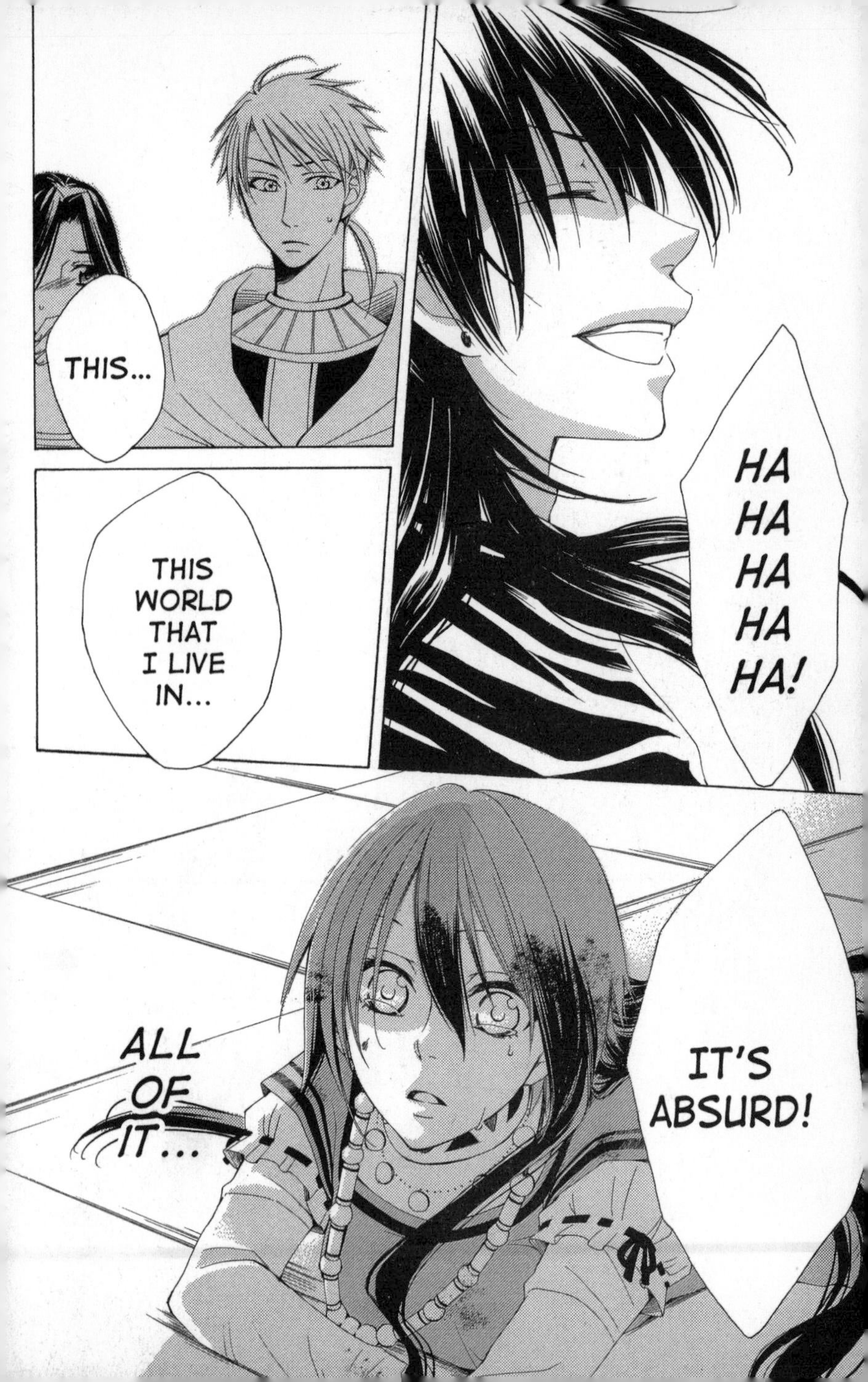
HA HA HA HA HA!
THIS...
THIS WORLD THAT I LIVE IN...
IT'S ABSURD!
ALL OF IT...

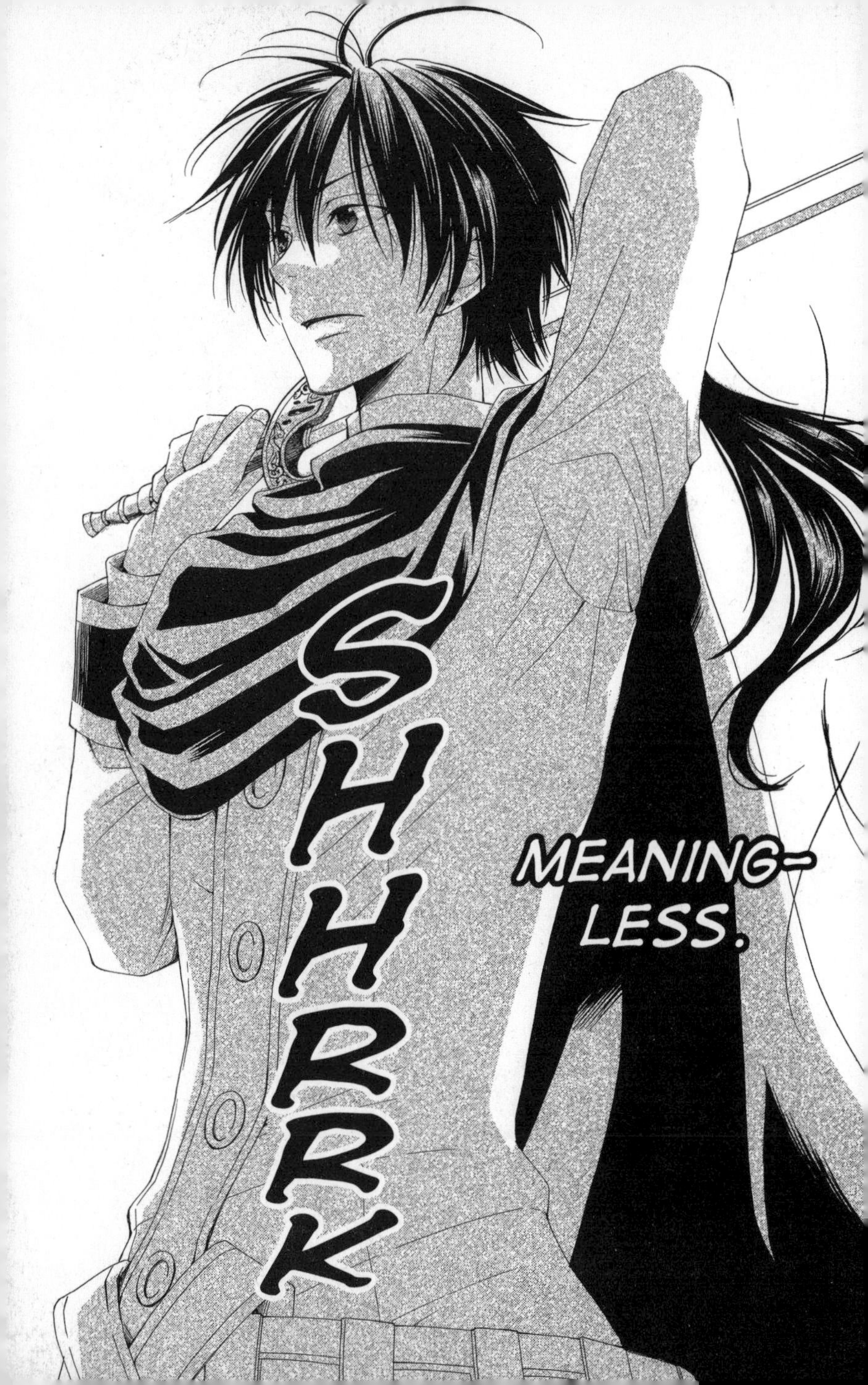
SHHHRRK
MEANING-
LESS.

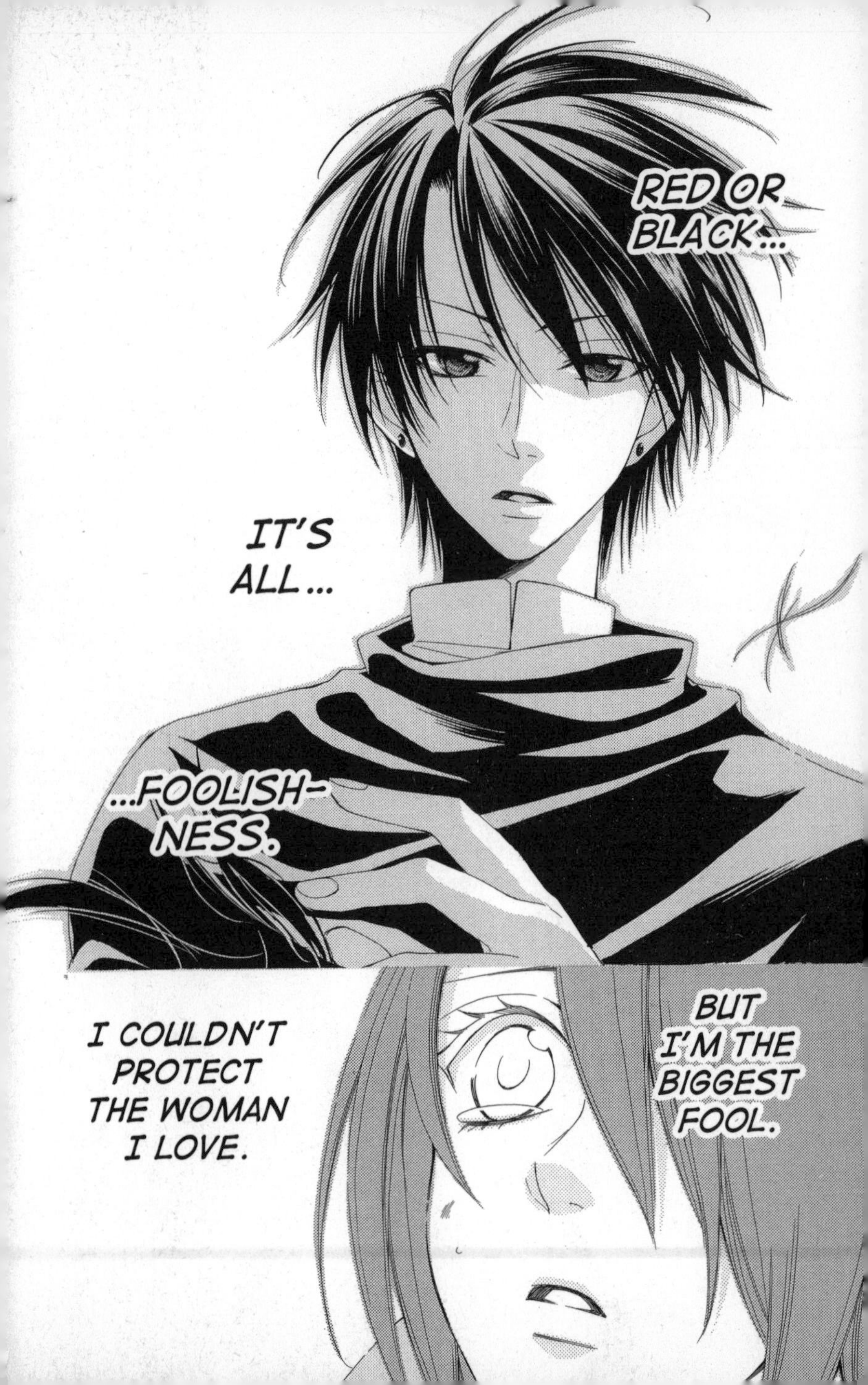
RED OR BLACK...
IT'S ALL...
...FOOLISH-NESS.
BUT I'M THE BIGGEST FOOL.
I COULDN'T PROTECT THE WOMAN I LOVE.

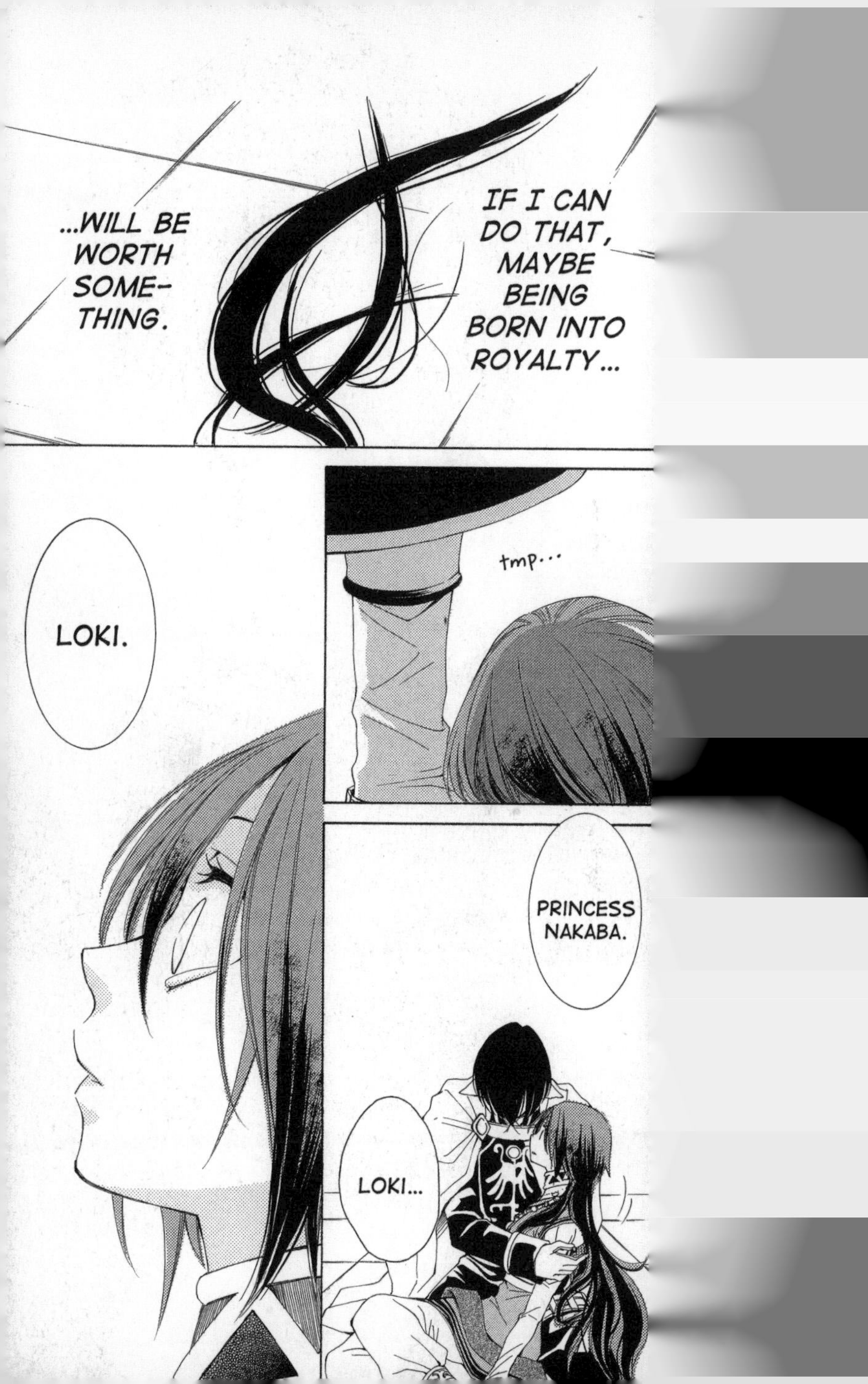
IF I CAN DO THAT, MAYBE BEING BORN INTO ROYALTY...
...WILL BE WORTH SOME-THING.
tmp...
PRINCESS NAKABA.
LOKI...
LOKI.

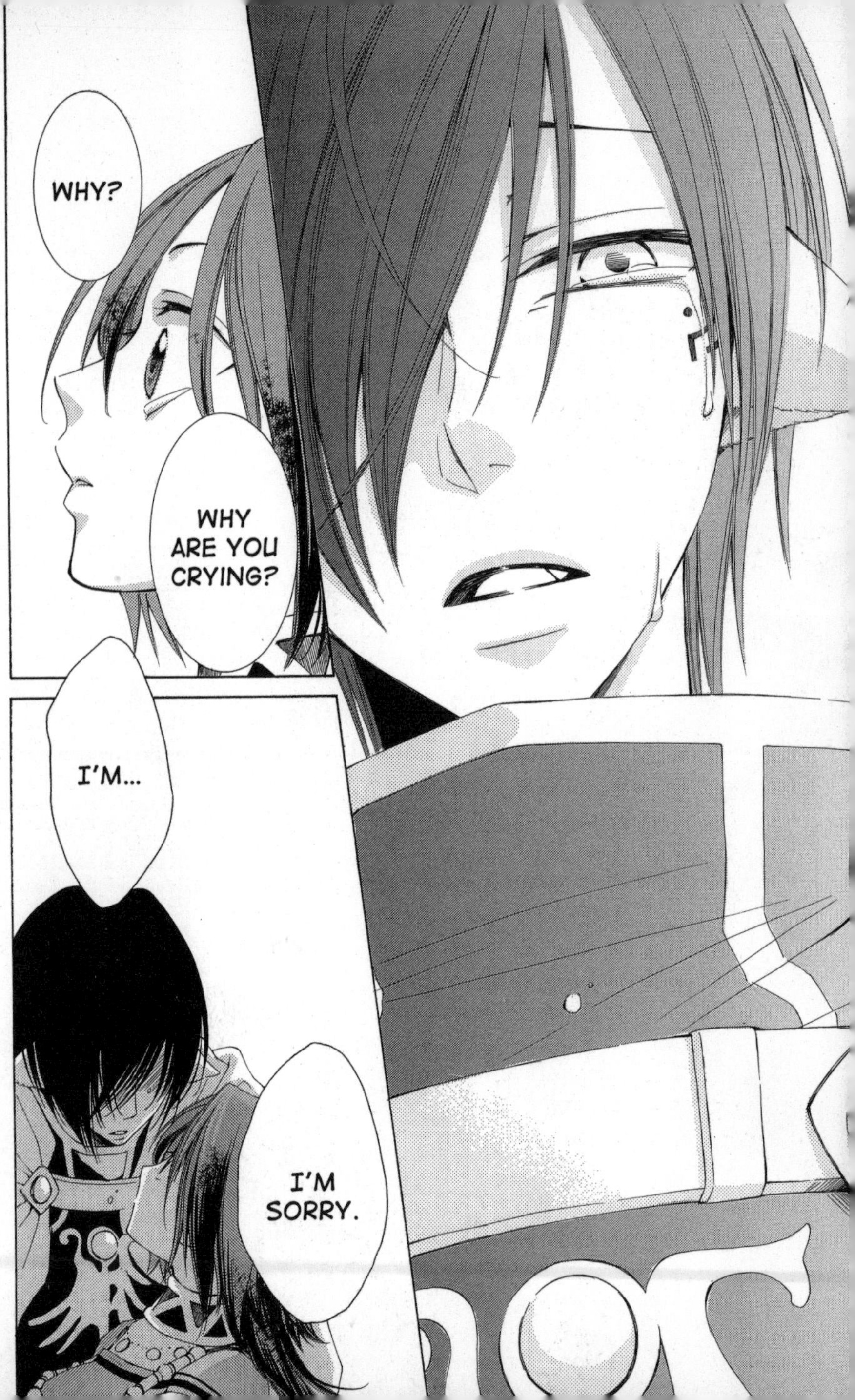
WHY?
WHY ARE YOU CRYING?
I'M...
I'M SORRY.

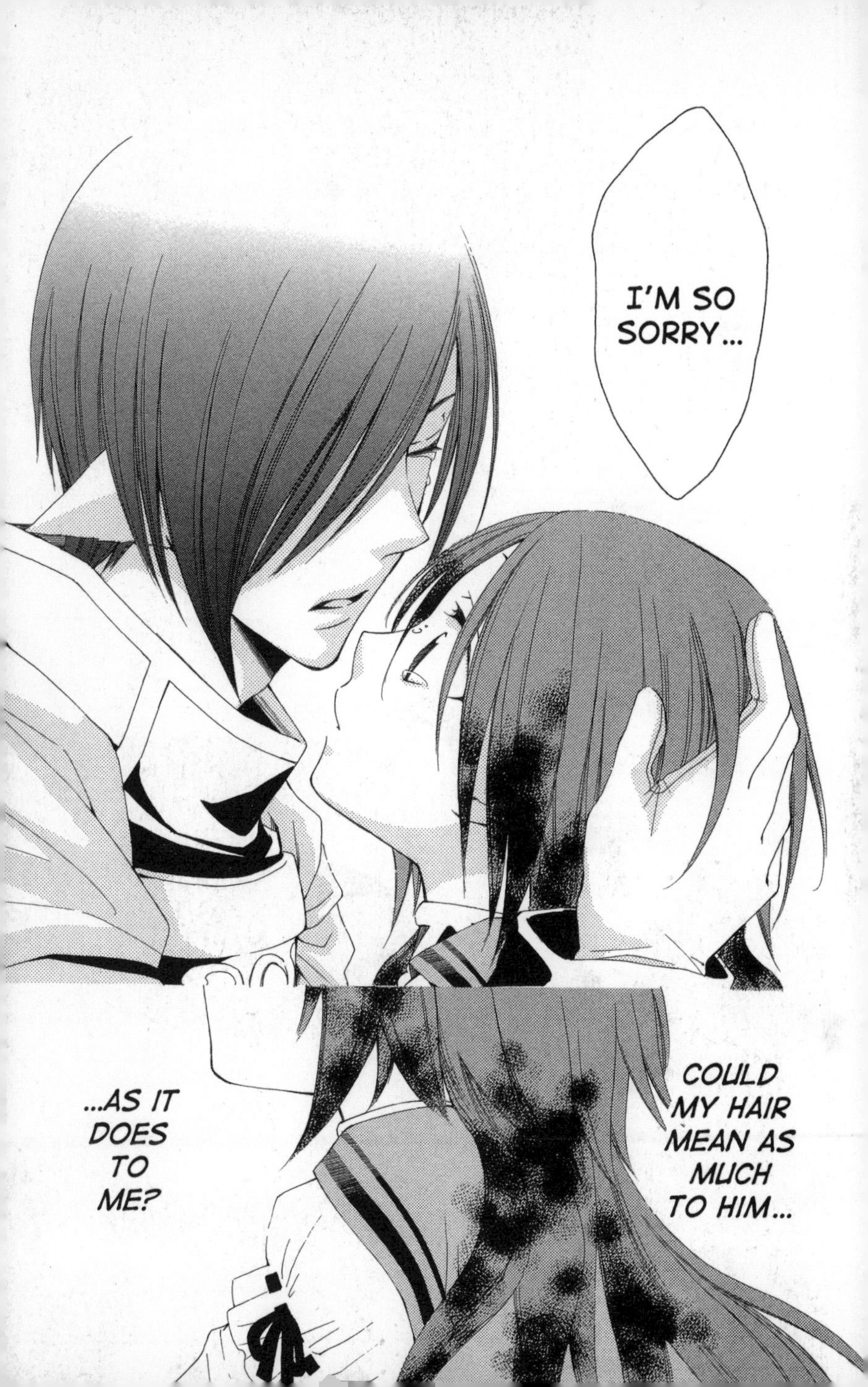
I'M SO SORRY...
COULD MY HAIR MEAN AS MUCH TO HIM...
...AS IT DOES TO ME?

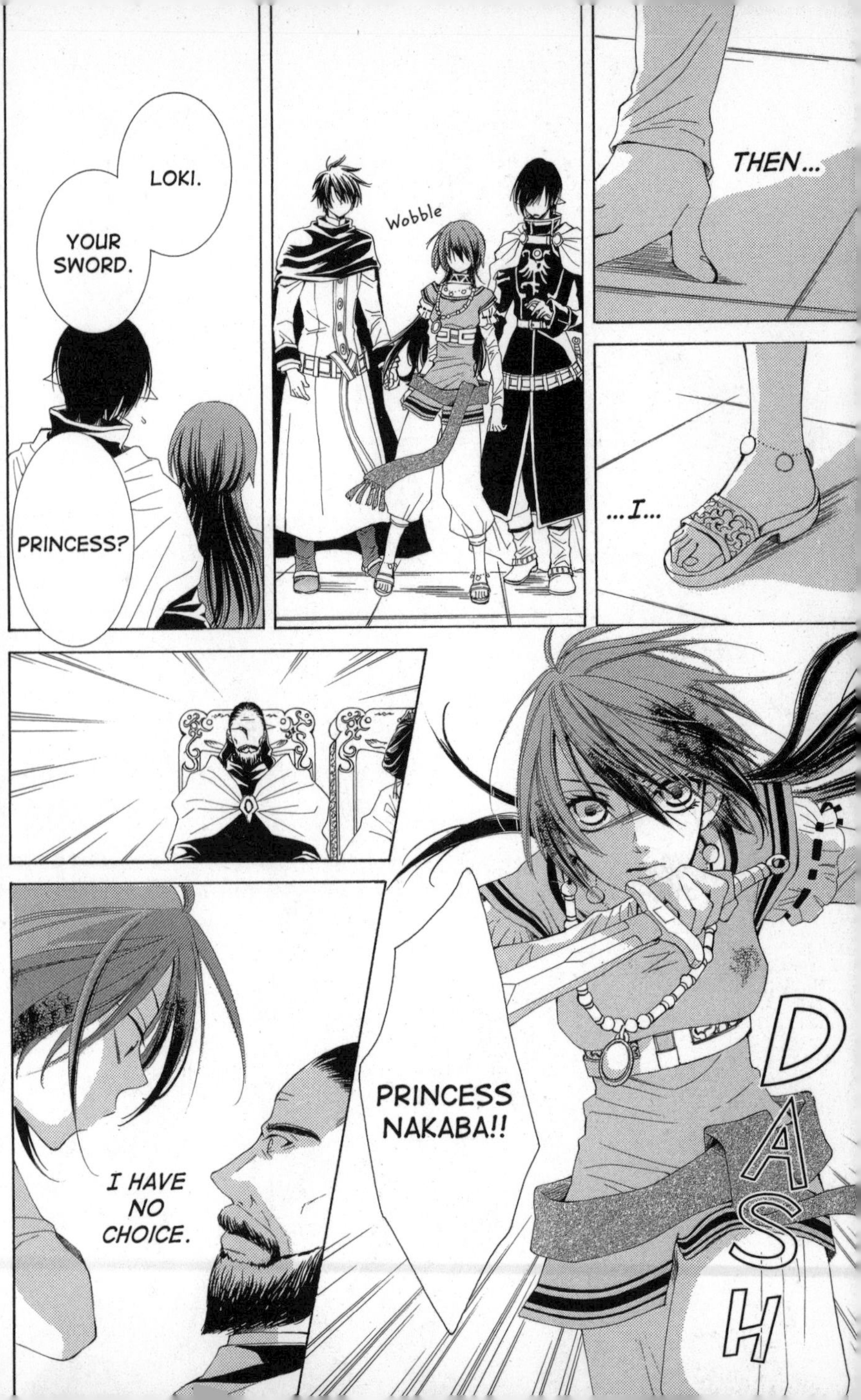
THEN...
...I...
Wobble
LOKI.
YOUR SWORD.
PRINCESS?
PRINCESS NAKABA!!
DASH
I HAVE NO CHOICE.

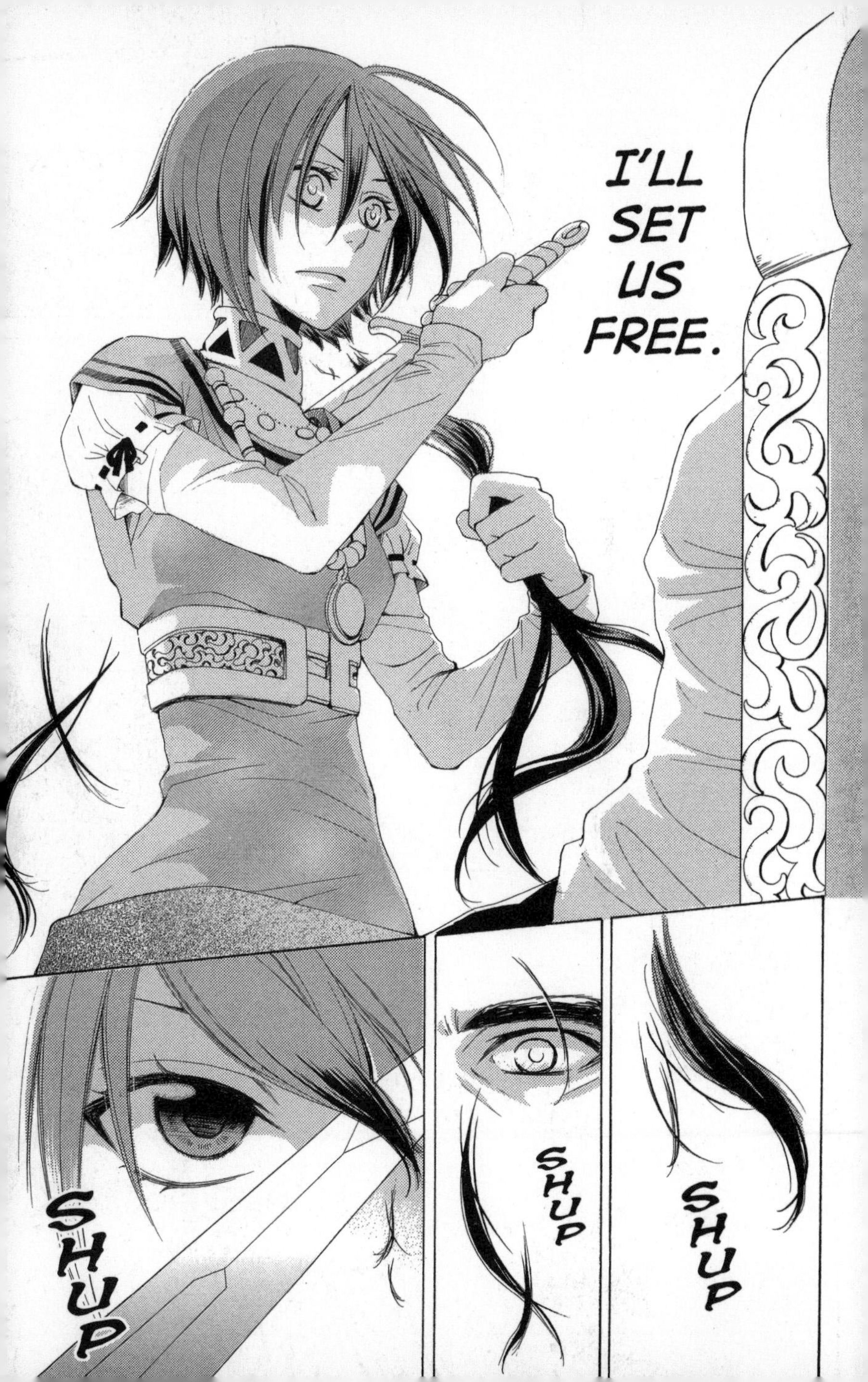
I'LL SET US FREE.
SHUP
SHUP
SHUP

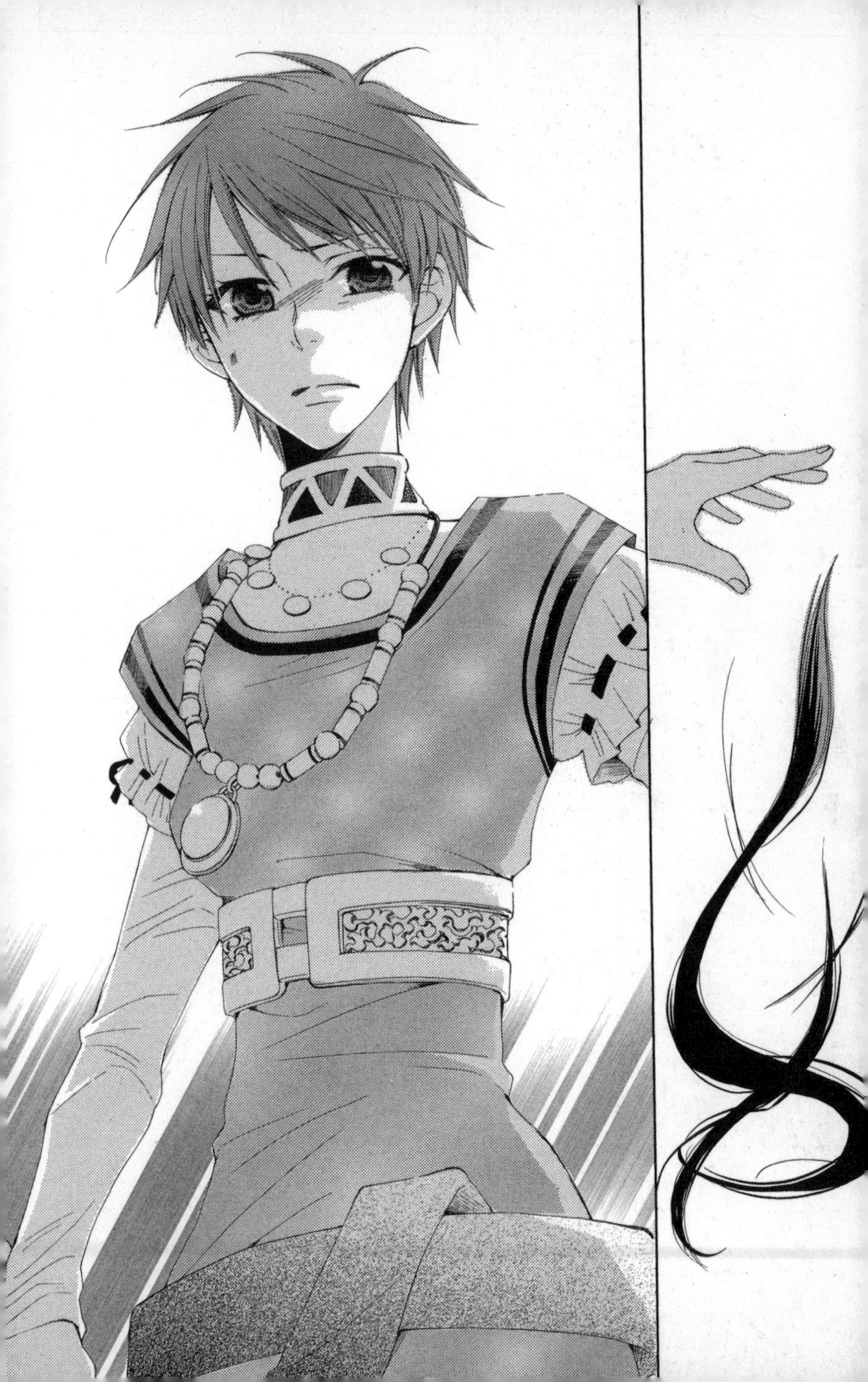

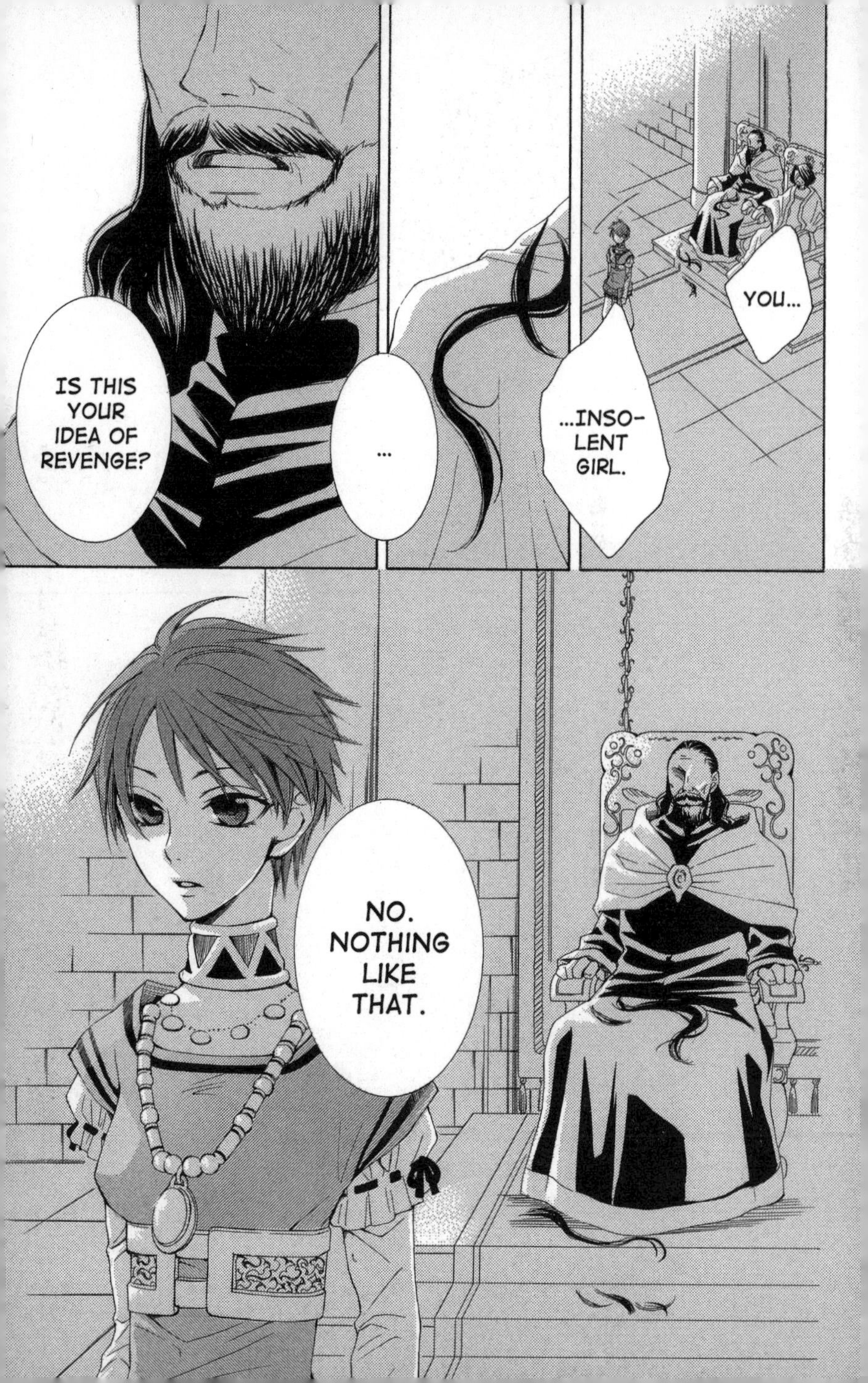
YOU...
...INSO-LENT GIRL.
...
IS THIS YOUR IDEA OF REVENGE?
NO. NOTHING LIKE THAT.

I WANT ONLY TO LIVE.
RED HAIR AND ALL.
TO LIVE THE ONLY WAY I KNOW HOW.

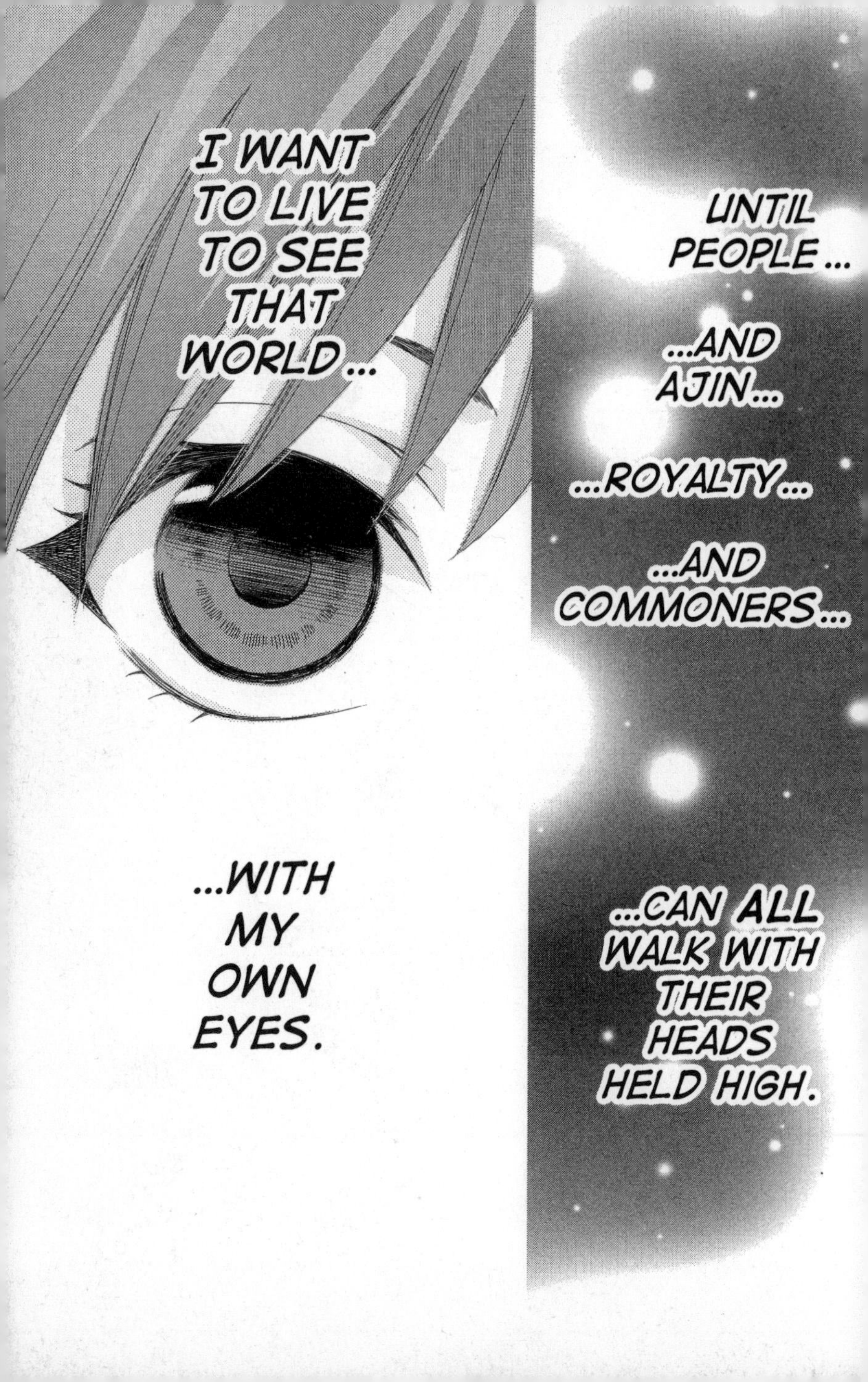
UNTIL PEOPLE...
...AND AJIN...
...ROYALTY...
...AND COMMONERS...
...CAN ALL WALK WITH THEIR HEADS HELD HIGH.
I WANT TO LIVE TO SEE THAT WORLD...
...WITH MY OWN EYES.

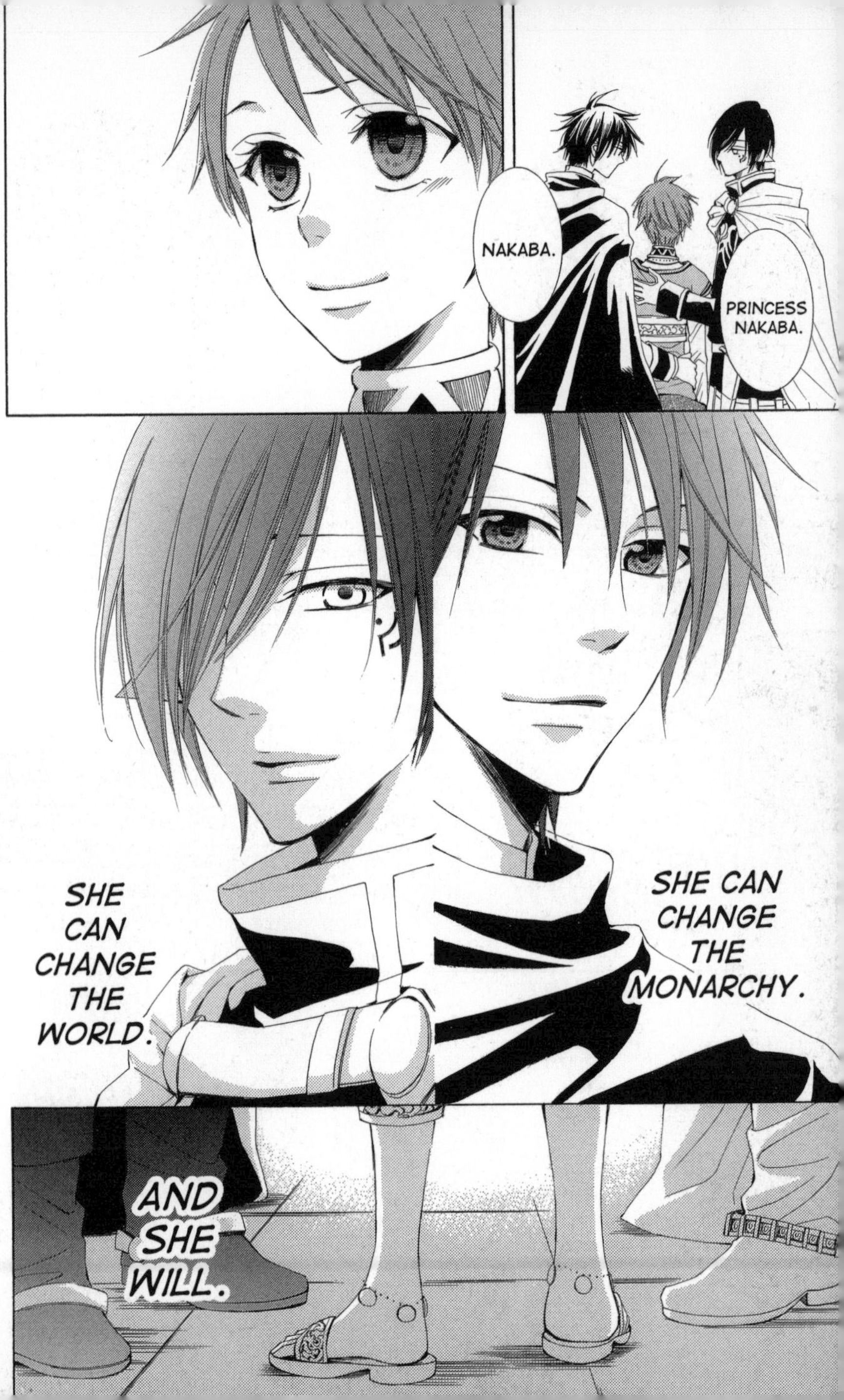
NAKABA.
PRINCESS NAKABA.
SHE CAN CHANGE THE MONARCHY.
SHE CAN CHANGE THE WORLD.
AND SHE WILL.

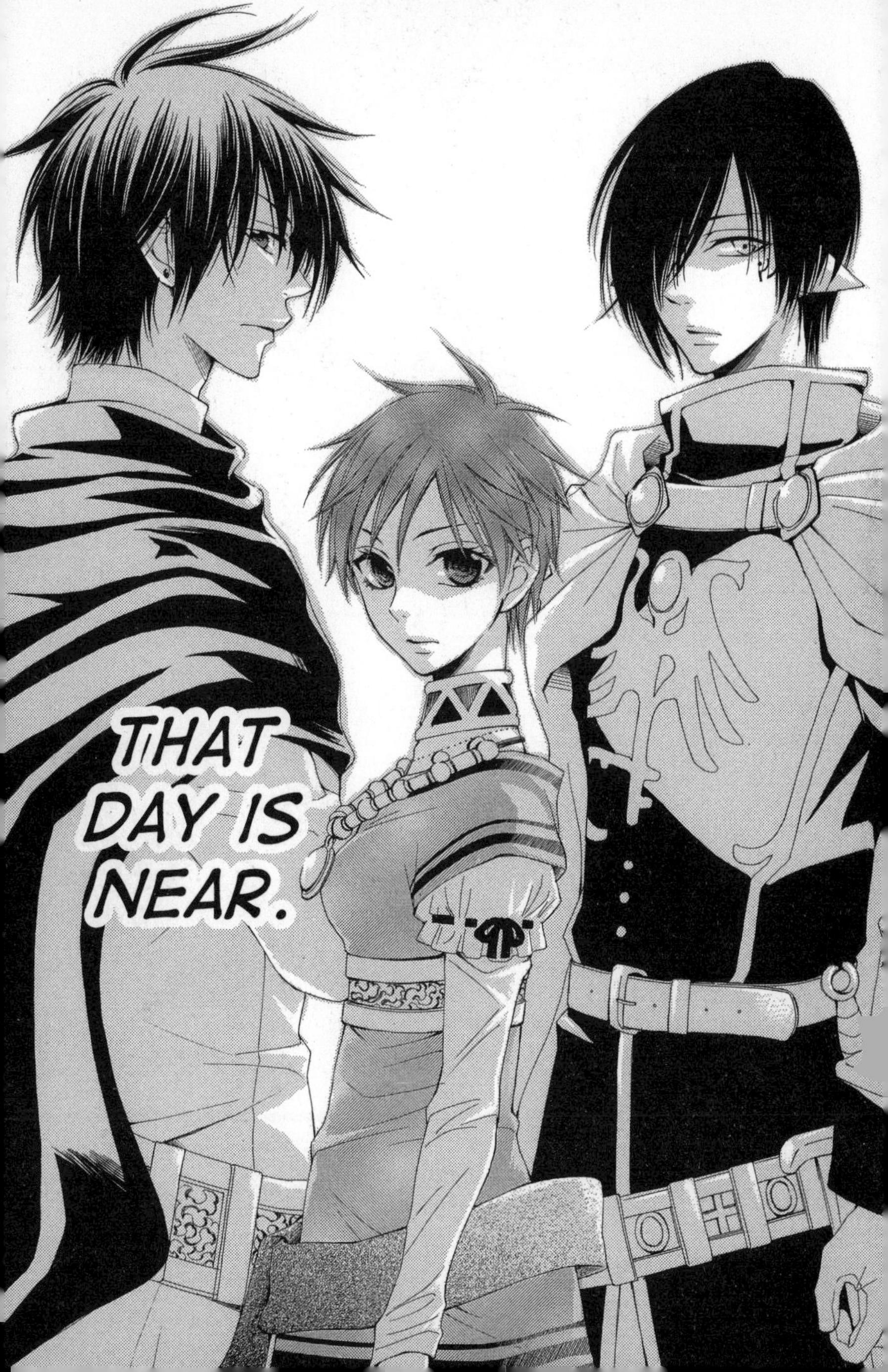
THAT DAY IS NEAR.

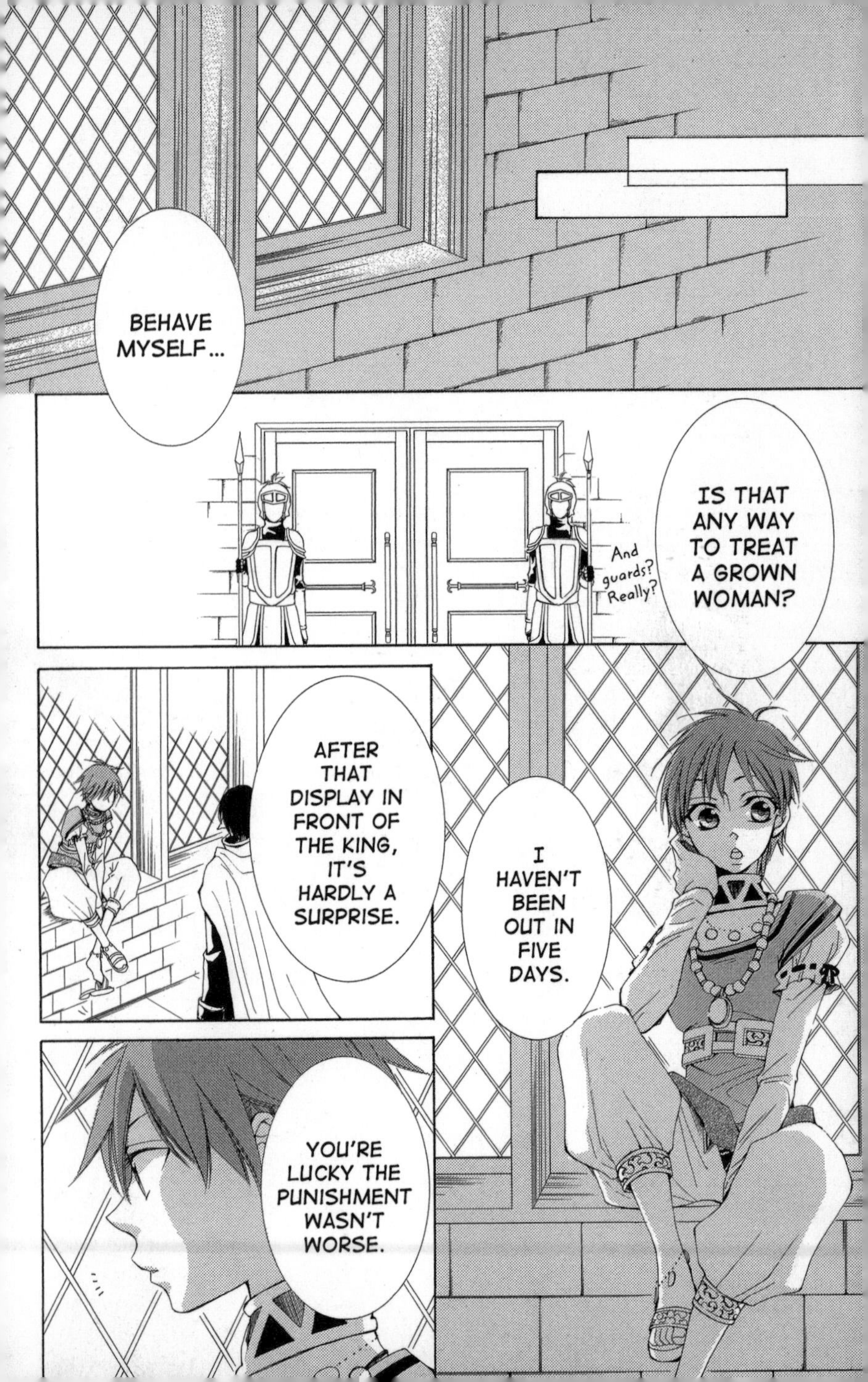

BEHAVE MYSELF...
IS THAT ANY WAY TO TREAT A GROWN WOMAN?
And guards? Really?
I HAVEN'T BEEN OUT IN FIVE DAYS.
AFTER THAT DISPLAY IN FRONT OF THE KING, IT'S HARDLY A SURPRISE.
YOU'RE LUCKY THE PUNISHMENT WASN'T WORSE.

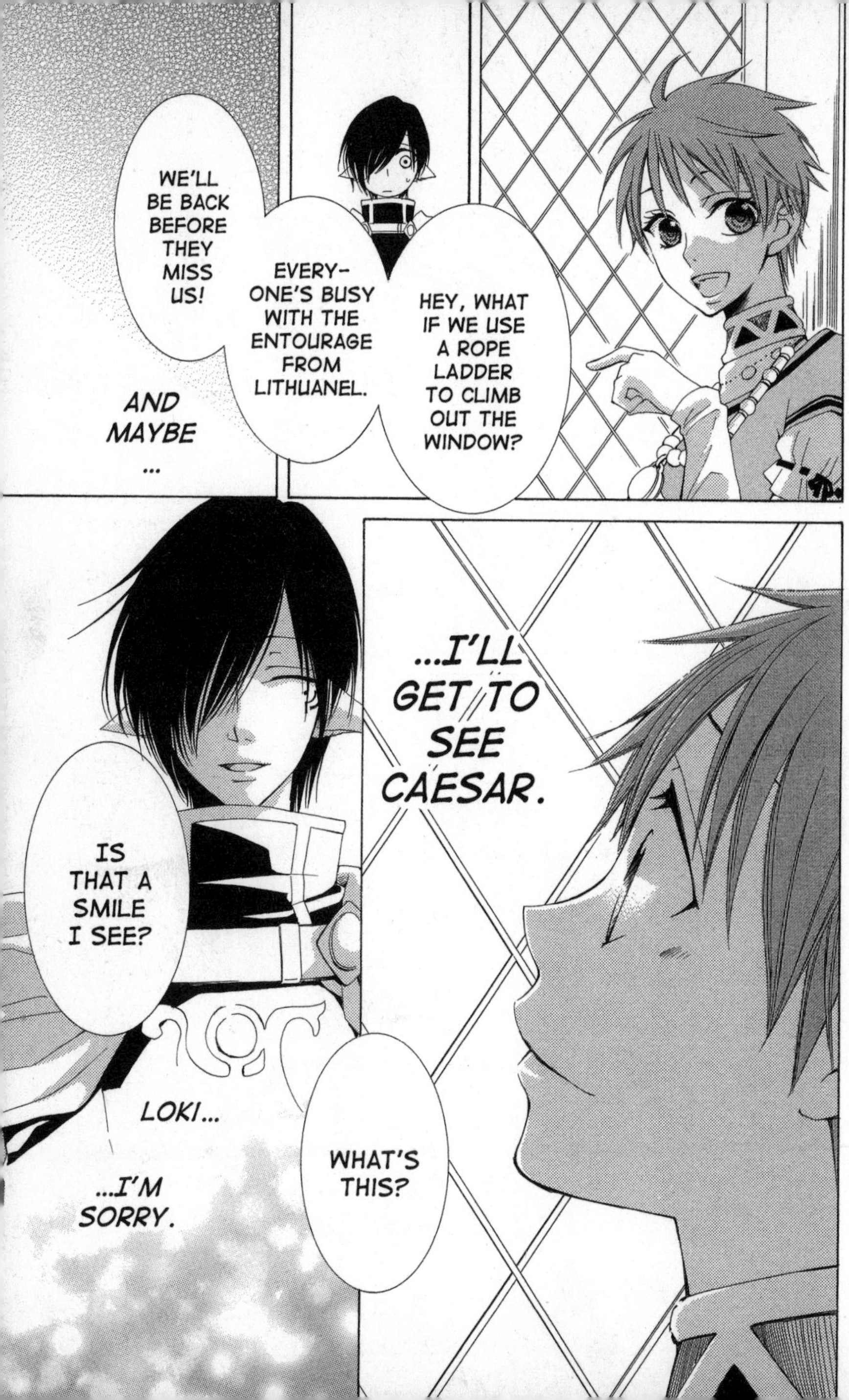
HEY, WHAT IF WE USE A ROPE LADDER TO CLIMB OUT THE WINDOW?
EVERY-ONE'S BUSY WITH THE ENTOURAGE FROM LITHUANEL.
WE'LL BE BACK BEFORE THEY MISS US!
AND MAYBE ...
...I'LL GET TO SEE CAESAR.
IS THAT A SMILE I SEE?
WHAT'S THIS?
LOKI...
...I'M SORRY.

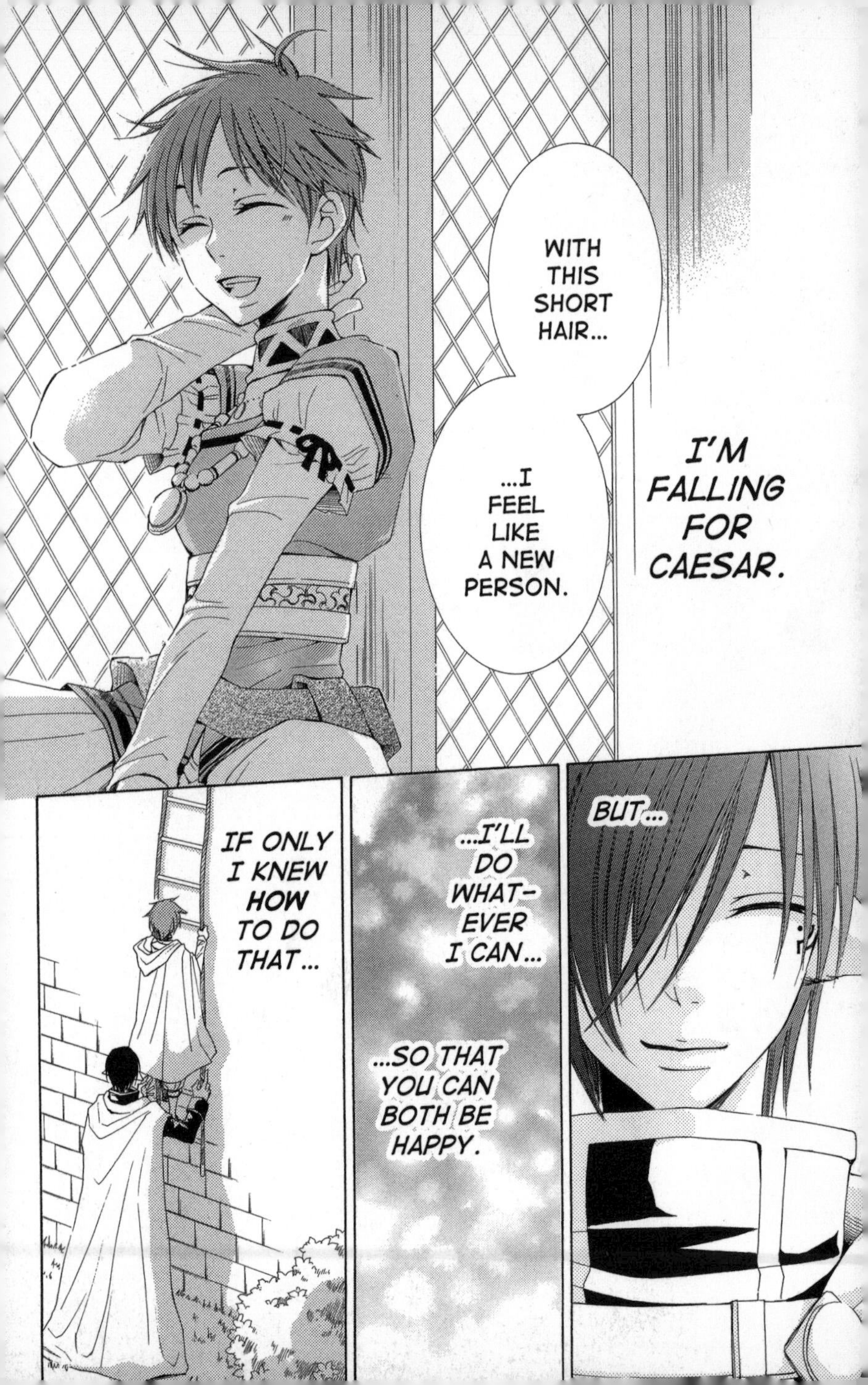
WITH THIS SHORT HAIR...
...I FEEL LIKE A NEW PERSON.
I'M FALLING FOR CAESAR.
BUT...
...I'LL DO WHATEVER I CAN...
...SO THAT YOU CAN BOTH BE HAPPY.
IF ONLY I KNEW HOW TO DO THAT...

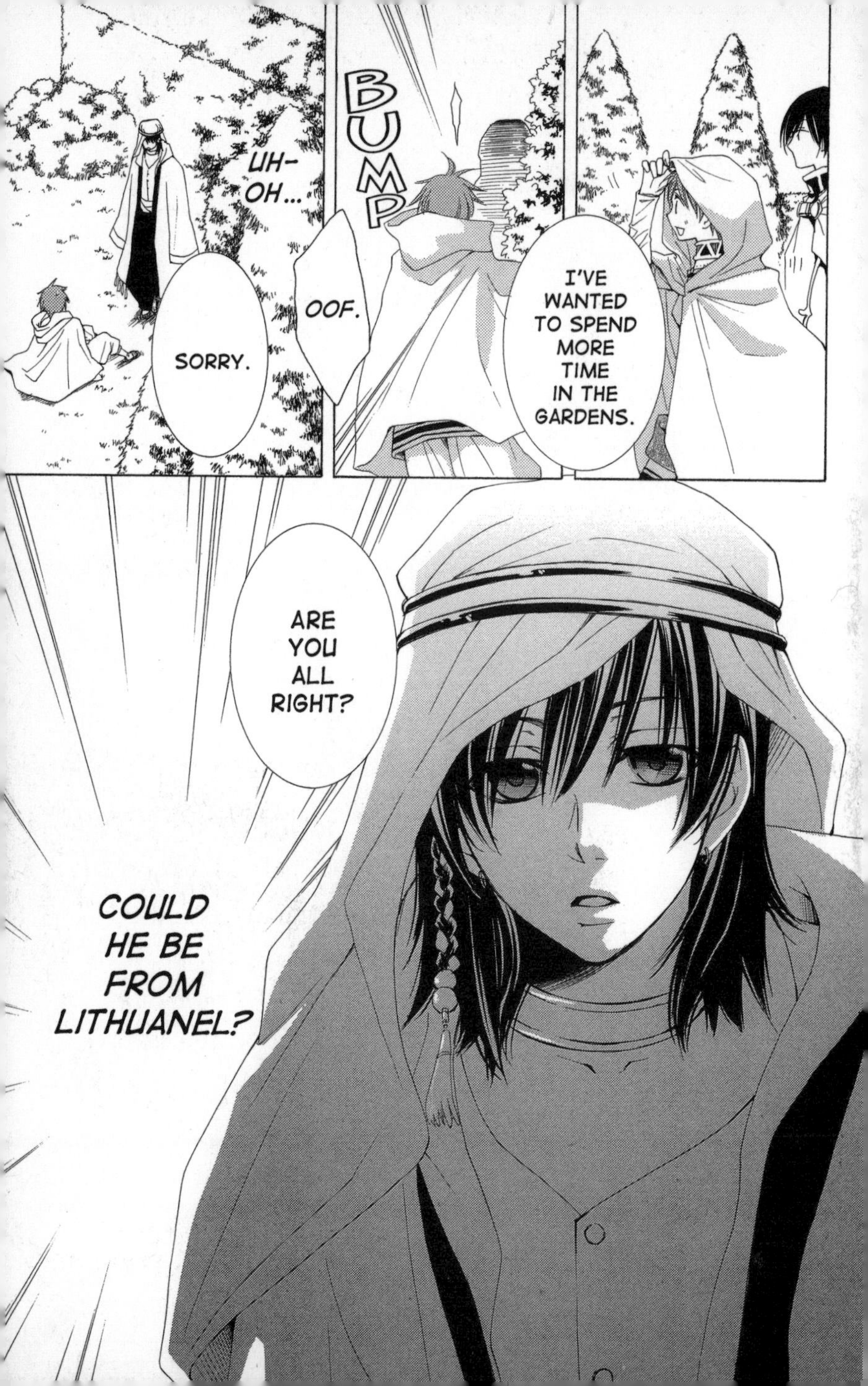
I'VE WANTED TO SPEND MORE TIME IN THE GARDENS.
BUMP
OOF.
UH-OH...
SORRY.
ARE YOU ALL RIGHT?
COULD HE BE FROM LITHUANEL?

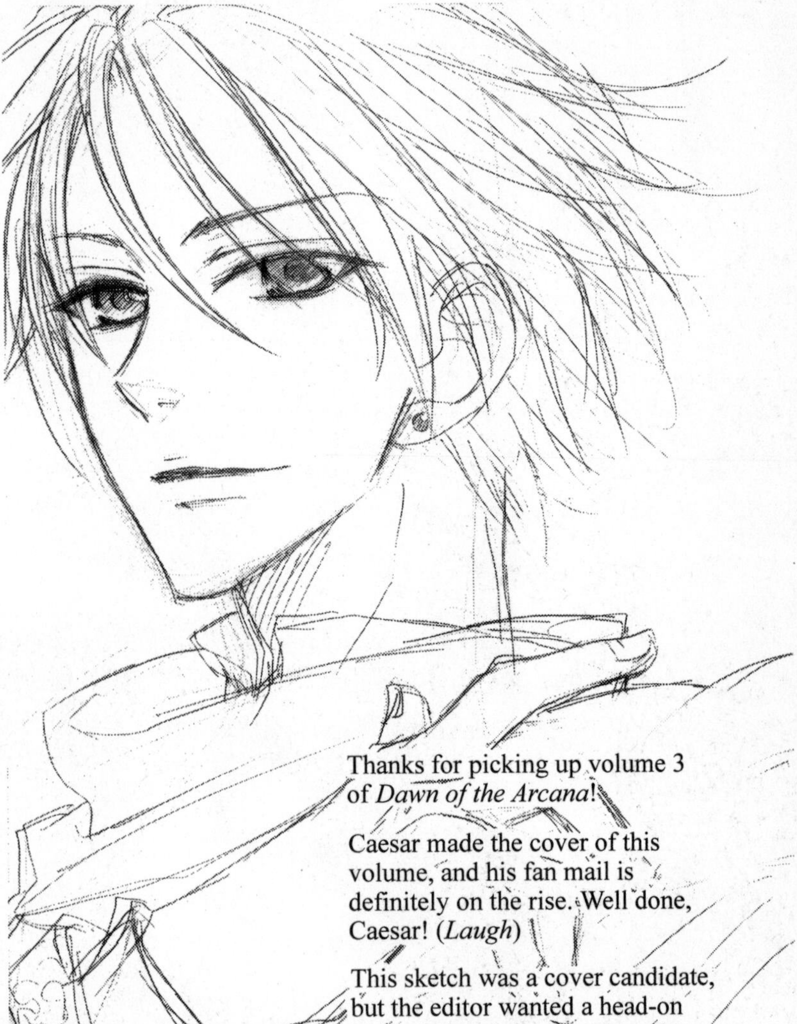

Thanks for picking up volume 3 of *Dawn of the Arcana*!

Caesar made the cover of this volume, and his fan mail is definitely on the rise. Well done, Caesar! (*Laugh*)

This sketch was a cover candidate, but the editor wanted a head-on view, so it got the axe. I hated to see it go to waste, so here it is. (´ω`)

Chapter 9

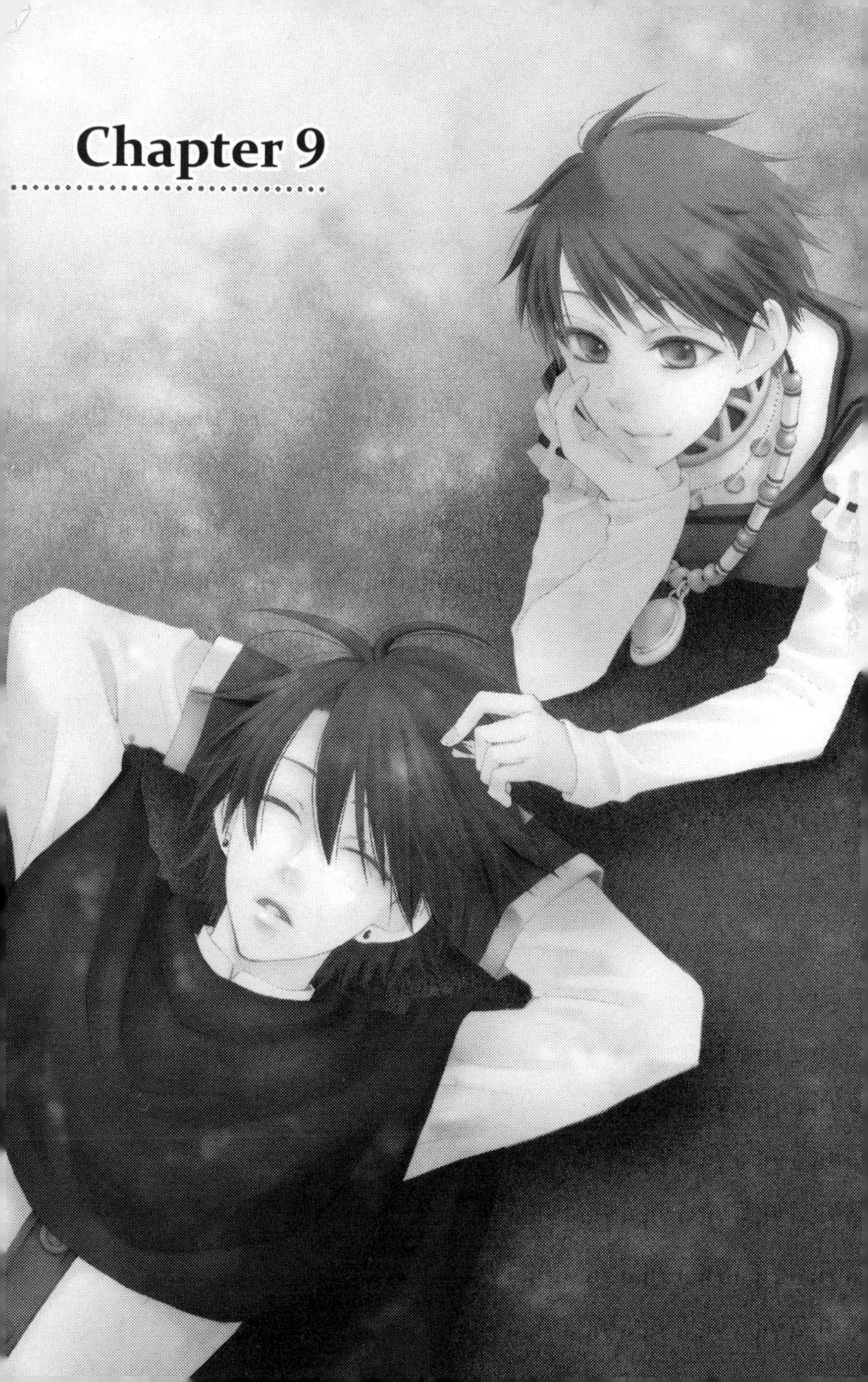

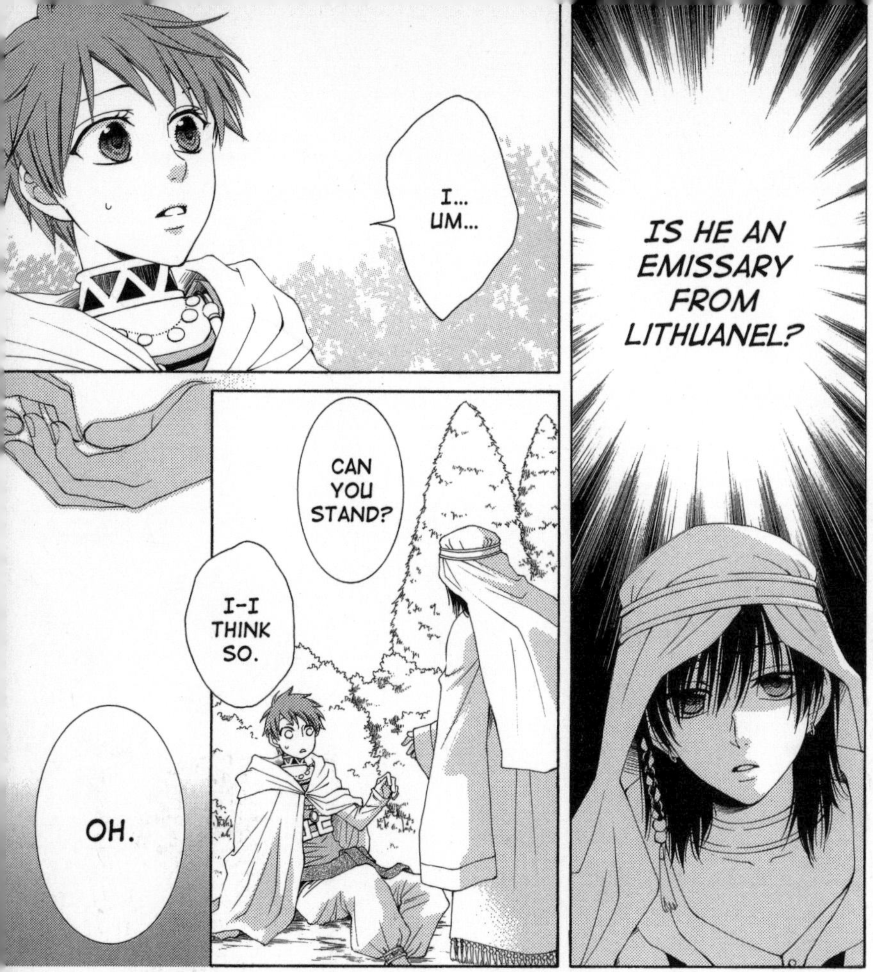
IS HE AN EMISSARY FROM LITHUANEL?
I... UM...
CAN YOU STAND?
I-I THINK SO.
OH.

Dawn of the Arcana

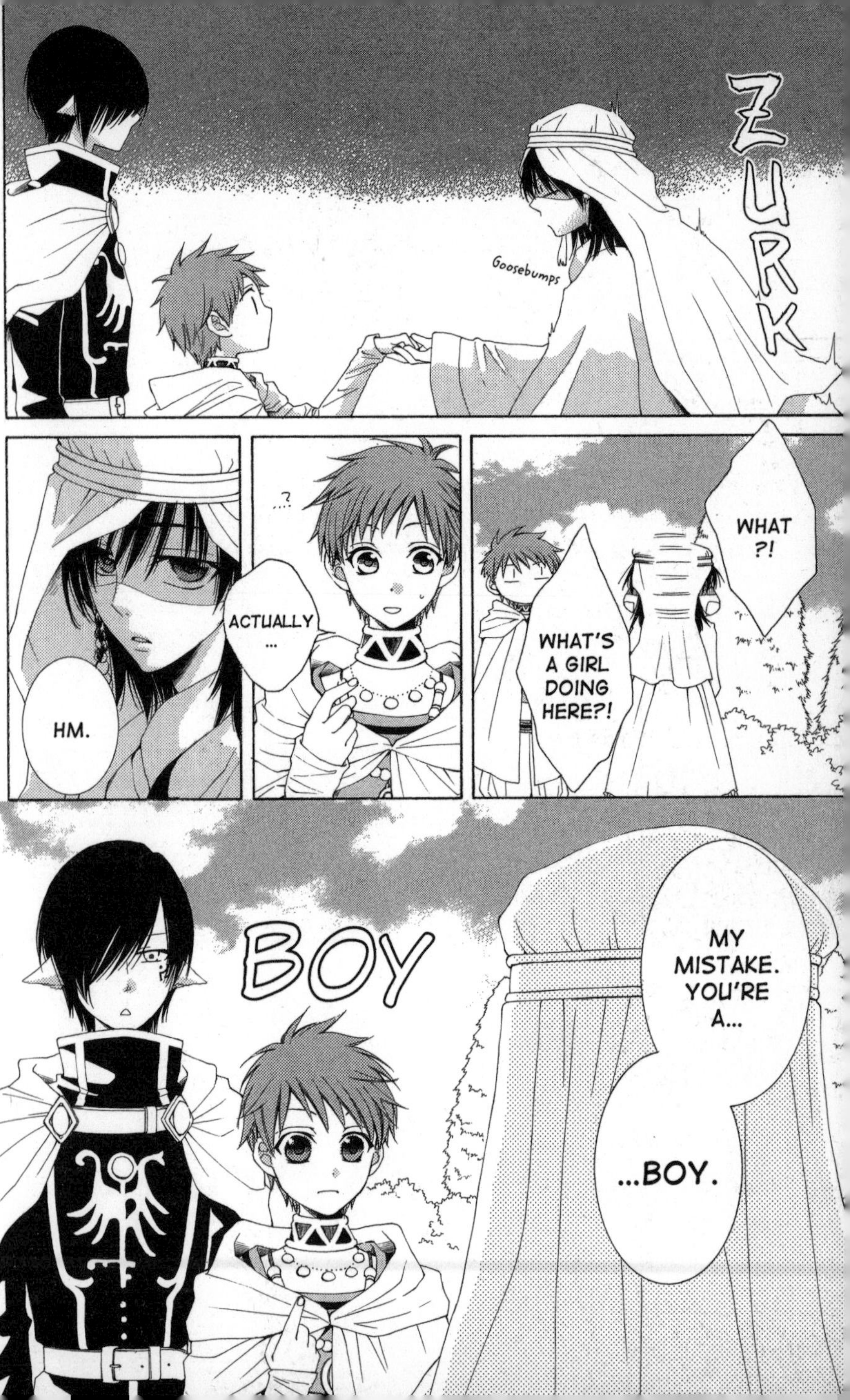
ZURK
Goosebumps
WHAT ?!
WHAT'S A GIRL DOING HERE?!
...?
ACTUALLY ...
HM.
MY MISTAKE. YOU'RE A...
BOY
...BOY.

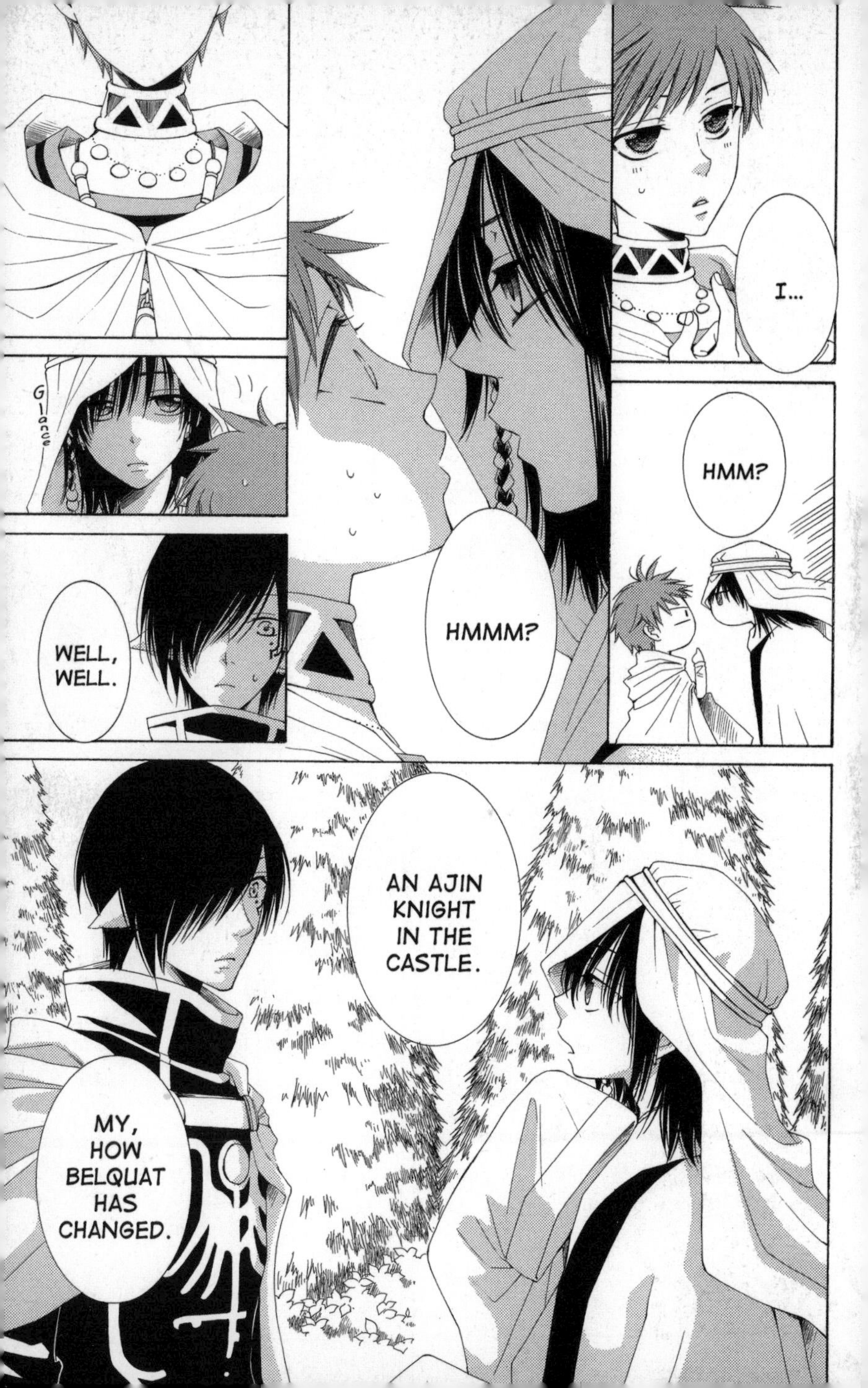

I...
HMM?
HMMM?
Glance
WELL, WELL.
AN AJIN KNIGHT IN THE CASTLE.
MY, HOW BELQUAT HAS CHANGED.

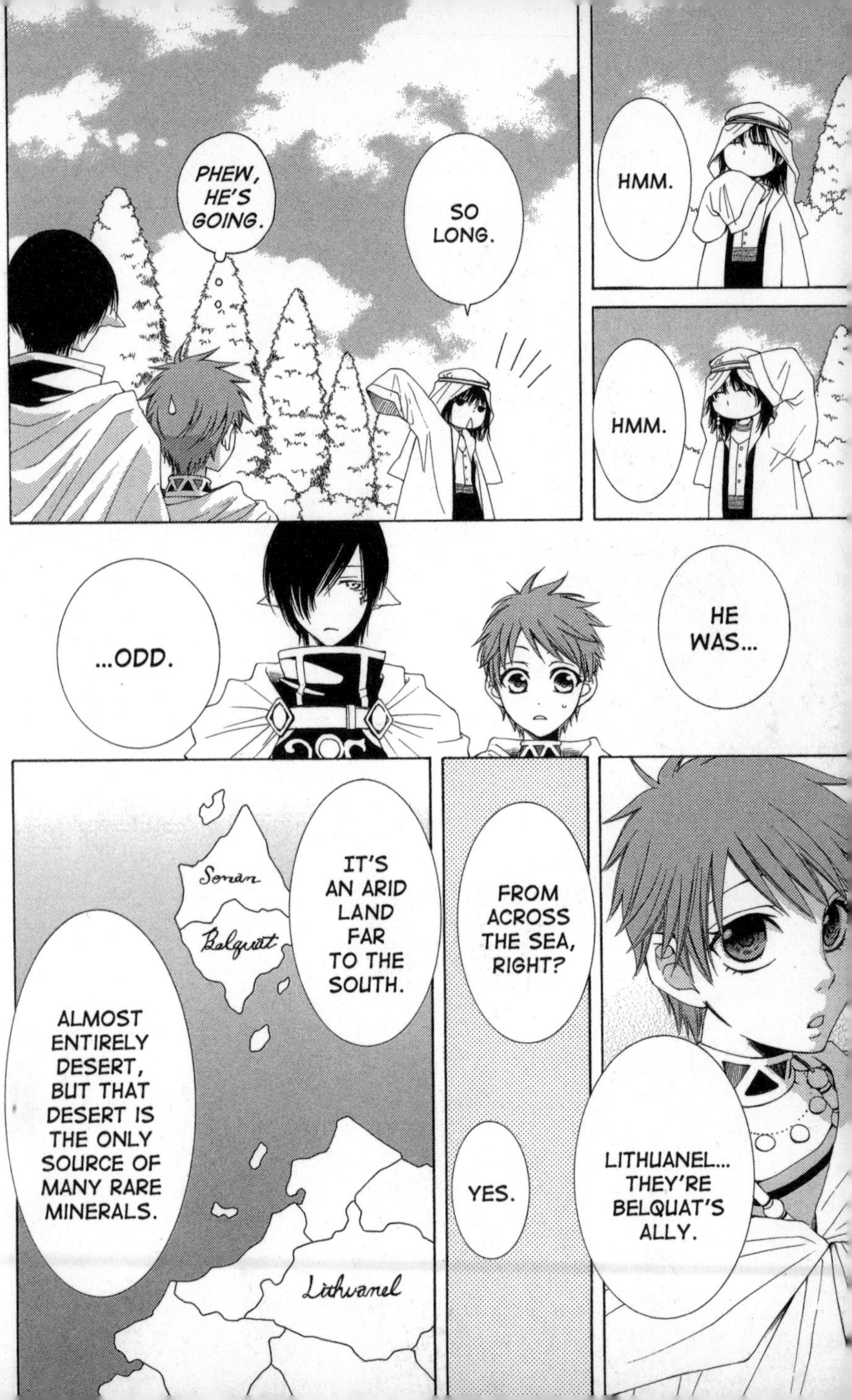
HMM.
HMM.
SO LONG.
PHEW, HE'S GOING.
HE WAS...
...ODD.
LITHUANEL... THEY'RE BELQUAT'S ALLY.
FROM ACROSS THE SEA, RIGHT?
YES.
IT'S AN ARID LAND FAR TO THE SOUTH.
ALMOST ENTIRELY DESERT, BUT THAT DESERT IS THE ONLY SOURCE OF MANY RARE MINERALS.
Soran
Belquat
Lithuanel

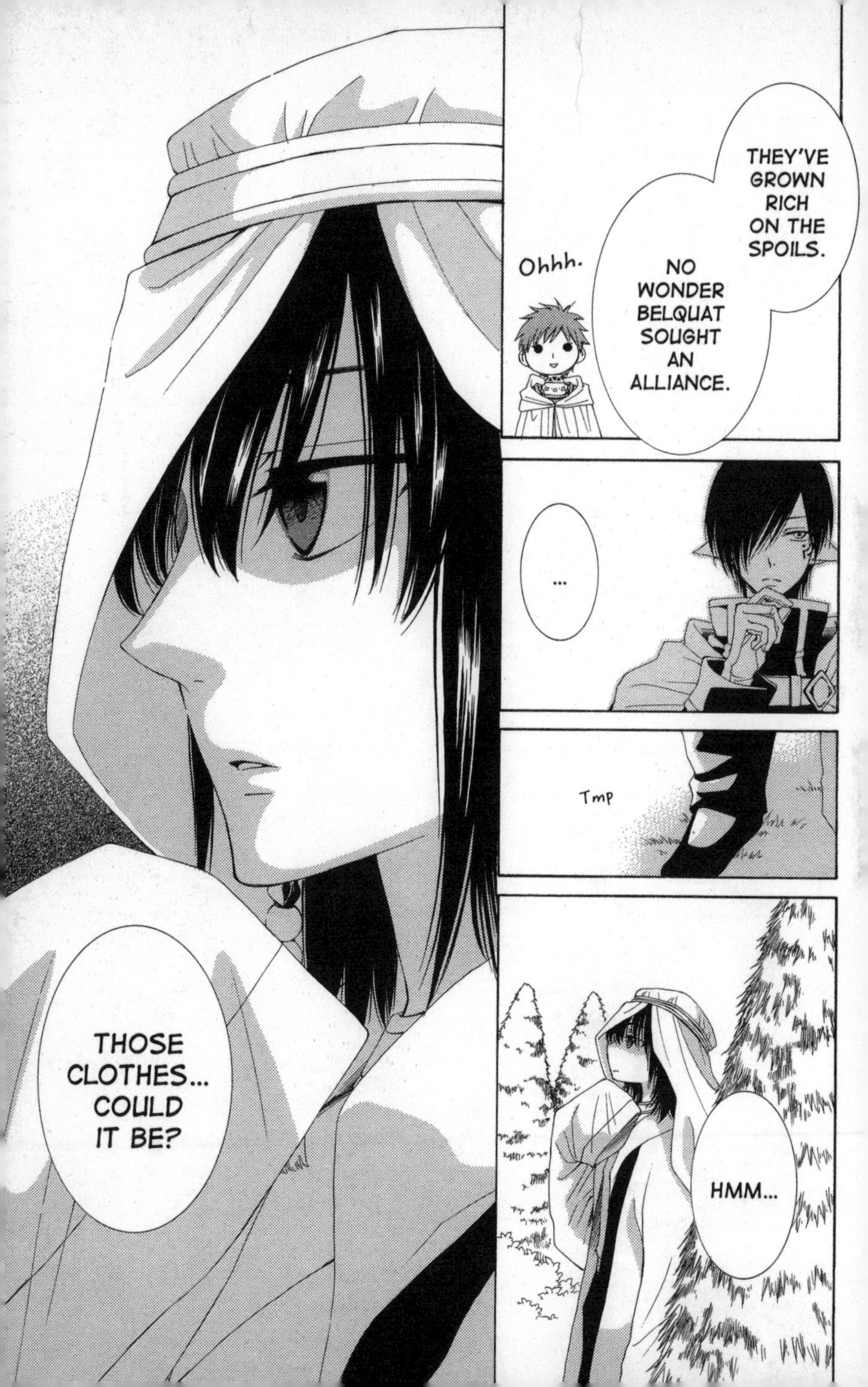
THEY'VE GROWN RICH ON THE SPOILS.
NO WONDER BELQUAT SOUGHT AN ALLIANCE.
Ohhh.
...
Tmp
HMM...
THOSE CLOTHES... COULD IT BE?

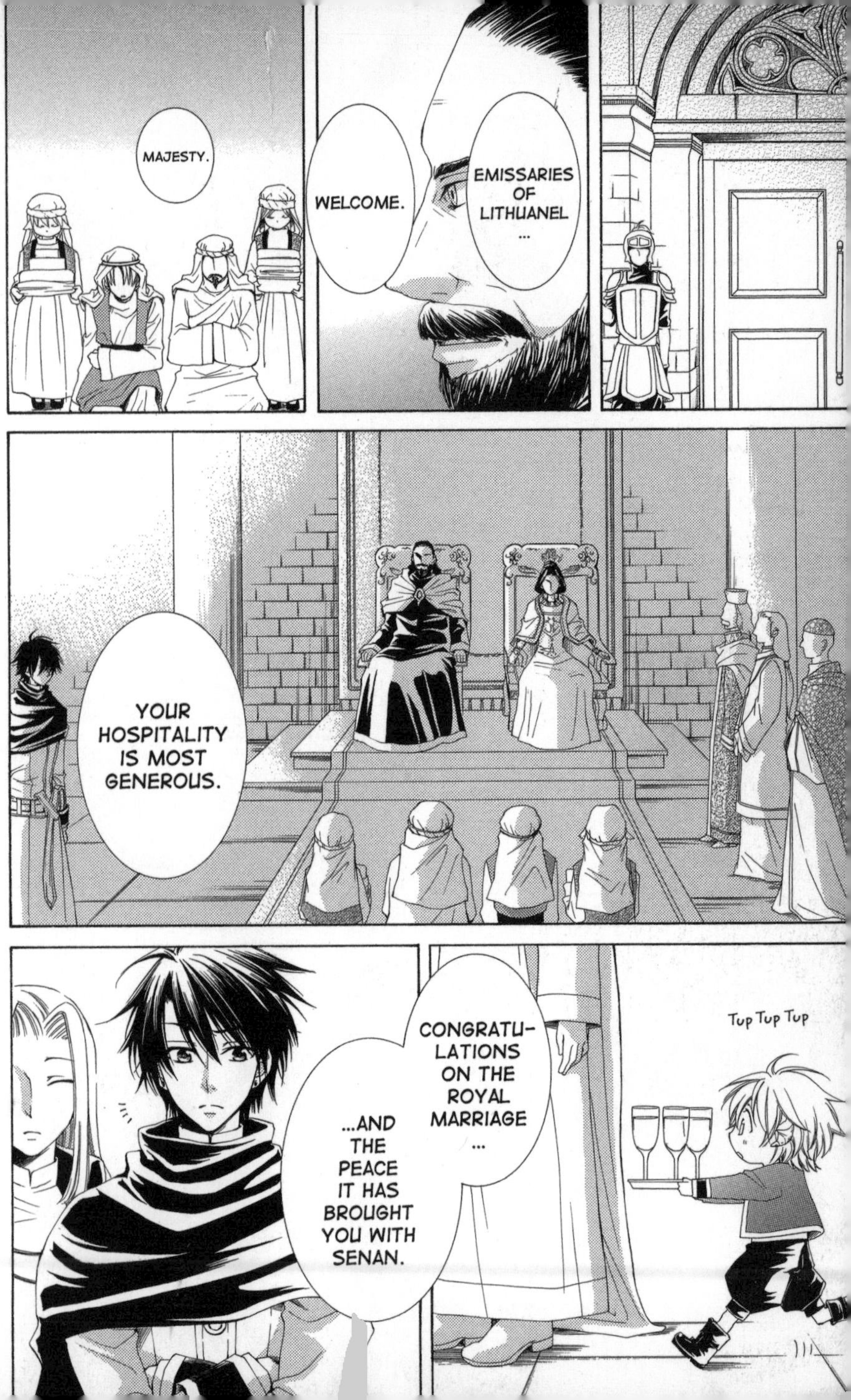
EMISSARIES OF LITHUANEL ...
WELCOME.
MAJESTY.
YOUR HOSPITALITY IS MOST GENEROUS.
Tup Tup Tup
CONGRATU-LATIONS ON THE ROYAL MARRIAGE ...
...AND THE PEACE IT HAS BROUGHT YOU WITH SENAN.

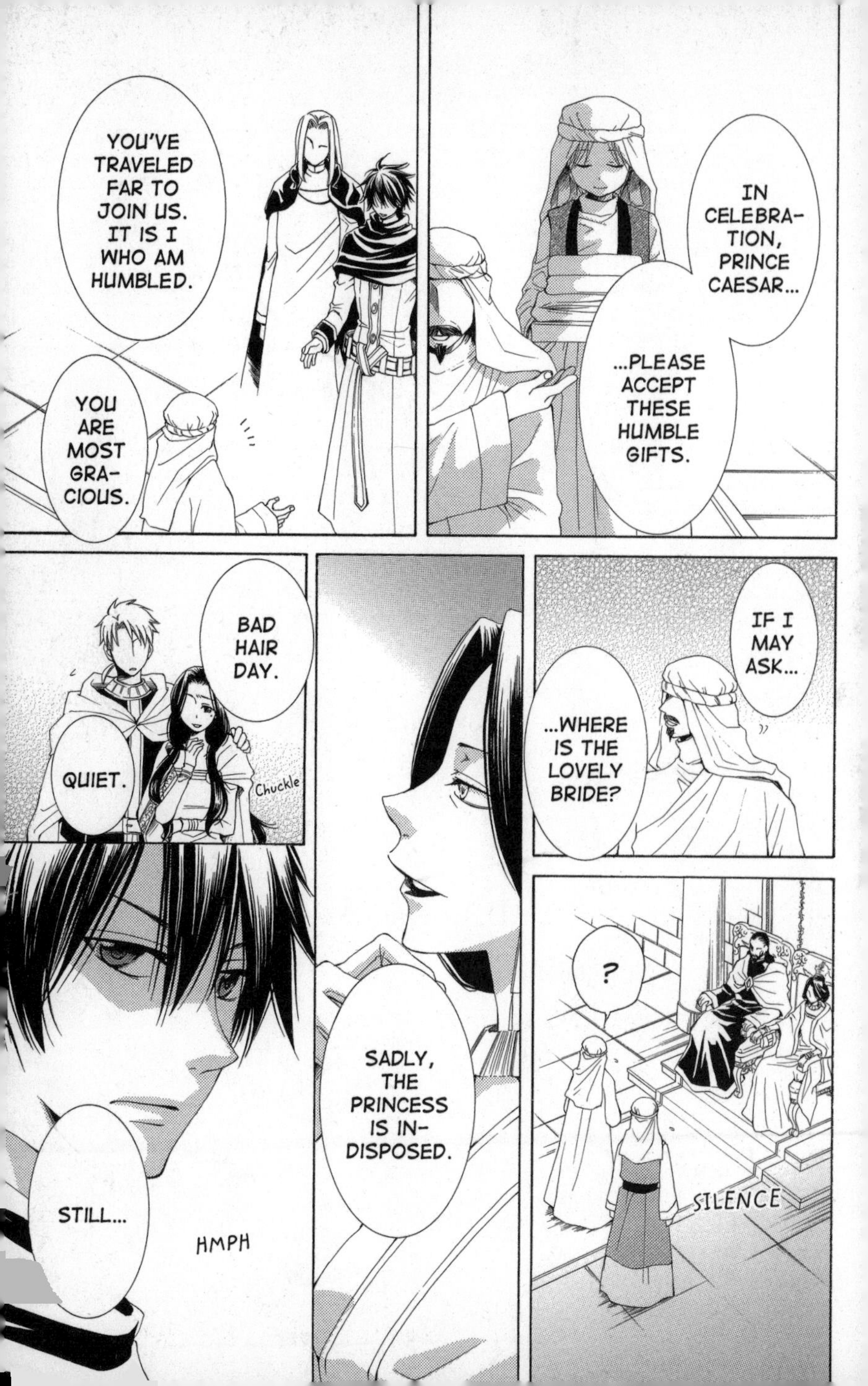
IN CELEBRATION, PRINCE CAESAR...
...PLEASE ACCEPT THESE HUMBLE GIFTS.
YOU'VE TRAVELED FAR TO JOIN US. IT IS I WHO AM HUMBLED.
YOU ARE MOST GRACIOUS.
IF I MAY ASK...
...WHERE IS THE LOVELY BRIDE?
?
SILENCE
SADLY, THE PRINCESS IS INDISPOSED.
BAD HAIR DAY.
QUIET.
Chuckle
STILL...
HMPH

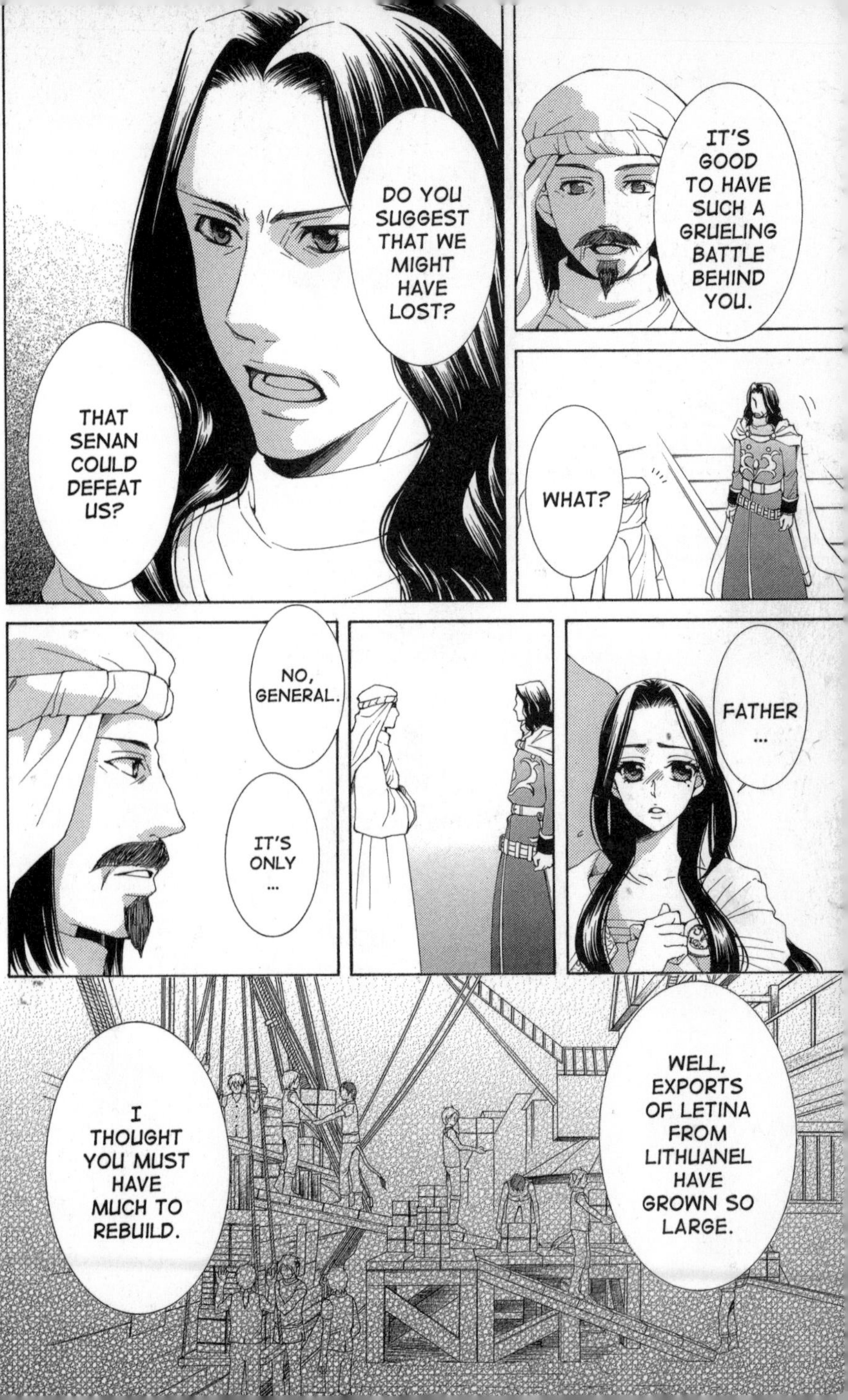
IT'S GOOD TO HAVE SUCH A GRUELING BATTLE BEHIND YOU.
WHAT?
DO YOU SUGGEST THAT WE MIGHT HAVE LOST?
THAT SENAN COULD DEFEAT US?
FATHER ...
NO, GENERAL.
IT'S ONLY ...
WELL, EXPORTS OF LETINA FROM LITHUANEL HAVE GROWN SO LARGE.
I THOUGHT YOU MUST HAVE MUCH TO REBUILD.

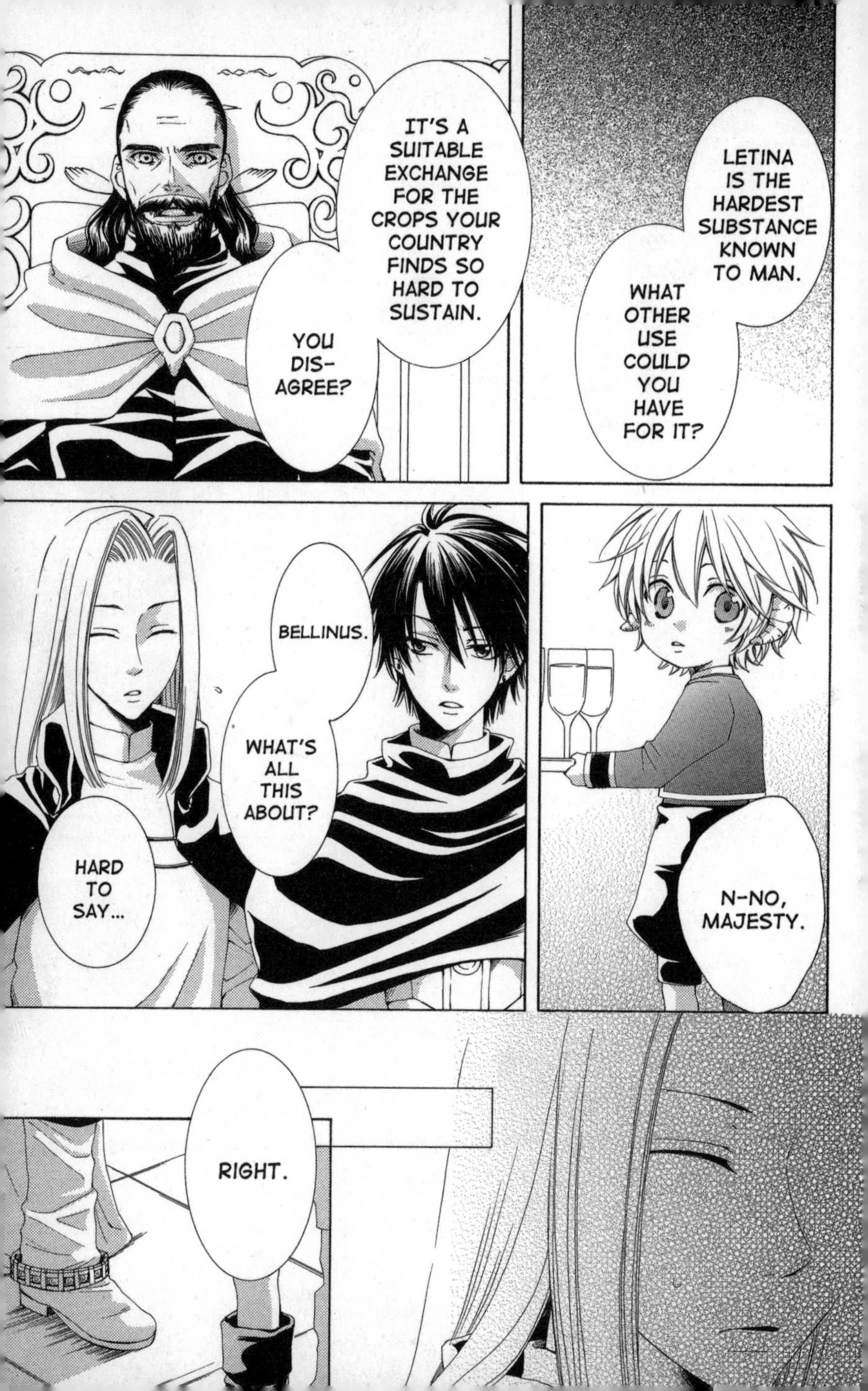
LETINA IS THE HARDEST SUBSTANCE KNOWN TO MAN.
WHAT OTHER USE COULD YOU HAVE FOR IT?
IT'S A SUITABLE EXCHANGE FOR THE CROPS YOUR COUNTRY FINDS SO HARD TO SUSTAIN.
YOU DIS-AGREE?
N-NO, MAJESTY.
BELLINUS.
WHAT'S ALL THIS ABOUT?
HARD TO SAY...
RIGHT.

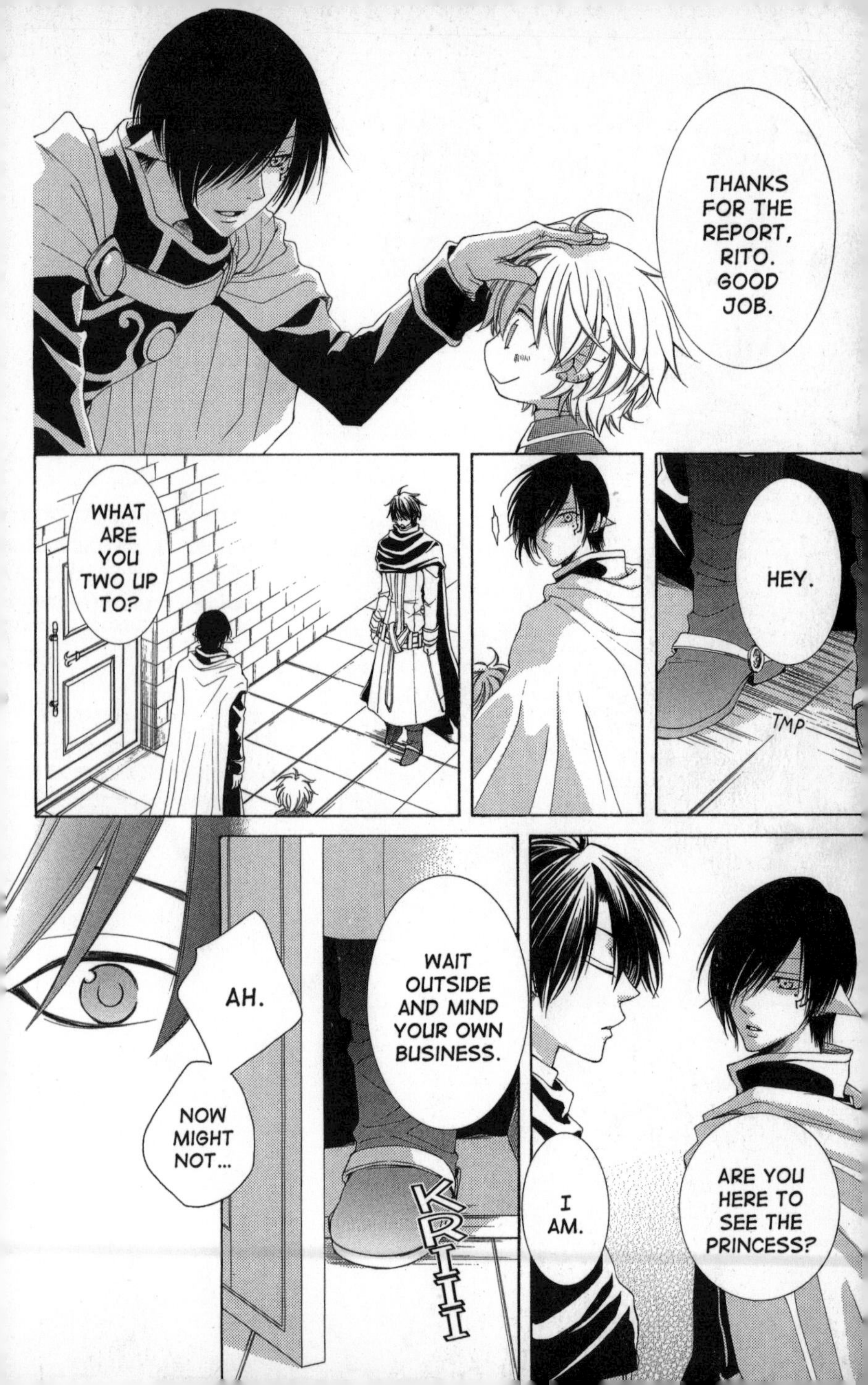
THANKS FOR THE REPORT, RITO. GOOD JOB.
HEY.
TMP
WHAT ARE YOU TWO UP TO?
ARE YOU HERE TO SEE THE PRINCESS?
I AM.
WAIT OUTSIDE AND MIND YOUR OWN BUSINESS.
KRIII
AH.
NOW MIGHT NOT...

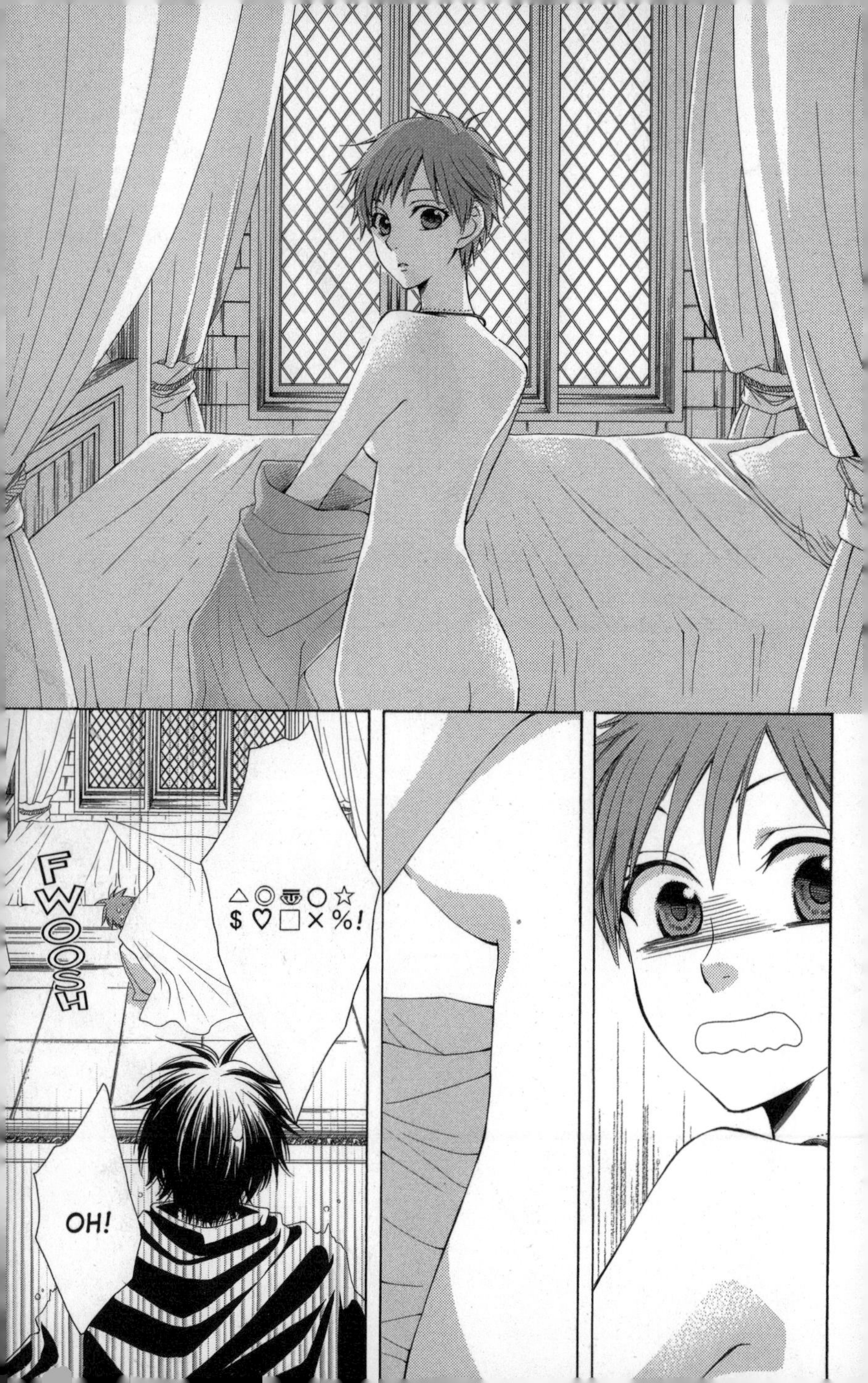
△◎〒○☆
$♡□×%!
FWOOSH
OH!

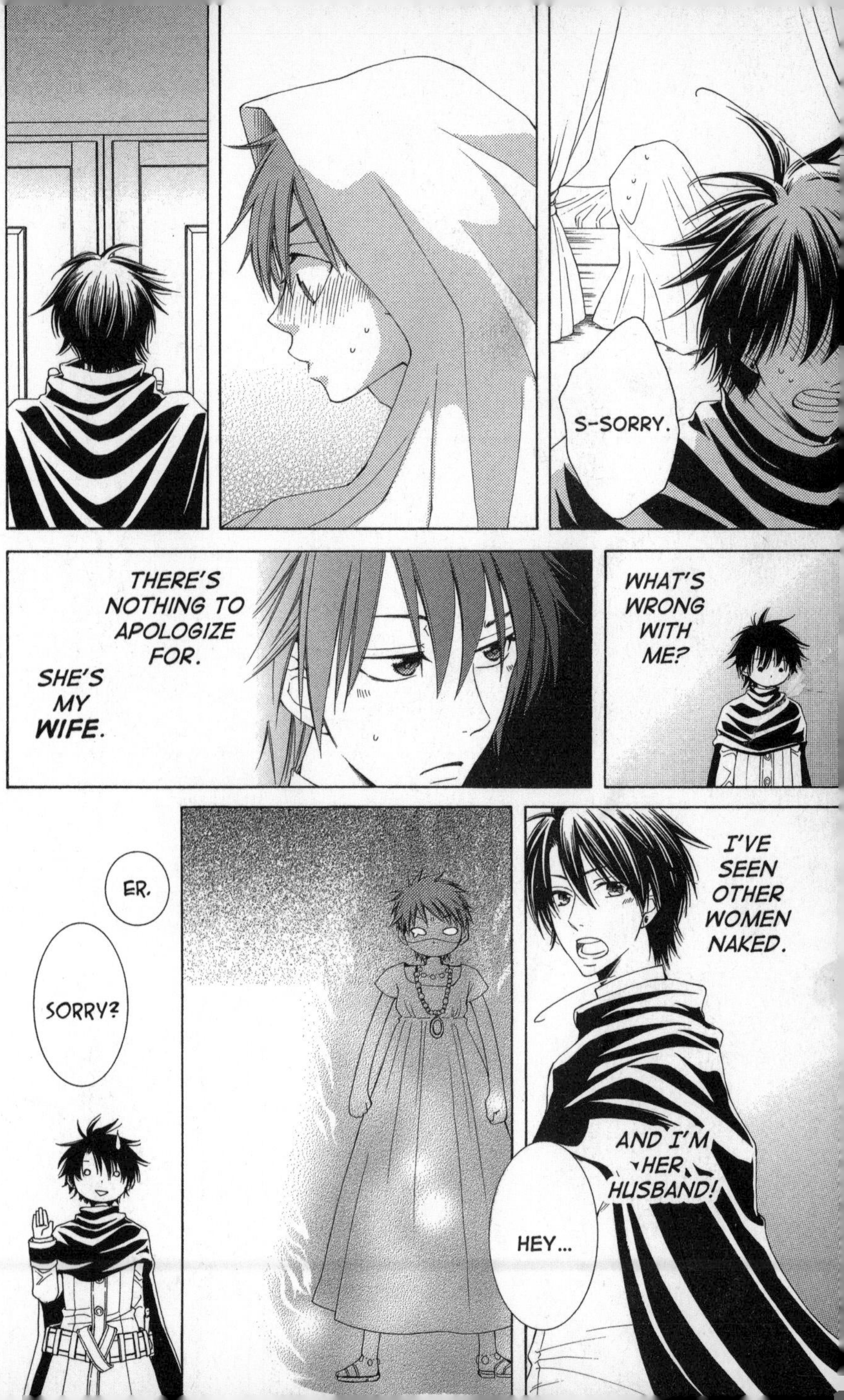
S-SORRY.
WHAT'S WRONG WITH ME?
THERE'S NOTHING TO APOLOGIZE FOR.
SHE'S MY WIFE.
I'VE SEEN OTHER WOMEN NAKED.
AND I'M HER HUSBAND!
HEY...
ER.
SORRY?

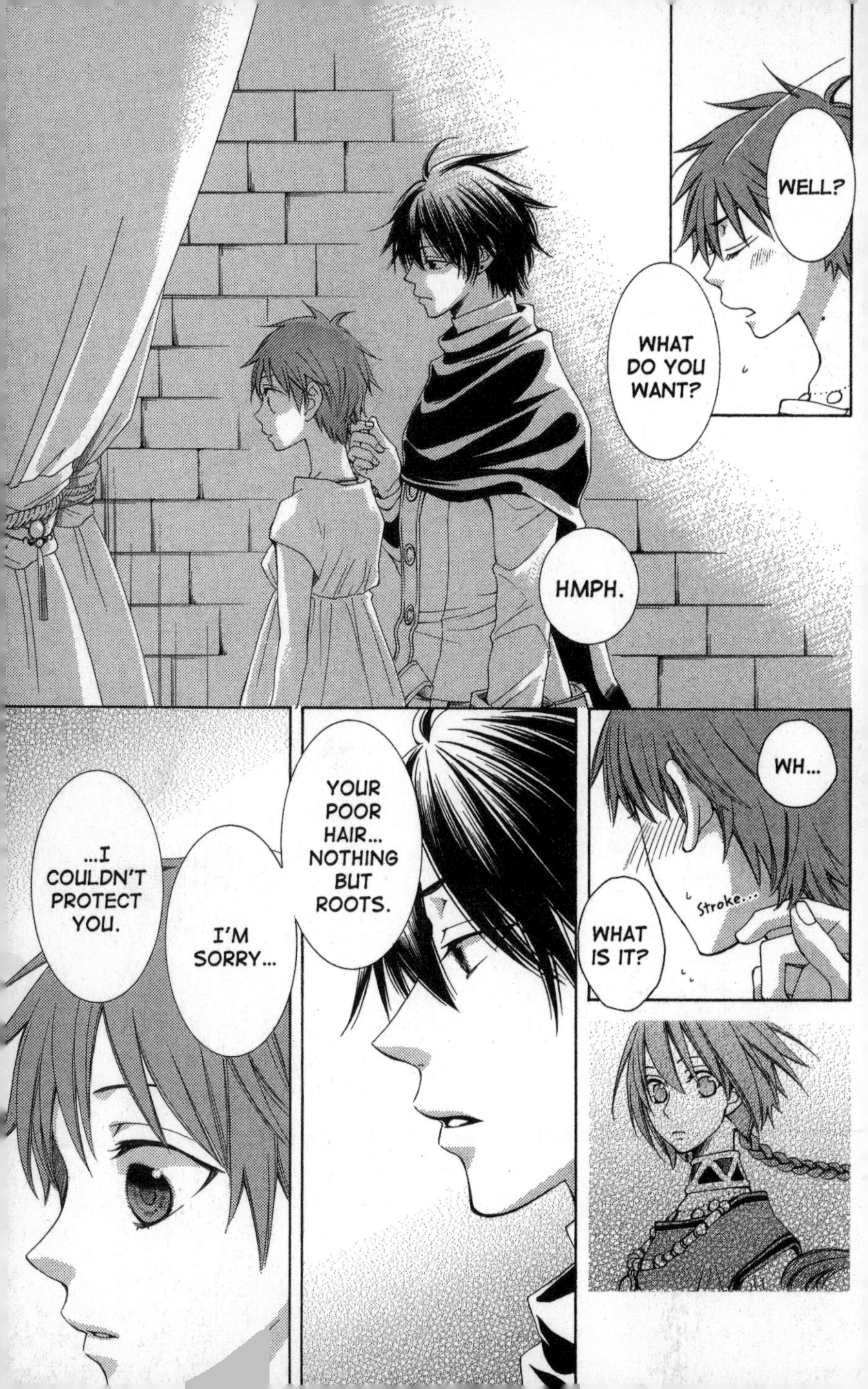

WELL?
WHAT DO YOU WANT?
HMPH.
WH...
Stroke...
WHAT IS IT?
YOUR POOR HAIR... NOTHING BUT ROOTS.
I'M SORRY...
...I COULDN'T PROTECT YOU.

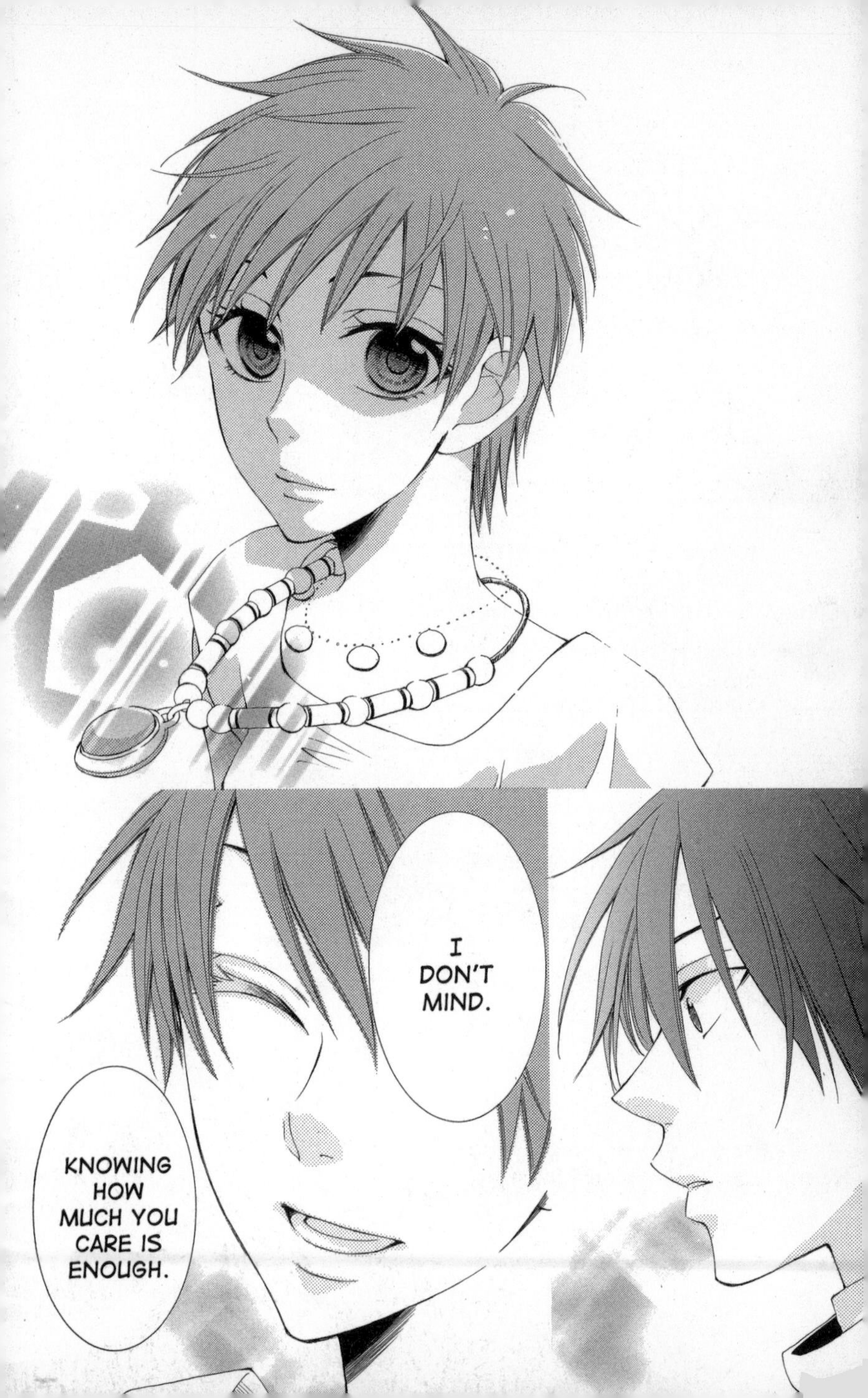
I DON'T MIND.
KNOWING HOW MUCH YOU CARE IS ENOUGH.

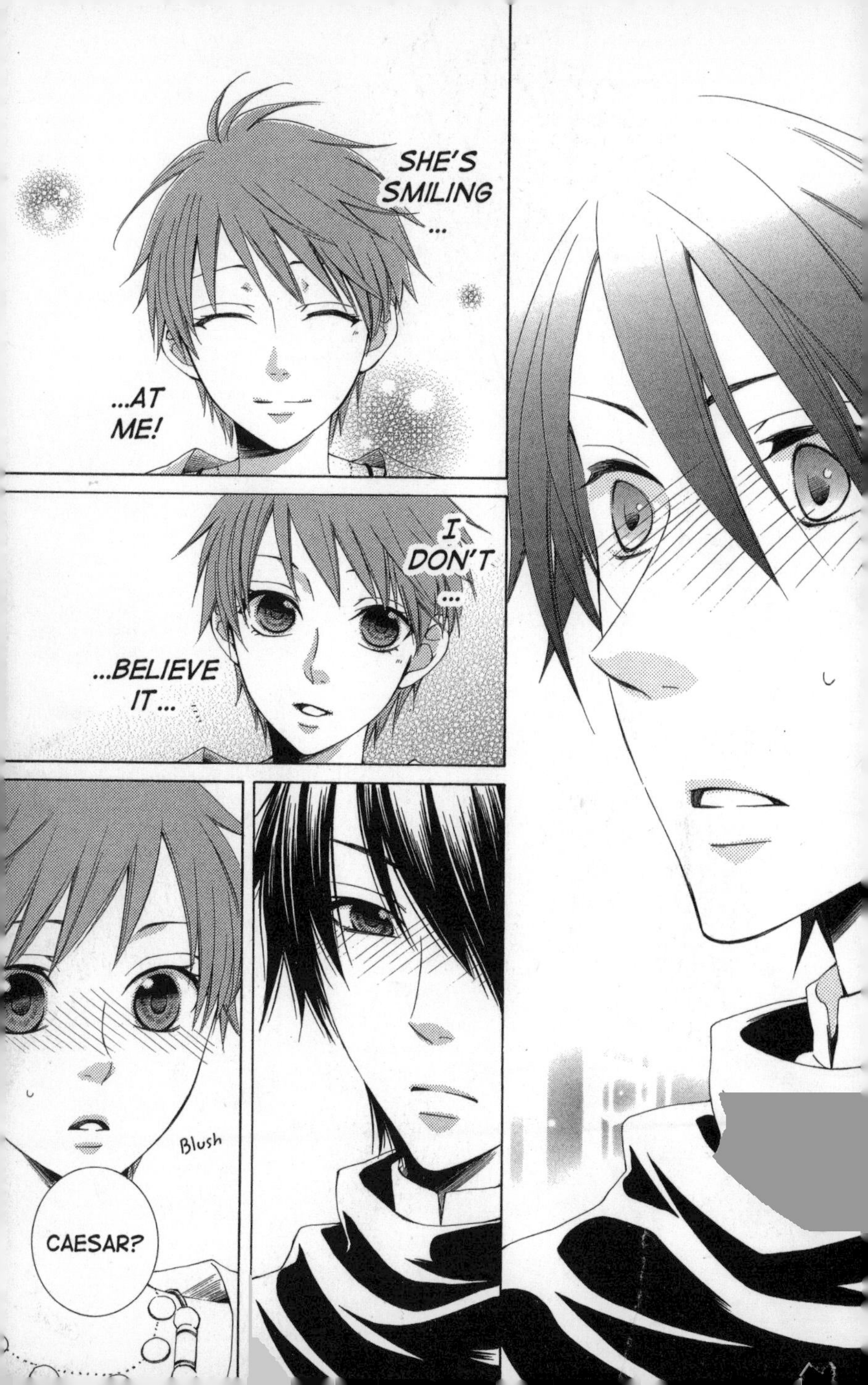
SHE'S SMILING ...
...AT ME!
I DON'T ...
...BELIEVE IT ...
Blush
CAESAR?

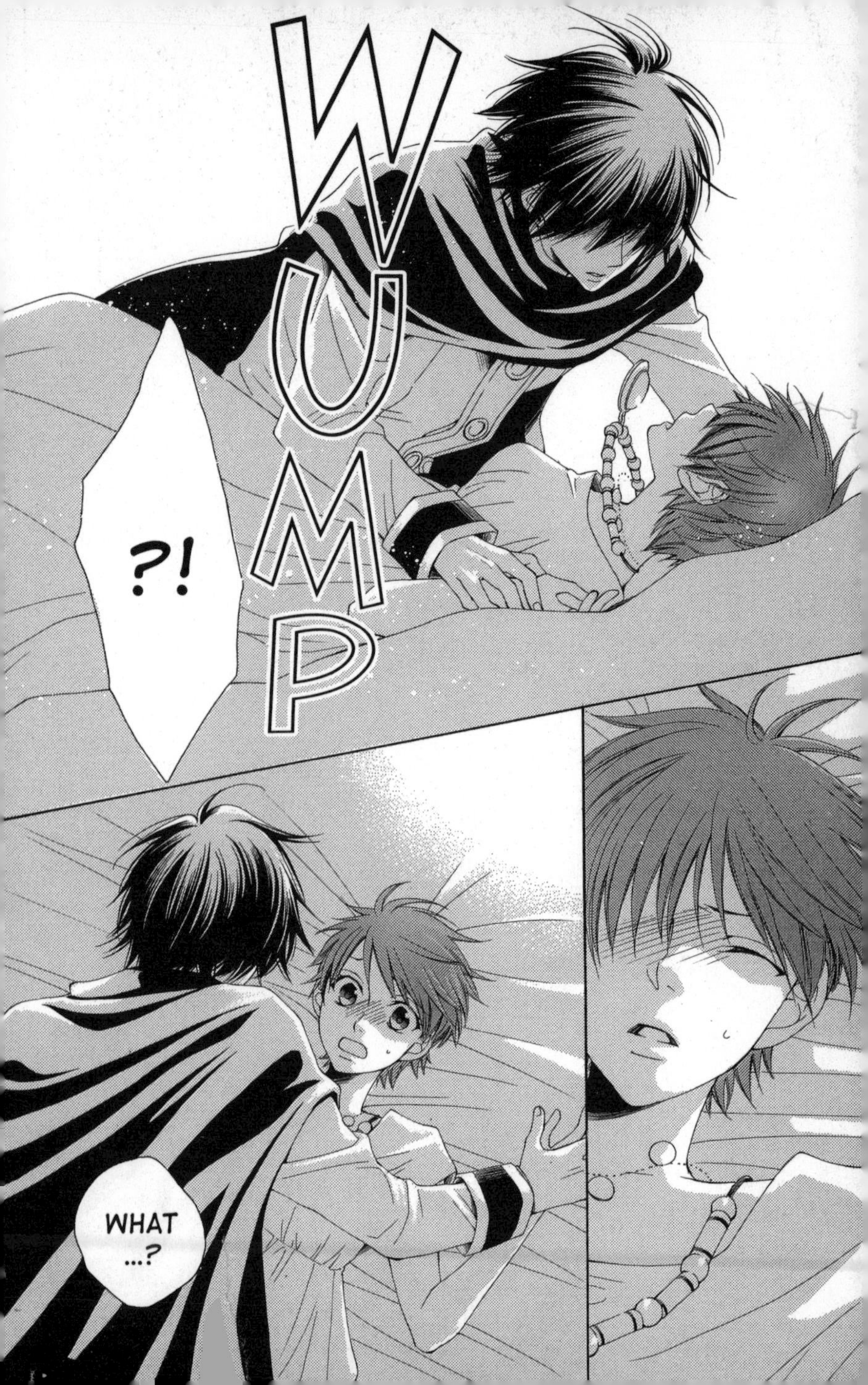
WUMP
?!
WHAT ...?

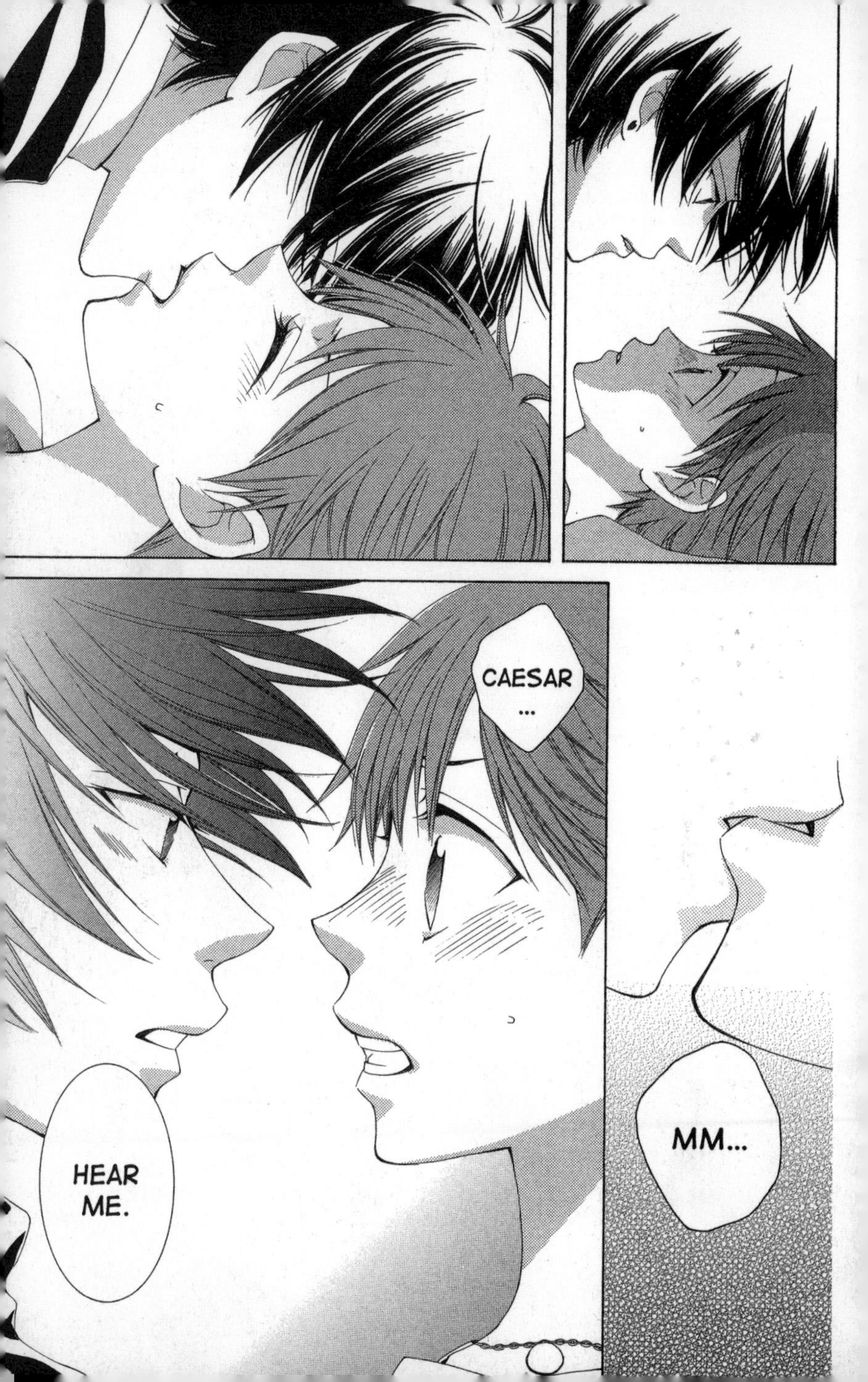
MM...
CAESAR ...
HEAR ME.

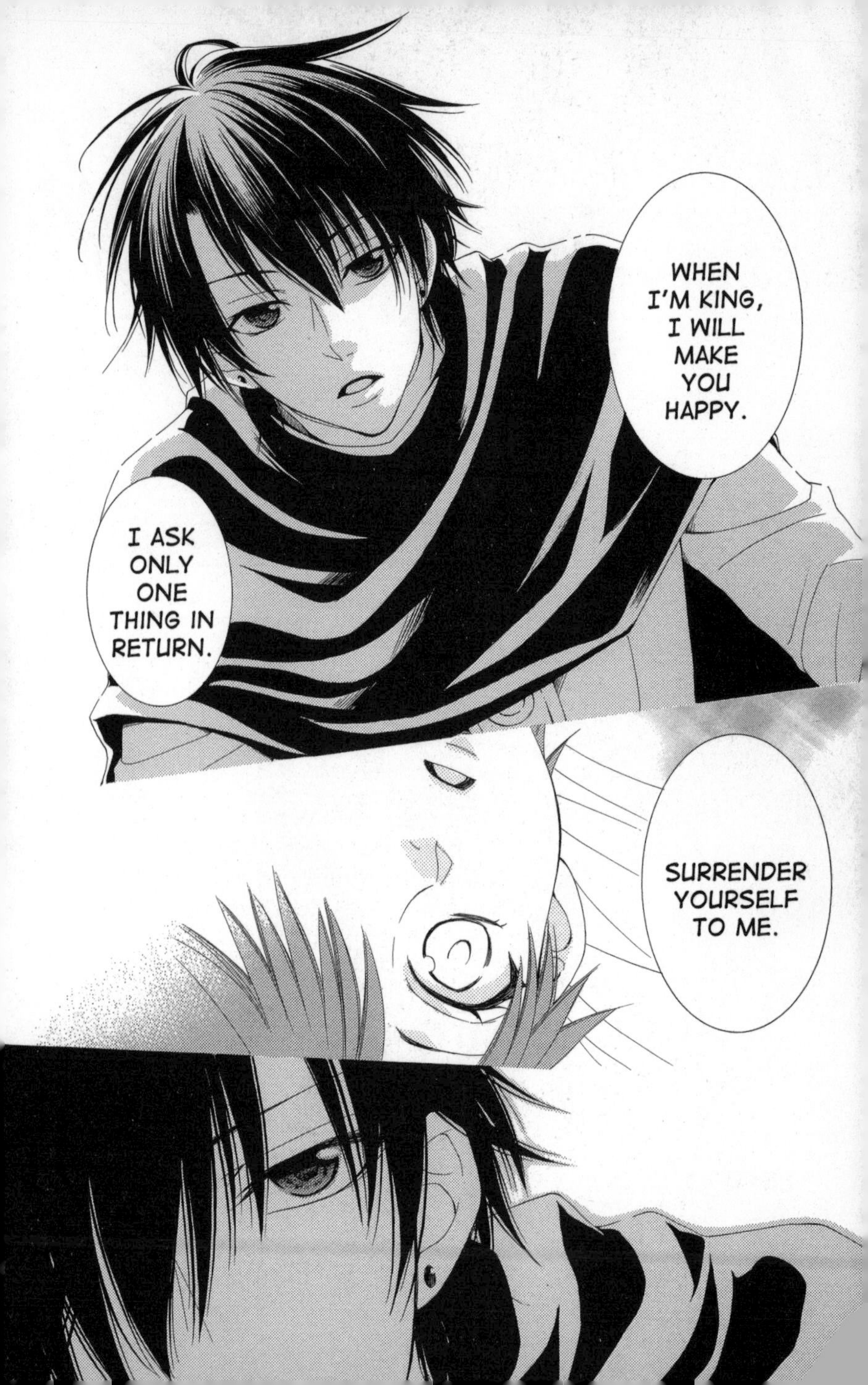
WHEN I'M KING, I WILL MAKE YOU HAPPY.
I ASK ONLY ONE THING IN RETURN.
SURRENDER YOURSELF TO ME.

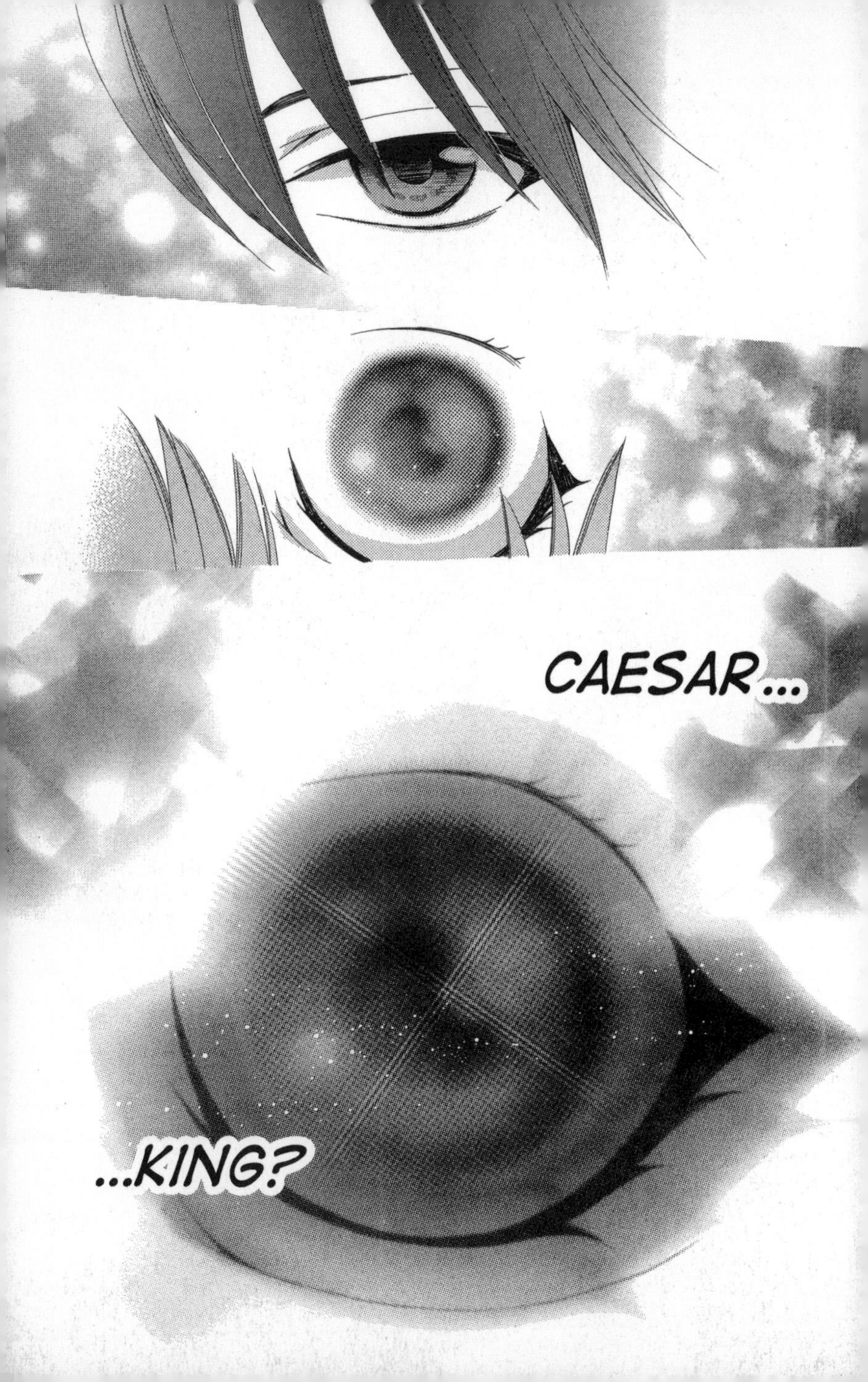
CAESAR...
...KING?

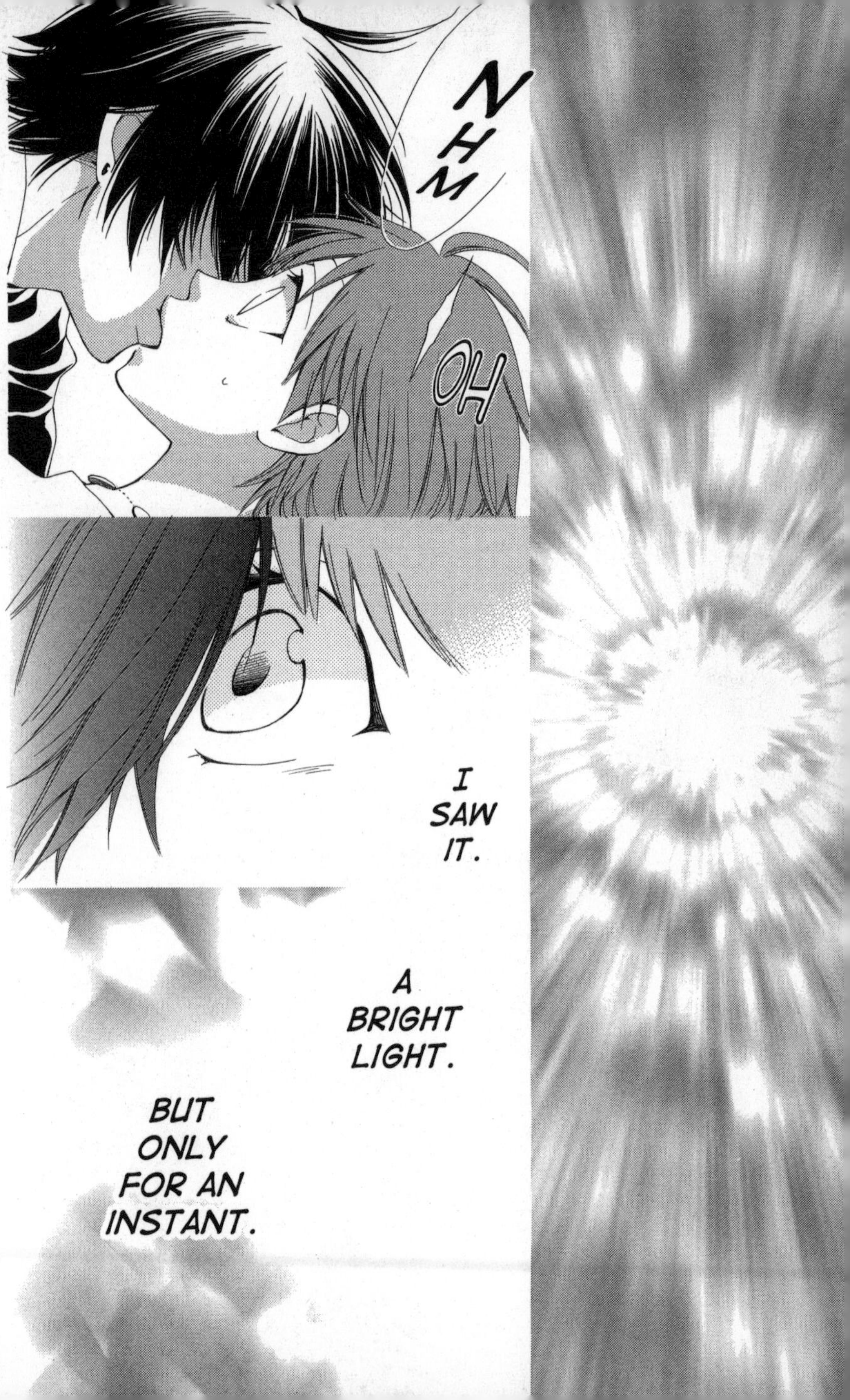
NHM
OH
I SAW IT.
A BRIGHT LIGHT.
BUT ONLY FOR AN INSTANT.

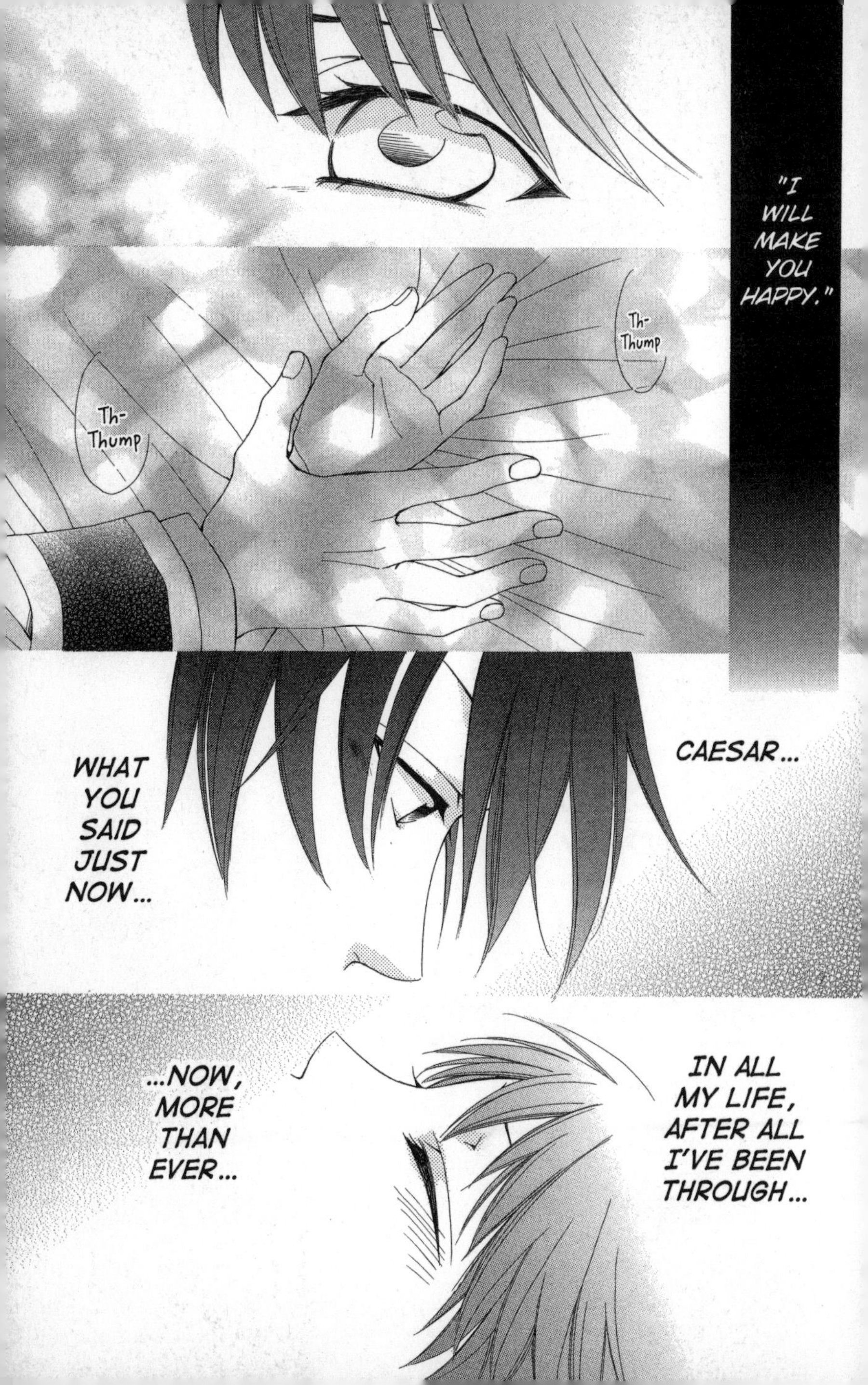
"I WILL MAKE YOU HAPPY."
Th-Thump
Th-Thump
CAESAR...
WHAT YOU SAID JUST NOW...
IN ALL MY LIFE, AFTER ALL I'VE BEEN THROUGH...
...NOW, MORE THAN EVER...

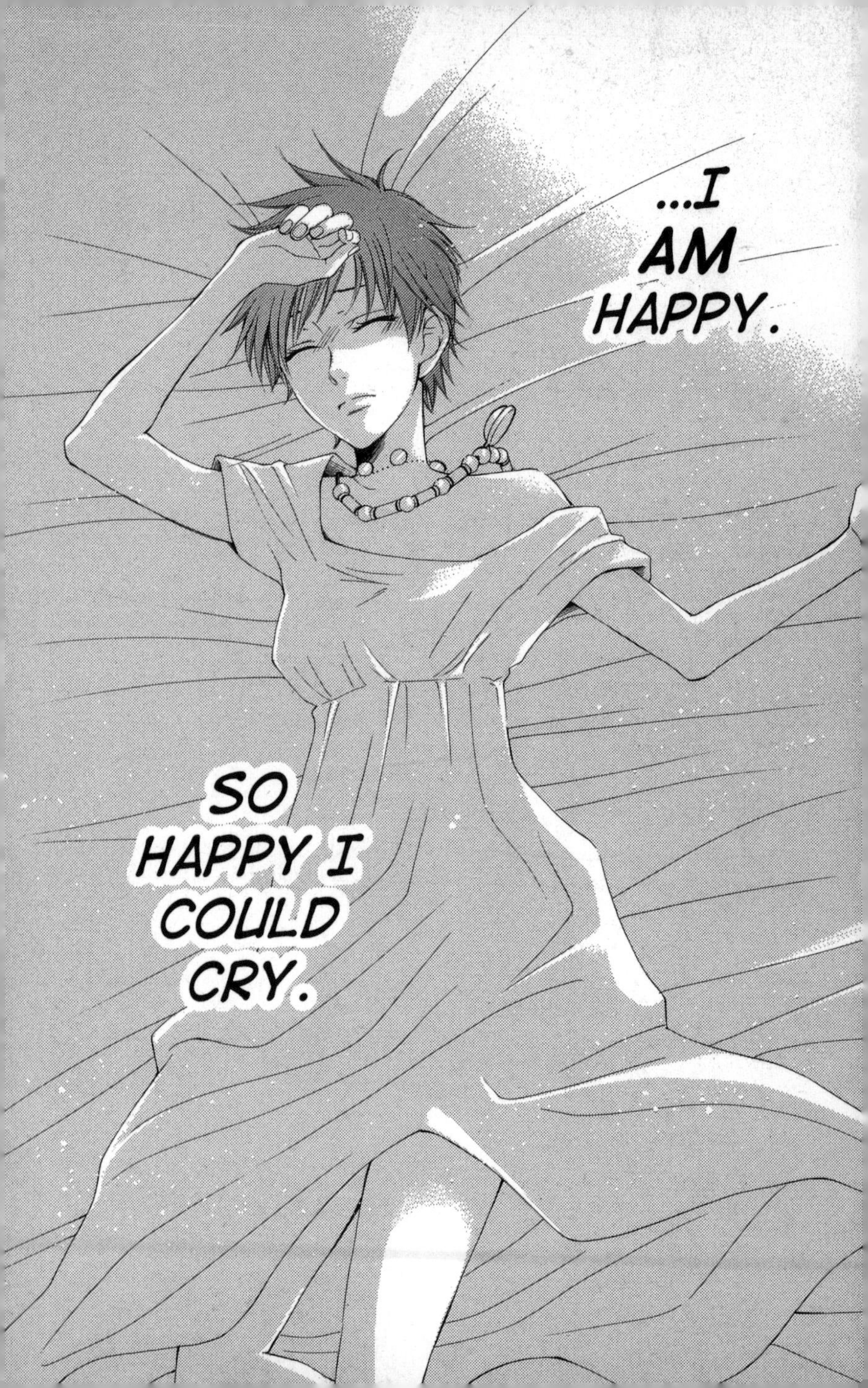
...I AM HAPPY.
SO HAPPY I COULD CRY.

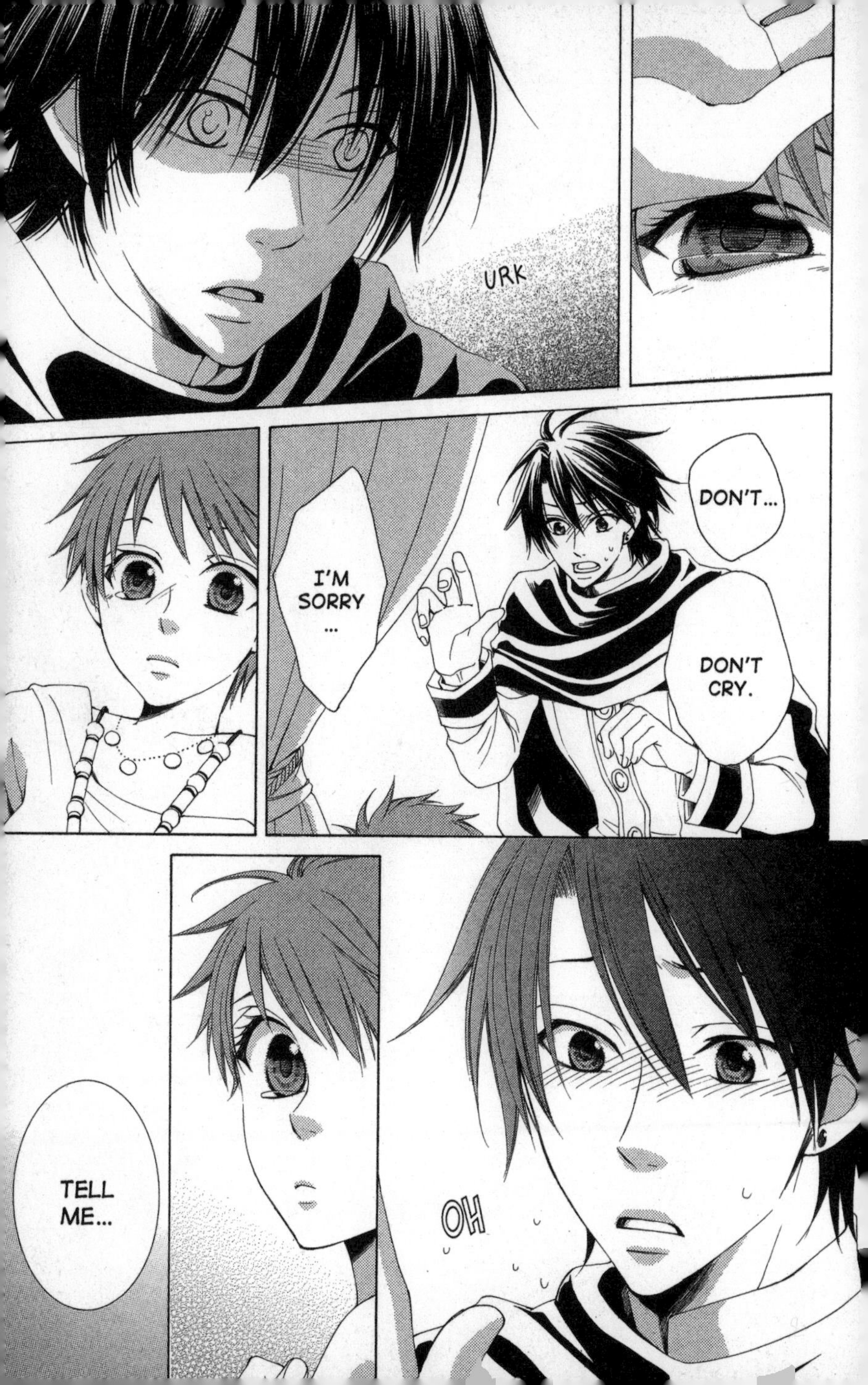
URK
DON'T...
DON'T CRY.
I'M SORRY ...
OH
TELL ME...

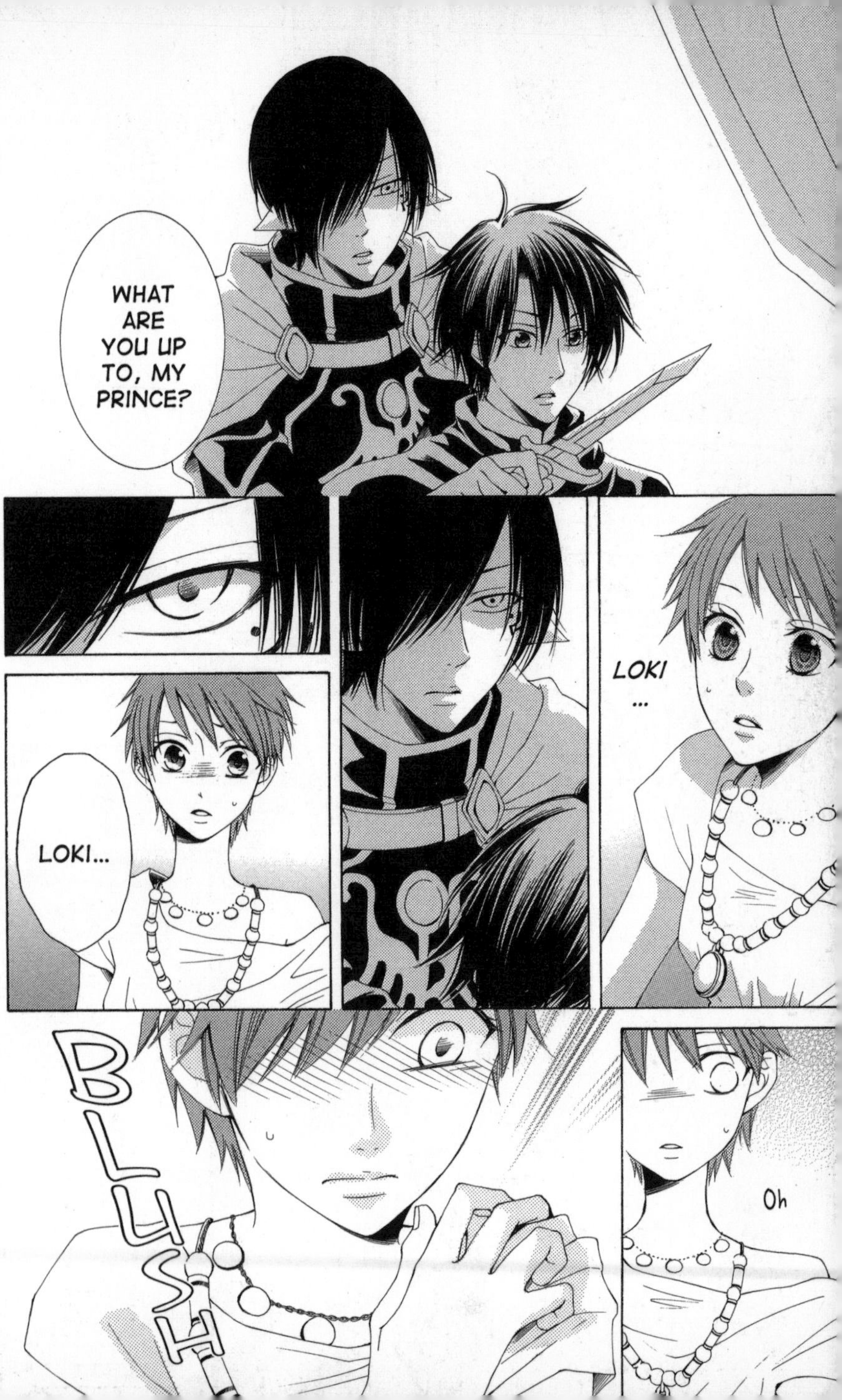
WHAT ARE YOU UP TO, MY PRINCE?
LOKI ...
LOKI...
Oh
BLUSH

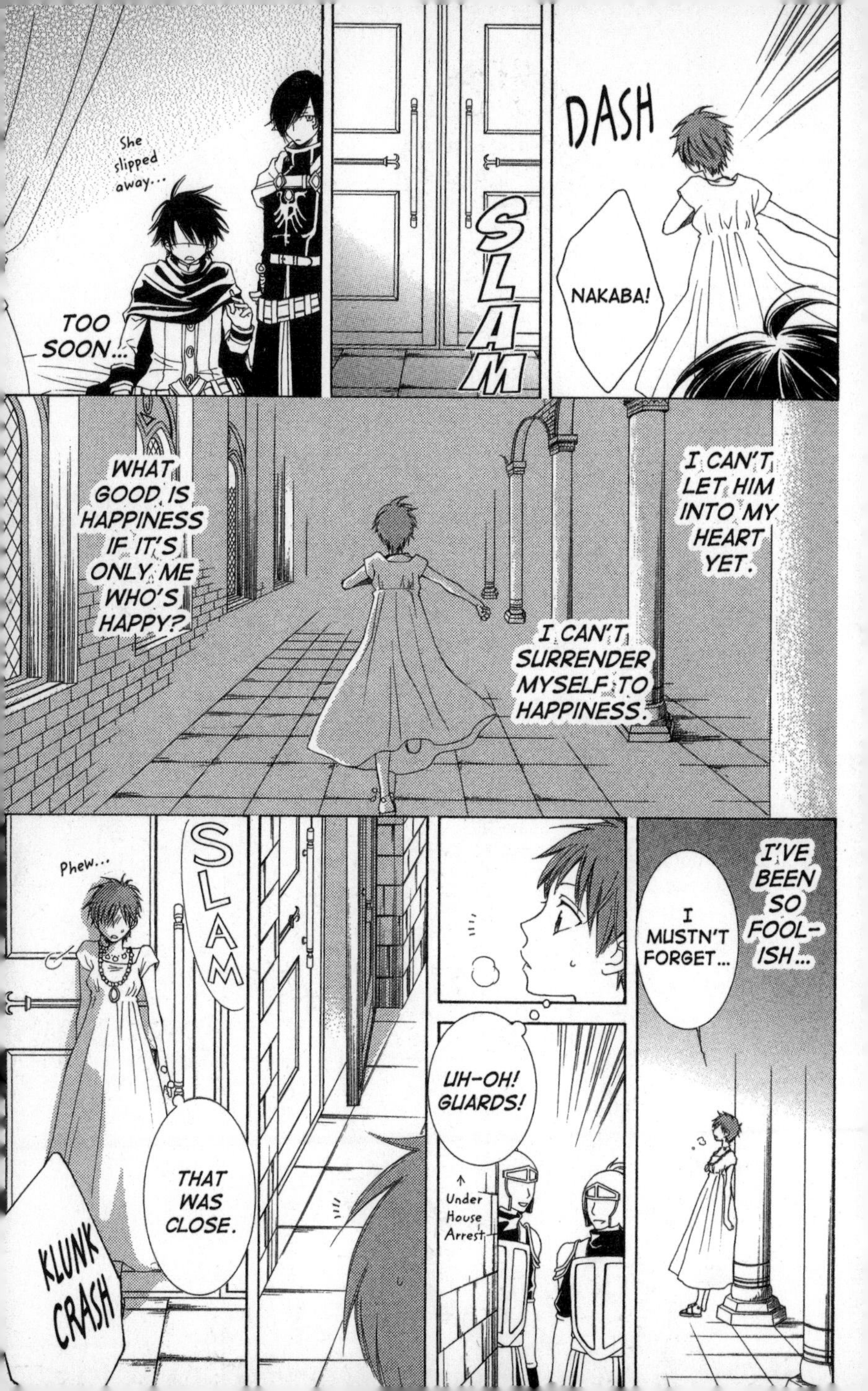
DASH
NAKABA!
SLAM
She slipped away...
TOO SOON...
I CAN'T LET HIM INTO MY HEART YET.
I CAN'T SURRENDER MYSELF TO HAPPINESS.
WHAT GOOD IS HAPPINESS IF IT'S ONLY ME WHO'S HAPPY?
I'VE BEEN SO FOOL-ISH...
I MUSTN'T FORGET...
UH-OH! GUARDS!
↑ Under House Arrest
SLAM
Phew...
THAT WAS CLOSE.
KLUNK CRASH

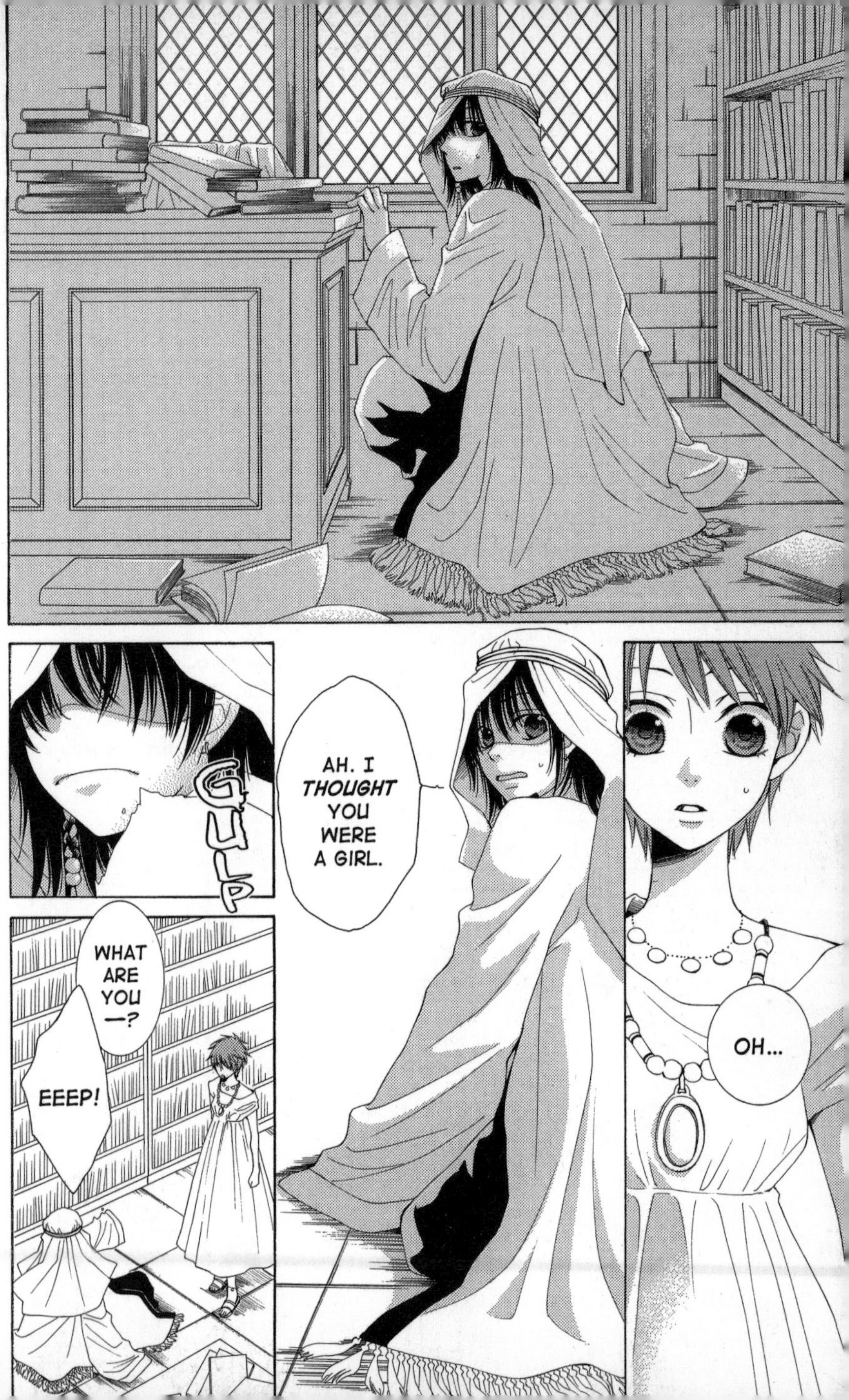
OH...
AH. I *THOUGHT* YOU WERE A GIRL.
GULP
WHAT ARE YOU—?
EEEP!

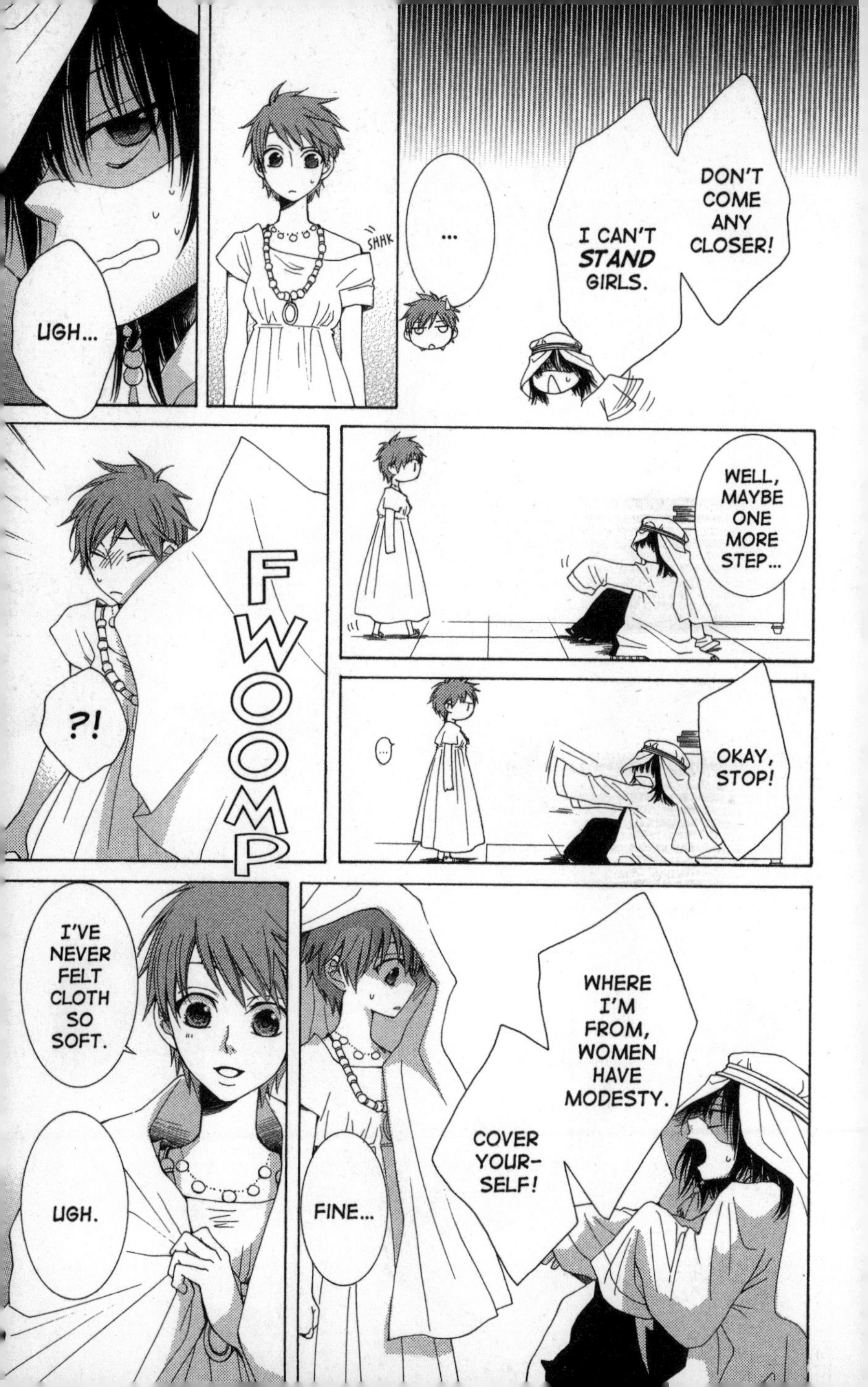
DON'T COME ANY CLOSER!
I CAN'T STAND GIRLS.
...
SHHK
UGH...
WELL, MAYBE ONE MORE STEP...
OKAY, STOP!
...
FWOOMP
?!
WHERE I'M FROM, WOMEN HAVE MODESTY.
COVER YOUR-SELF!
FINE...
I'VE NEVER FELT CLOTH SO SOFT.
UGH.

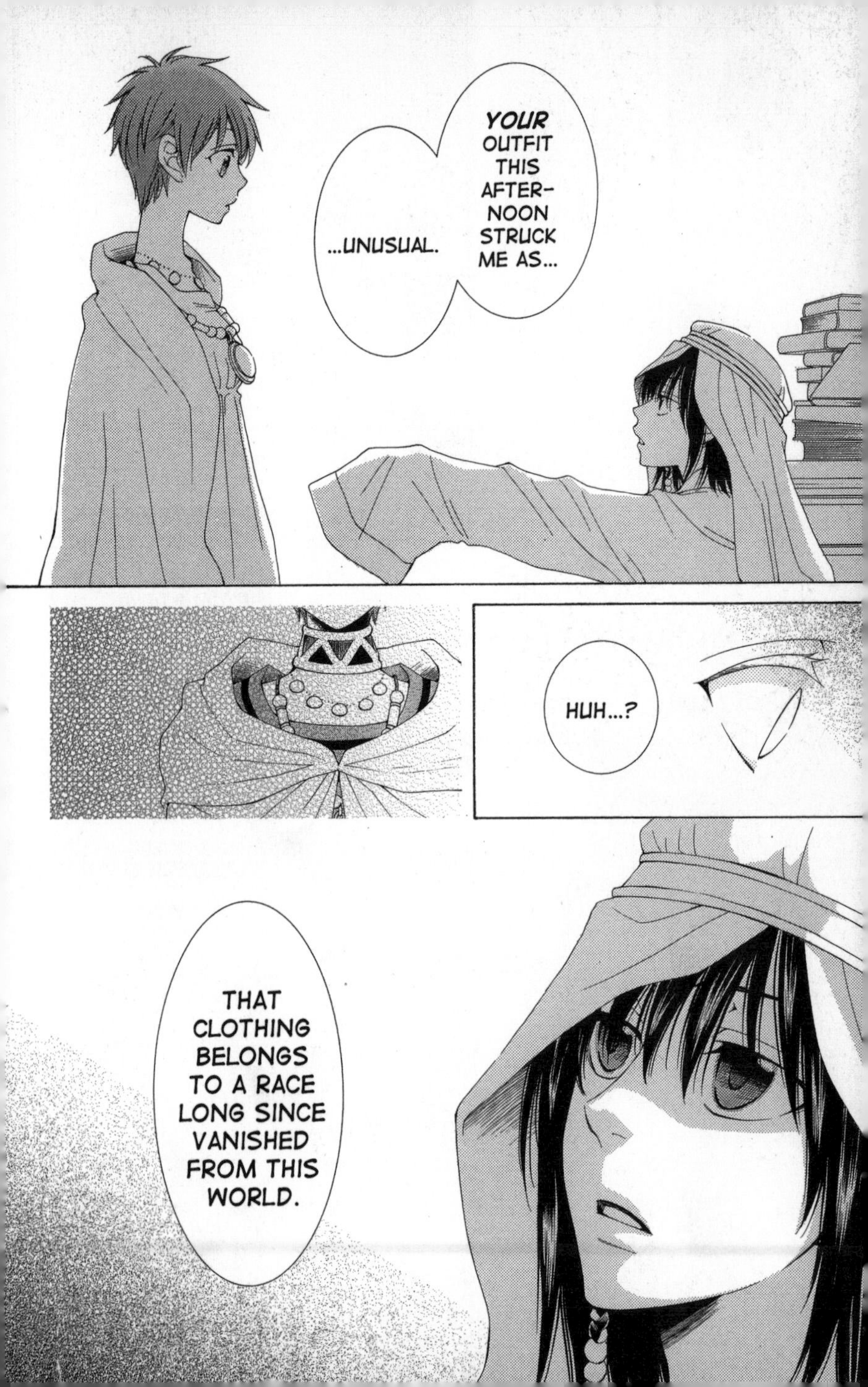
YOUR OUTFIT THIS AFTERNOON STRUCK ME AS...
...UNUSUAL.
HUH...?
THAT CLOTHING BELONGS TO A RACE LONG SINCE VANISHED FROM THIS WORLD.

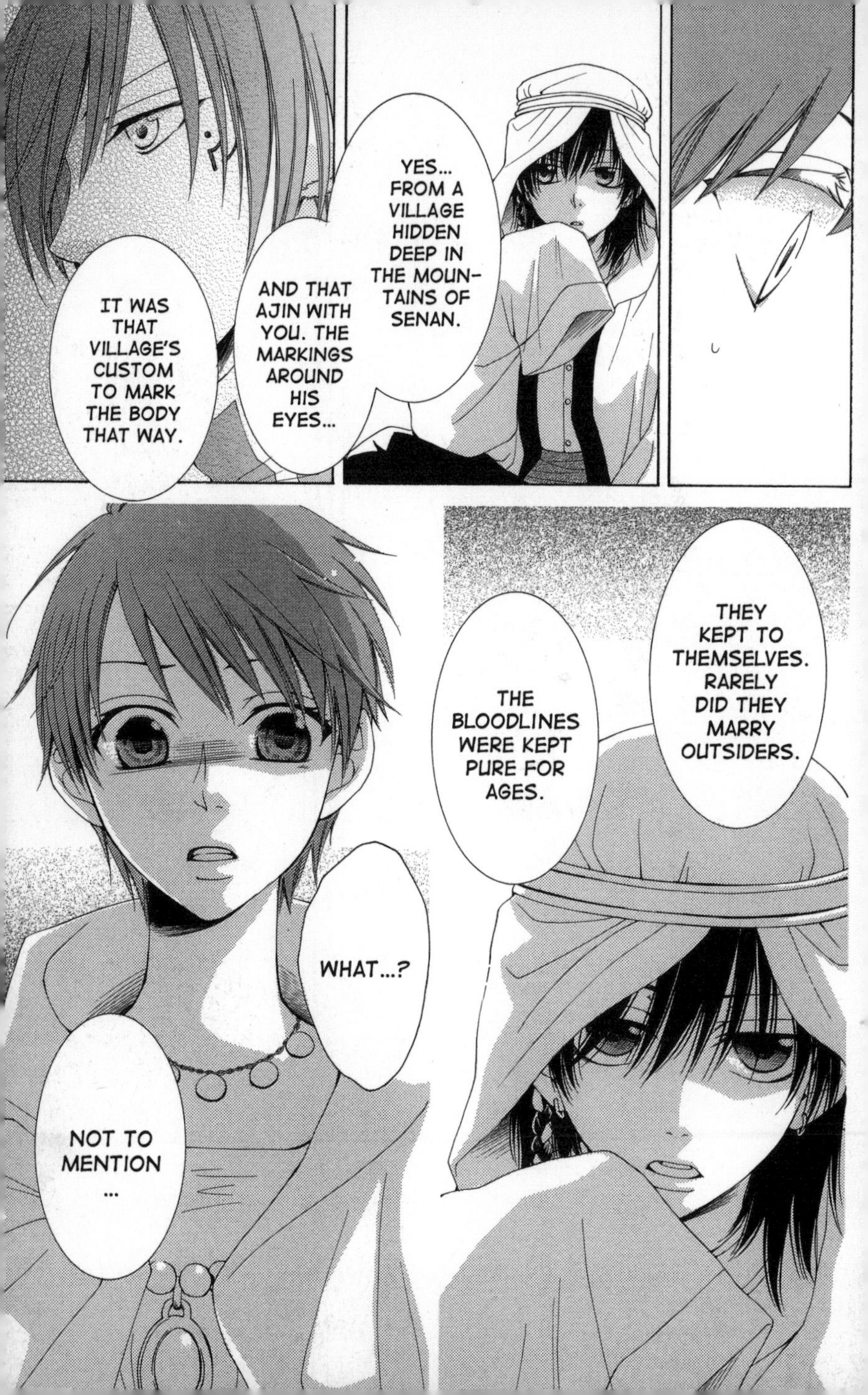
YES... FROM A VILLAGE HIDDEN DEEP IN THE MOUN-TAINS OF SENAN.
AND THAT AJIN WITH YOU. THE MARKINGS AROUND HIS EYES...
IT WAS THAT VILLAGE'S CUSTOM TO MARK THE BODY THAT WAY.
THEY KEPT TO THEMSELVES. RARELY DID THEY MARRY OUTSIDERS.
THE BLOODLINES WERE KEPT PURE FOR AGES.
WHAT...?
NOT TO MENTION ...

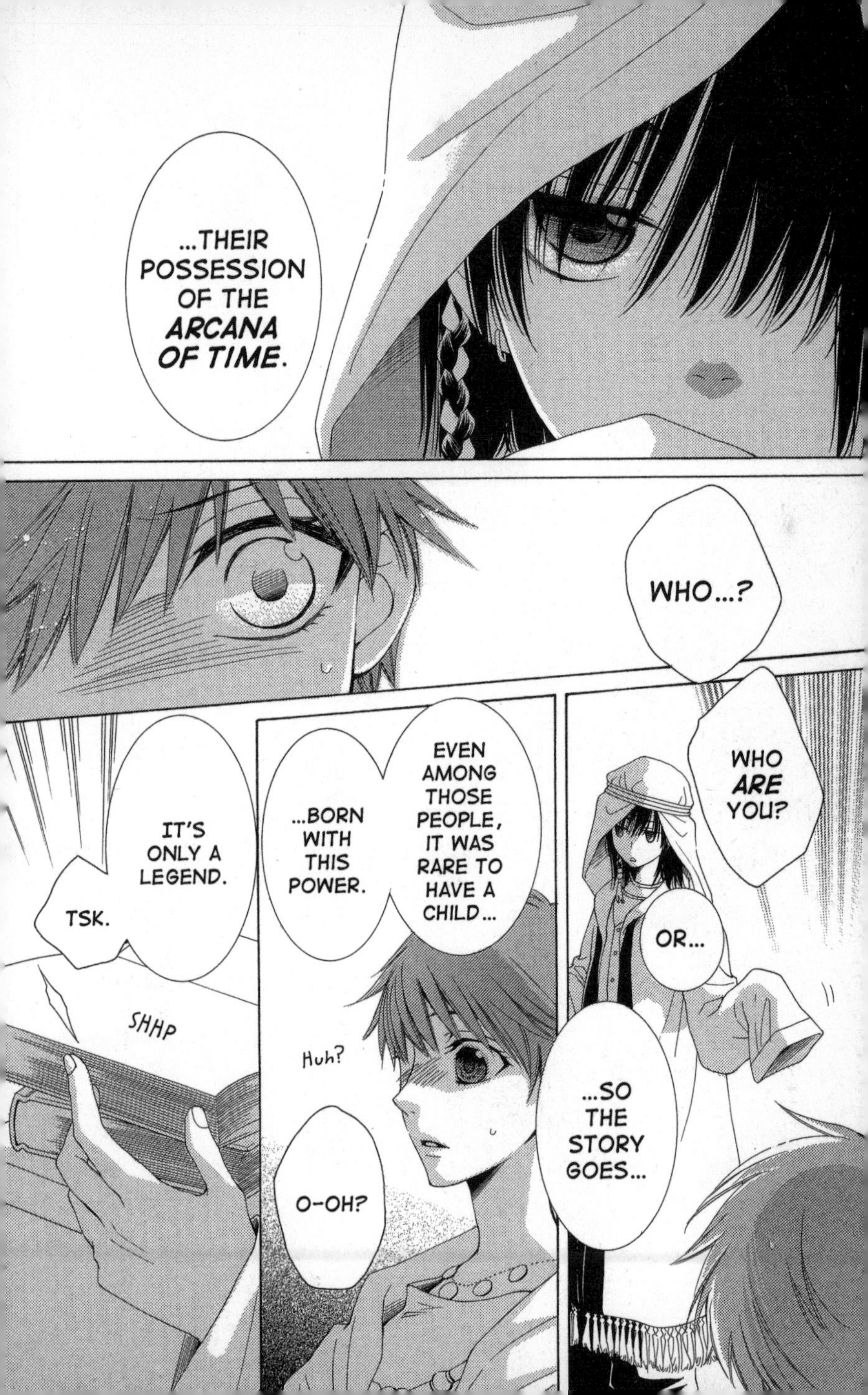
...THEIR POSSESSION OF THE *ARCANA OF TIME*.
WHO...?
WHO *ARE* YOU?
OR...
...SO THE STORY GOES...
EVEN AMONG THOSE PEOPLE, IT WAS RARE TO HAVE A CHILD...
...BORN WITH THIS POWER.
Huh?
O-OH?
IT'S ONLY A LEGEND.
TSK.
SHHP

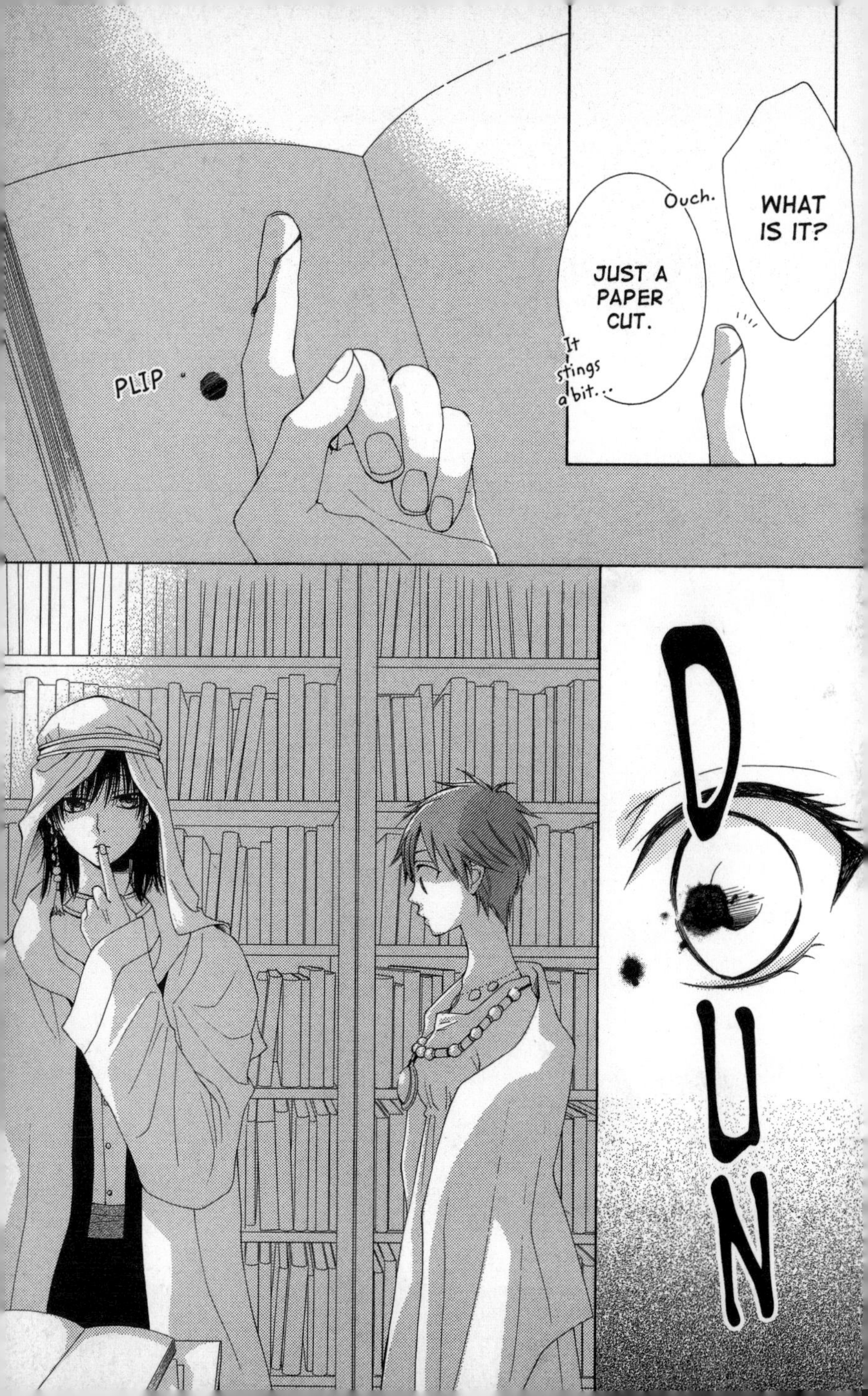
WHAT IS IT?
Ouch.
JUST A PAPER CUT.
It stings a bit...
PLIP
DUN

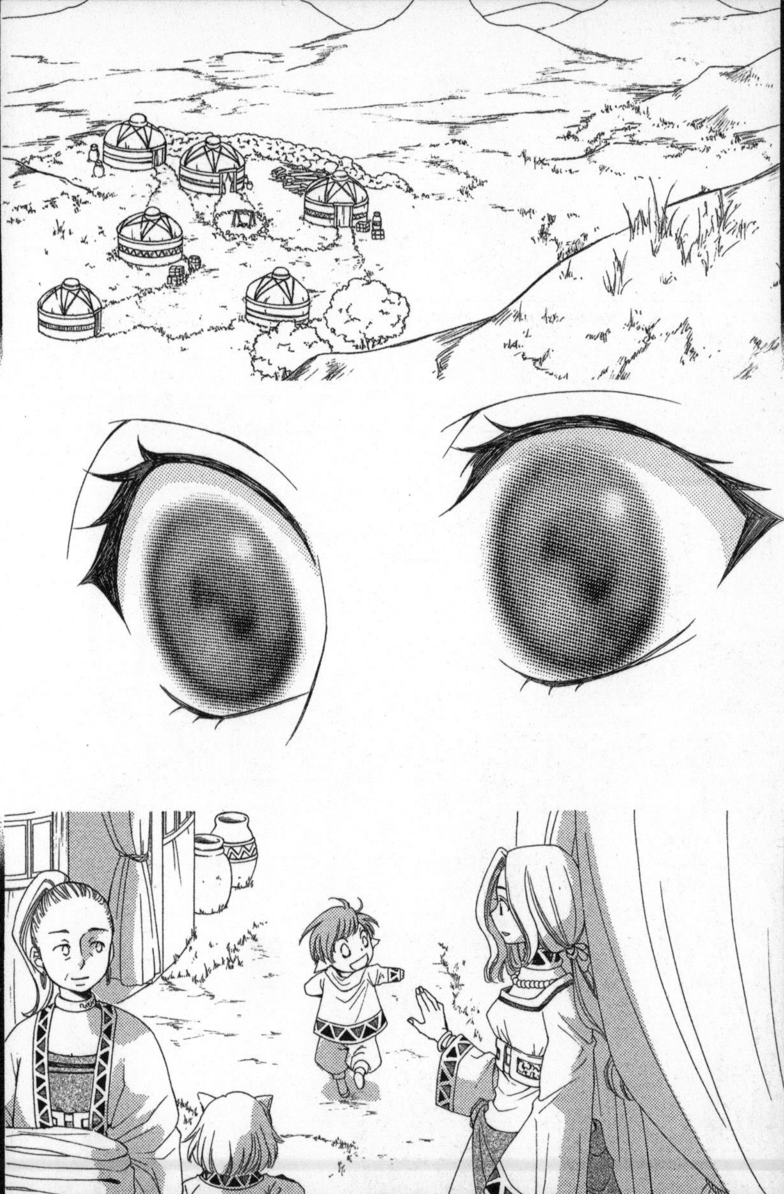

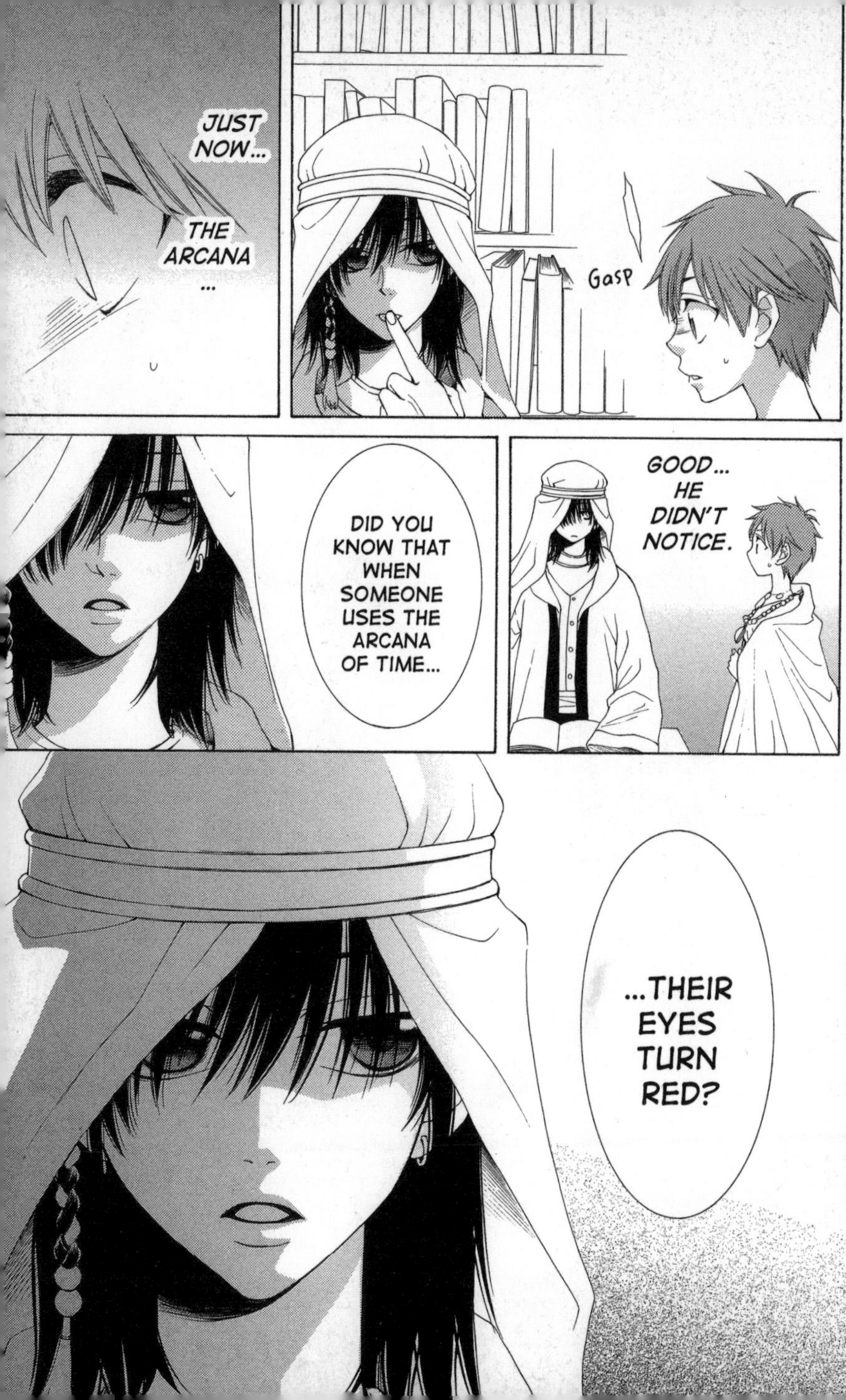
Gasp
JUST NOW...
THE ARCANA ...
GOOD... HE DIDN'T NOTICE.
DID YOU KNOW THAT WHEN SOMEONE USES THE ARCANA OF TIME...
...THEIR EYES TURN RED?

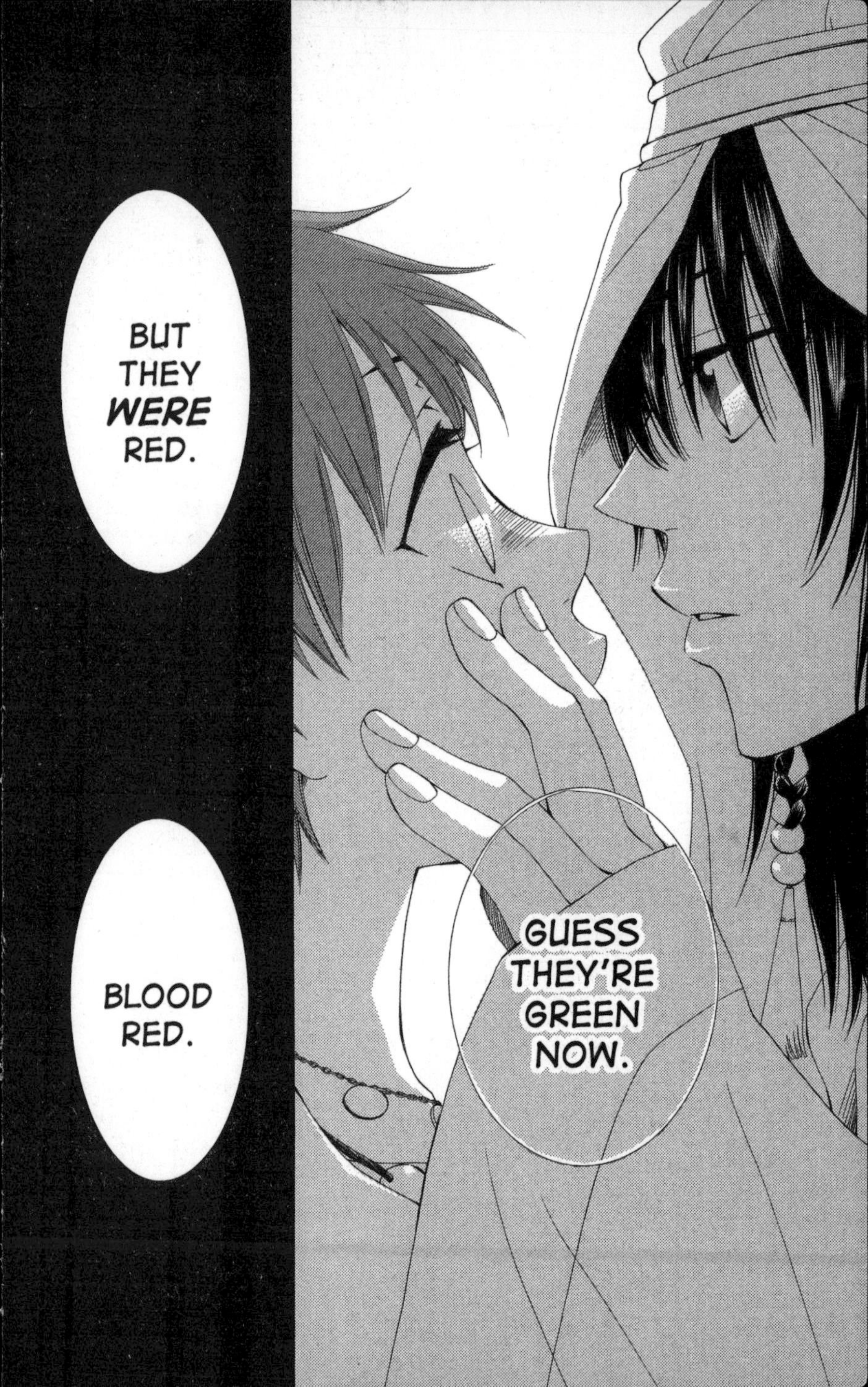
GUESS THEY'RE GREEN NOW.
BUT THEY *WERE* RED.
BLOOD RED.

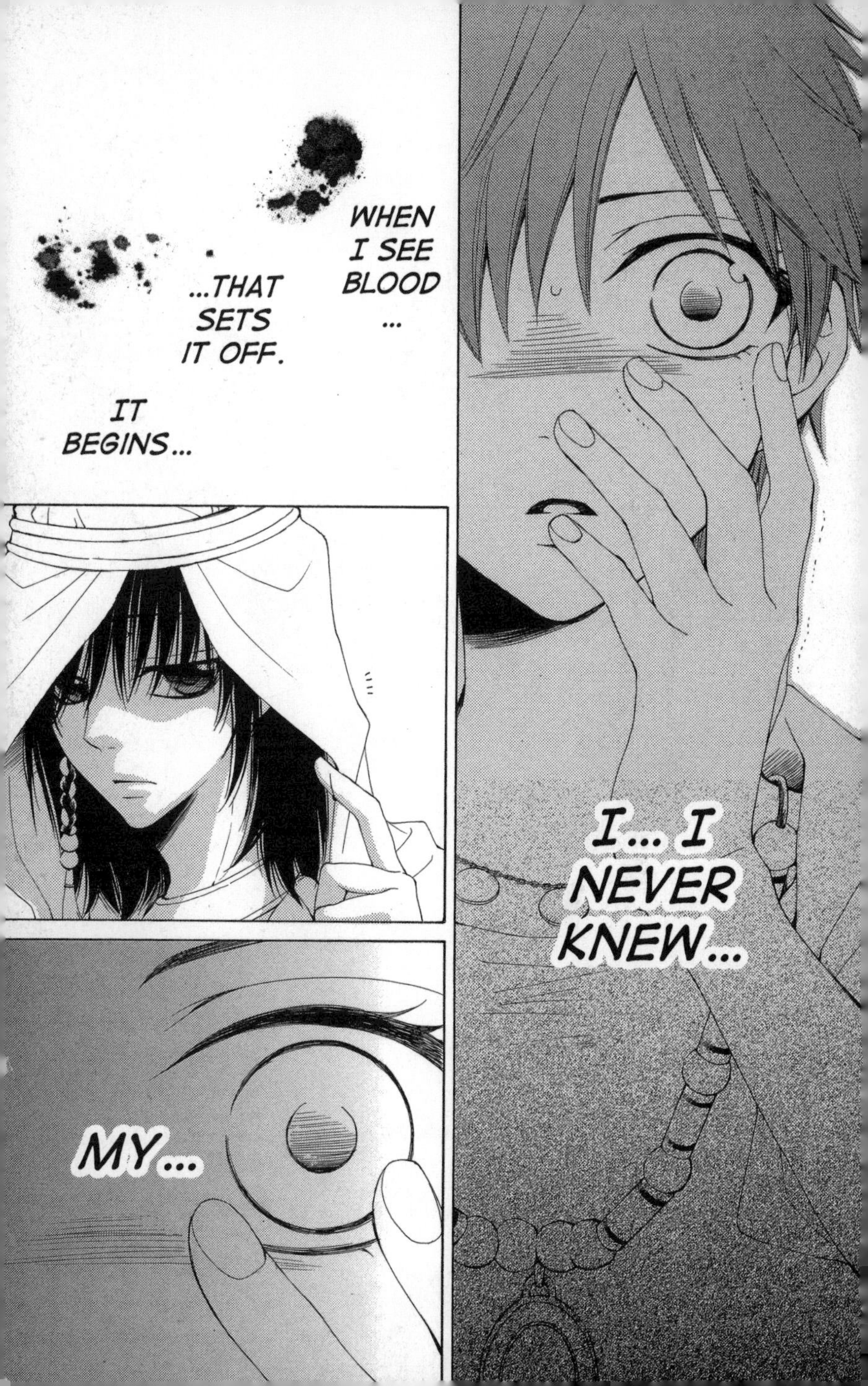
I... I NEVER KNEW...
WHEN I SEE BLOOD ...
...THAT SETS IT OFF.
IT BEGINS...
MY...

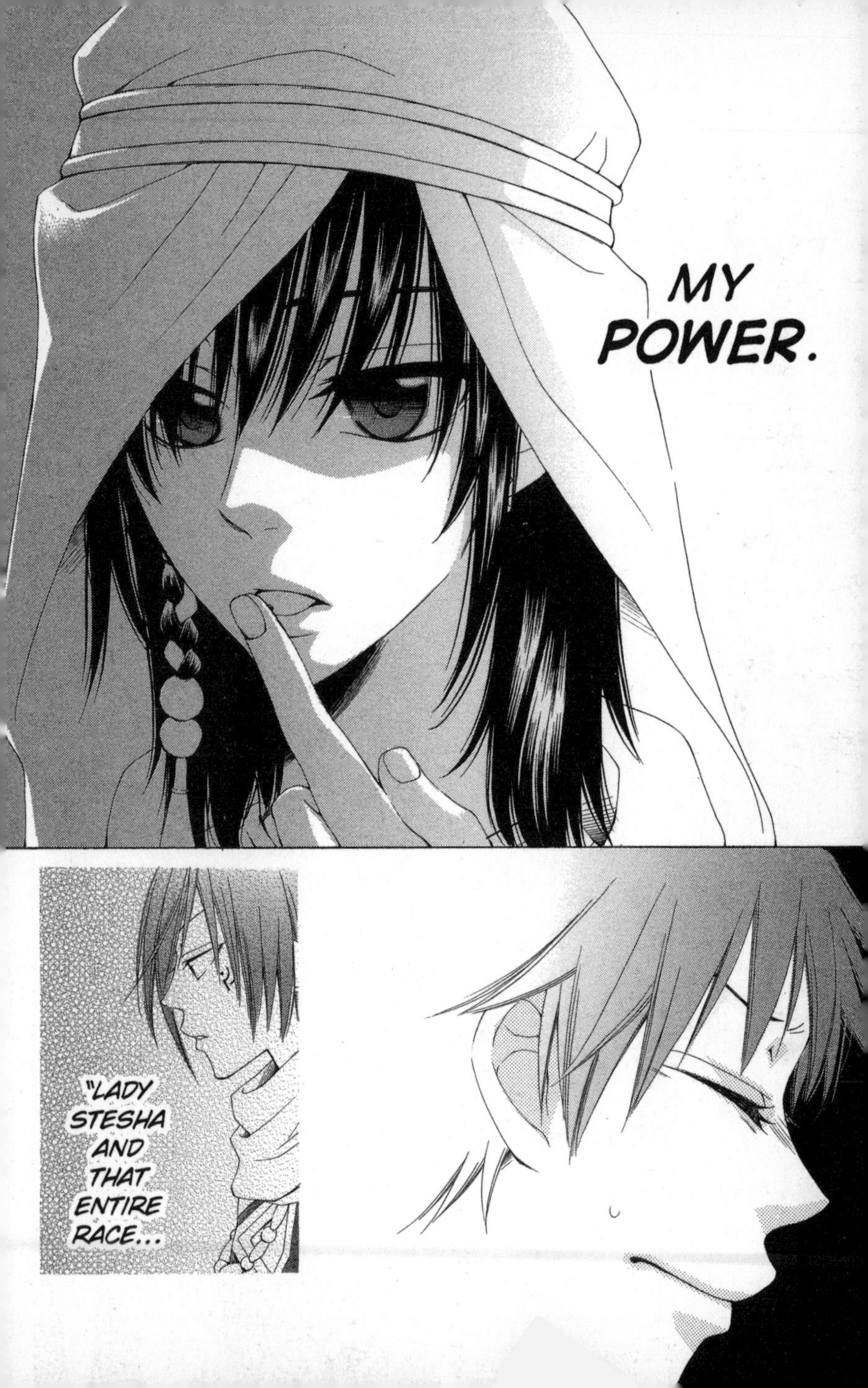
MY POWER.
"LADY STESHA AND THAT ENTIRE RACE...

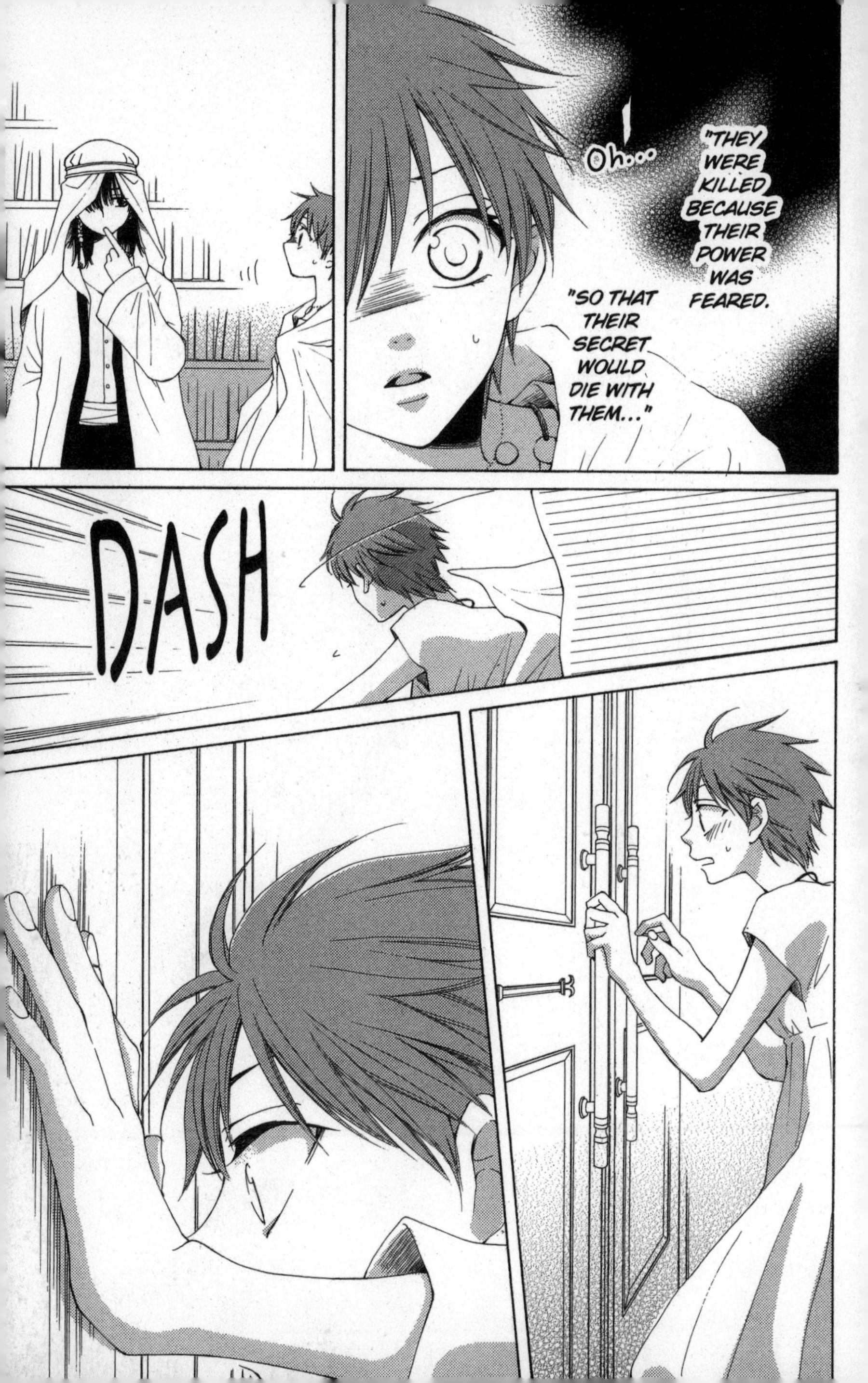
Oh...
"THEY WERE KILLED BECAUSE THEIR POWER WAS FEARED.
"SO THAT THEIR SECRET WOULD DIE WITH THEM..."
DASH

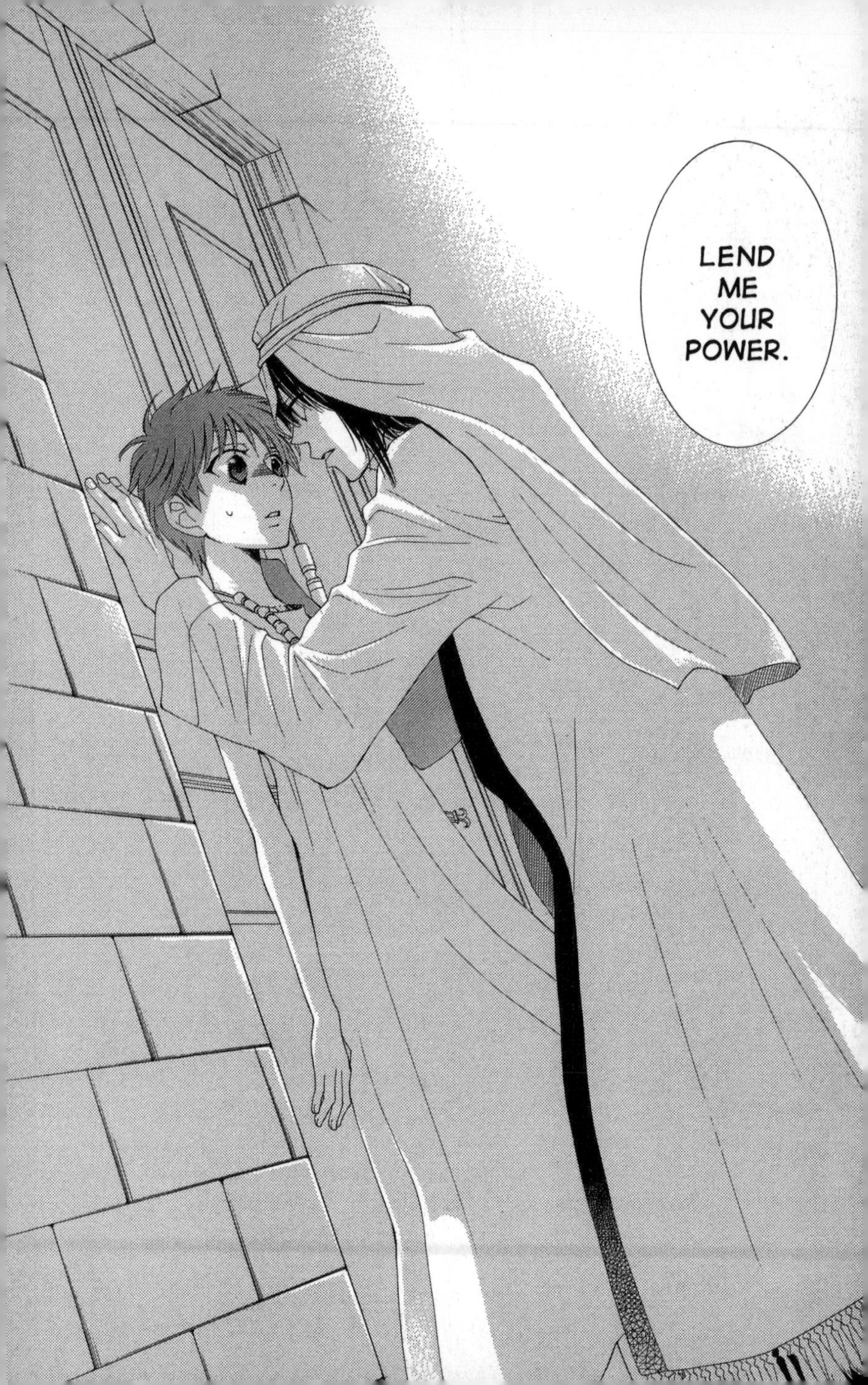
LEND ME YOUR POWER.

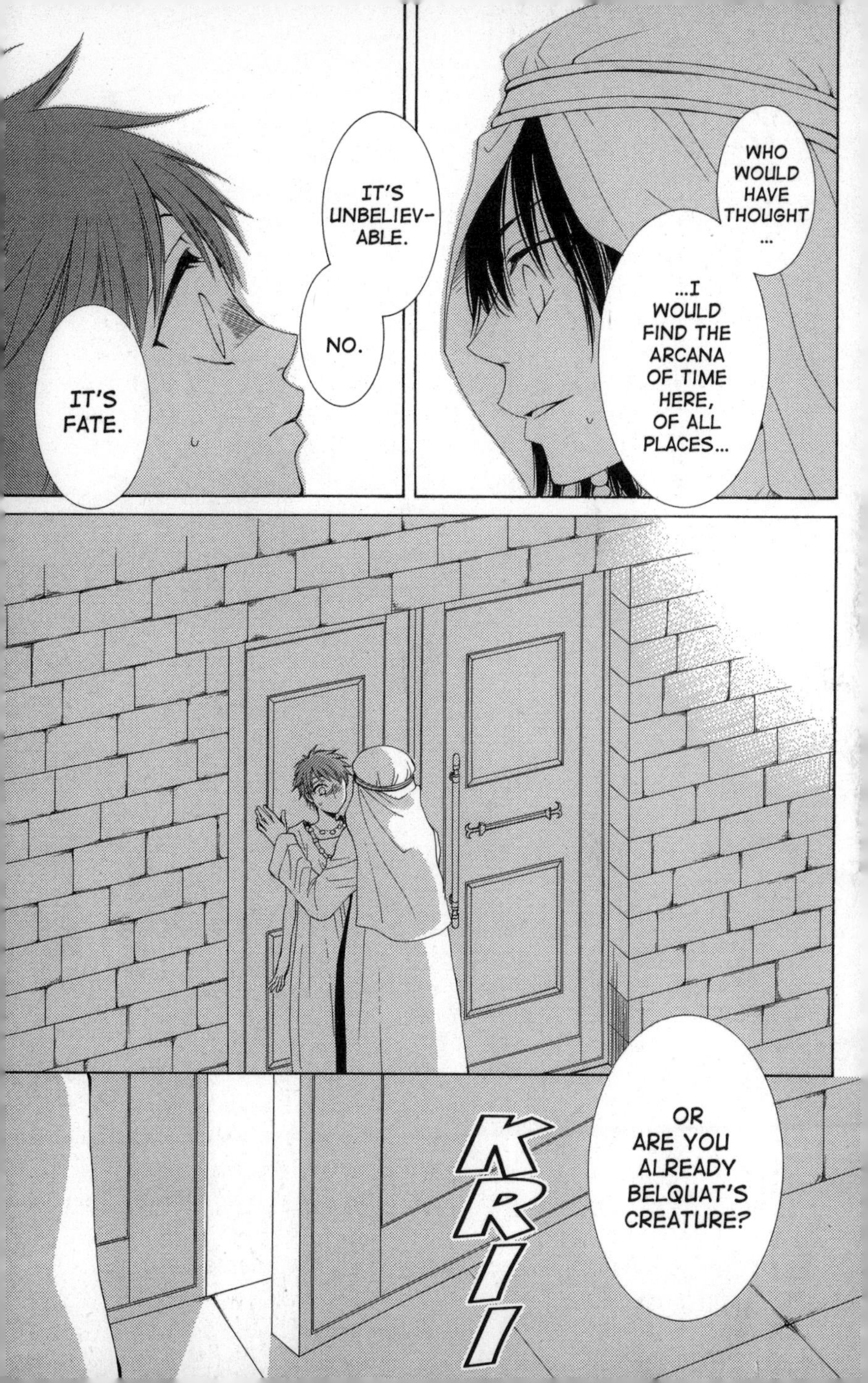
WHO WOULD HAVE THOUGHT...
...I WOULD FIND THE ARCANA OF TIME HERE, OF ALL PLACES...
IT'S UNBELIEV-ABLE.
NO.
IT'S FATE.
OR ARE YOU ALREADY BELQUAT'S CREATURE?
KRII

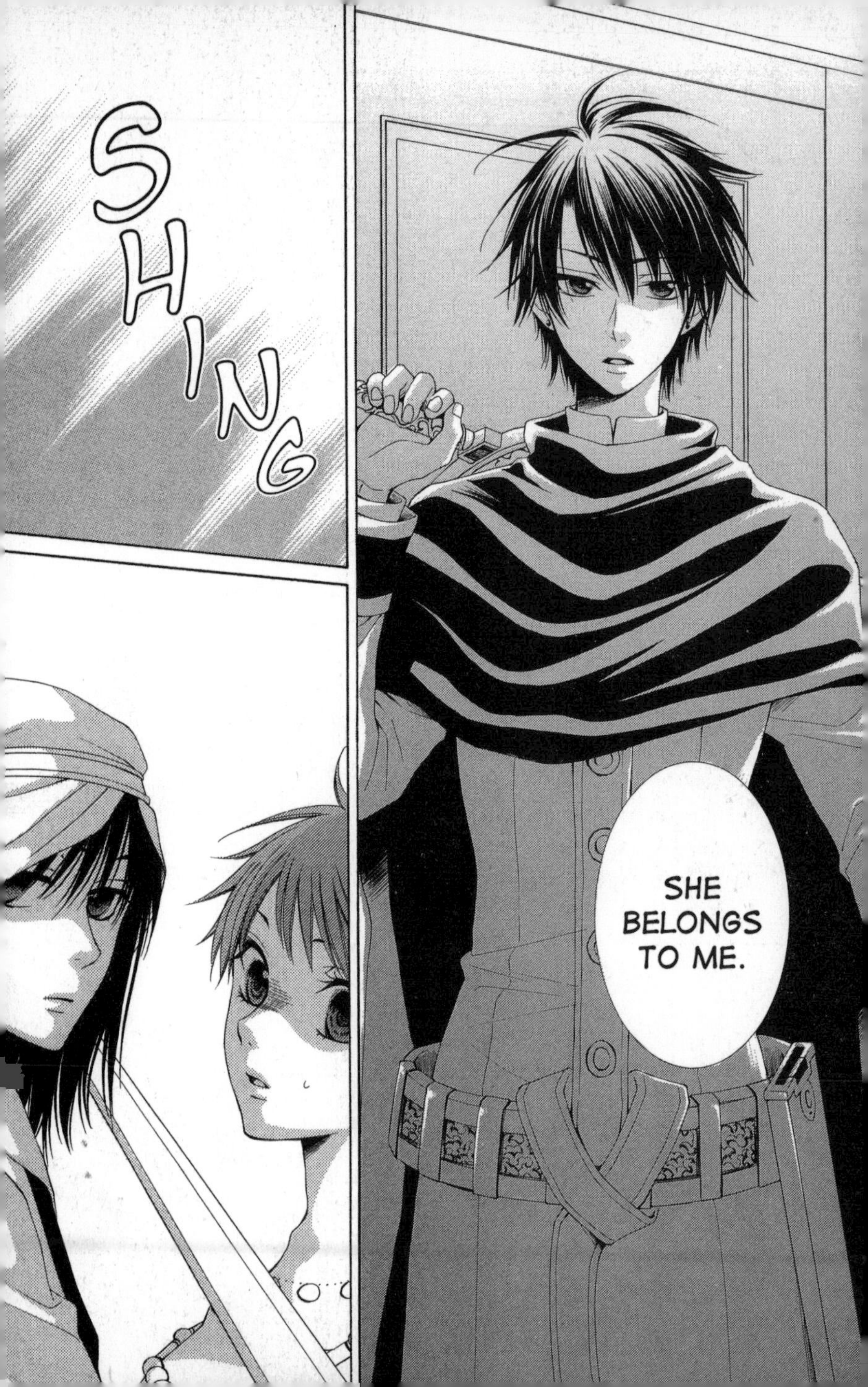
SHE BELONGS TO ME.
SHING

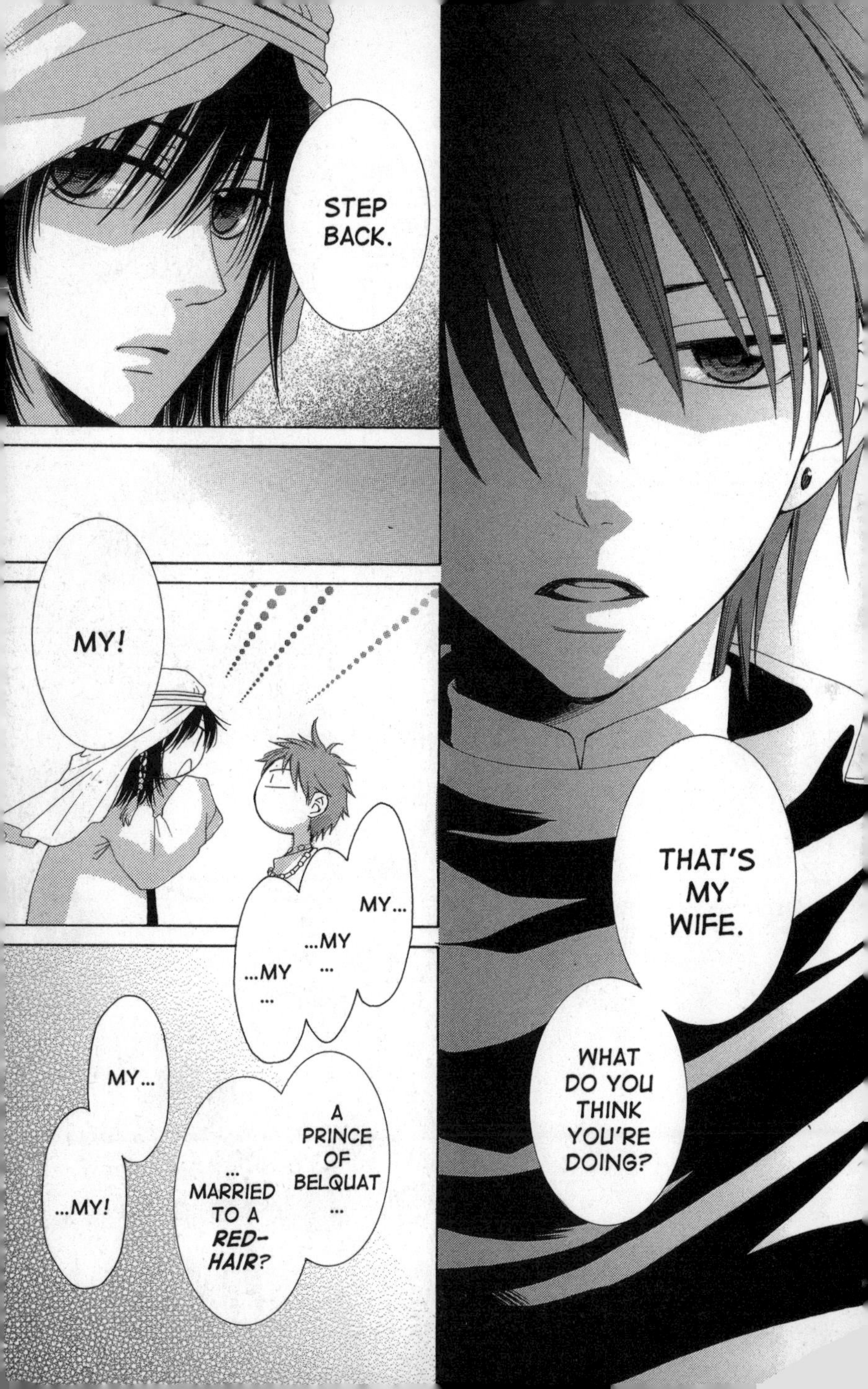
THAT'S MY WIFE.
WHAT DO YOU THINK YOU'RE DOING?
STEP BACK.
MY!
MY... ...MY ... ...MY ...
A PRINCE OF BELQUAT ... ... MARRIED TO A *RED-HAIR?*
MY... ...MY!

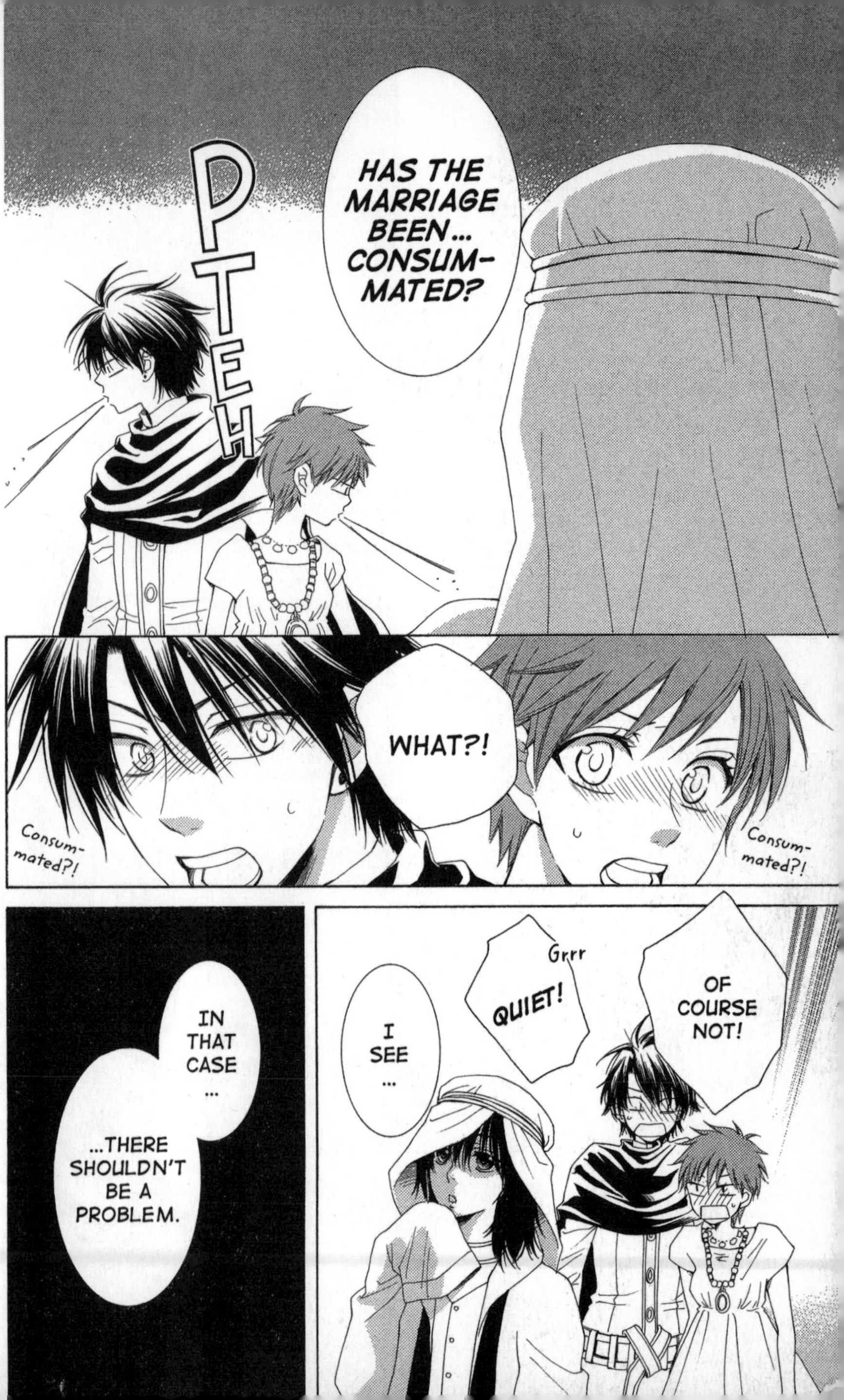
HAS THE MARRIAGE BEEN... CONSUMMATED?
PTEH
Consummated?!
WHAT?!
Consummated?!
OF COURSE NOT!
Grrr
QUIET!
I SEE...
IN THAT CASE...
...THERE SHOULDN'T BE A PROBLEM.

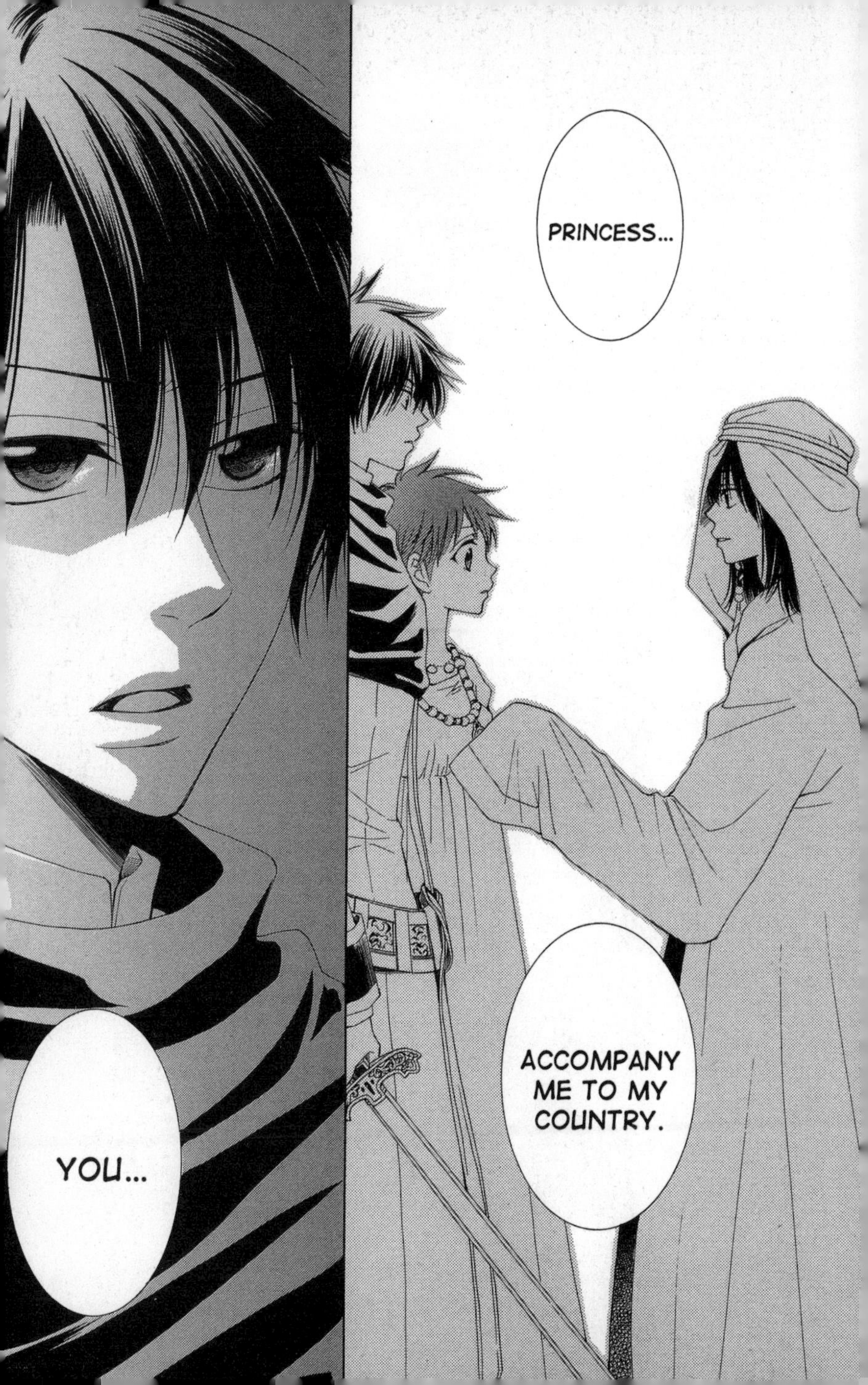
PRINCESS...
ACCOMPANY ME TO MY COUNTRY.
YOU...

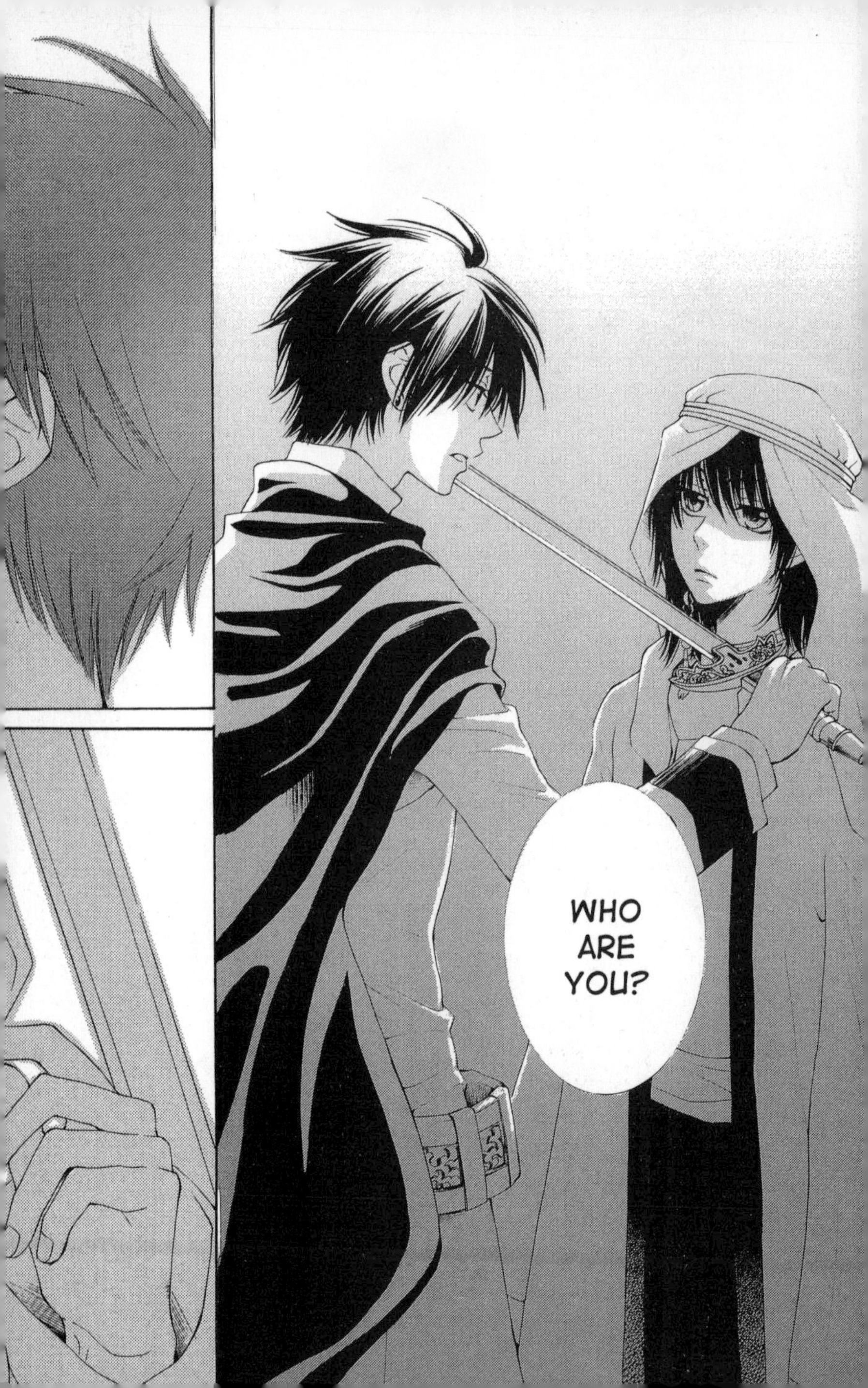
WHO ARE YOU?

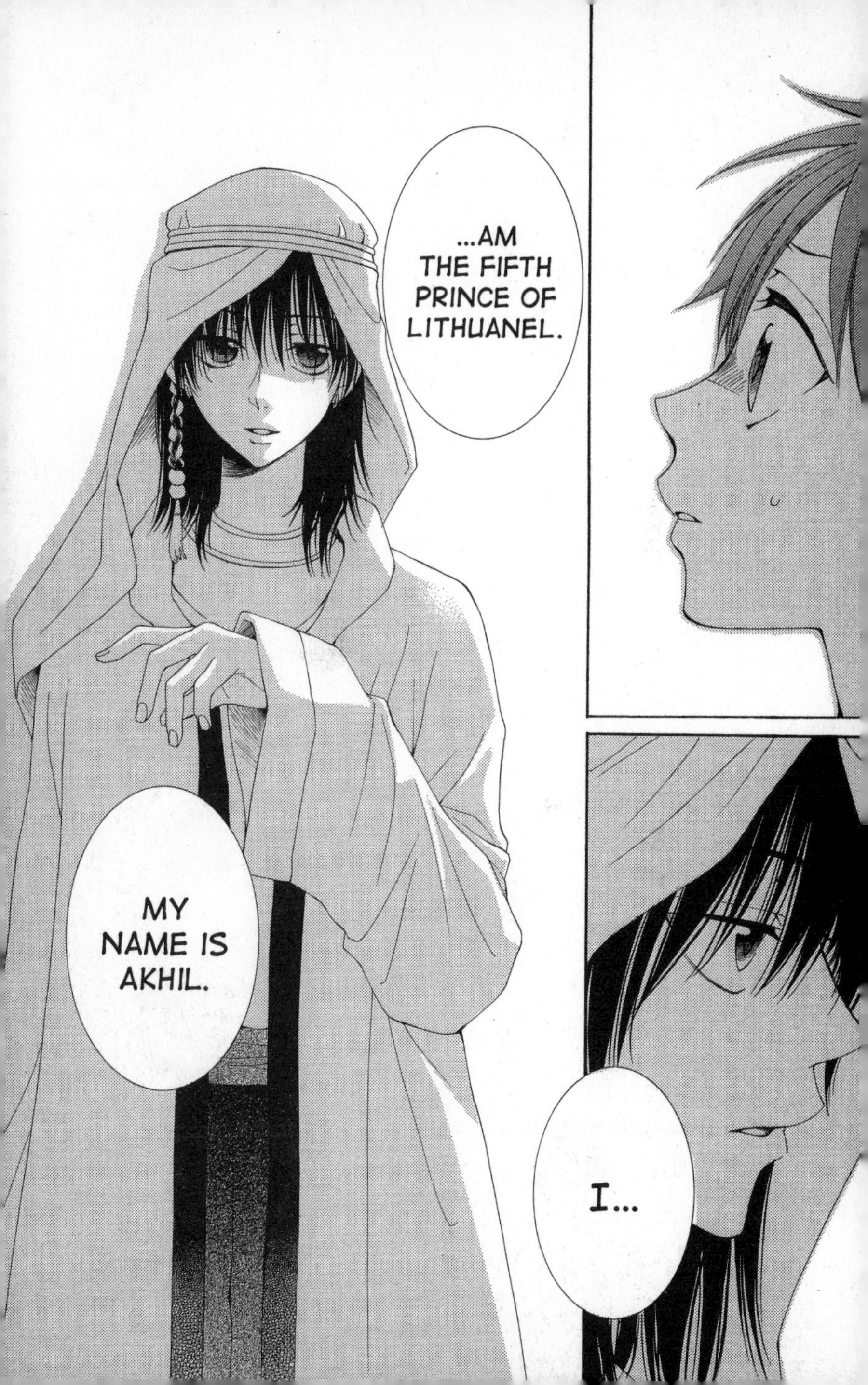
I...
...AM THE FIFTH PRINCE OF LITHUANEL.
MY NAME IS AKHIL.

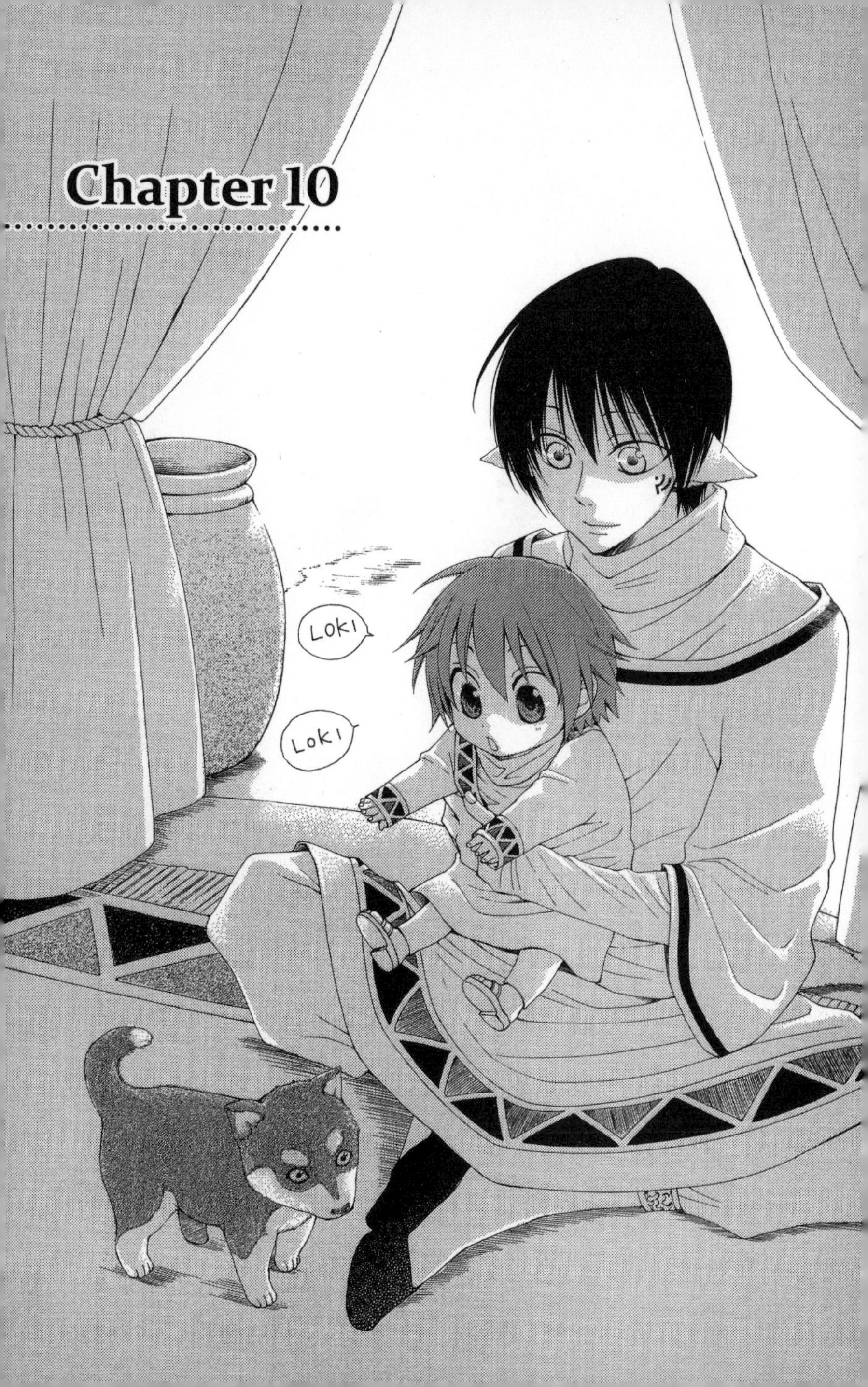
Chapter 10
LOKI
LOKI

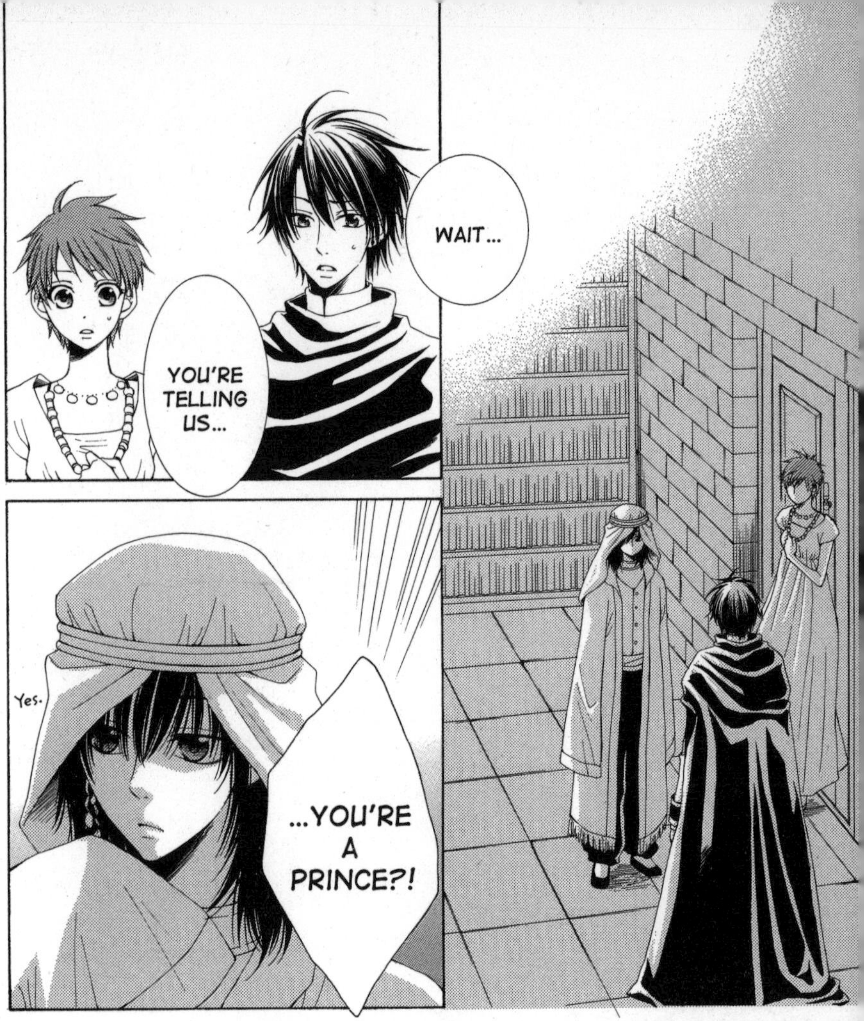
WAIT...
YOU'RE TELLING US...
...YOU'RE A PRINCE?!
Yes.

Dawn of the Arcana

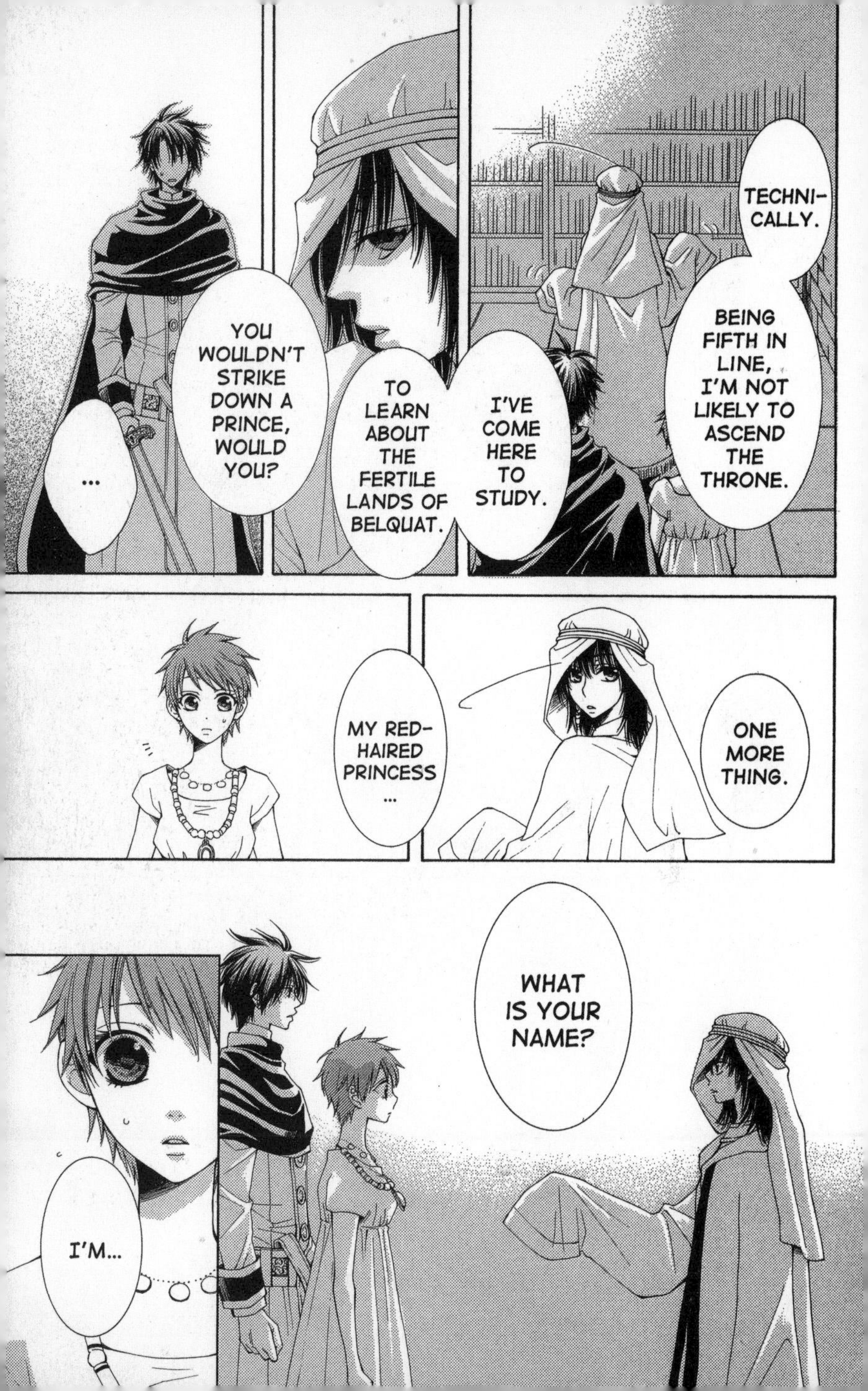
TECHNI-CALLY.
BEING FIFTH IN LINE, I'M NOT LIKELY TO ASCEND THE THRONE.
I'VE COME HERE TO STUDY.
TO LEARN ABOUT THE FERTILE LANDS OF BELQUAT.
YOU WOULDN'T STRIKE DOWN A PRINCE, WOULD YOU?
...
ONE MORE THING.
MY RED-HAIRED PRINCESS ...
WHAT IS YOUR NAME?
I'M...

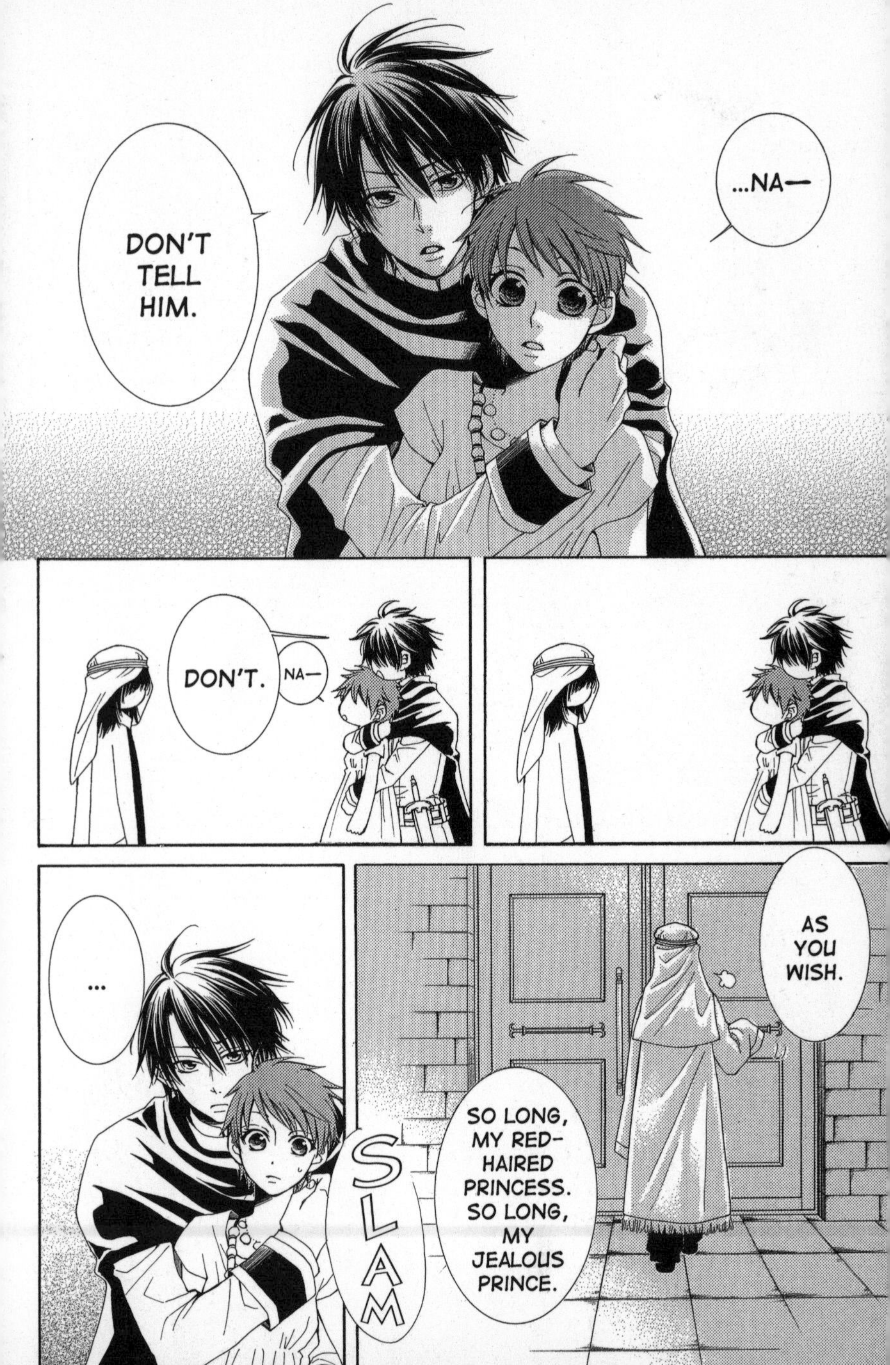
...NA—
DON'T TELL HIM.
NA—
DON'T.
AS YOU WISH.
SO LONG, MY RED-HAIRED PRINCESS. SO LONG, MY JEALOUS PRINCE.
SLAM
...

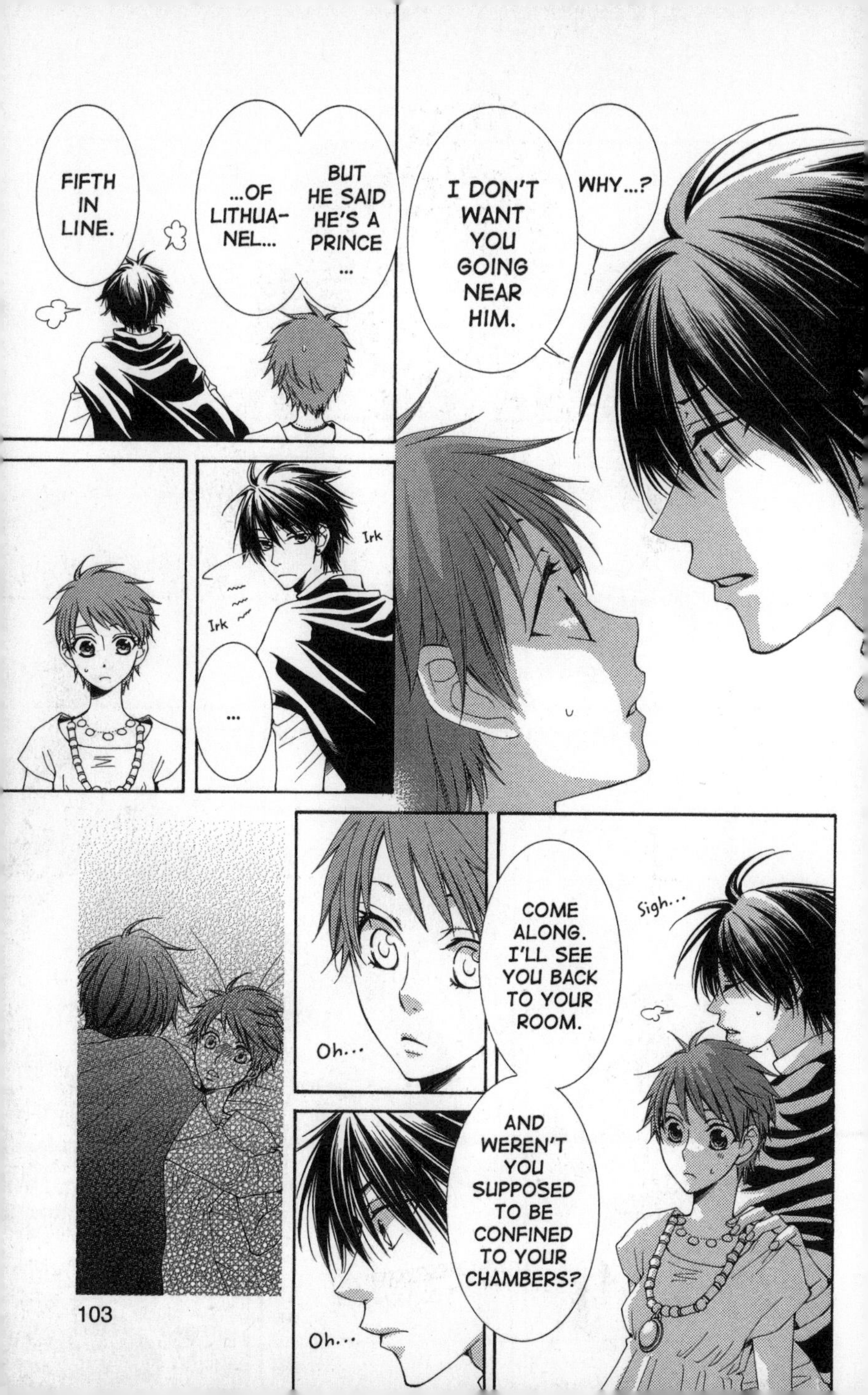
WHY...?
I DON'T WANT YOU GOING NEAR HIM.
BUT HE SAID HE'S A PRINCE ...
...OF LITHUA-NEL...
FIFTH IN LINE.
Irk
Irk
...
Sigh...
COME ALONG. I'LL SEE YOU BACK TO YOUR ROOM.
AND WEREN'T YOU SUPPOSED TO BE CONFINED TO YOUR CHAMBERS?
Oh...
Oh...

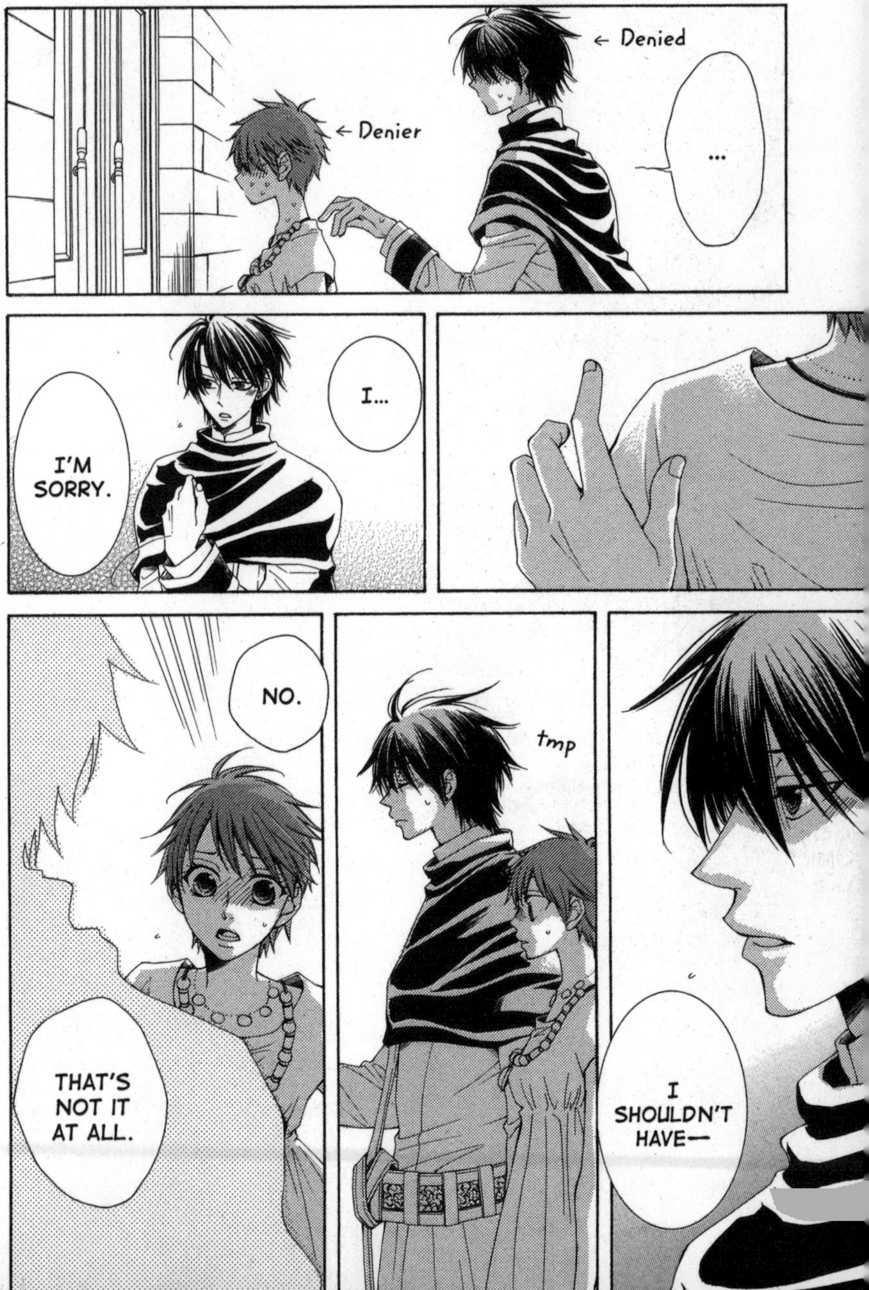

← Denied
...
← Denier
I...
I'M SORRY.
I SHOULDN'T HAVE—
tmp
NO.
THAT'S NOT IT AT ALL.

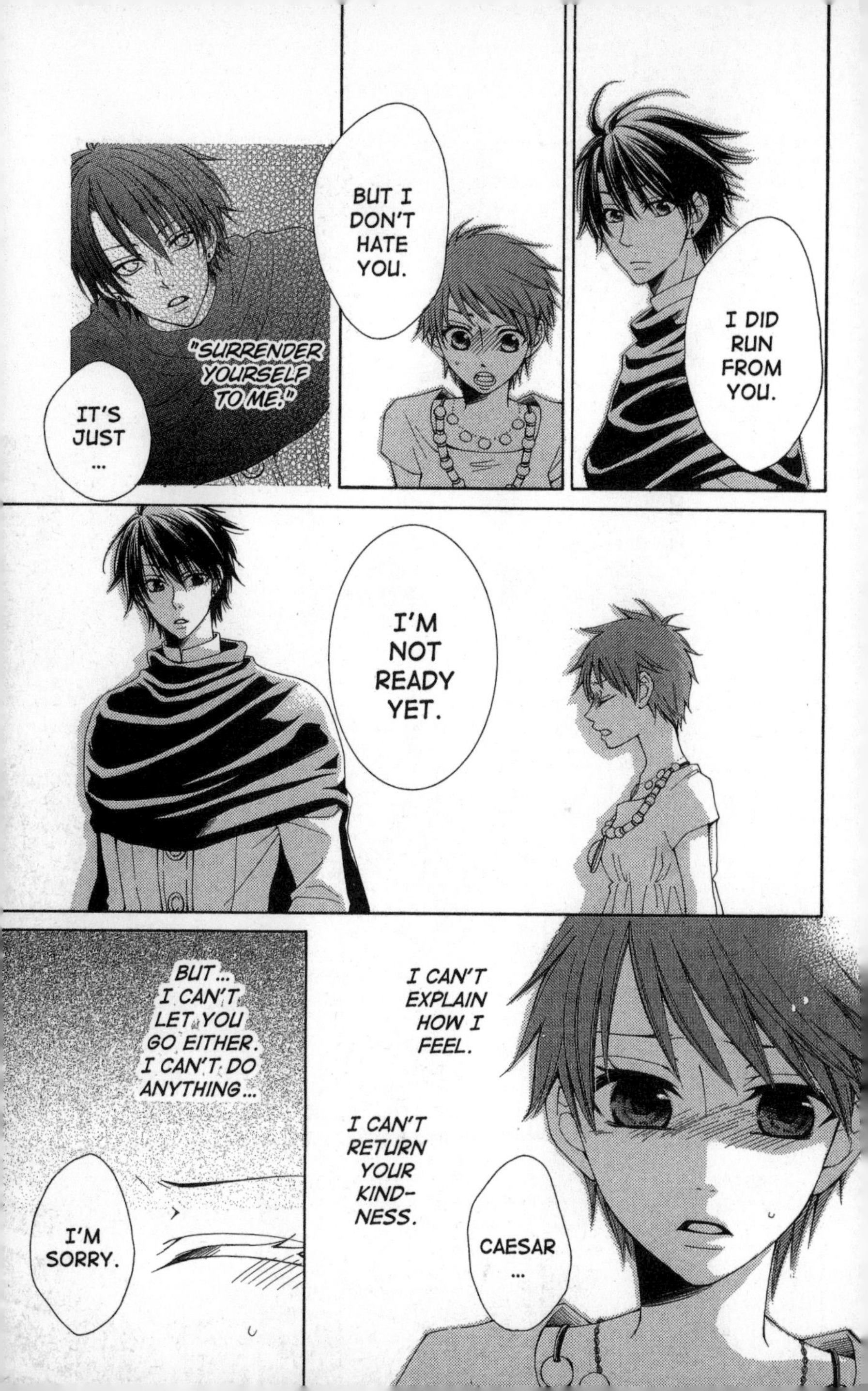
I DID RUN FROM YOU.
BUT I DON'T HATE YOU.
"SURRENDER YOURSELF TO ME."
IT'S JUST ...
I'M NOT READY YET.
I CAN'T EXPLAIN HOW I FEEL.
I CAN'T RETURN YOUR KINDNESS.
CAESAR ...
BUT... I CAN'T LET YOU GO EITHER. I CAN'T DO ANYTHING...
I'M SORRY.

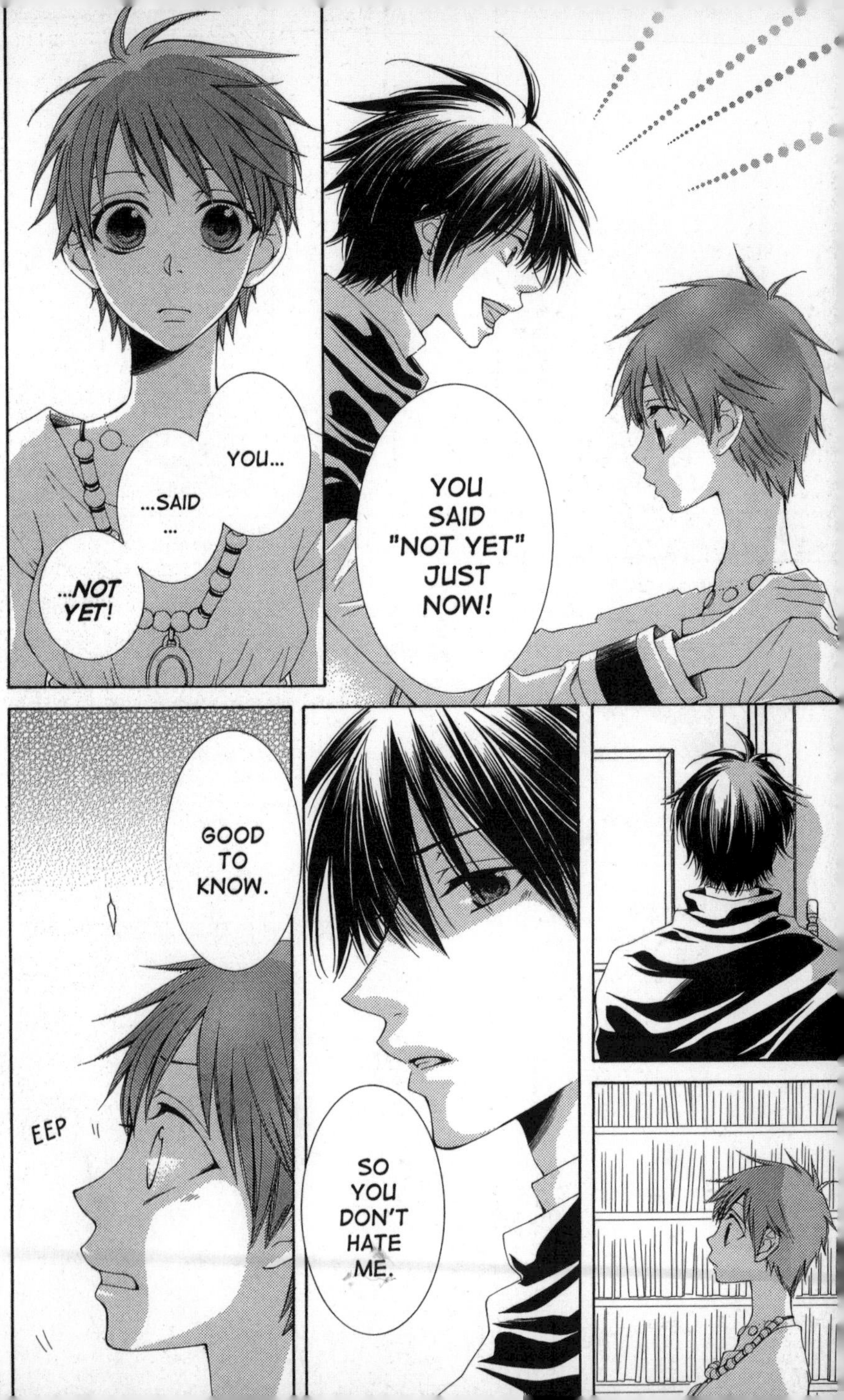

YOU SAID "NOT YET" JUST NOW!
YOU...
...SAID ...
...NOT YET!
SO YOU DON'T HATE ME.
GOOD TO KNOW.
EEP

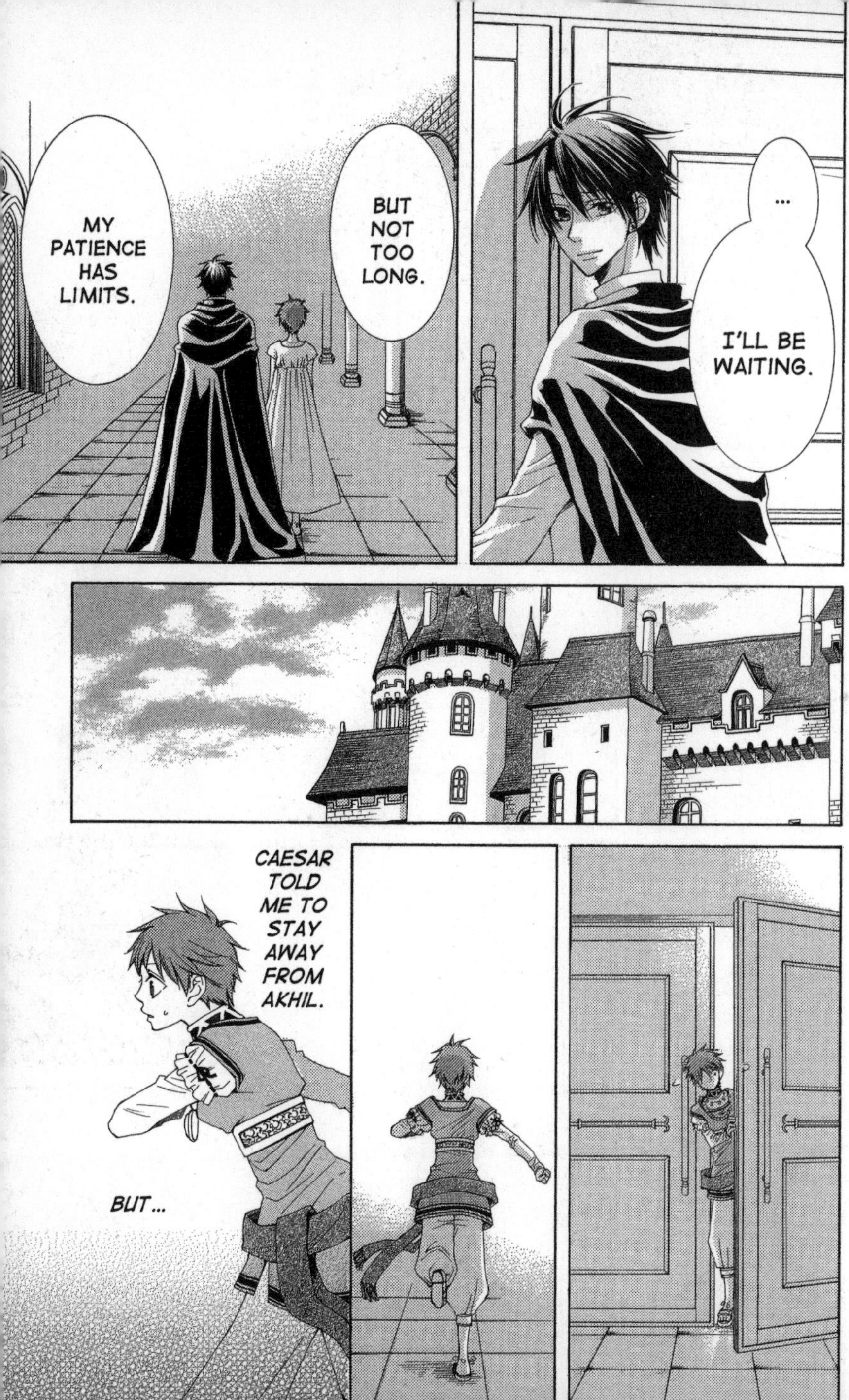
...
I'LL BE WAITING.
BUT NOT TOO LONG.
MY PATIENCE HAS LIMITS.
CAESAR TOLD ME TO STAY AWAY FROM AKHIL.
BUT...

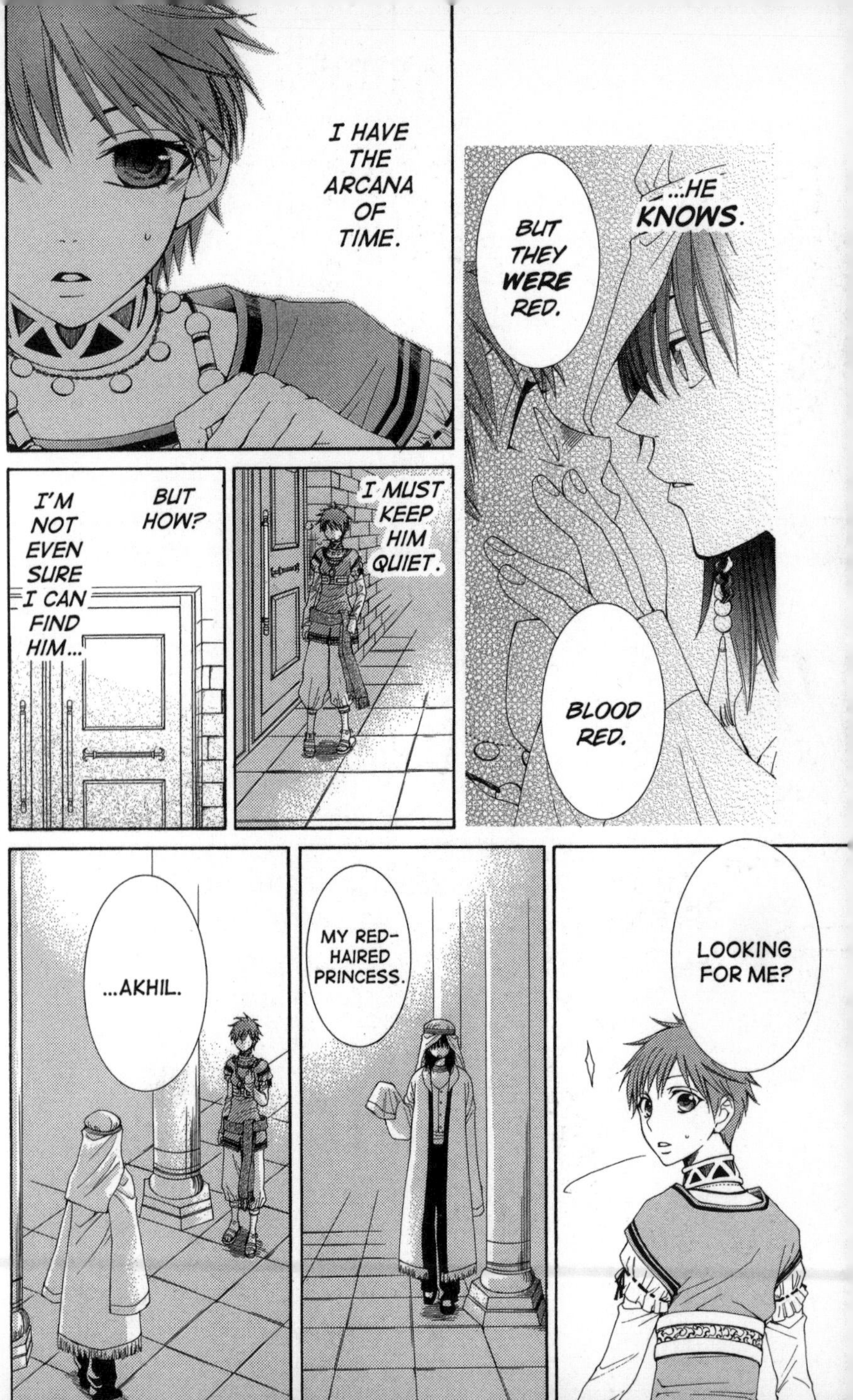
...HE KNOWS.
BUT THEY WERE RED.
BLOOD RED.
I HAVE THE ARCANA OF TIME.
I MUST KEEP HIM QUIET.
BUT HOW?
I'M NOT EVEN SURE I CAN FIND HIM...
LOOKING FOR ME?
MY RED-HAIRED PRINCESS.
...AKHIL.

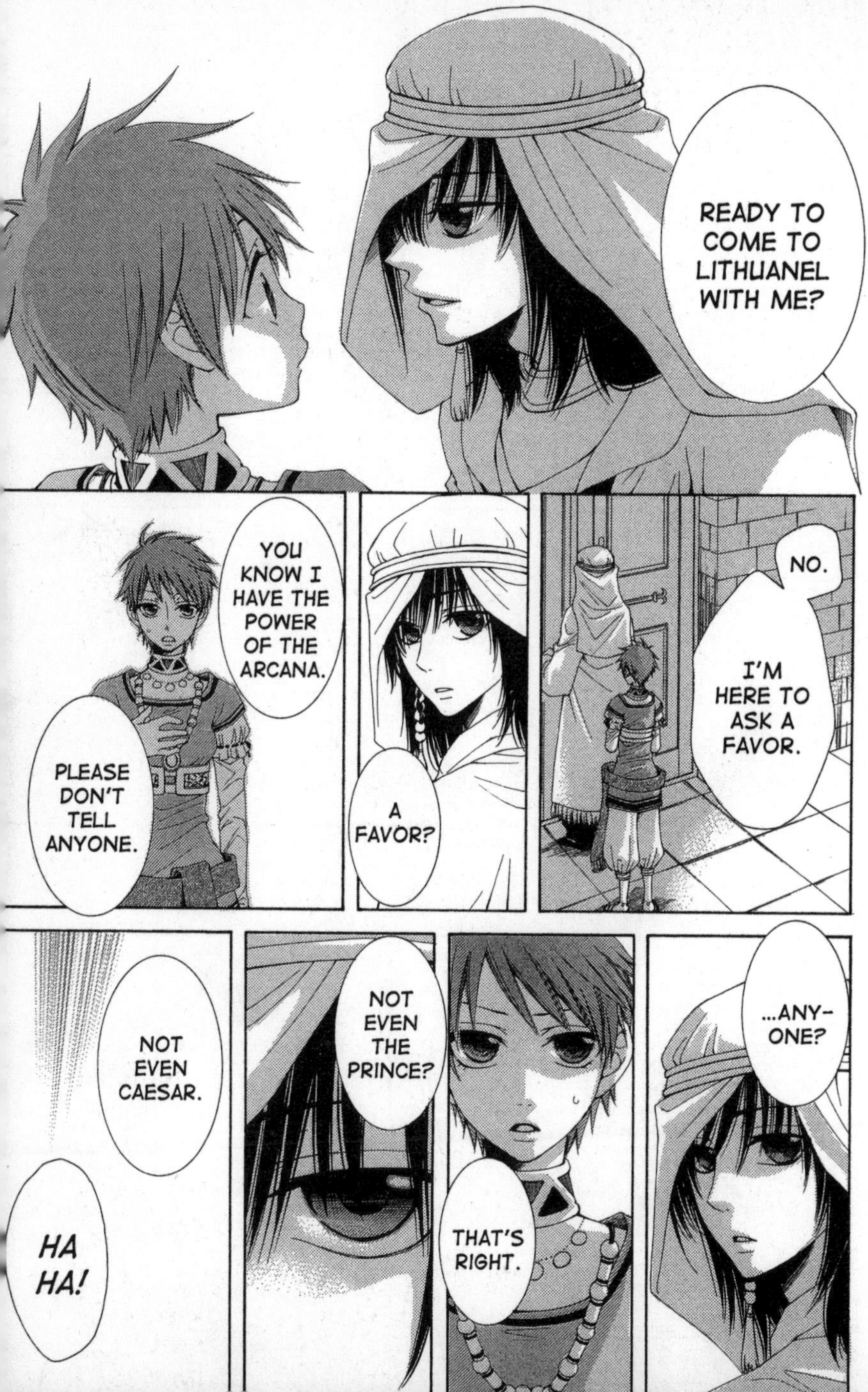
READY TO COME TO LITHUANEL WITH ME?
NO.
I'M HERE TO ASK A FAVOR.
A FAVOR?
YOU KNOW I HAVE THE POWER OF THE ARCANA.
PLEASE DON'T TELL ANYONE.
...ANY-ONE?
NOT EVEN THE PRINCE?
THAT'S RIGHT.
NOT EVEN CAESAR.
HA HA!

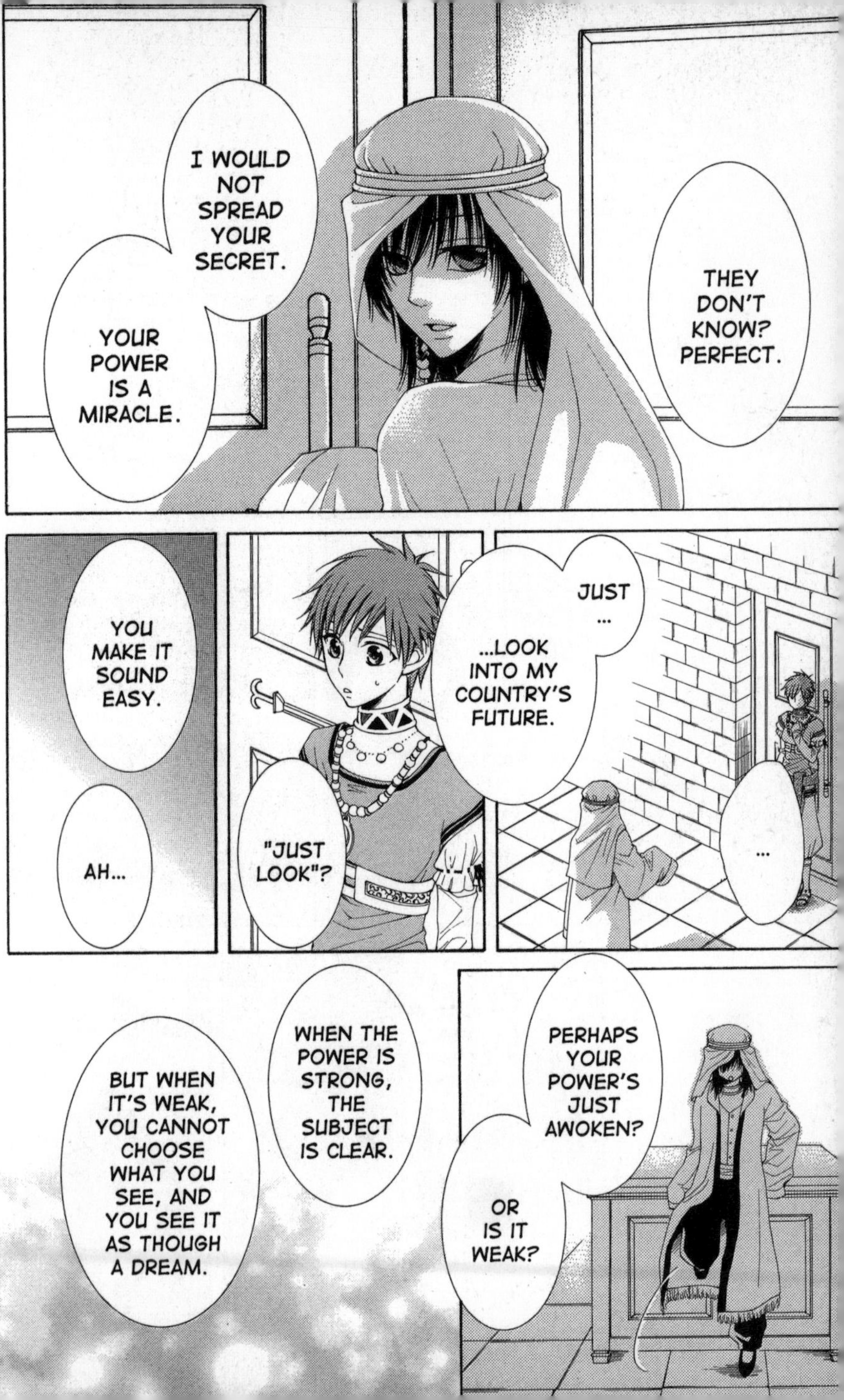
THEY DON'T KNOW? PERFECT.
I WOULD NOT SPREAD YOUR SECRET.
YOUR POWER IS A MIRACLE.
JUST ...
...LOOK INTO MY COUNTRY'S FUTURE.
...
"JUST LOOK"?
YOU MAKE IT SOUND EASY.
AH...
PERHAPS YOUR POWER'S JUST AWOKEN?
OR IS IT WEAK?
WHEN THE POWER IS STRONG, THE SUBJECT IS CLEAR.
BUT WHEN IT'S WEAK, YOU CANNOT CHOOSE WHAT YOU SEE, AND YOU SEE IT AS THOUGH A DREAM.

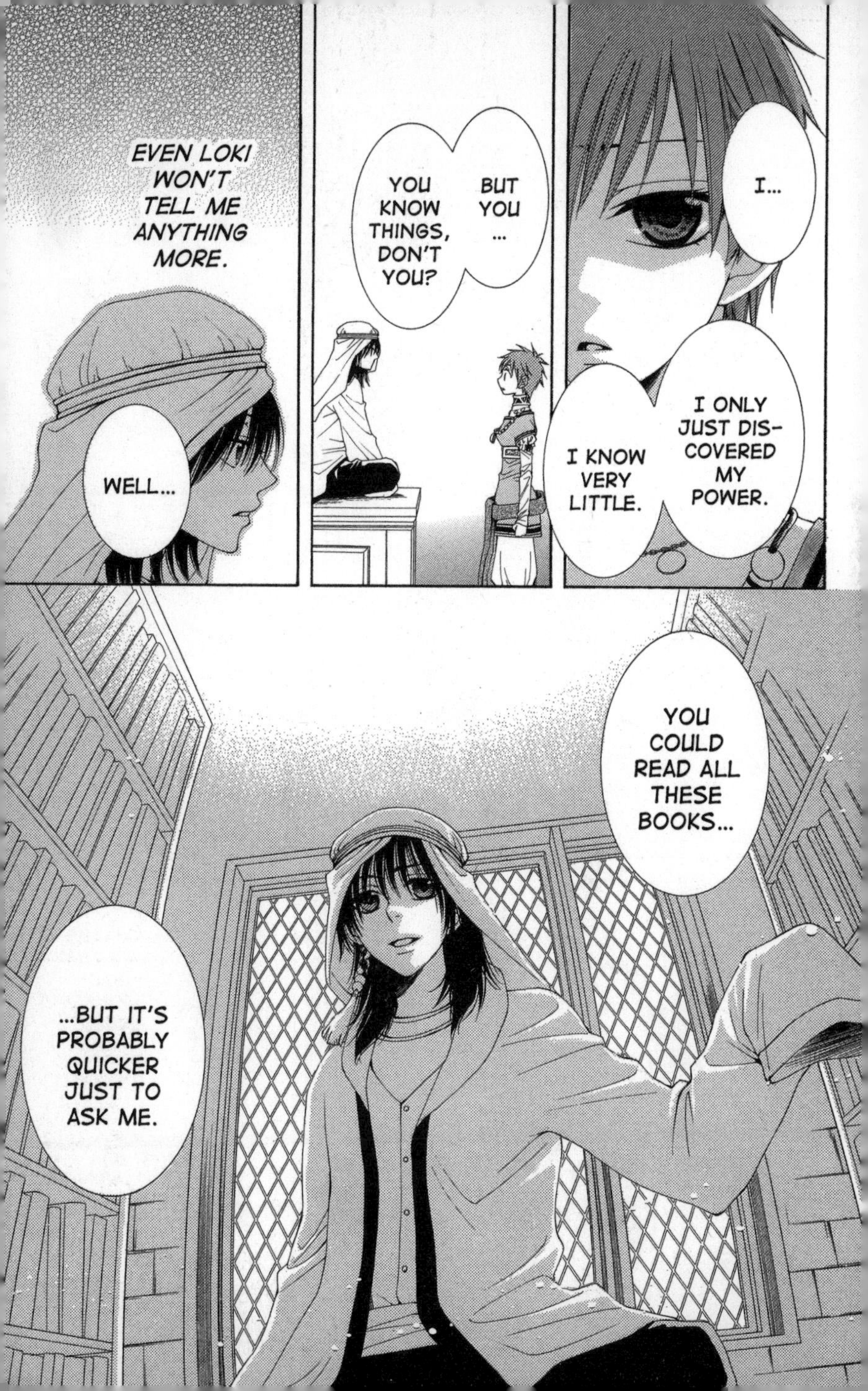
I...
I ONLY JUST DIS-COVERED MY POWER.
I KNOW VERY LITTLE.
BUT YOU ...
YOU KNOW THINGS, DON'T YOU?
EVEN LOKI WON'T TELL ME ANYTHING MORE.
WELL...
YOU COULD READ ALL THESE BOOKS...
...BUT IT'S PROBABLY QUICKER JUST TO ASK ME.

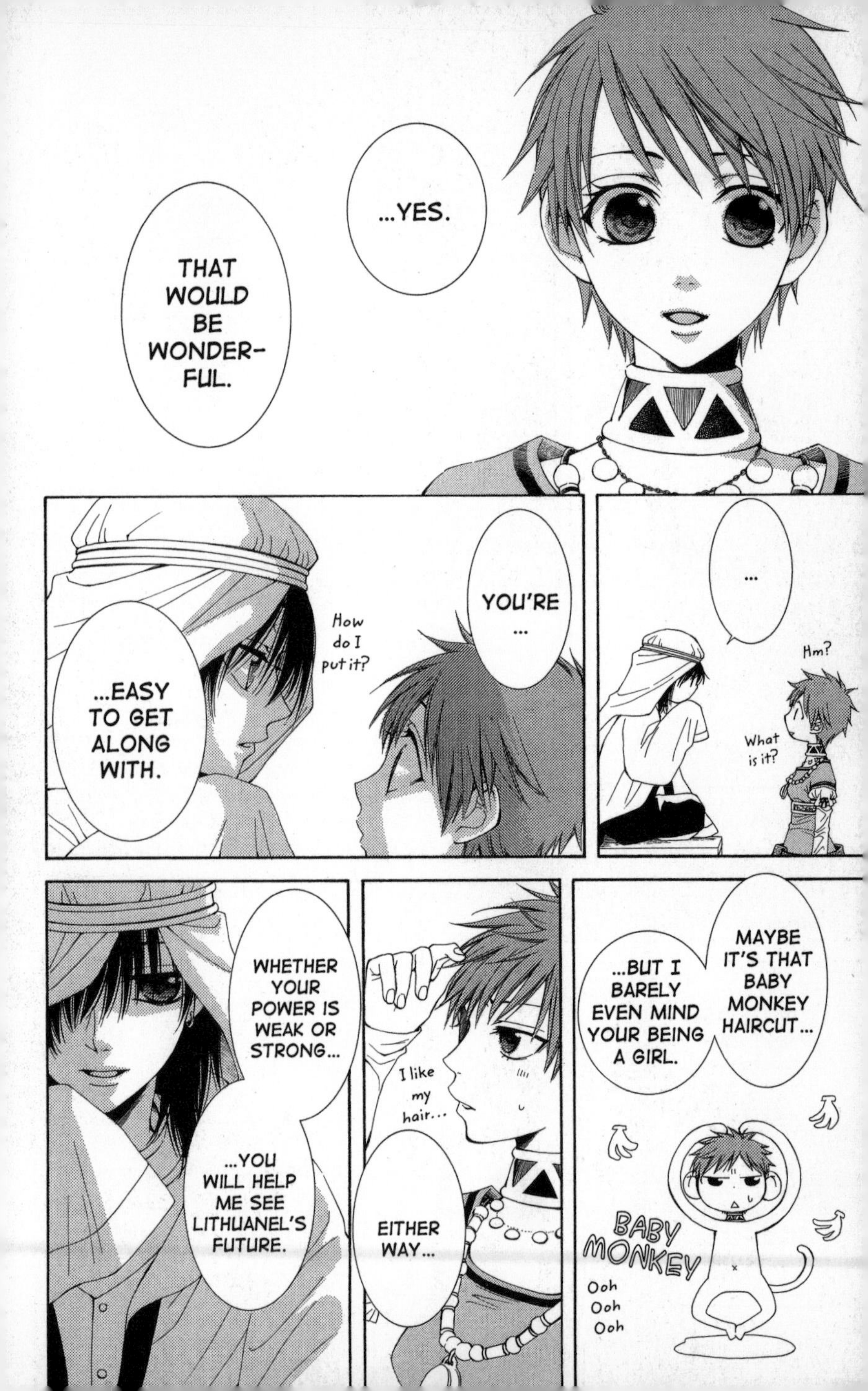
...YES.
THAT WOULD BE WONDER-FUL.
...
Hm?
What is it?
YOU'RE ...
How do I put it?
...EASY TO GET ALONG WITH.
MAYBE IT'S THAT BABY MONKEY HAIRCUT...
...BUT I BARELY EVEN MIND YOUR BEING A GIRL.
BABY MONKEY
Ooh Ooh Ooh
I like my hair...
EITHER WAY...
WHETHER YOUR POWER IS WEAK OR STRONG...
...YOU WILL HELP ME SEE LITHUANEL'S FUTURE.

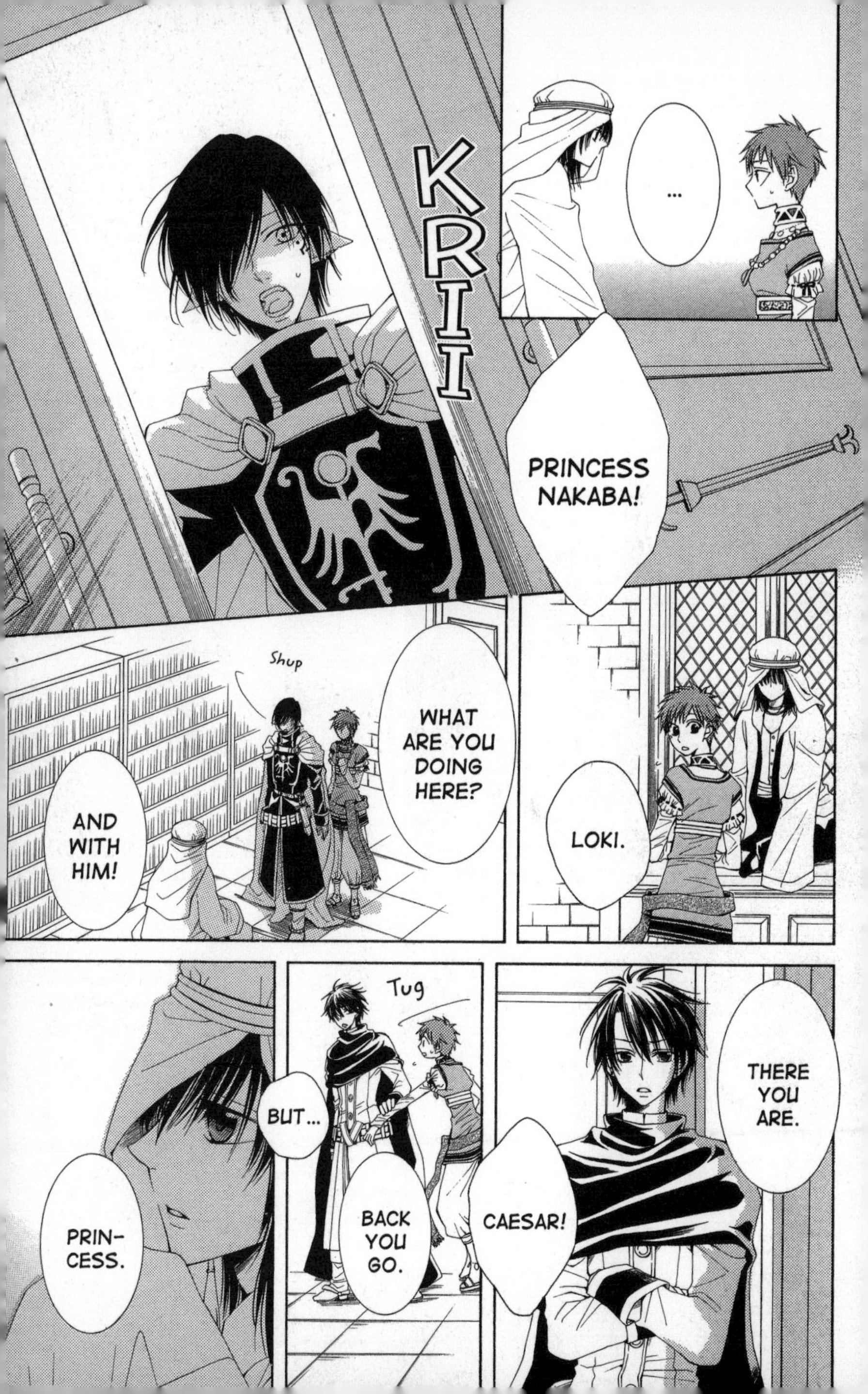
...
PRINCESS NAKABA!
KRII
LOKI.
Shup
WHAT ARE YOU DOING HERE?
AND WITH HIM!
THERE YOU ARE.
CAESAR!
Tug
BUT...
BACK YOU GO.
PRIN-CESS.

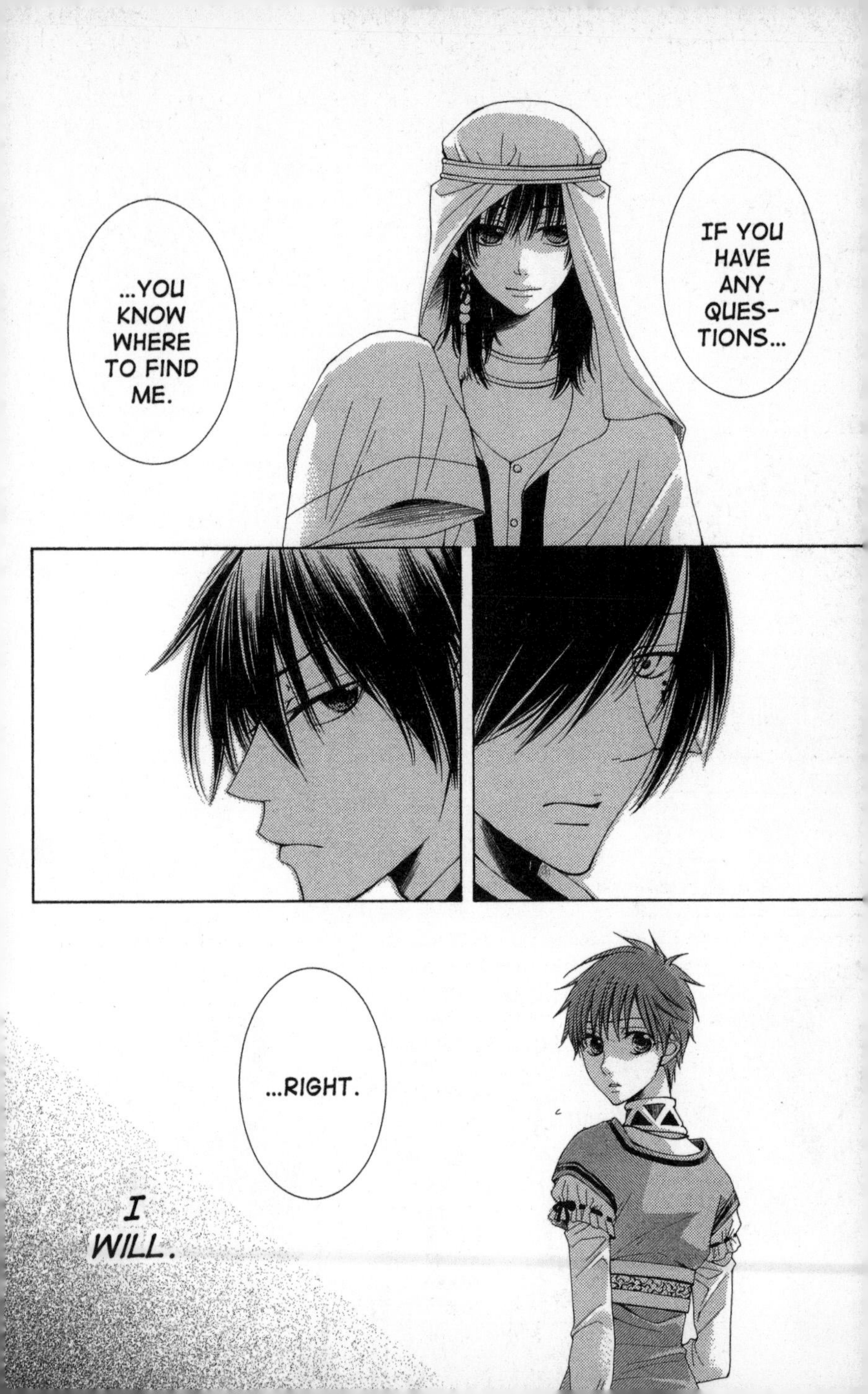
IF YOU HAVE ANY QUES-TIONS...
...YOU KNOW WHERE TO FIND ME.
...RIGHT.
I WILL.

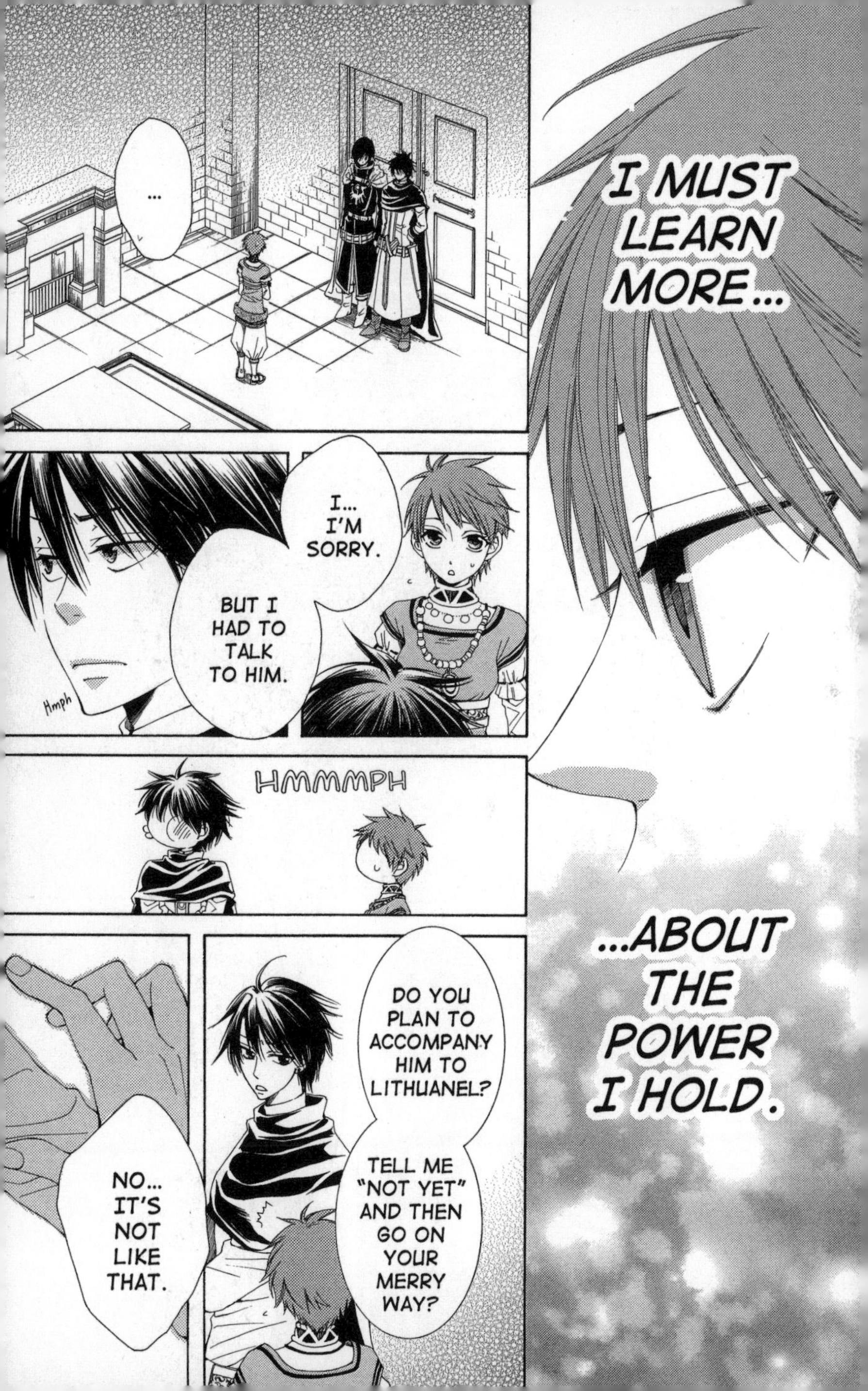
I MUST LEARN MORE...
...ABOUT THE POWER I HOLD.
...
I... I'M SORRY.
BUT I HAD TO TALK TO HIM.
Hmph
HMMMPH
DO YOU PLAN TO ACCOMPANY HIM TO LITHUANEL?
TELL ME "NOT YET" AND THEN GO ON YOUR MERRY WAY?
NO... IT'S NOT LIKE THAT.

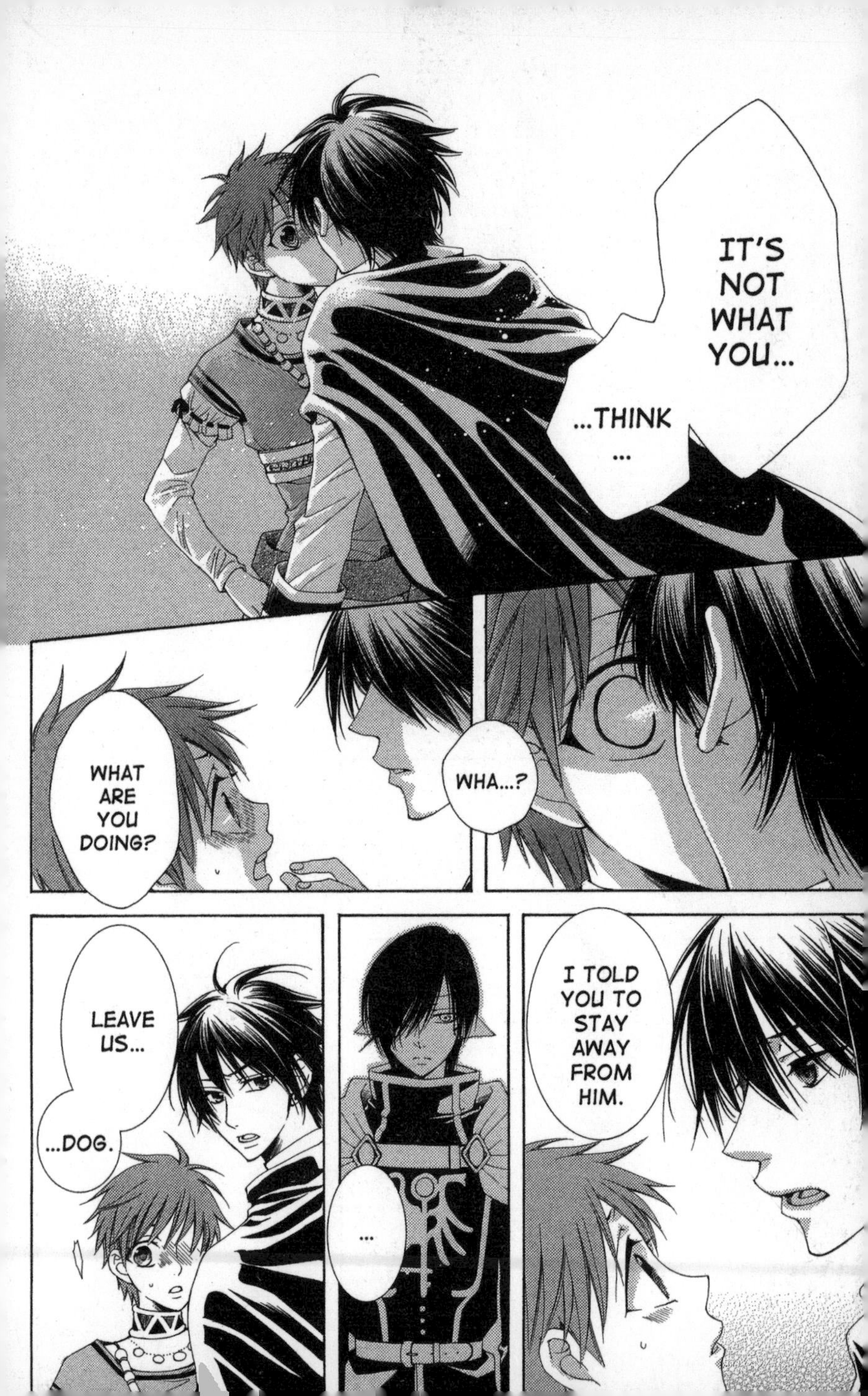
IT'S NOT WHAT YOU...
...THINK ...
WHA...?
WHAT ARE YOU DOING?
I TOLD YOU TO STAY AWAY FROM HIM.
...
LEAVE US...
...DOG.

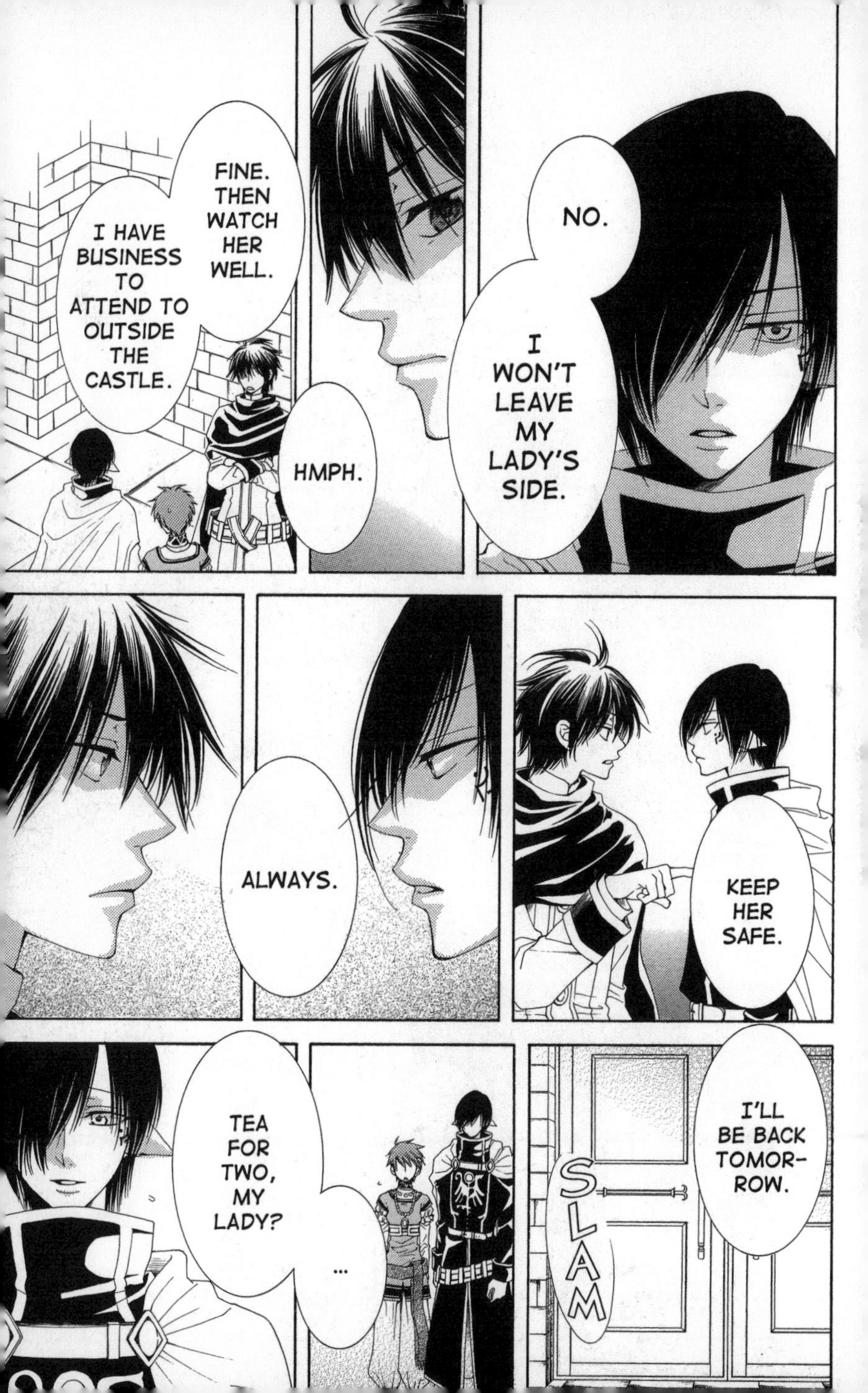
NO.
I WON'T LEAVE MY LADY'S SIDE.
HMPH.
FINE. THEN WATCH HER WELL.
I HAVE BUSINESS TO ATTEND TO OUTSIDE THE CASTLE.
KEEP HER SAFE.
ALWAYS.
I'LL BE BACK TOMOR-ROW.
SLAM
...
TEA FOR TWO, MY LADY?

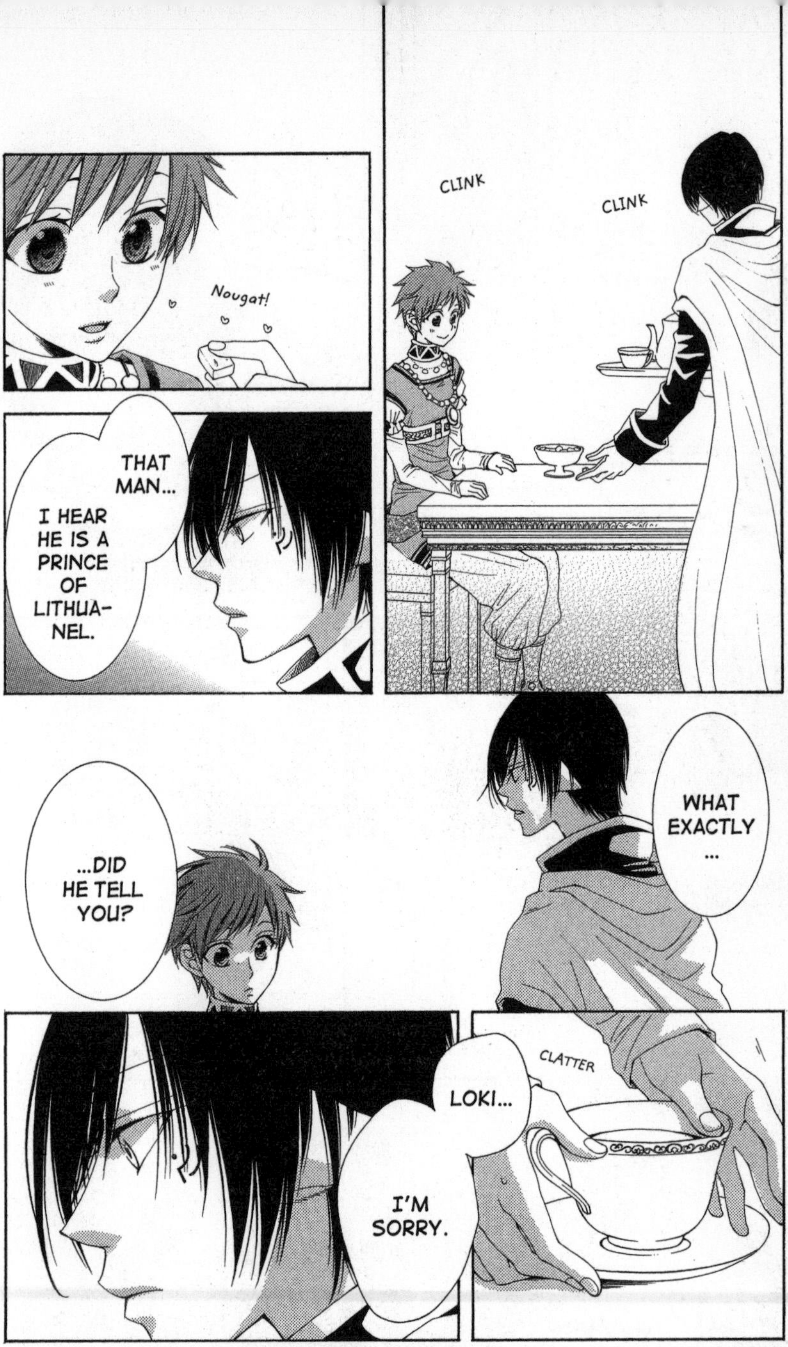
CLINK
CLINK
Nougat!
THAT MAN...
I HEAR HE IS A PRINCE OF LITHUA-NEL.
WHAT EXACTLY ...
...DID HE TELL YOU?
CLATTER
LOKI...
I'M SORRY.

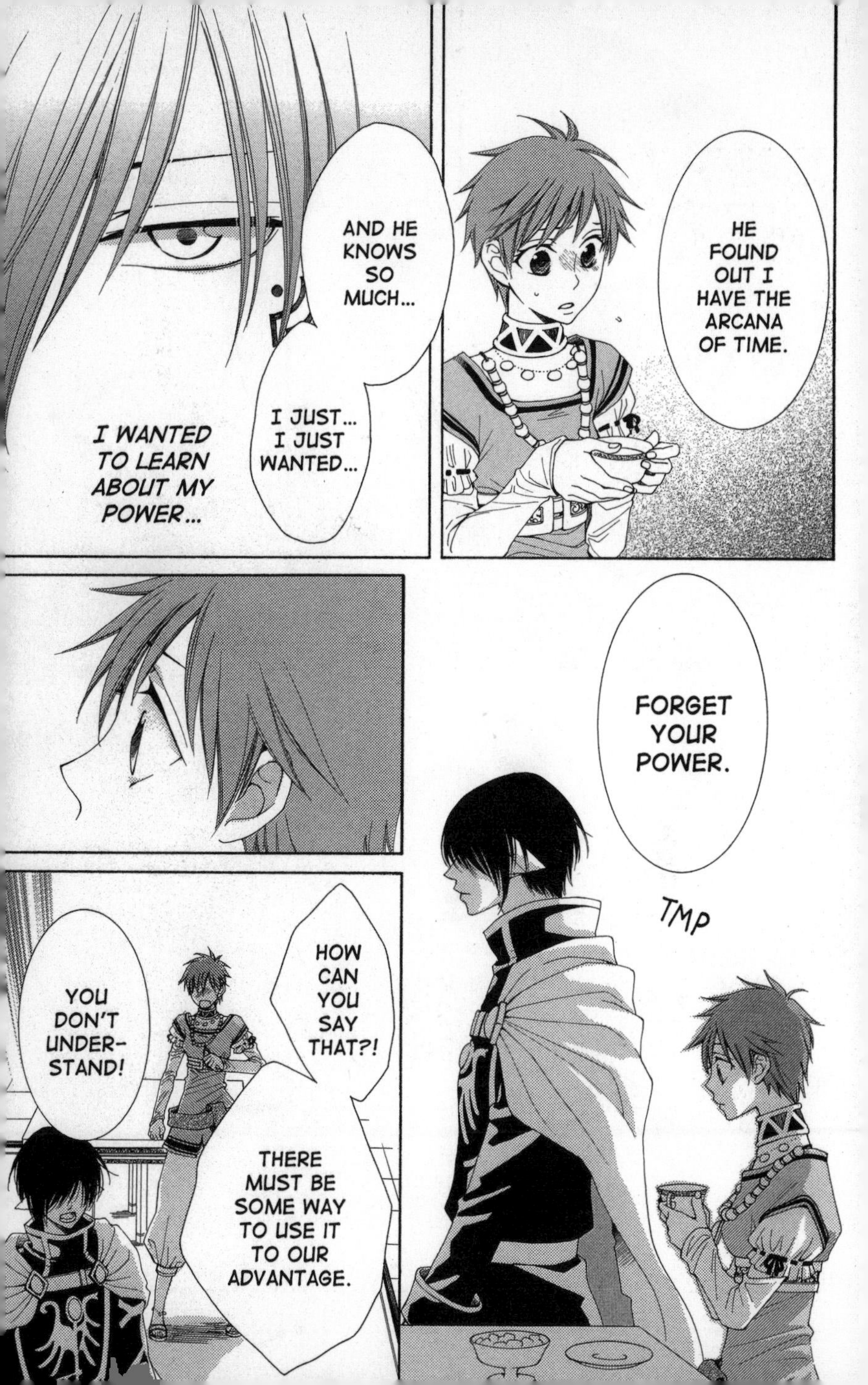
HE FOUND OUT I HAVE THE ARCANA OF TIME.
AND HE KNOWS SO MUCH...
I JUST... I JUST WANTED...
I WANTED TO LEARN ABOUT MY POWER...
FORGET YOUR POWER.
TMP
HOW CAN YOU SAY THAT?!
YOU DON'T UNDER-STAND!
THERE MUST BE SOME WAY TO USE IT TO OUR ADVANTAGE.

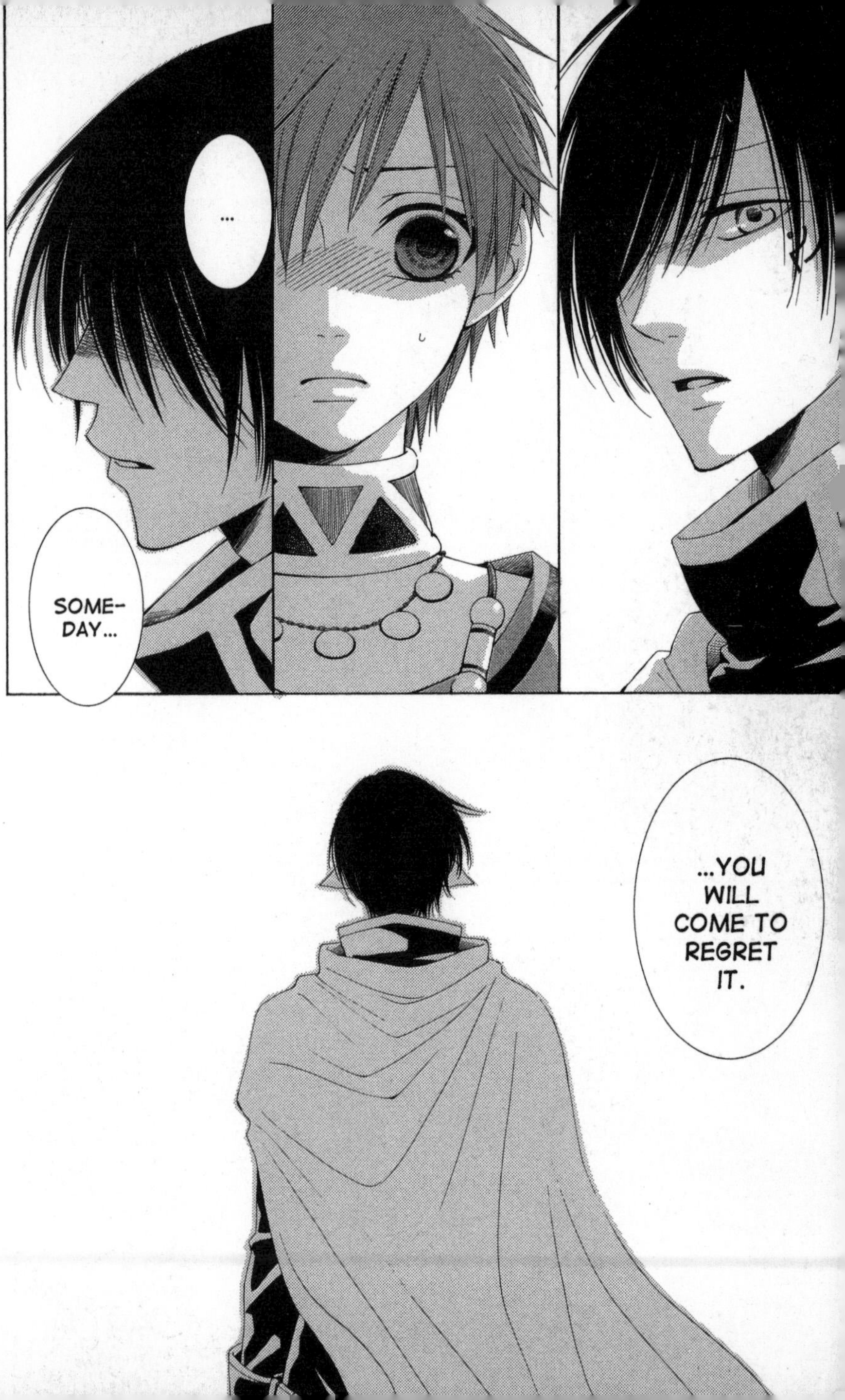
...
SOME-DAY...
...YOU WILL COME TO REGRET IT.

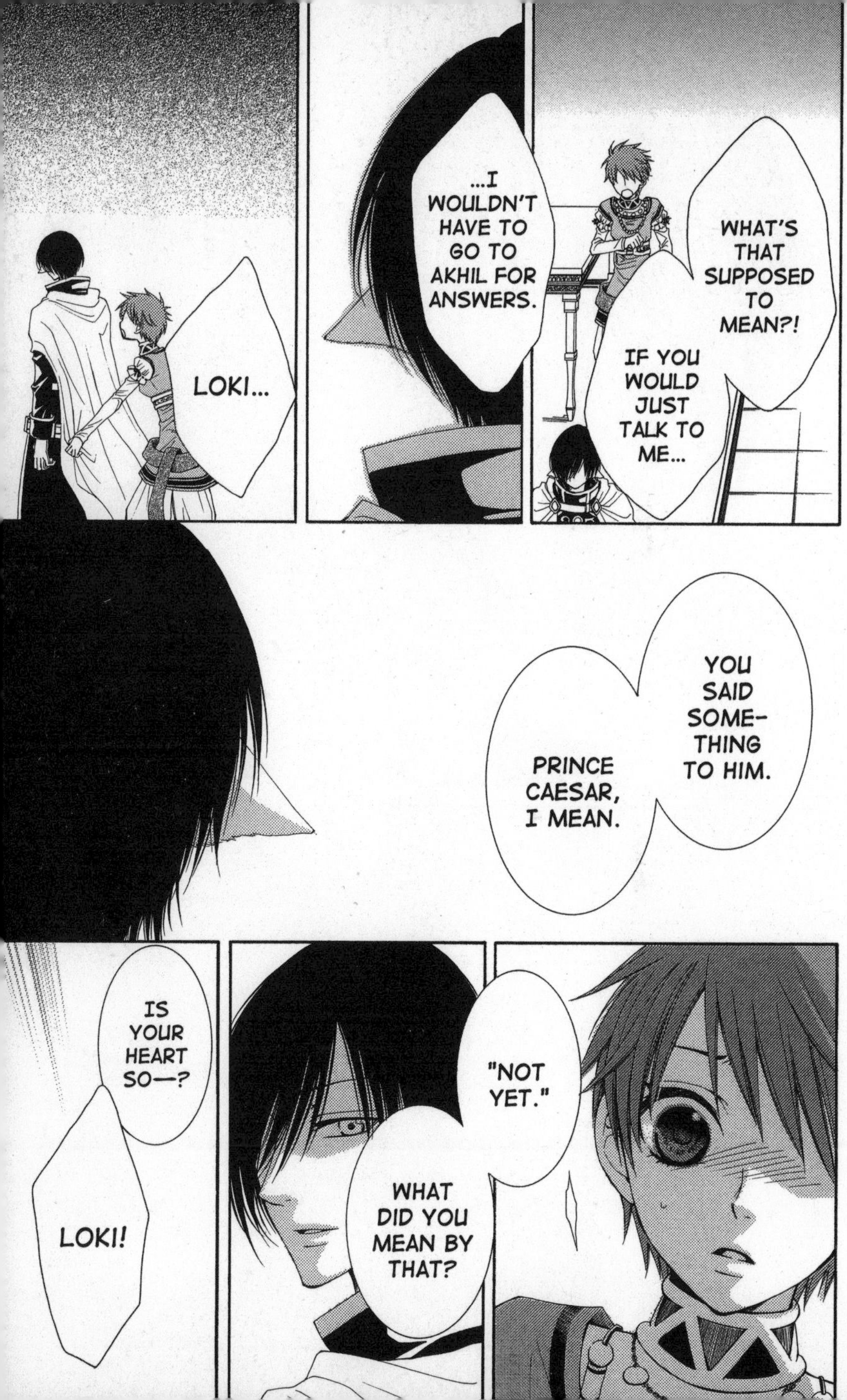
WHAT'S THAT SUPPOSED TO MEAN?!
IF YOU WOULD JUST TALK TO ME...
...I WOULDN'T HAVE TO GO TO AKHIL FOR ANSWERS.
LOKI...
YOU SAID SOME-THING TO HIM.
PRINCE CAESAR, I MEAN.
"NOT YET."
WHAT DID YOU MEAN BY THAT?
IS YOUR HEART SO—?
LOKI!

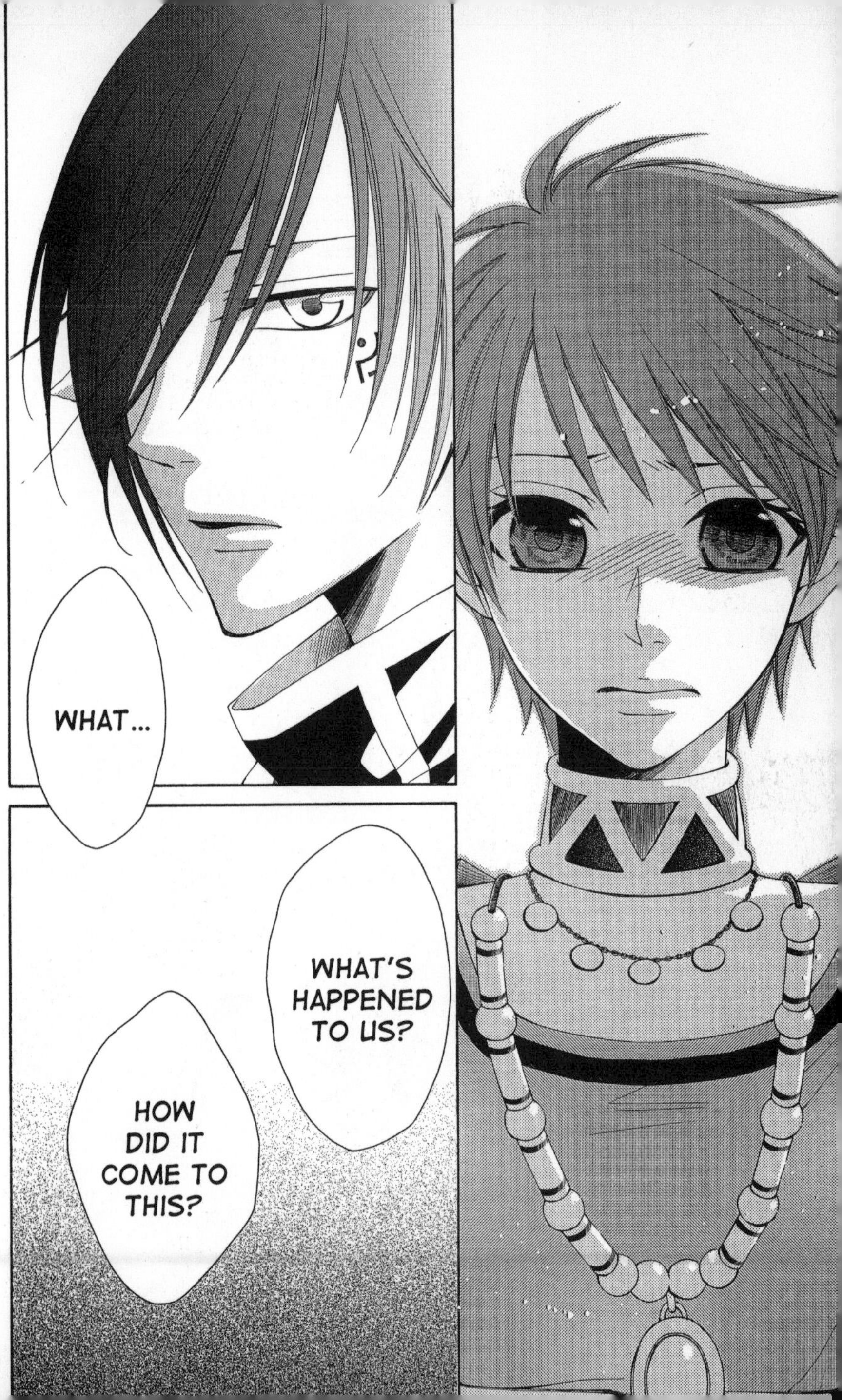
WHAT...
WHAT'S HAPPENED TO US?
HOW DID IT COME TO THIS?

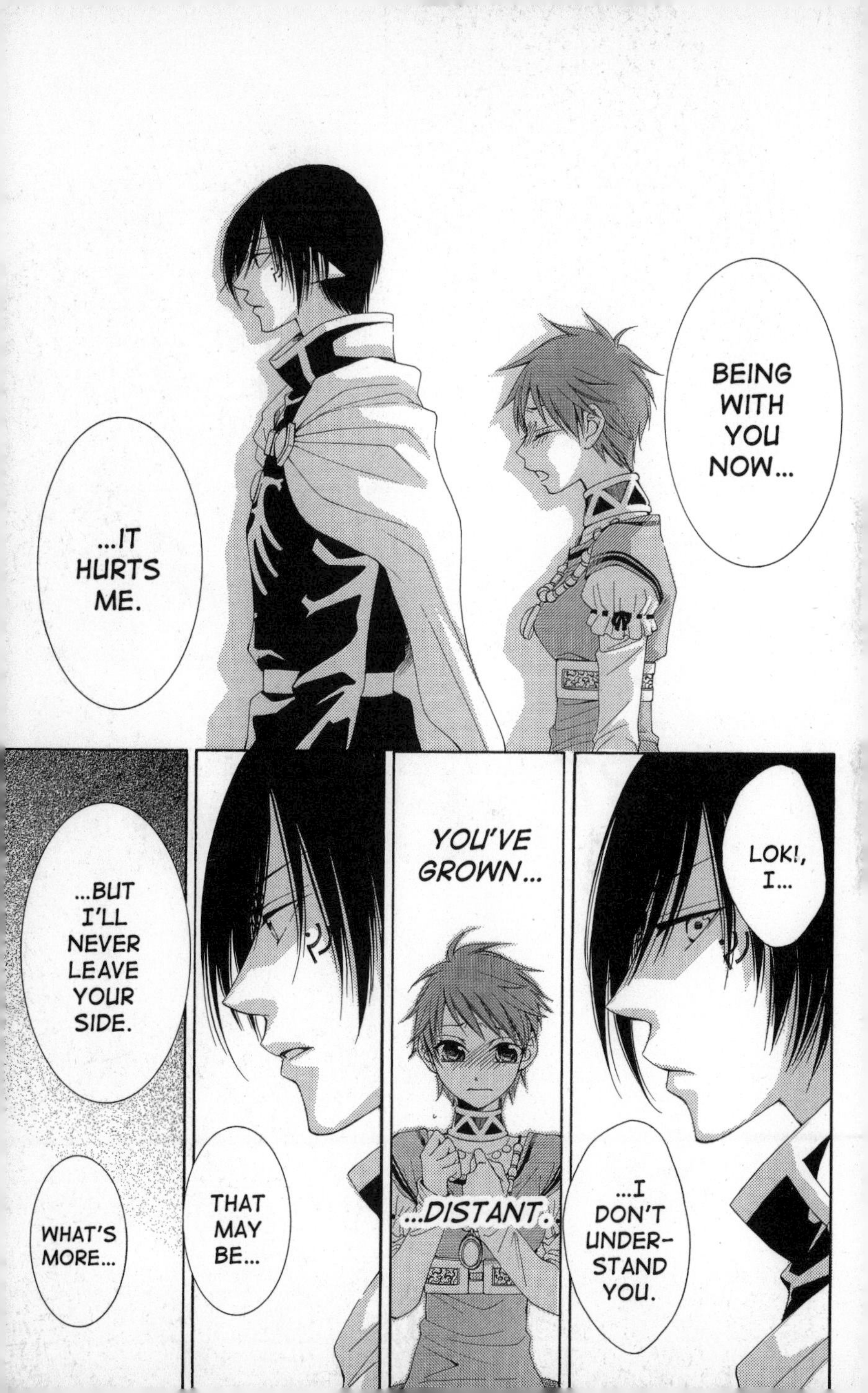
BEING WITH YOU NOW...
...IT HURTS ME.
LOKI, I...
...I DON'T UNDER-STAND YOU.
YOU'VE GROWN...
...DISTANT.
THAT MAY BE...
...BUT I'LL NEVER LEAVE YOUR SIDE.
WHAT'S MORE...

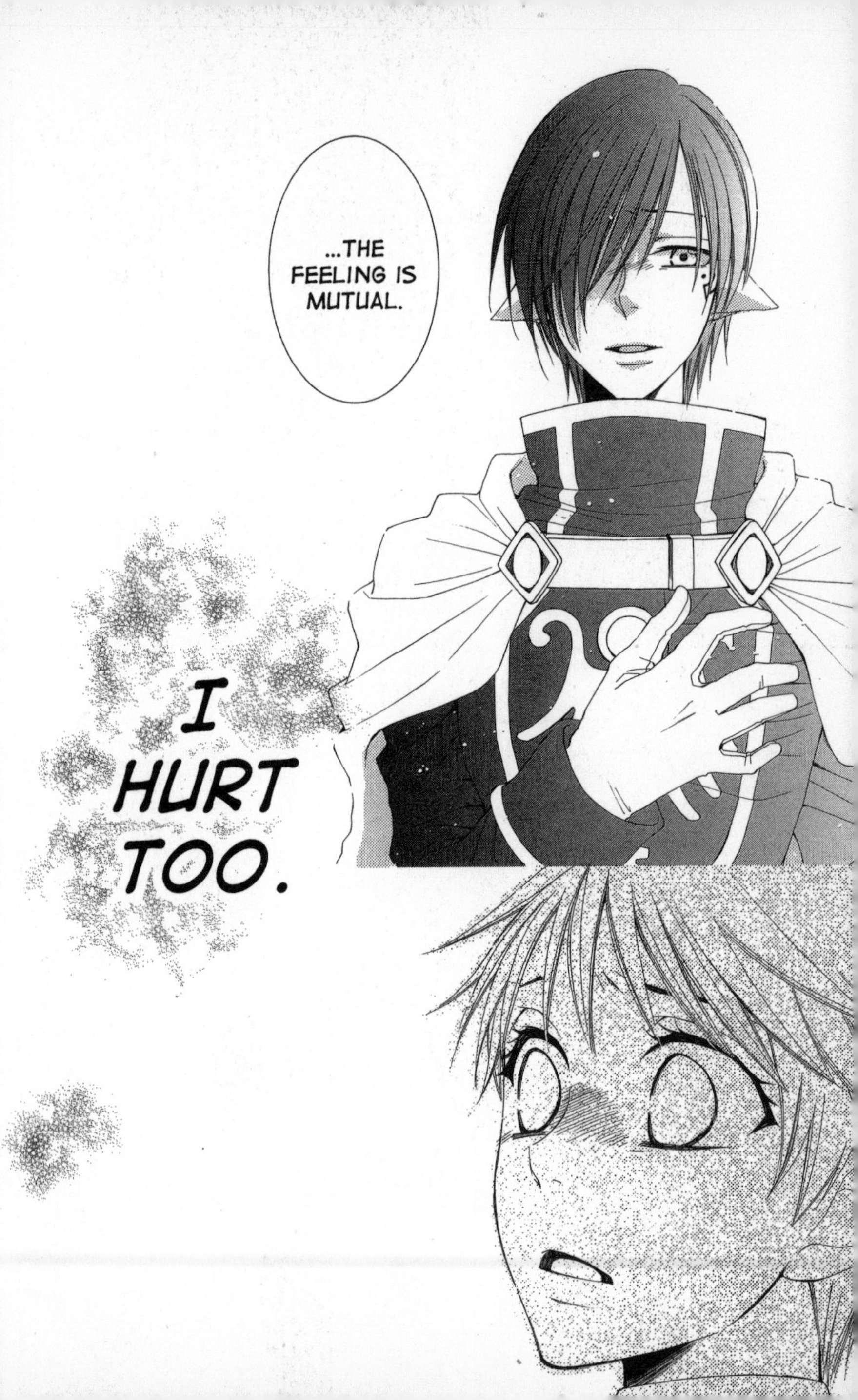
...THE FEELING IS MUTUAL.
I HURT TOO.

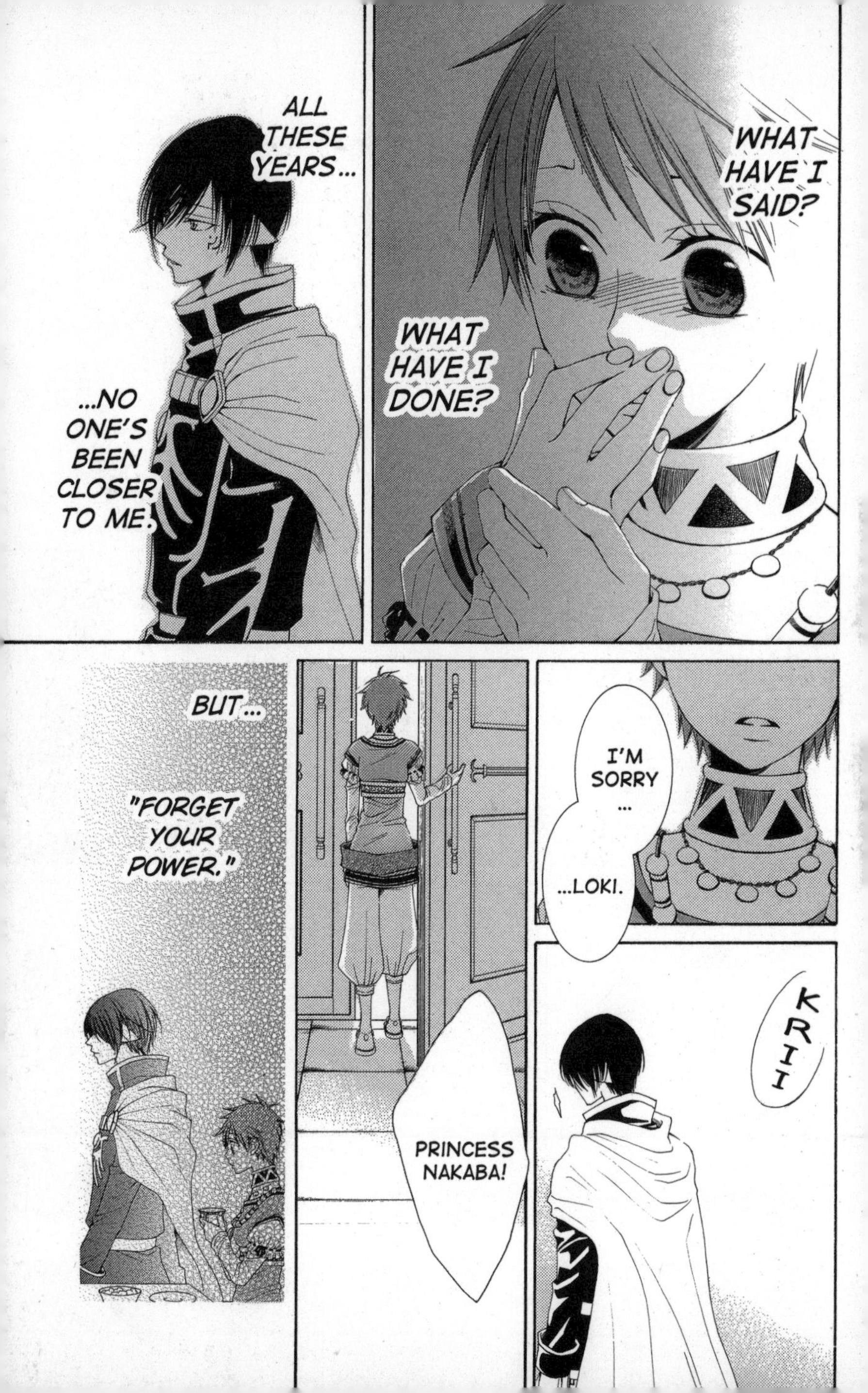
WHAT HAVE I SAID?
WHAT HAVE I DONE?
ALL THESE YEARS...
...NO ONE'S BEEN CLOSER TO ME.
I'M SORRY ...
...LOKI.
KRII
PRINCESS NAKABA!
BUT...
"FORGET YOUR POWER."

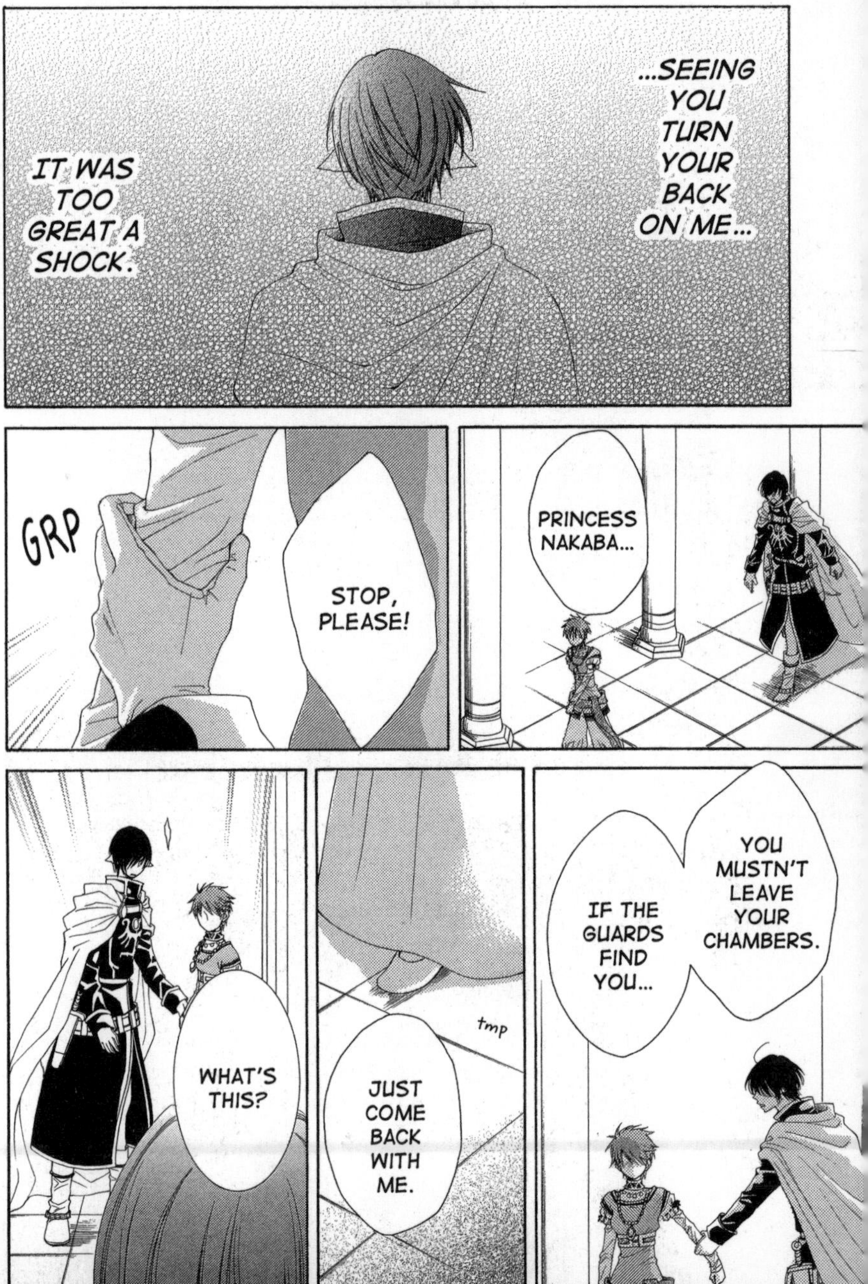
...SEEING YOU TURN YOUR BACK ON ME...
IT WAS TOO GREAT A SHOCK.
PRINCESS NAKABA...
STOP, PLEASE!
GRP
YOU MUSTN'T LEAVE YOUR CHAMBERS.
IF THE GUARDS FIND YOU...
tmp
JUST COME BACK WITH ME.
WHAT'S THIS?

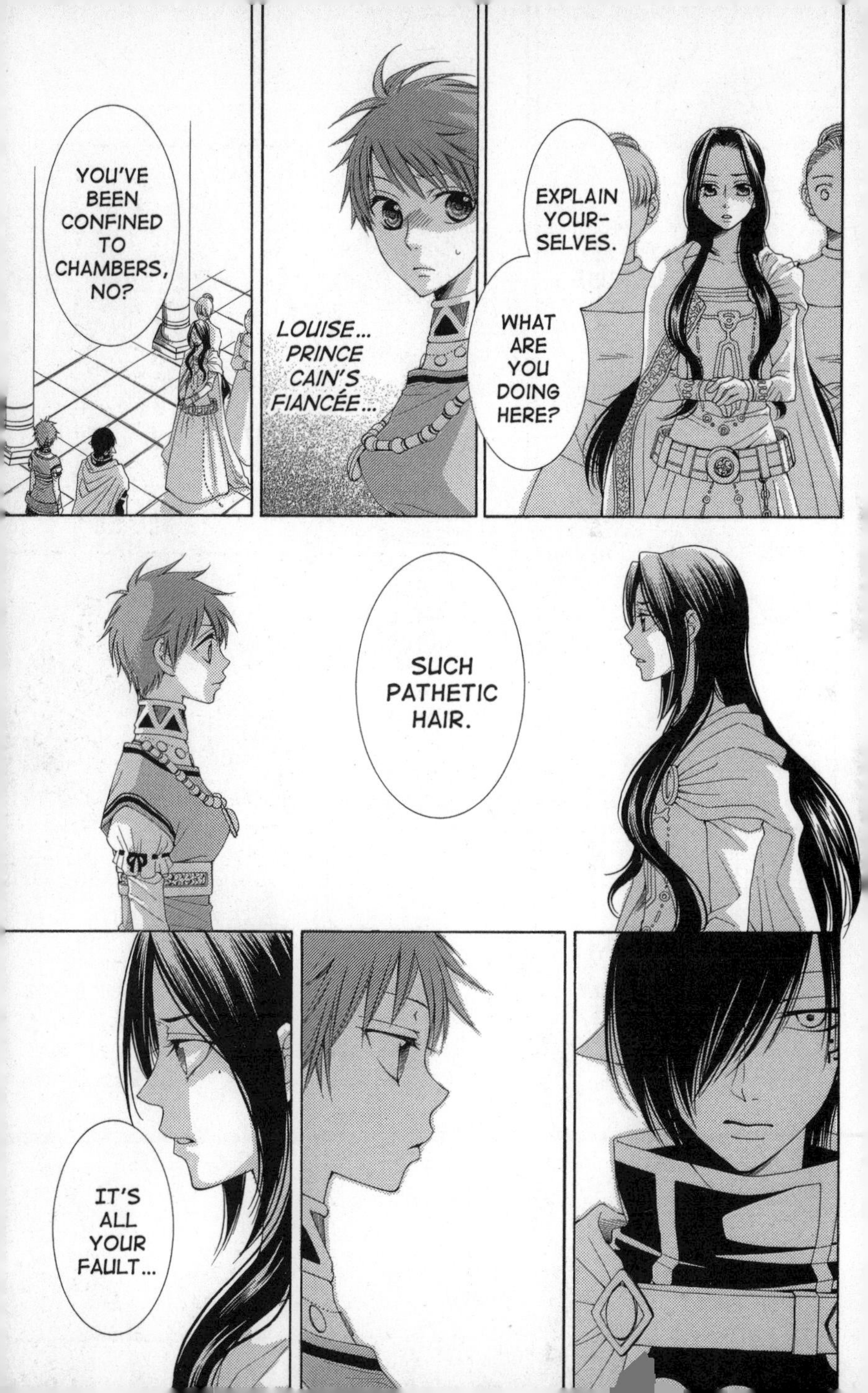
EXPLAIN YOUR-SELVES.
WHAT ARE YOU DOING HERE?
LOUISE... PRINCE CAIN'S FIANCÉE...
YOU'VE BEEN CONFINED TO CHAMBERS, NO?
SUCH PATHETIC HAIR.
IT'S ALL YOUR FAULT...

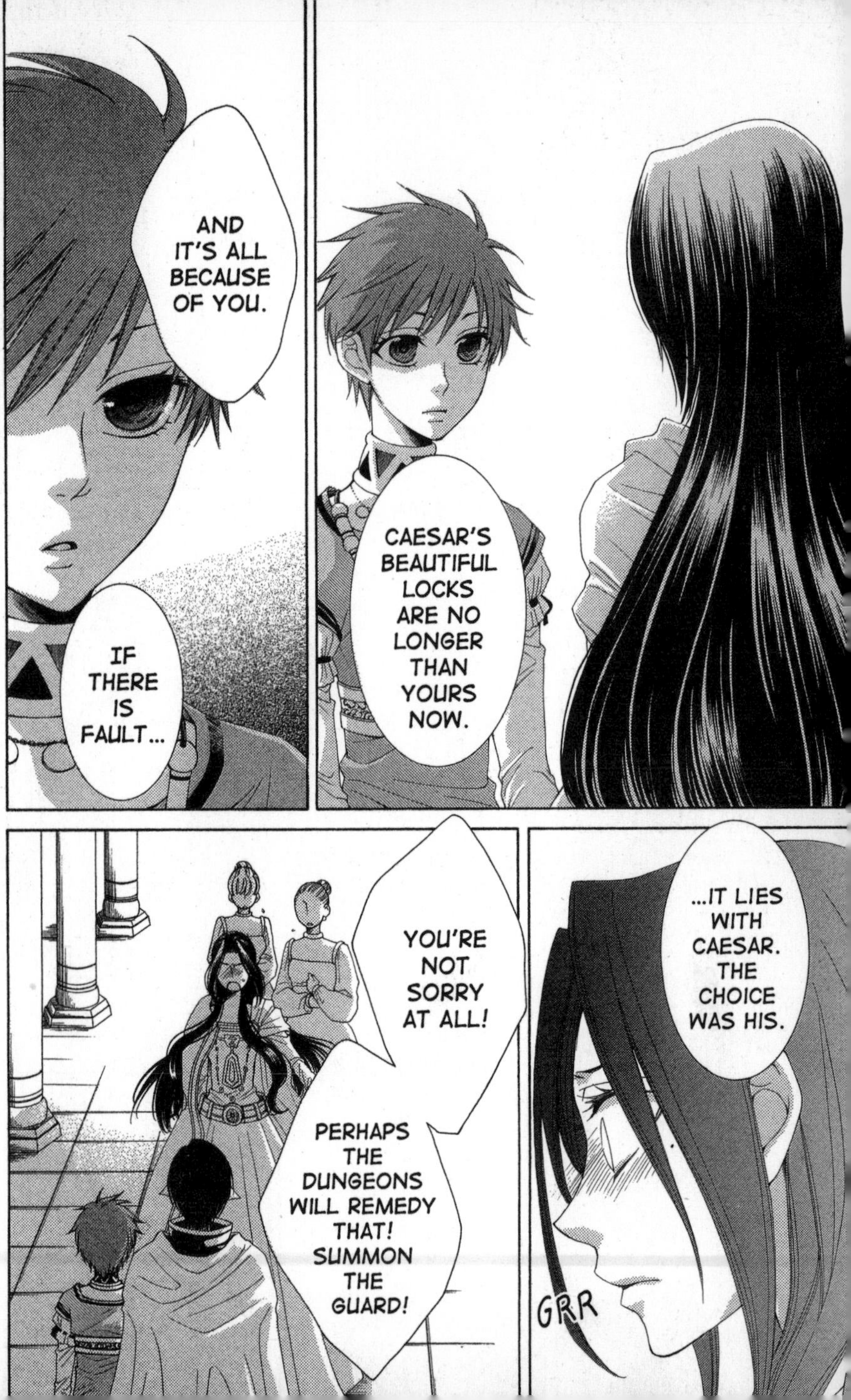
CAESAR'S BEAUTIFUL LOCKS ARE NO LONGER THAN YOURS NOW.
AND IT'S ALL BECAUSE OF YOU.
IF THERE IS FAULT...
...IT LIES WITH CAESAR. THE CHOICE WAS HIS.
GRR
YOU'RE NOT SORRY AT ALL!
PERHAPS THE DUNGEONS WILL REMEDY THAT! SUMMON THE GUARD!

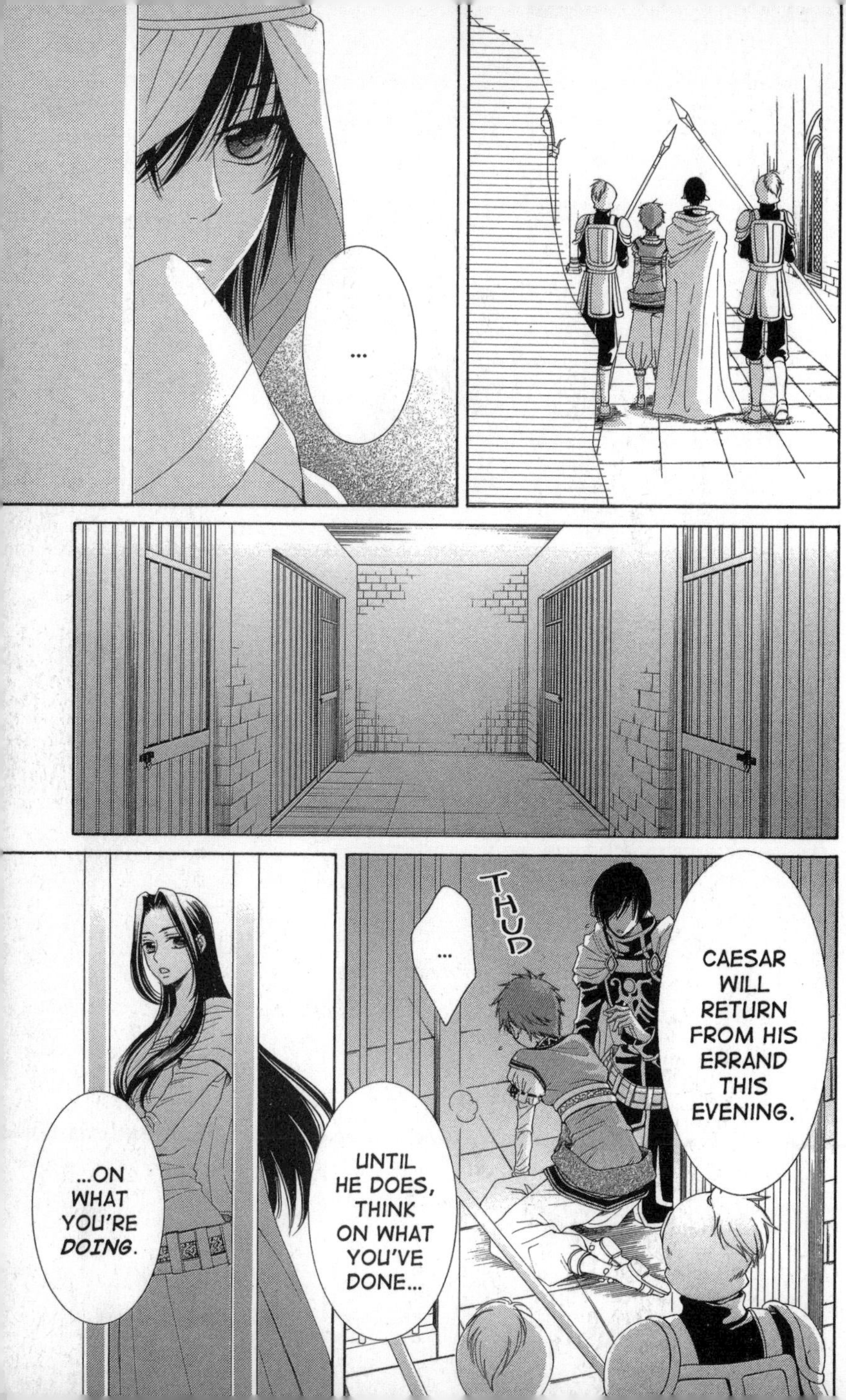
...
CAESAR WILL RETURN FROM HIS ERRAND THIS EVENING.
THUD
...
UNTIL HE DOES, THINK ON WHAT YOU'VE DONE...
...ON WHAT YOU'RE *DOING*.

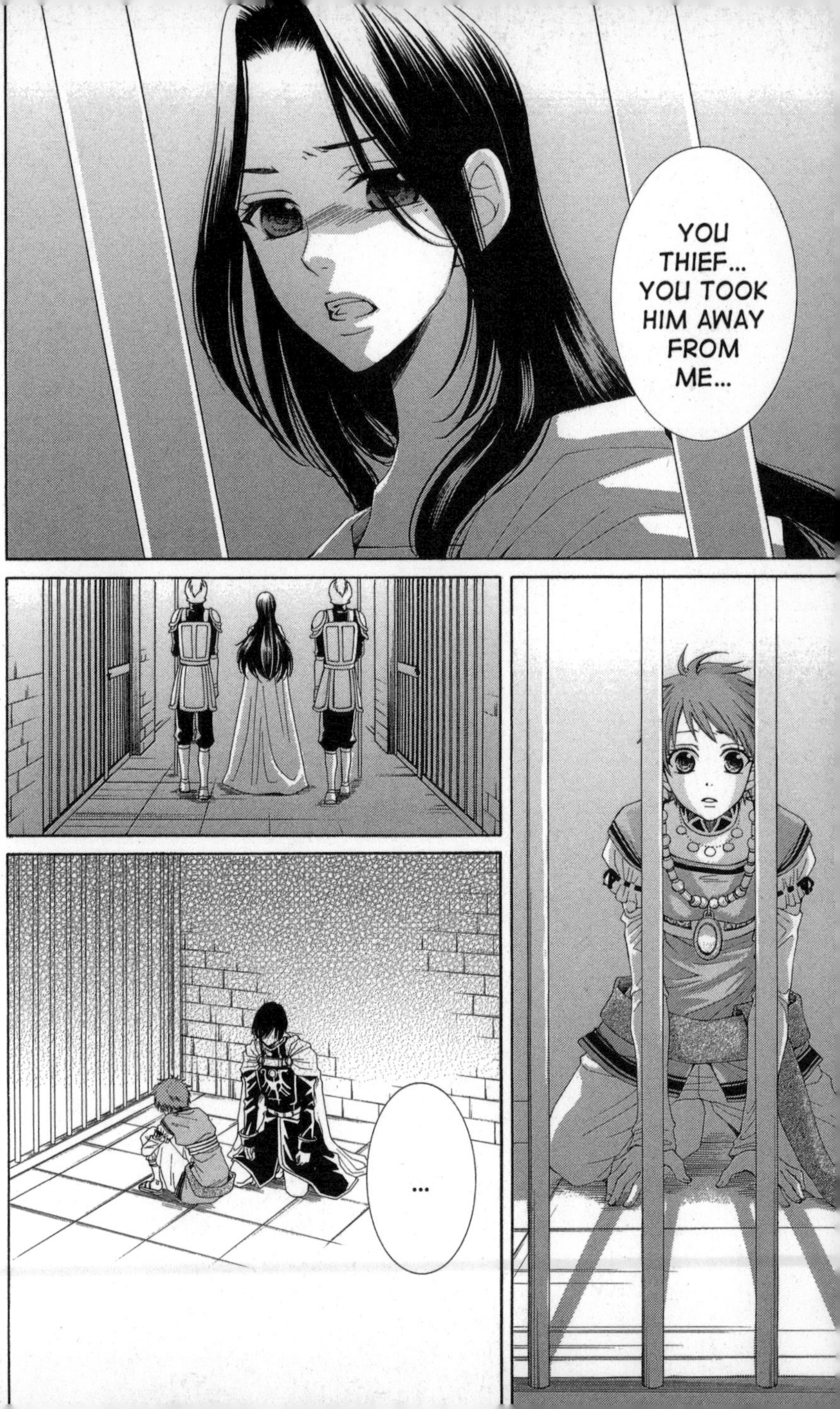
YOU THIEF... YOU TOOK HIM AWAY FROM ME...
...

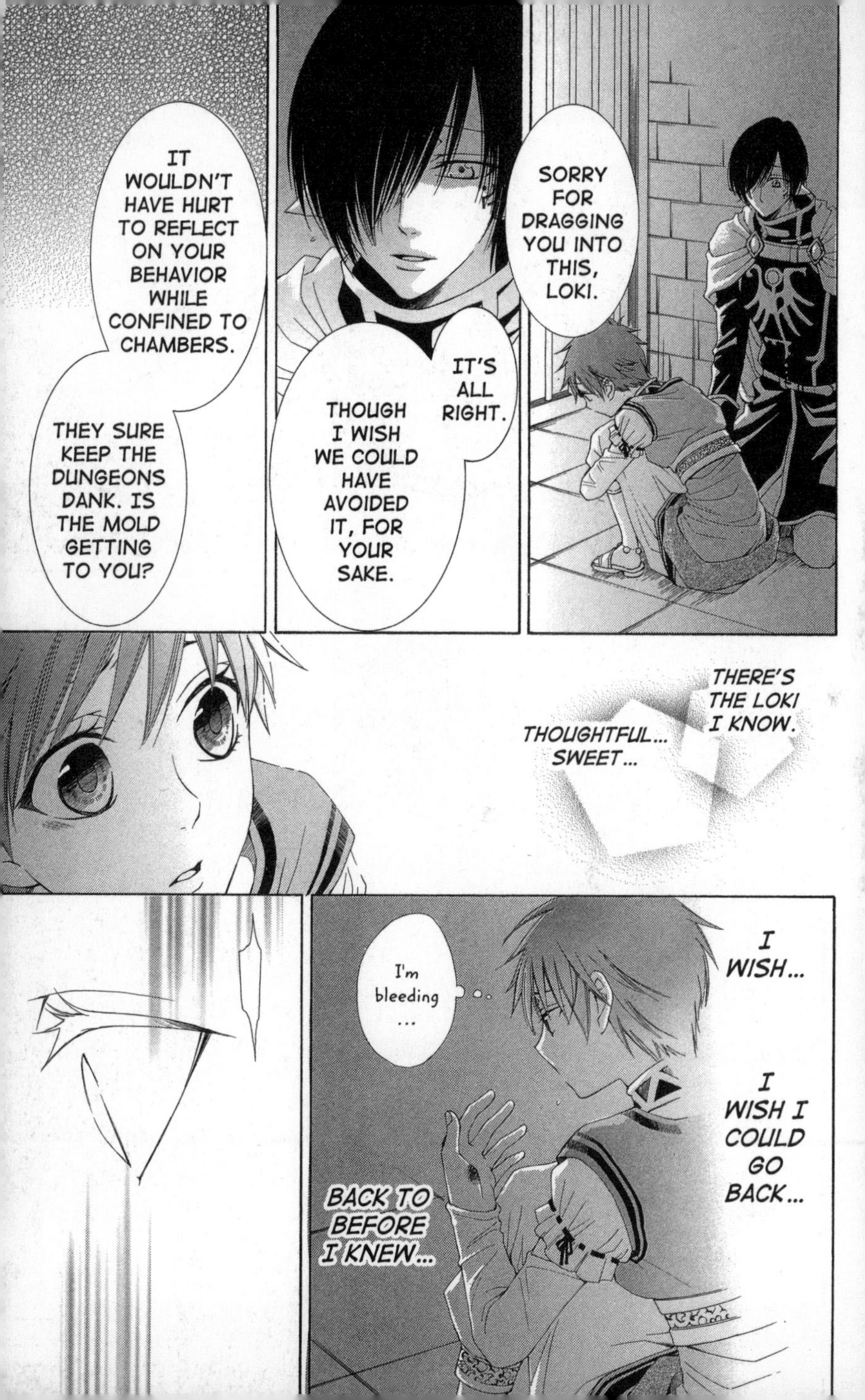
SORRY FOR DRAGGING YOU INTO THIS, LOKI.
IT'S ALL RIGHT.
THOUGH I WISH WE COULD HAVE AVOIDED IT, FOR YOUR SAKE.
IT WOULDN'T HAVE HURT TO REFLECT ON YOUR BEHAVIOR WHILE CONFINED TO CHAMBERS.
THEY SURE KEEP THE DUNGEONS DANK. IS THE MOLD GETTING TO YOU?
THERE'S THE LOKI I KNOW.
THOUGHTFUL... SWEET...
I WISH...
I WISH I COULD GO BACK...
I'm bleeding ...
BACK TO BEFORE I KNEW...

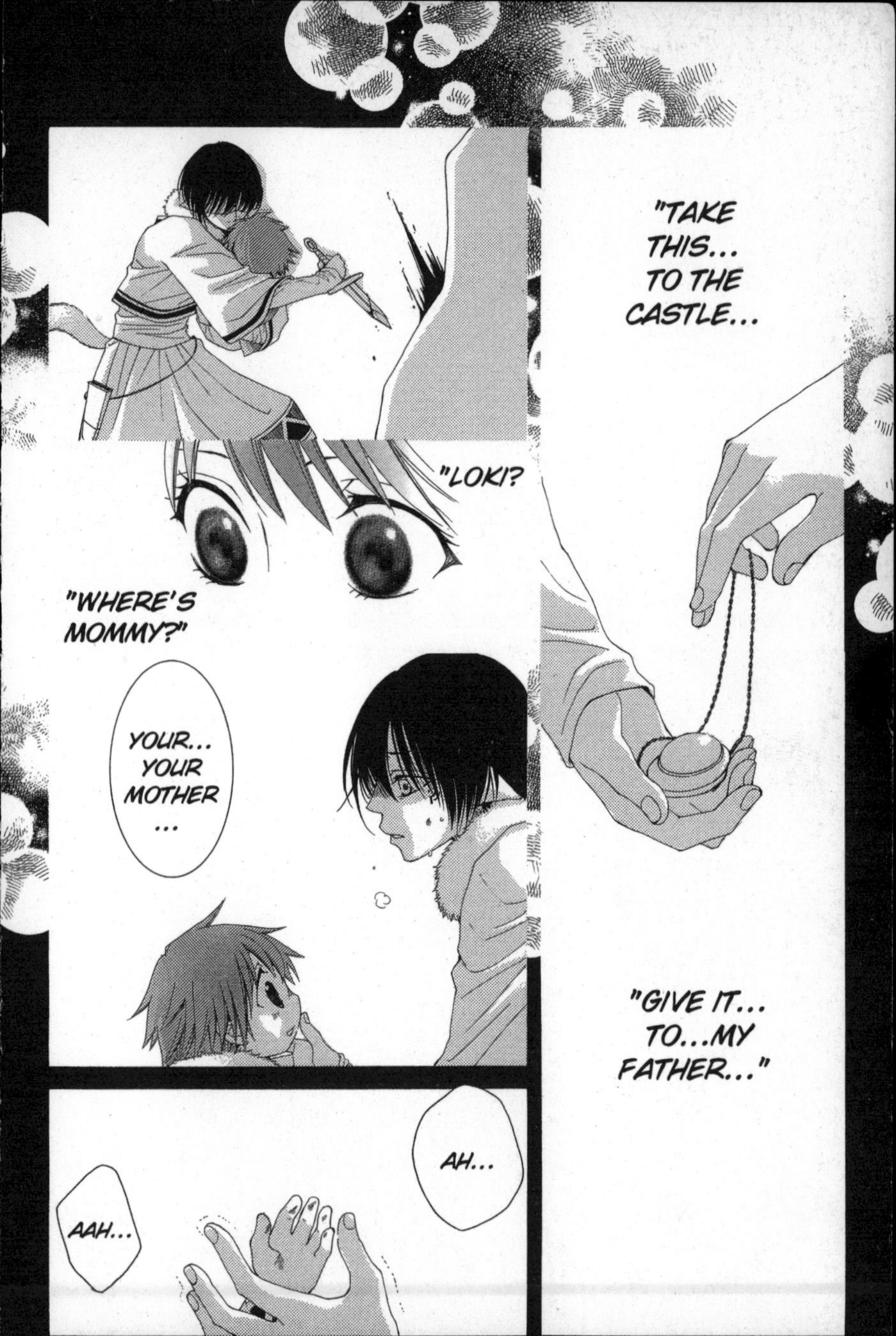
"TAKE THIS... TO THE CASTLE...
"GIVE IT... TO...MY FATHER..."
"LOKI?
"WHERE'S MOMMY?"
YOUR... YOUR MOTHER ...
AH...
AAH...

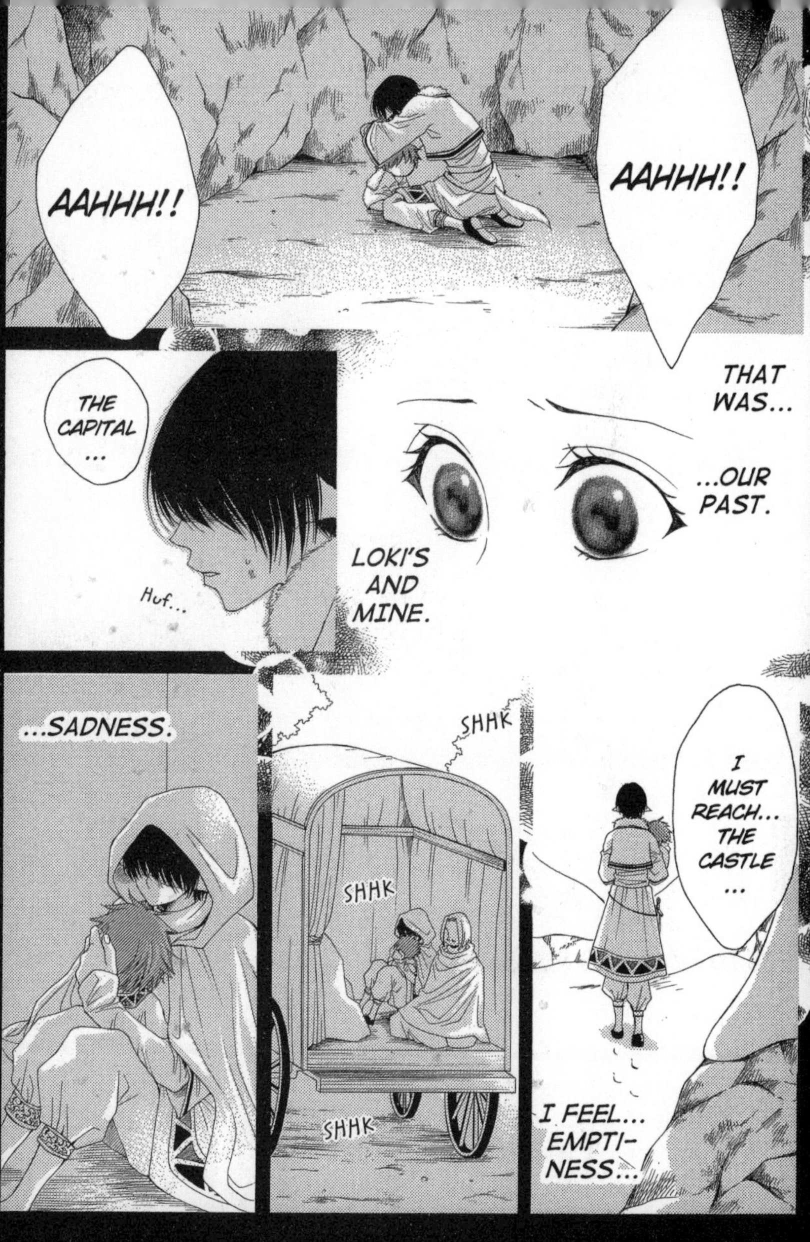
AAHHH!!
AAHHH!!
THAT WAS...
...OUR PAST.
LOKI'S AND MINE.
THE CAPITAL ...
Huf...
I MUST REACH... THE CASTLE ...
I FEEL... EMPTI-NESS...
SHHK
SHHK
SHHK
...SADNESS.

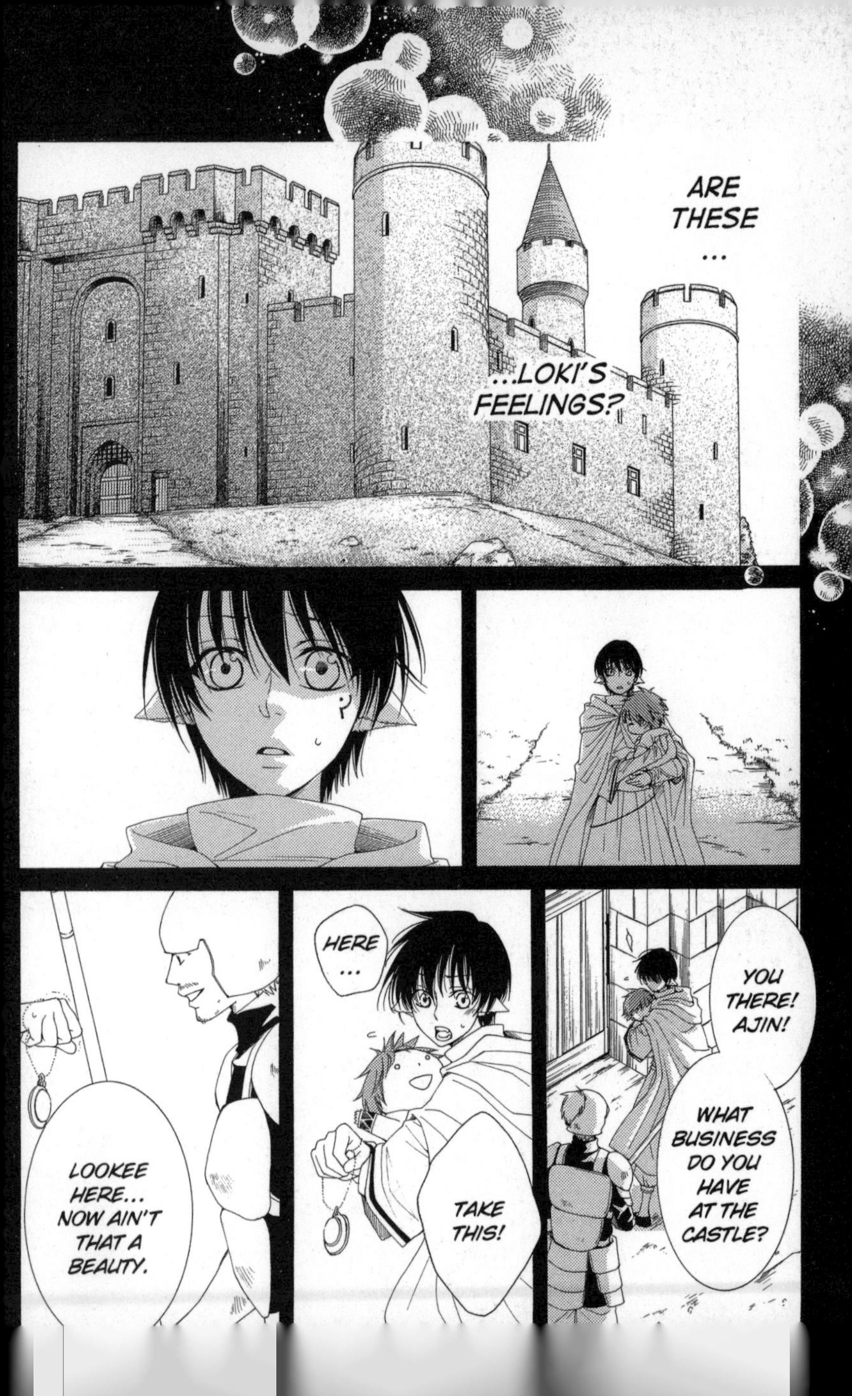
ARE THESE ...
...LOKI'S FEELINGS?
YOU THERE! AJIN!
WHAT BUSINESS DO YOU HAVE AT THE CASTLE?
HERE ...
TAKE THIS!
LOOKEE HERE... NOW AIN'T THAT A BEAUTY.

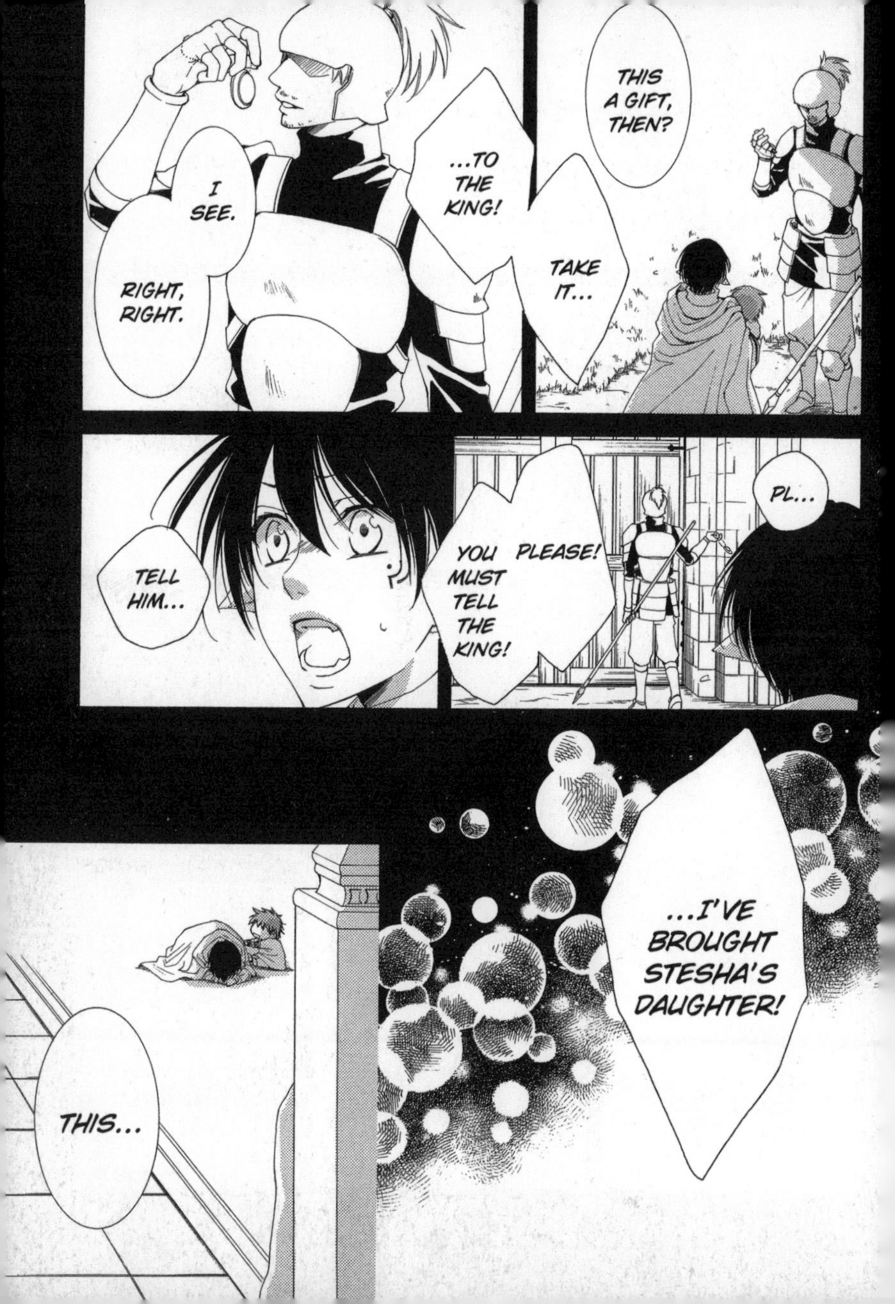
THIS A GIFT, THEN?
TAKE IT...
...TO THE KING!
I SEE.
RIGHT, RIGHT.
PL...
PLEASE!
YOU MUST TELL THE KING!
TELL HIM...
...I'VE BROUGHT STESHA'S DAUGHTER!
THIS...

THIS IS MY DAUGHTER'S CHILD?
YES... MY LORD.
SHE HAS MUCH OF HER FATHER IN HER.
HER HAIR BURNS LIKE A FLAME.
I DID NOT THINK BELQUAT WOULD... KILL THEM...

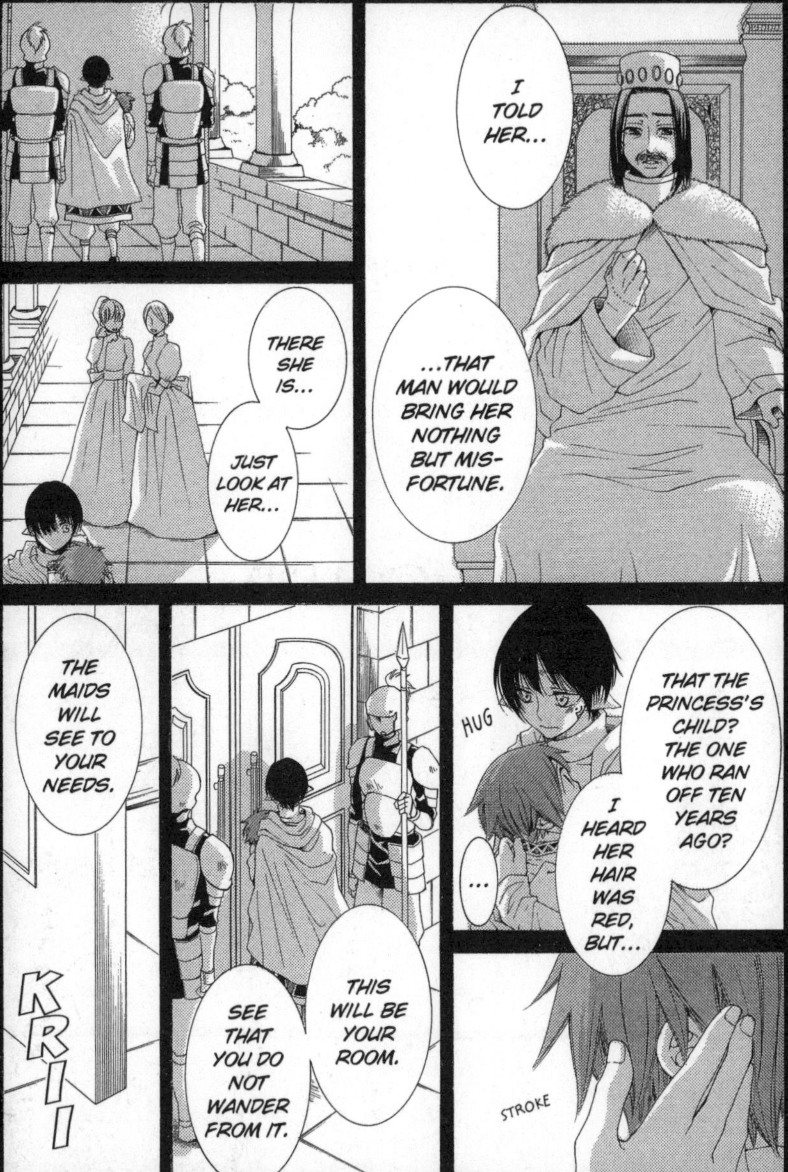
I TOLD HER...
...THAT MAN WOULD BRING HER NOTHING BUT MIS-FORTUNE.
THERE SHE IS...
JUST LOOK AT HER...
THAT THE PRINCESS'S CHILD? THE ONE WHO RAN OFF TEN YEARS AGO?
HUG
I HEARD HER HAIR WAS RED, BUT...
...
STROKE
THIS WILL BE YOUR ROOM.
SEE THAT YOU DO NOT WANDER FROM IT.
THE MAIDS WILL SEE TO YOUR NEEDS.
KRIII

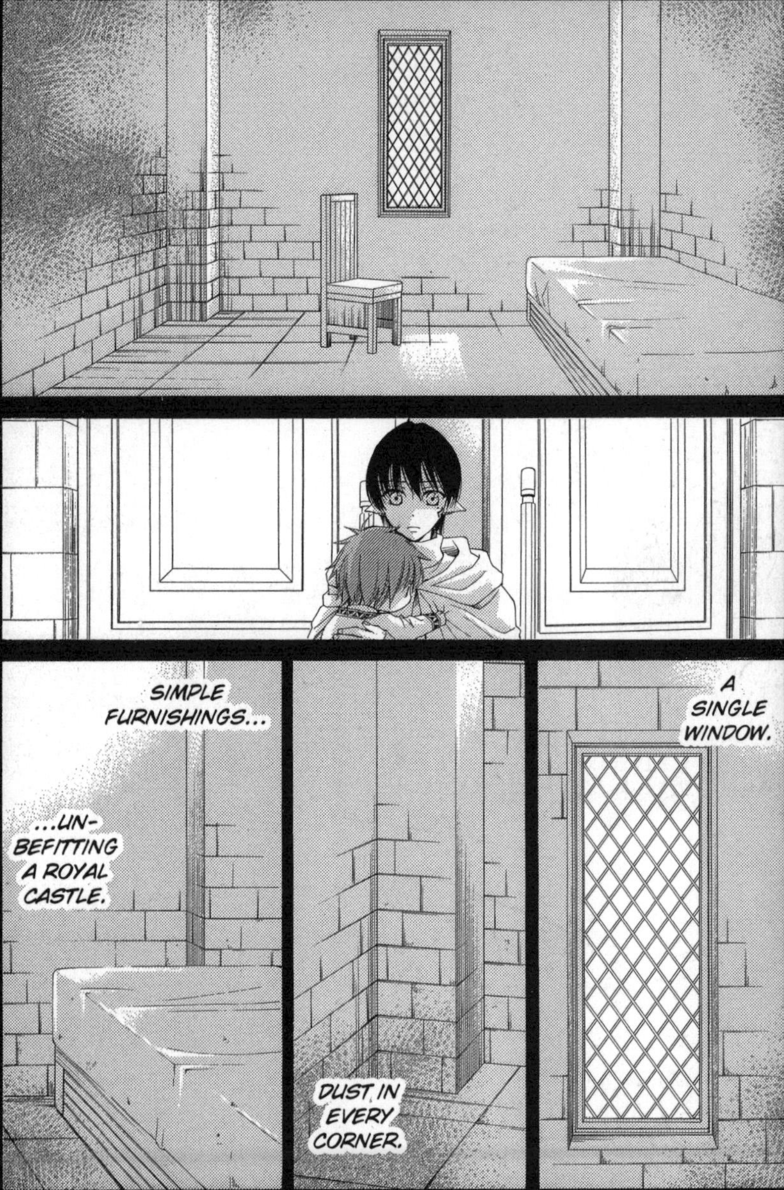
A SINGLE WINDOW.
DUST IN EVERY CORNER.
SIMPLE FURNISHINGS...
...UN-BEFITTING A ROYAL CASTLE.

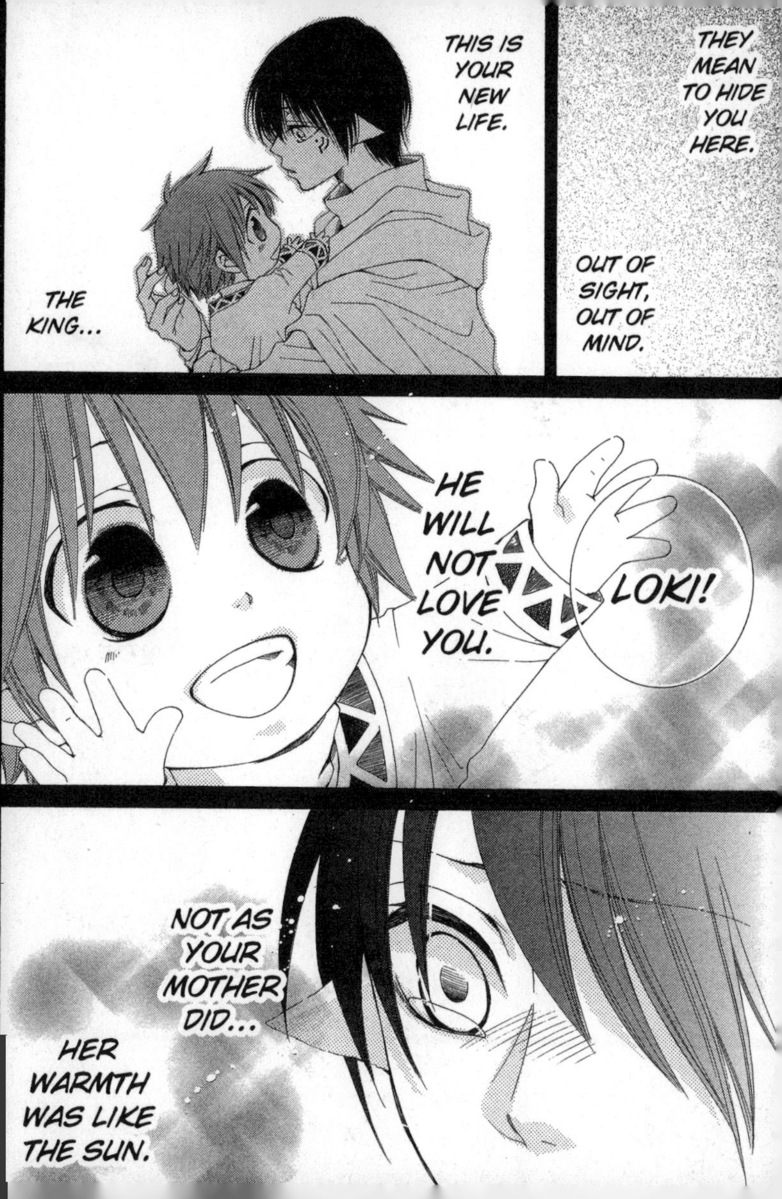
THEY MEAN TO HIDE YOU HERE.
OUT OF SIGHT, OUT OF MIND.
THIS IS YOUR NEW LIFE.
THE KING...
LOKI!
HE WILL NOT LOVE YOU.
NOT AS YOUR MOTHER DID...
HER WARMTH WAS LIKE THE SUN.

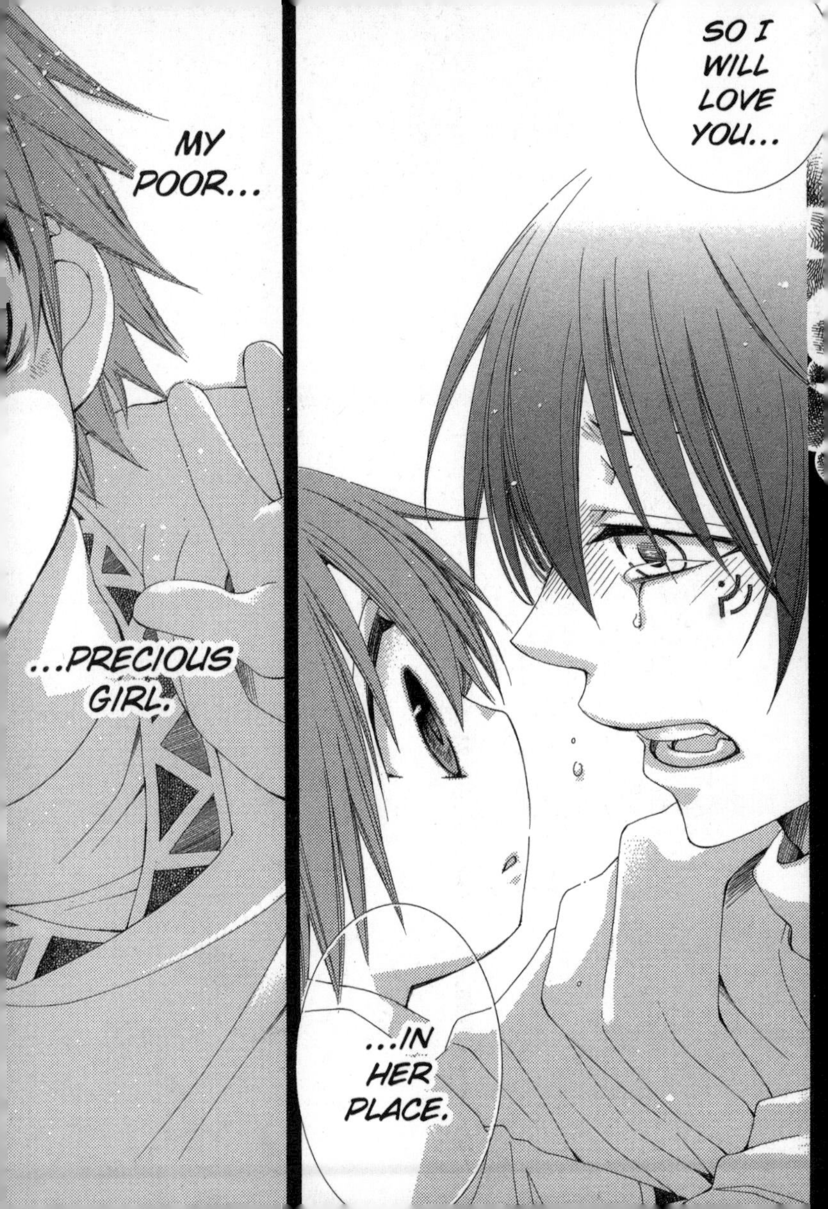
SO I WILL LOVE YOU...
...IN HER PLACE.
MY POOR...
...PRECIOUS GIRL.

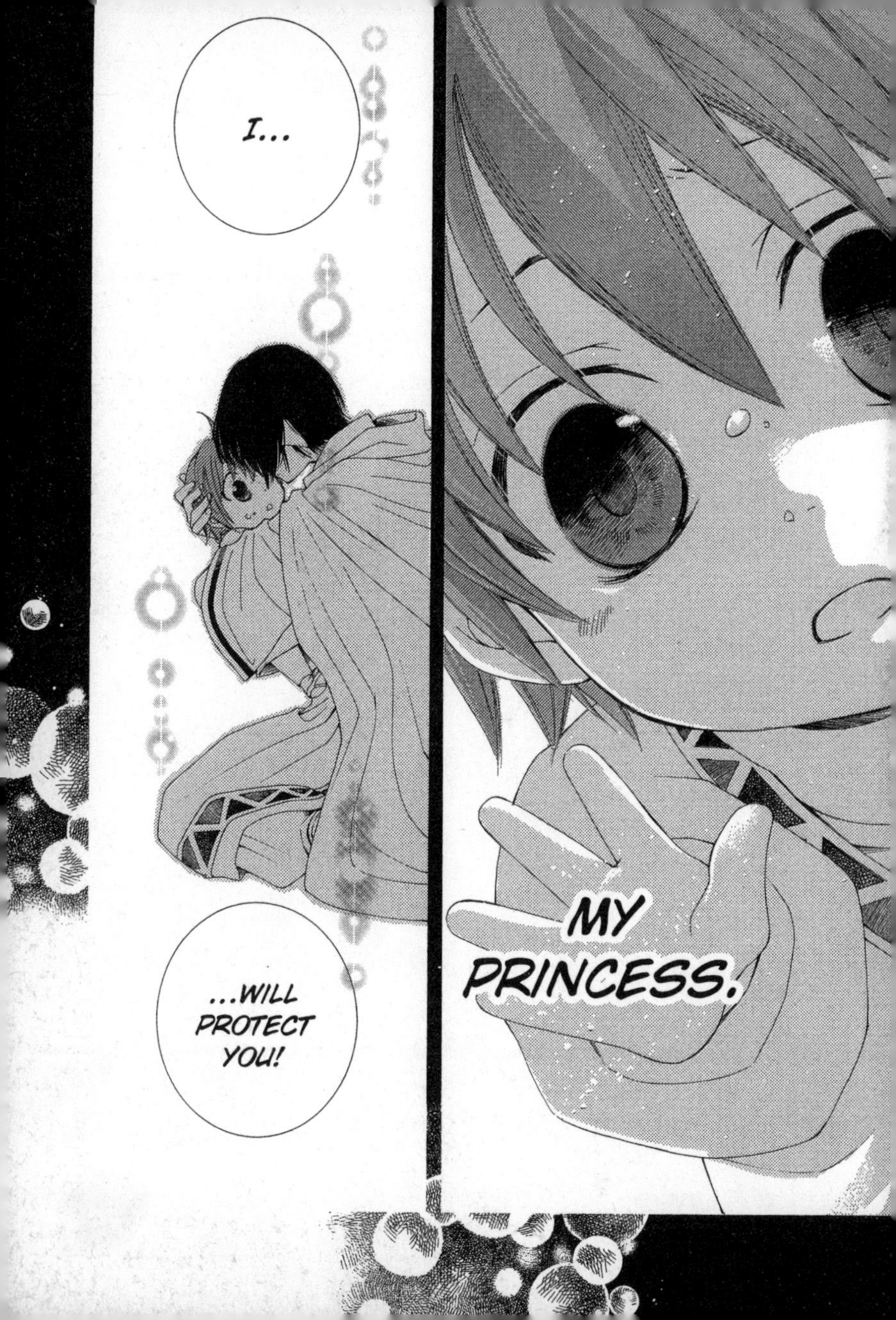
I...
...WILL PROTECT YOU!
MY PRINCESS.

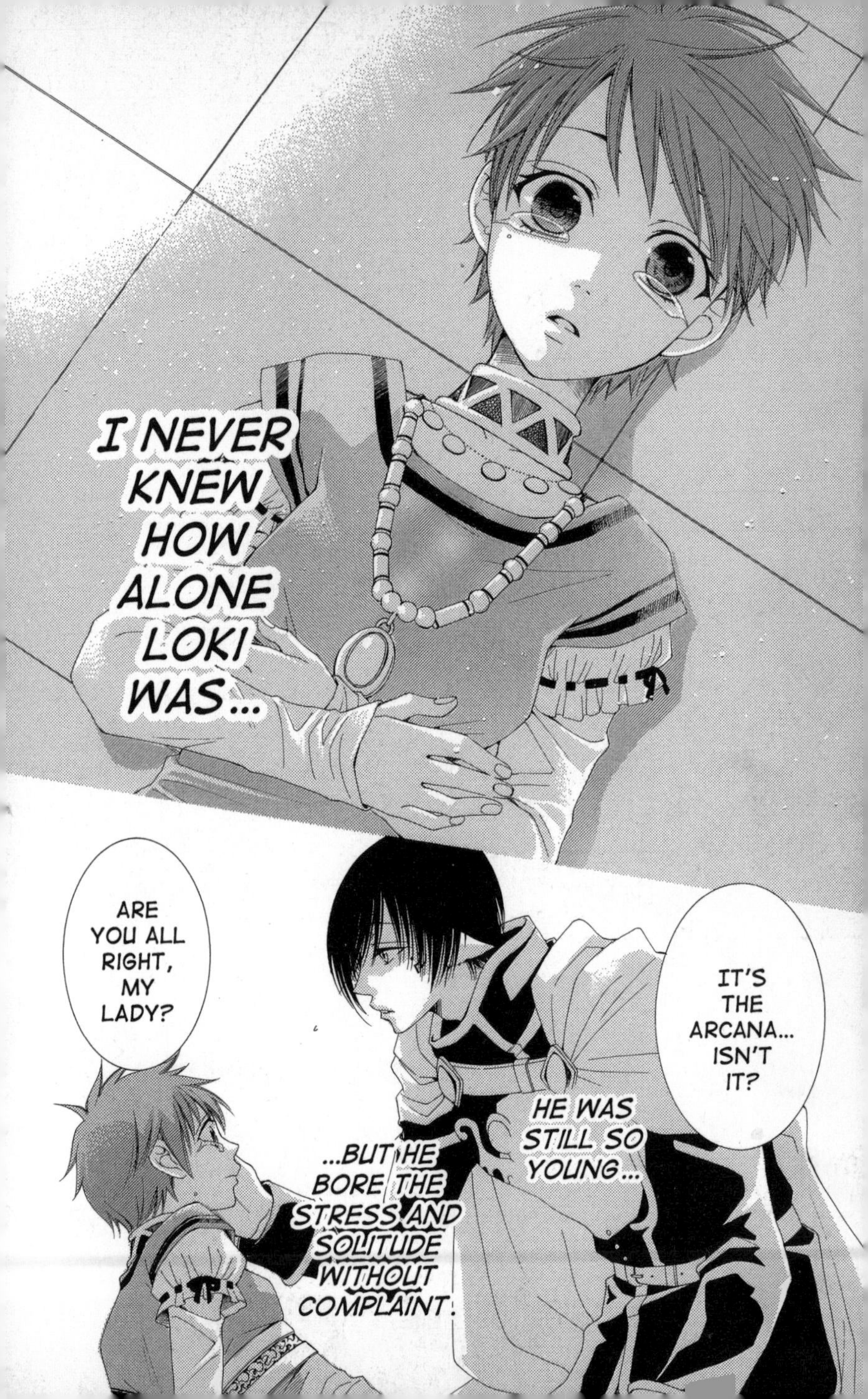
I NEVER KNEW HOW ALONE LOKI WAS...
IT'S THE ARCANA... ISN'T IT?
ARE YOU ALL RIGHT, MY LADY?
HE WAS STILL SO YOUNG...
...BUT HE BORE THE STRESS AND SOLITUDE WITHOUT COMPLAINT.

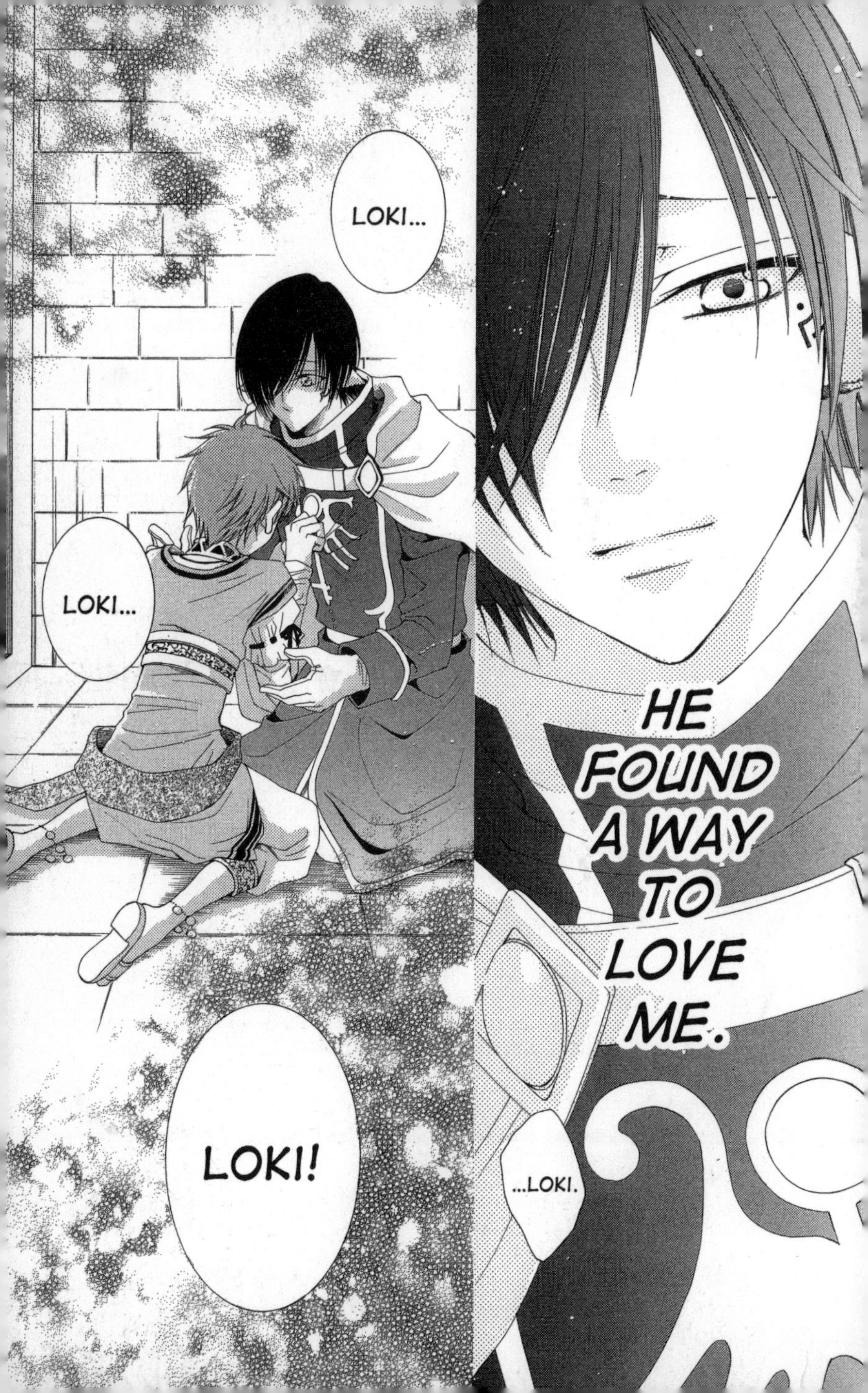
HE FOUND A WAY TO LOVE ME.
...LOKI.
LOKI...
LOKI...
LOKI!

So! The other day, I was flipping through volume 2, and I made a pretty shocking discovery. 「(Д) ˙ ˙」

My eyes literally popped out of my head. I forgot to draw the tattoo under Loki's eye! At first I tried to convince myself, "It's hidden by his hair. Heh heh…" But it was such an obvious place, so I have to admit I messed up. Eep! It's been fixed in the reprints, but if you bought the book right when it came out, you probably have a copy with the mistake. (*Laugh*) Sorry, no tattoo. (*Guffaw*)

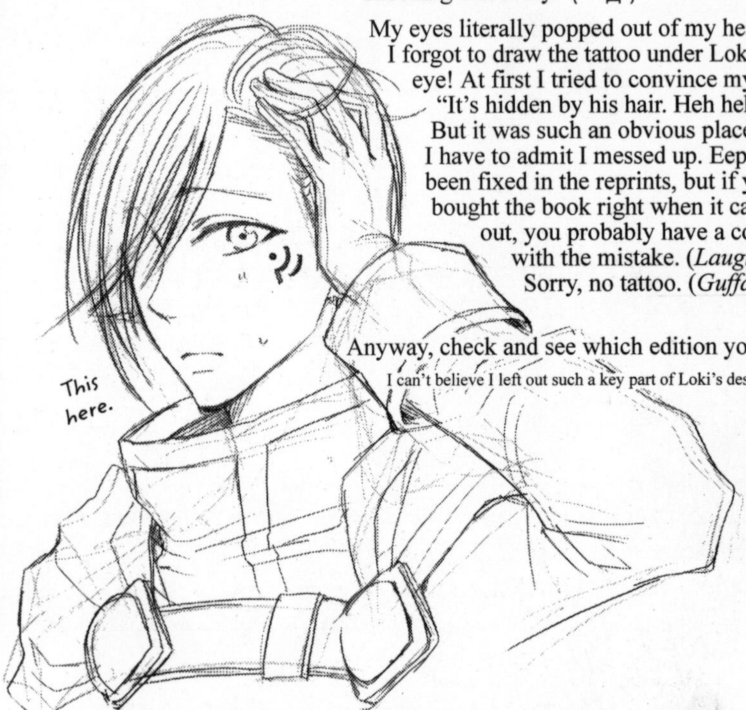
This here.

Anyway, check and see which edition you got!!!

I can't believe I left out such a key part of Loki's design... Eep!

I make plenty of mistakes in the initial sketches, like drawing Loki with human ears, or Caesar with dog ears... (*Laugh*) Usually I catch these and fix them right away...but I'm afraid that one of these days something big is gonna slip through! ＼ (ˆ O ˆ) ／

Send your letters to ↓

Rei Toma
c/o Dawn of the Arcana Editor
Viz Media
P.O. Box 77010
San Francisco, CA 94107

Chapter 11

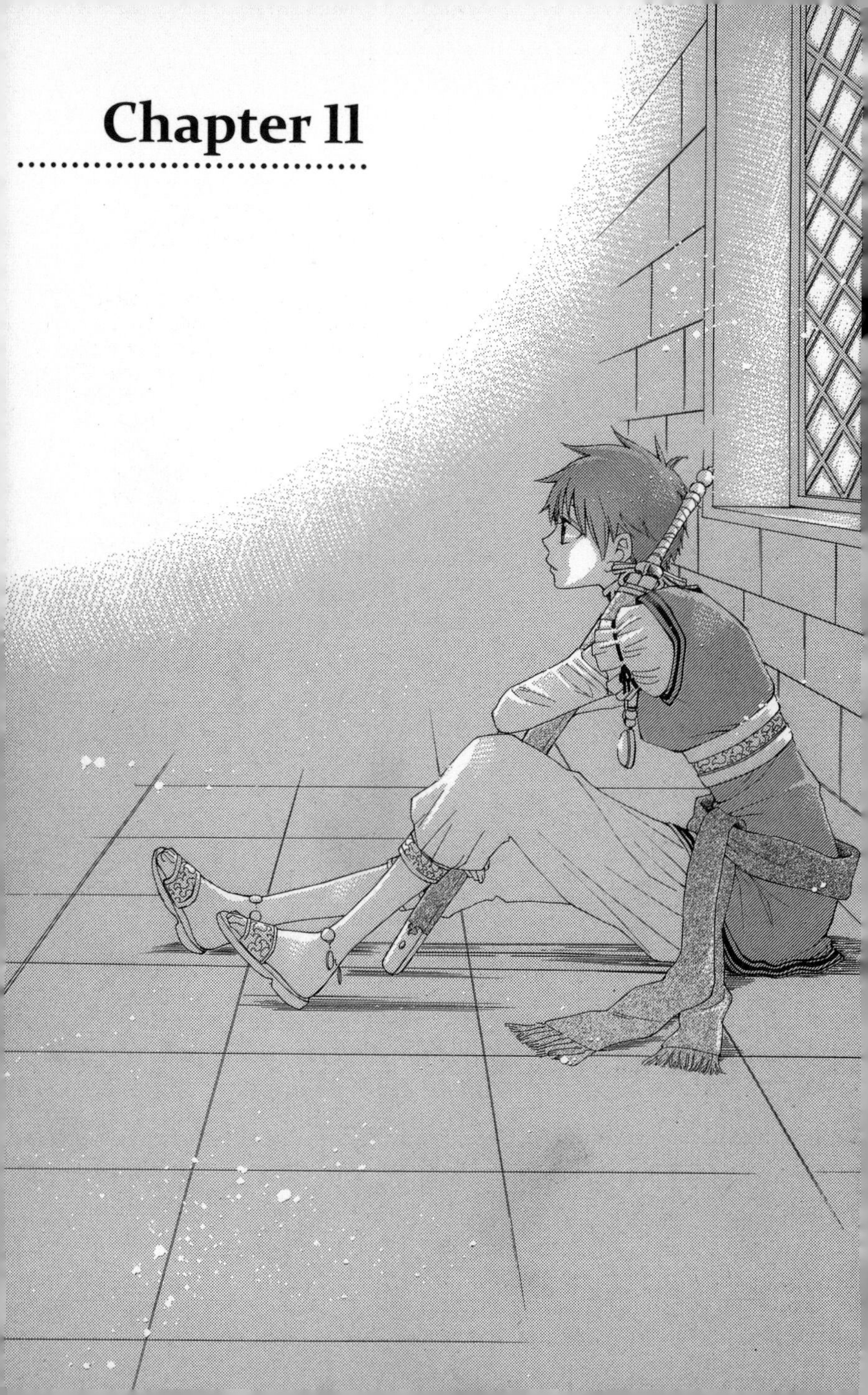

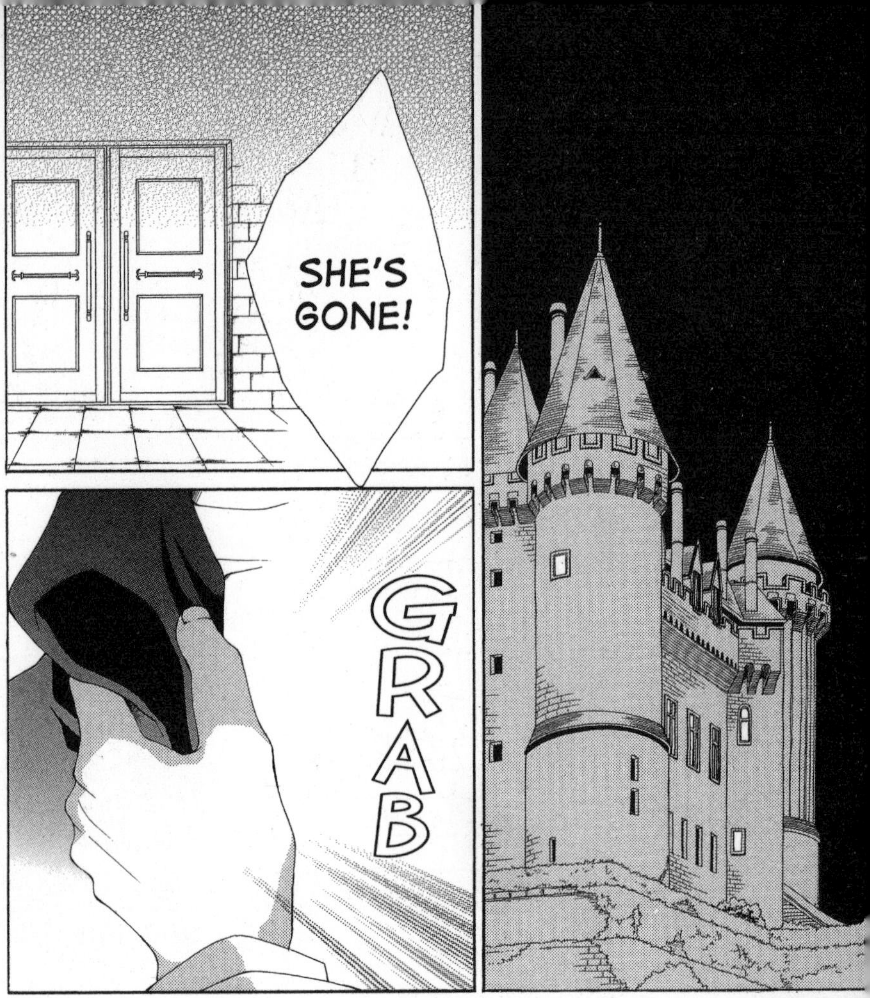
SHE'S GONE!
GRAB

Dawn of the Arcana

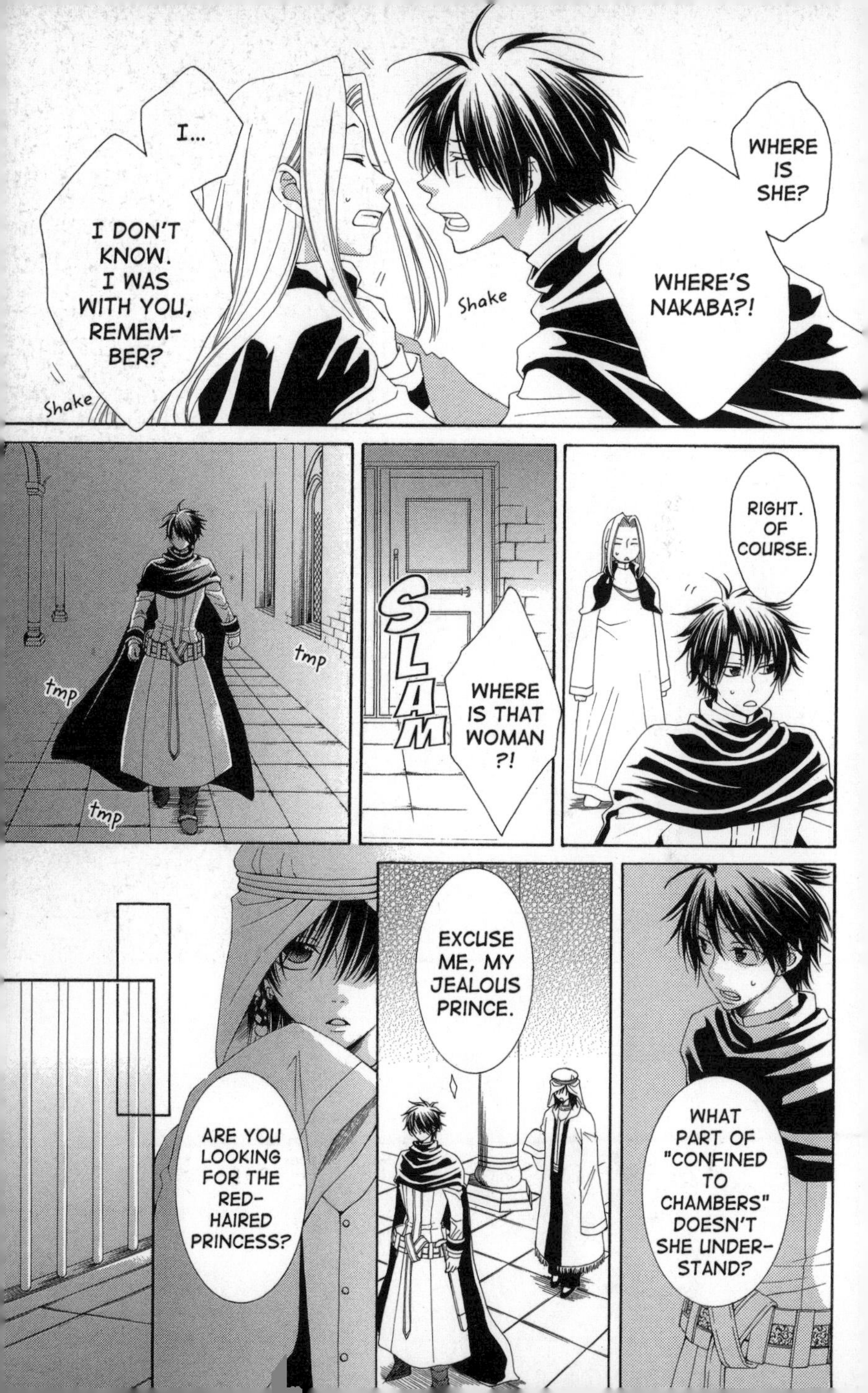
WHERE IS SHE?
WHERE'S NAKABA?!
Shake
I...
I DON'T KNOW. I WAS WITH YOU, REMEMBER?
Shake
RIGHT. OF COURSE.
SLAM
WHERE IS THAT WOMAN ?!
tmp
tmp
tmp
WHAT PART OF "CONFINED TO CHAMBERS" DOESN'T SHE UNDERSTAND?
EXCUSE ME, MY JEALOUS PRINCE.
ARE YOU LOOKING FOR THE RED-HAIRED PRINCESS?

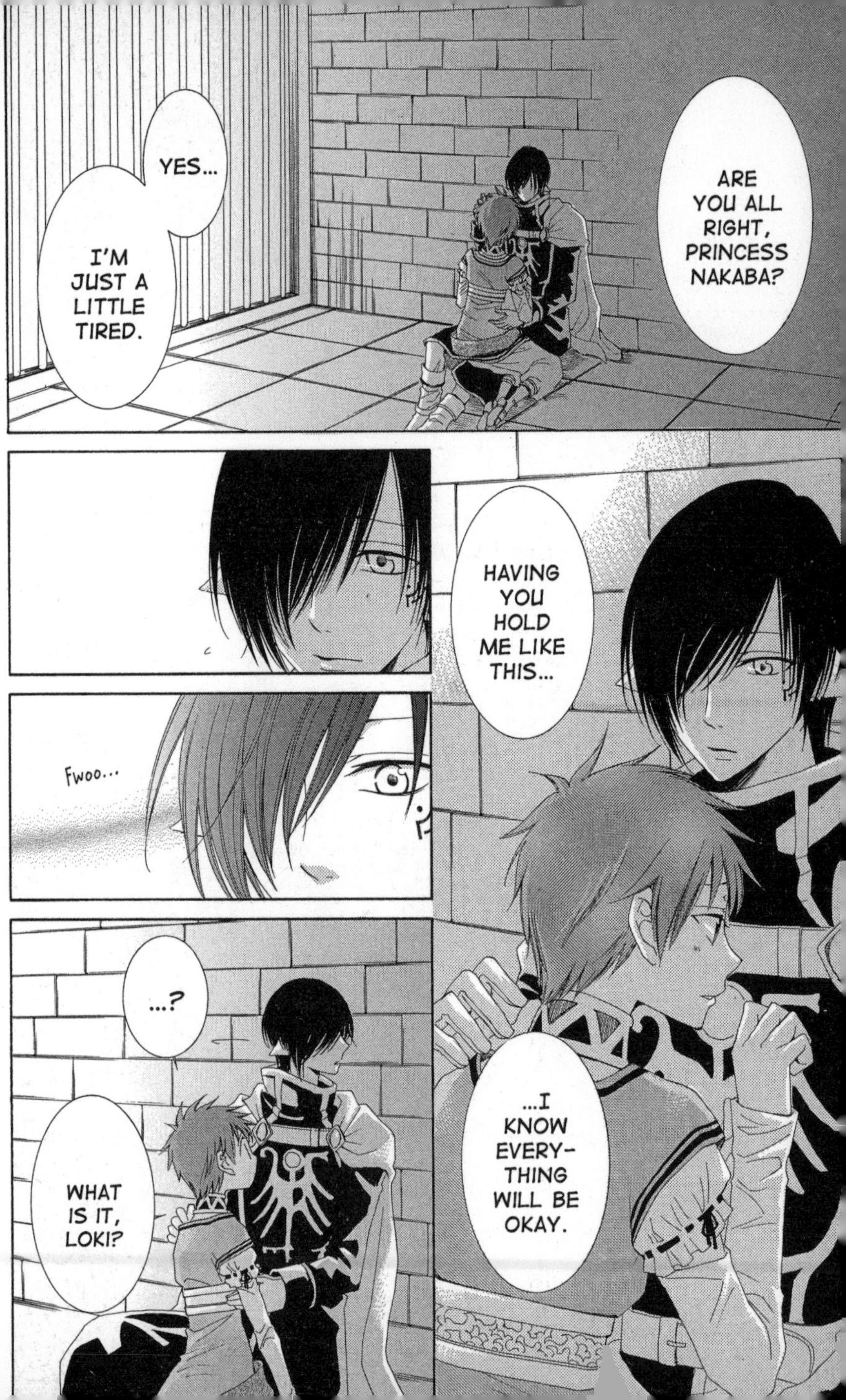
ARE YOU ALL RIGHT, PRINCESS NAKABA?
YES...
I'M JUST A LITTLE TIRED.
HAVING YOU HOLD ME LIKE THIS...
...I KNOW EVERY-THING WILL BE OKAY.
Fwoo...
...?
WHAT IS IT, LOKI?

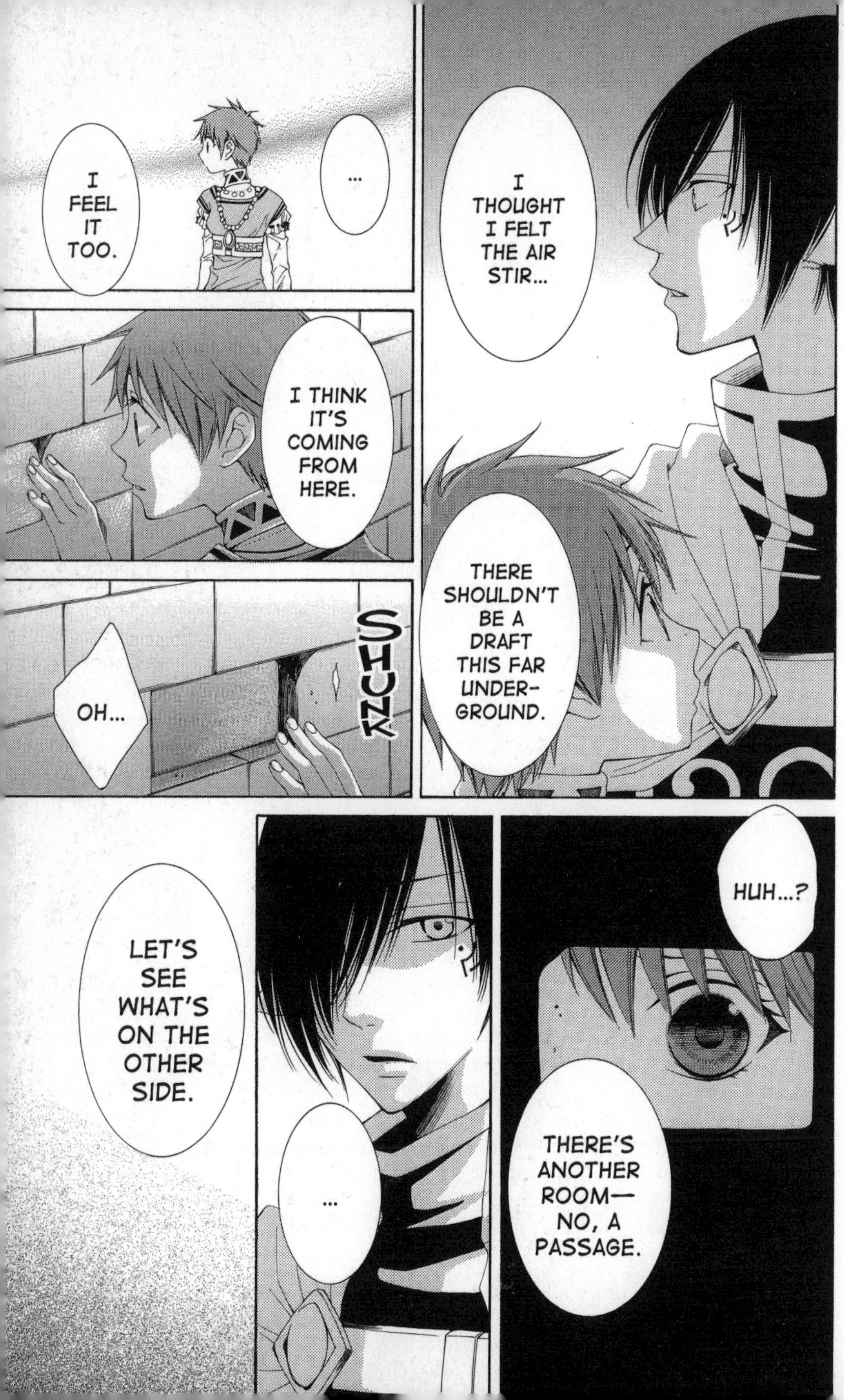
I THOUGHT I FELT THE AIR STIR...
THERE SHOULDN'T BE A DRAFT THIS FAR UNDER-GROUND.
...
I FEEL IT TOO.
I THINK IT'S COMING FROM HERE.
SHUNK
OH...
HUH...?
THERE'S ANOTHER ROOM—NO, A PASSAGE.
LET'S SEE WHAT'S ON THE OTHER SIDE.
...

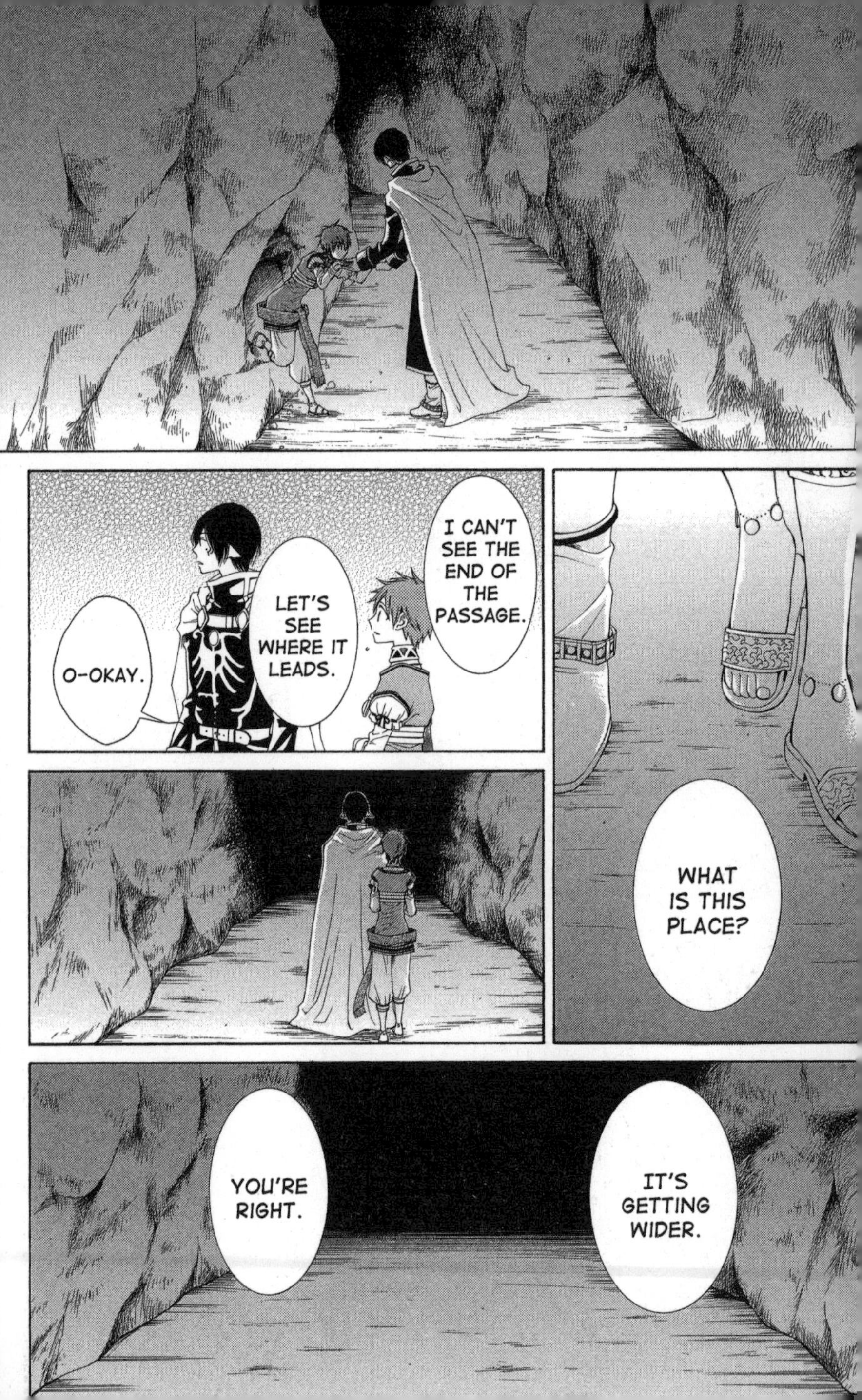
WHAT IS THIS PLACE?
I CAN'T SEE THE END OF THE PASSAGE.
LET'S SEE WHERE IT LEADS.
O-OKAY.
IT'S GETTING WIDER.
YOU'RE RIGHT.

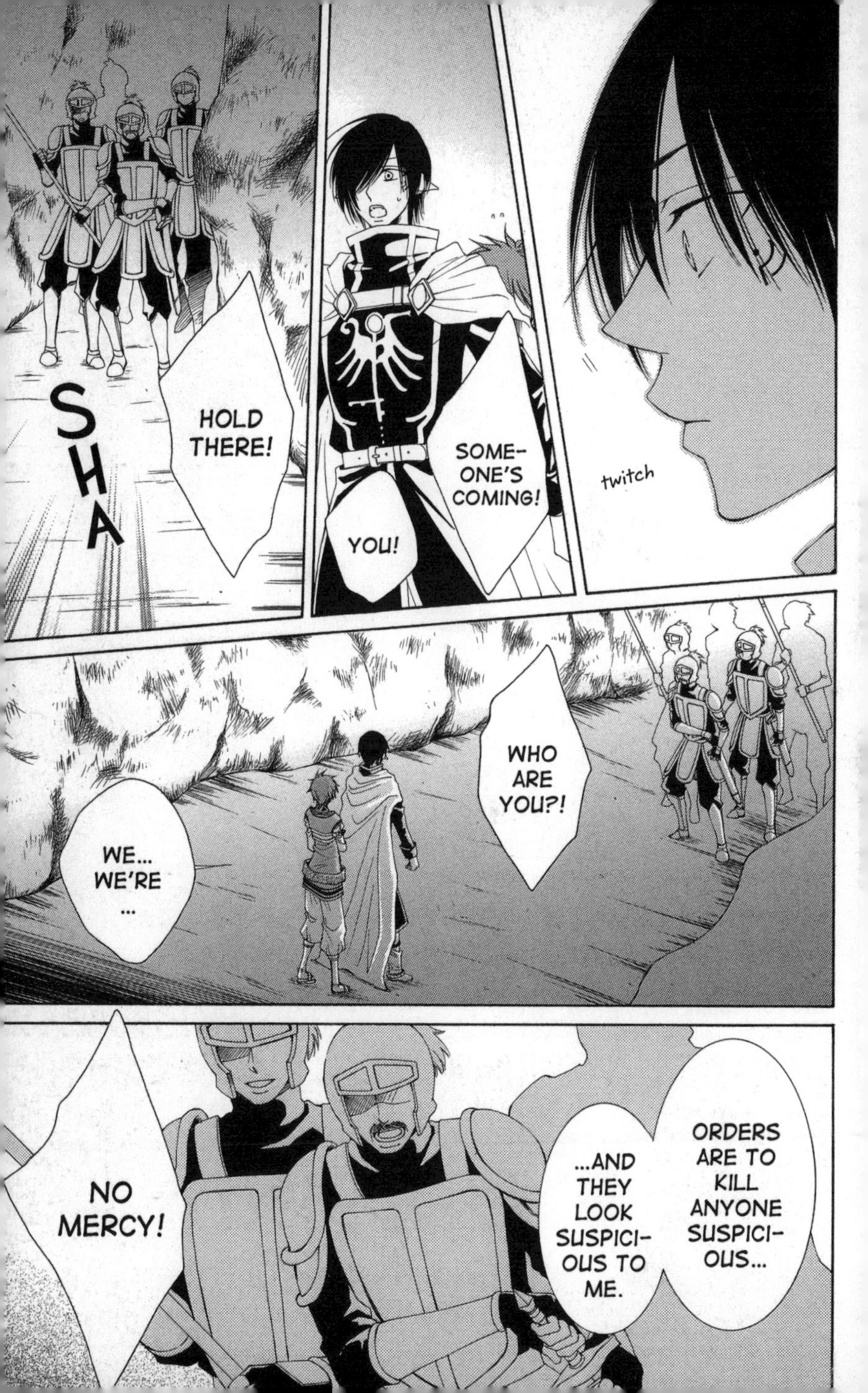
twitch
SOME-ONE'S COMING!
SHA
HOLD THERE!
YOU!
WHO ARE YOU?!
WE... WE'RE ...
ORDERS ARE TO KILL ANYONE SUSPICIOUS...
...AND THEY LOOK SUSPICIOUS TO ME.
NO MERCY!

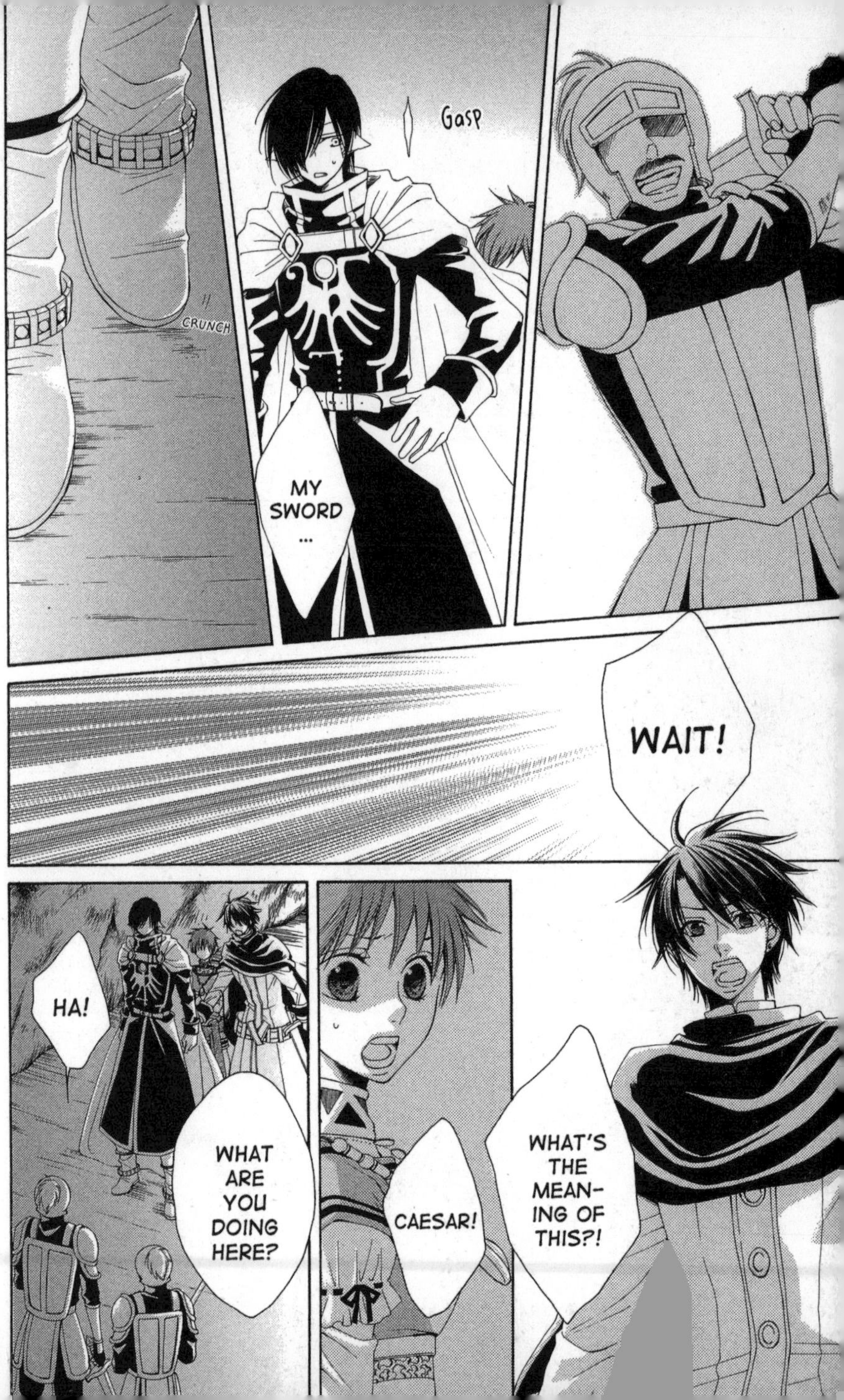
Gasp
MY SWORD ...
CRUNCH
WAIT!
WHAT'S THE MEAN- ING OF THIS?!
CAESAR!
HA!
WHAT ARE YOU DOING HERE?

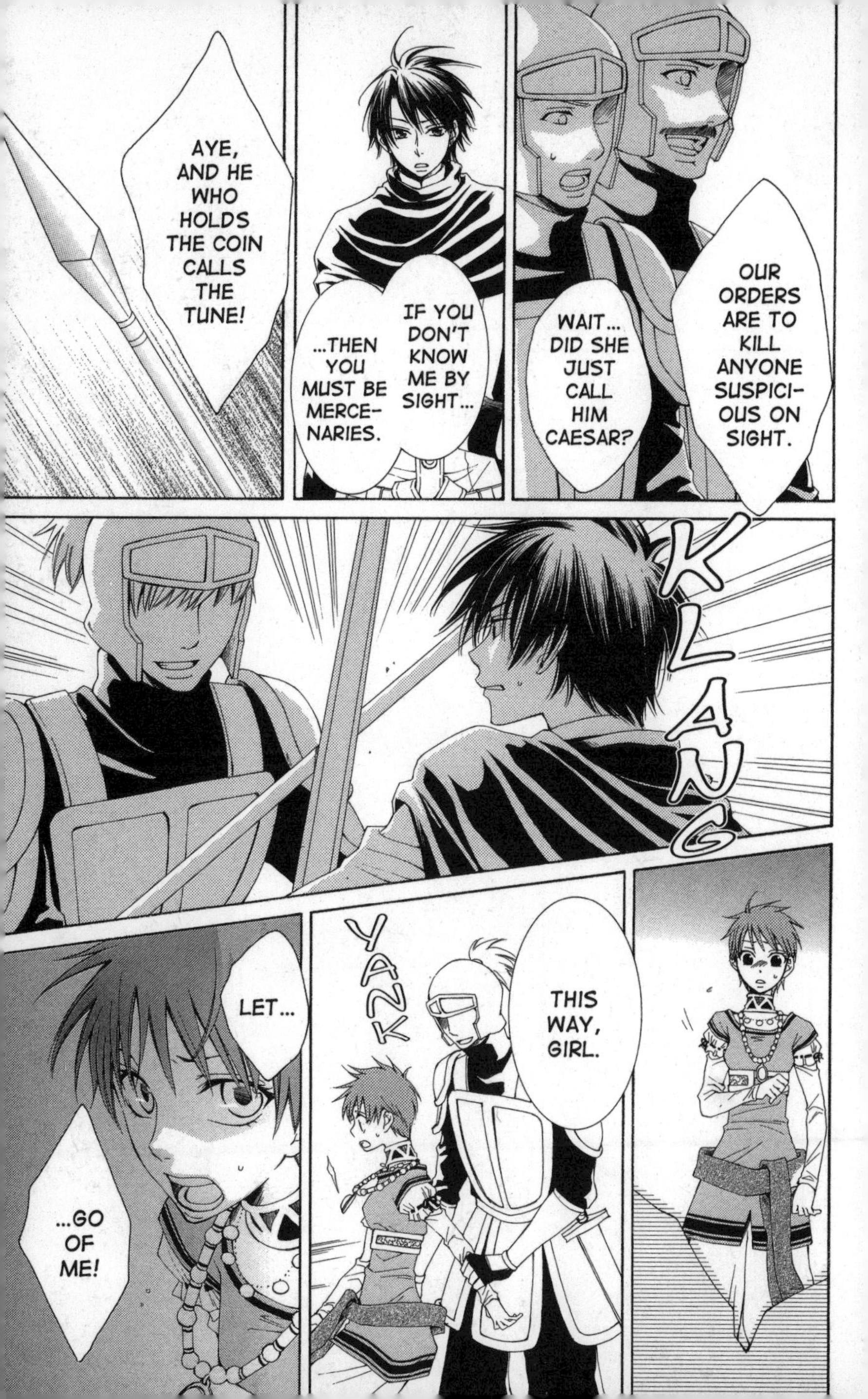
OUR ORDERS ARE TO KILL ANYONE SUSPICIOUS ON SIGHT.
WAIT... DID SHE JUST CALL HIM CAESAR?
IF YOU DON'T KNOW ME BY SIGHT...
...THEN YOU MUST BE MERCENARIES.
AYE, AND HE WHO HOLDS THE COIN CALLS THE TUNE!
KLANG
THIS WAY, GIRL.
YANK
LET...
...GO OF ME!

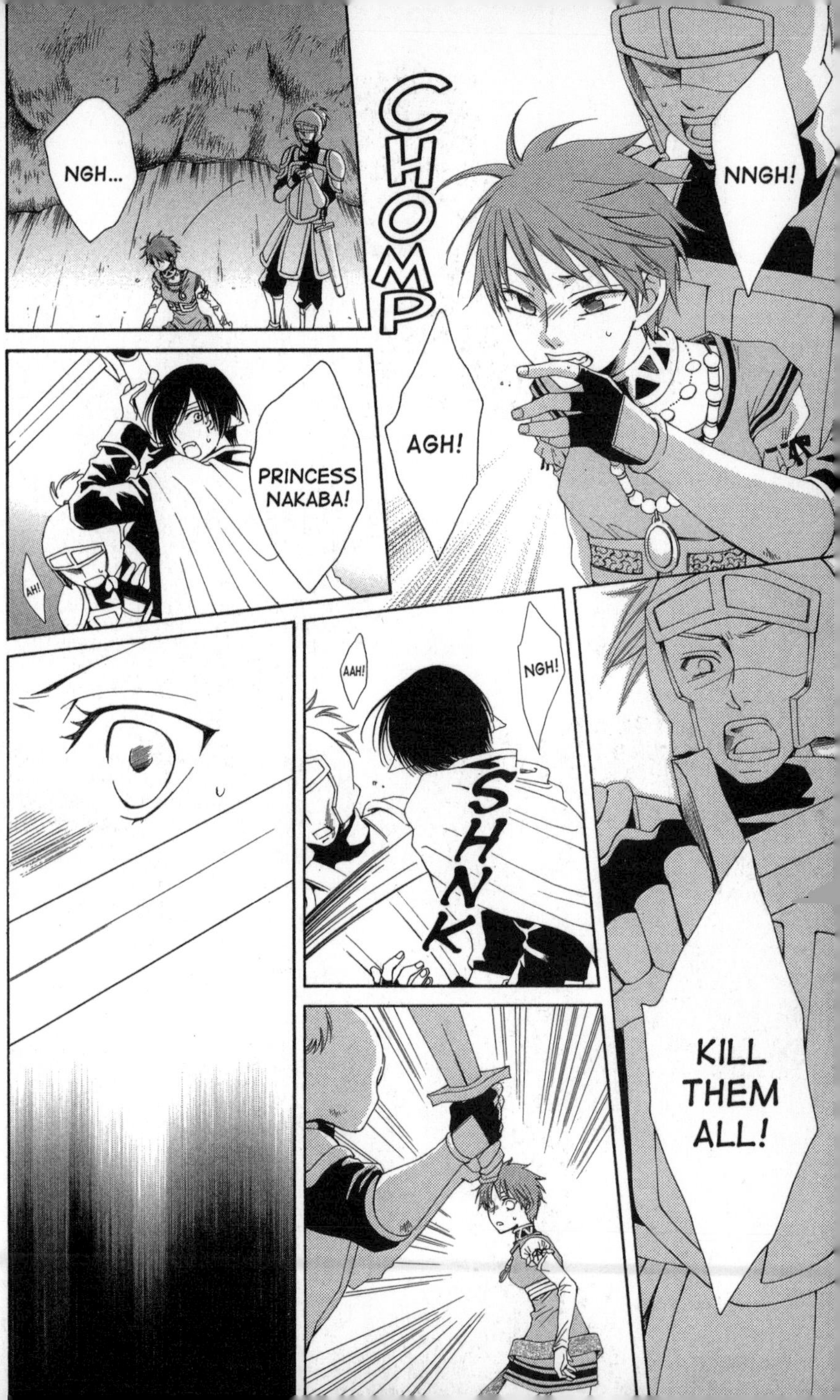
NNGH!
CHOMP
AGH!
NGH...
PRINCESS NAKABA!
AH!
KILL THEM ALL!
NGH!
SHNK
AAH!

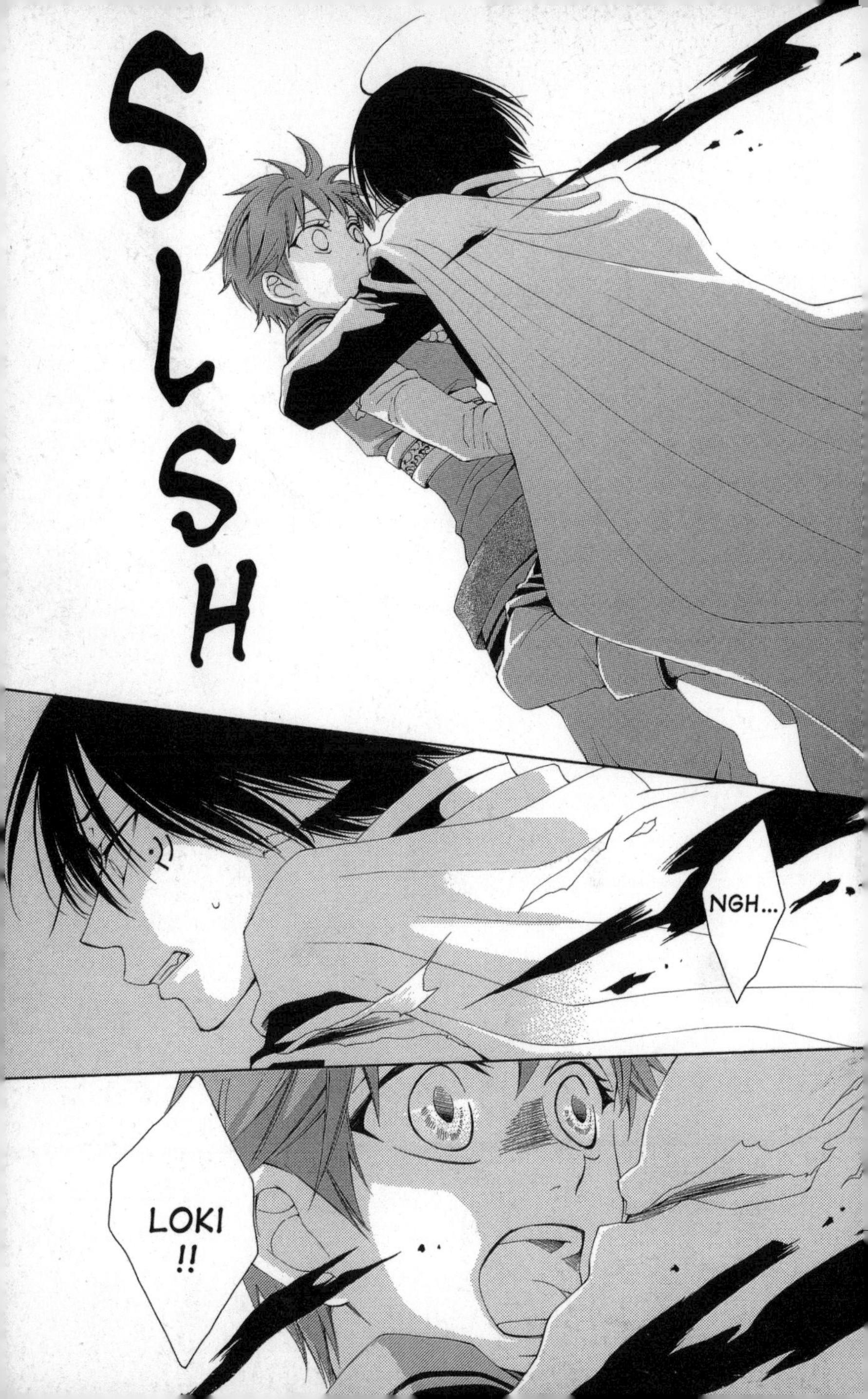
SLSH
NGH...
LOKI !!

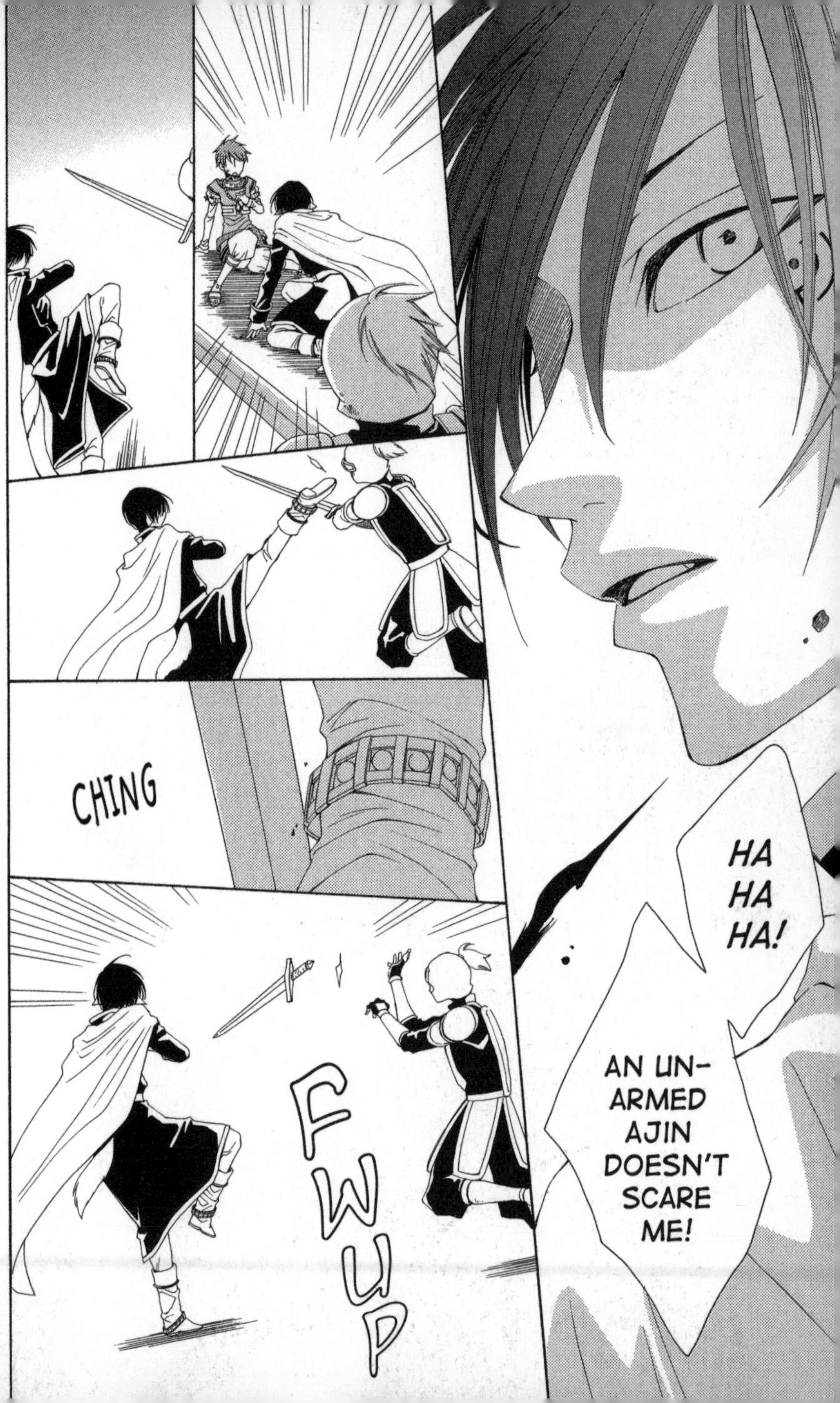
HA HA HA!
AN UN-ARMED AJIN DOESN'T SCARE ME!
CHING
FWUP

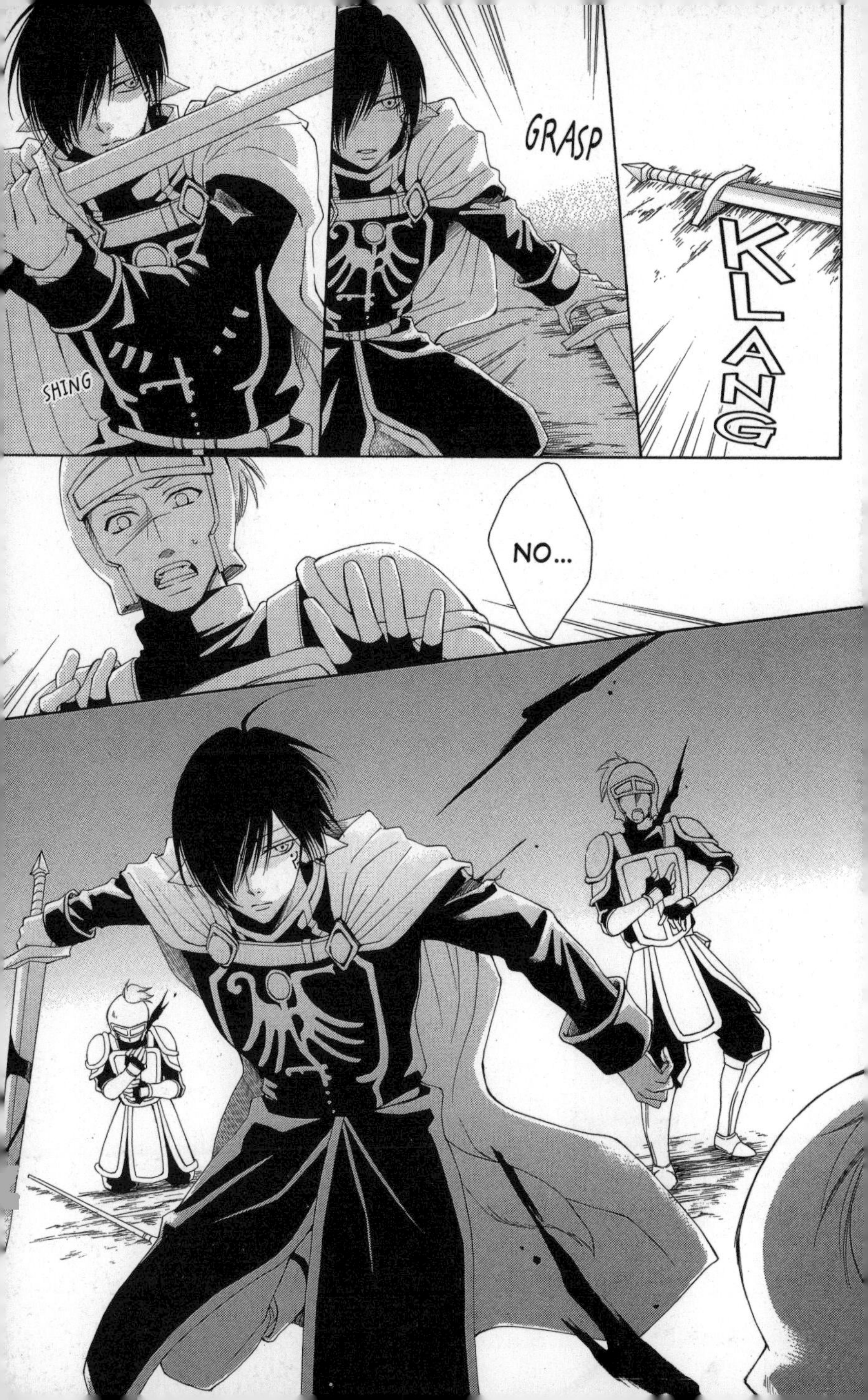
KLANG
GRASP
SHING
NO...

SSSS
Oh...
LOKI.
Feh.
...
OOF
THAT WAS A PRETTY DEEP CUT.
HOW'S YOUR ARM?
THE BLEEDING WILL STOP.

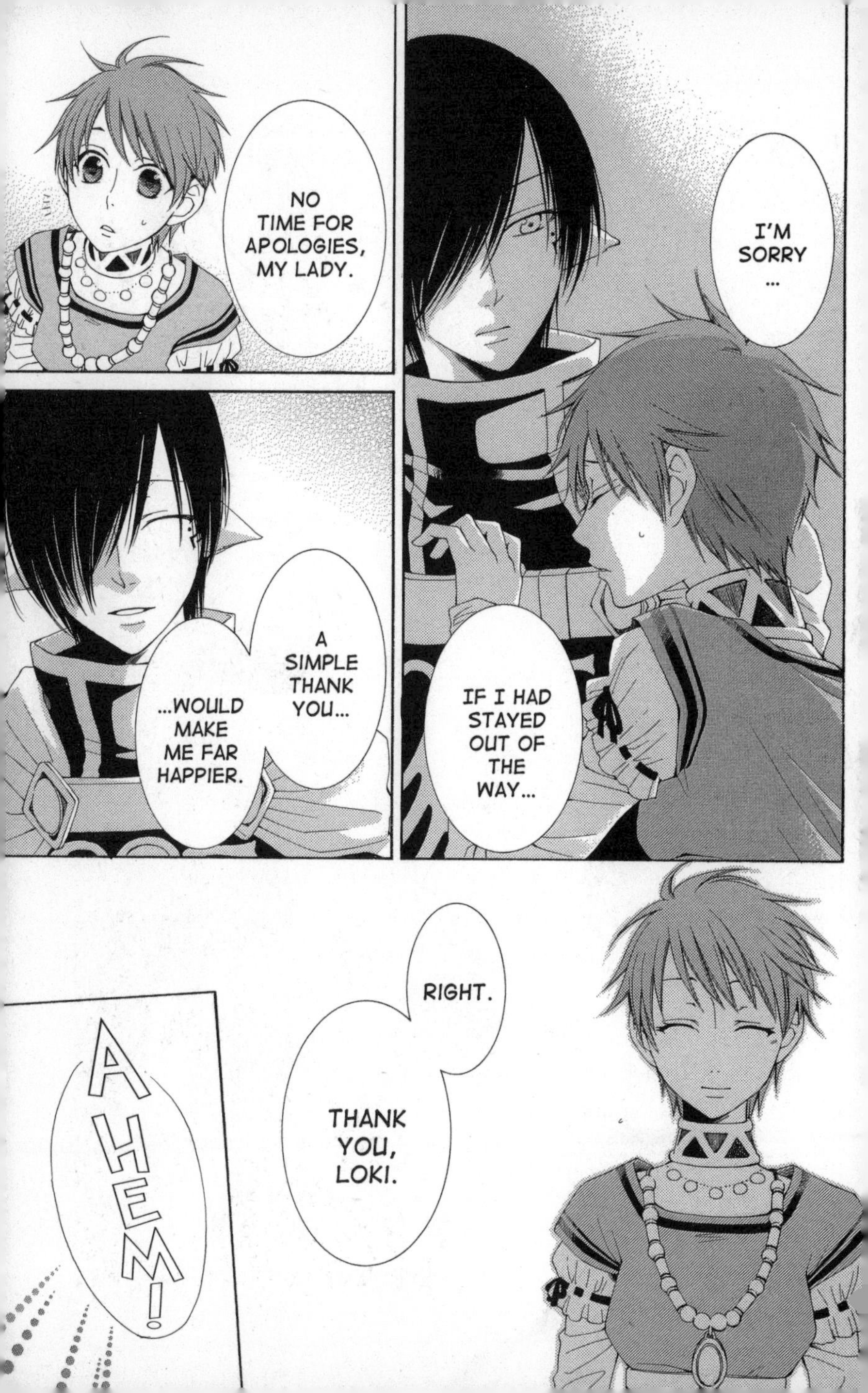
I'M SORRY ...
IF I HAD STAYED OUT OF THE WAY...
NO TIME FOR APOLOGIES, MY LADY.
A SIMPLE THANK YOU...
...WOULD MAKE ME FAR HAPPIER.
RIGHT.
THANK YOU, LOKI.
AHEM!

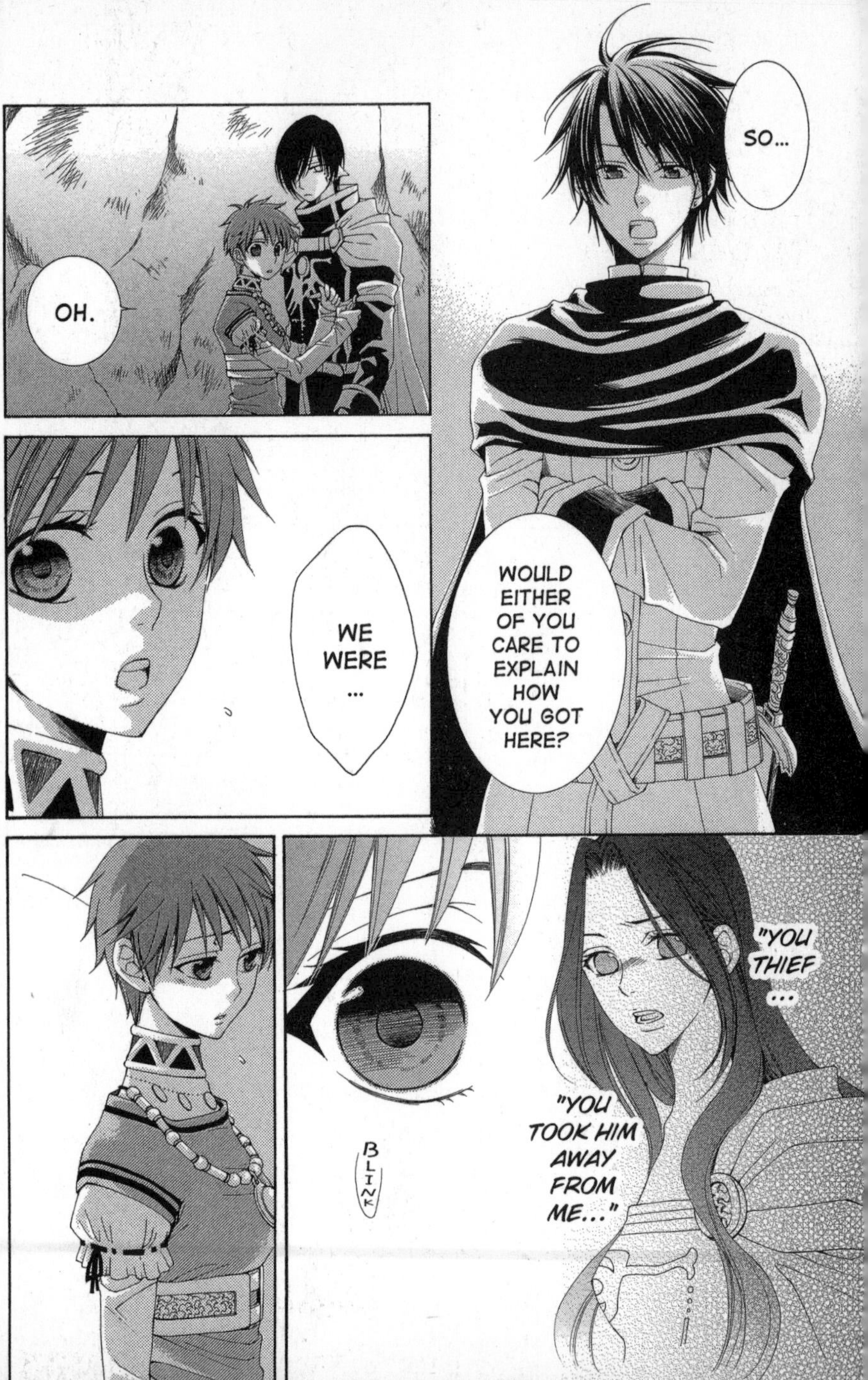
SO...
WOULD EITHER OF YOU CARE TO EXPLAIN HOW YOU GOT HERE?
OH.
WE WERE ...
"YOU THIEF ...
"YOU TOOK HIM AWAY FROM ME..."
BLINK

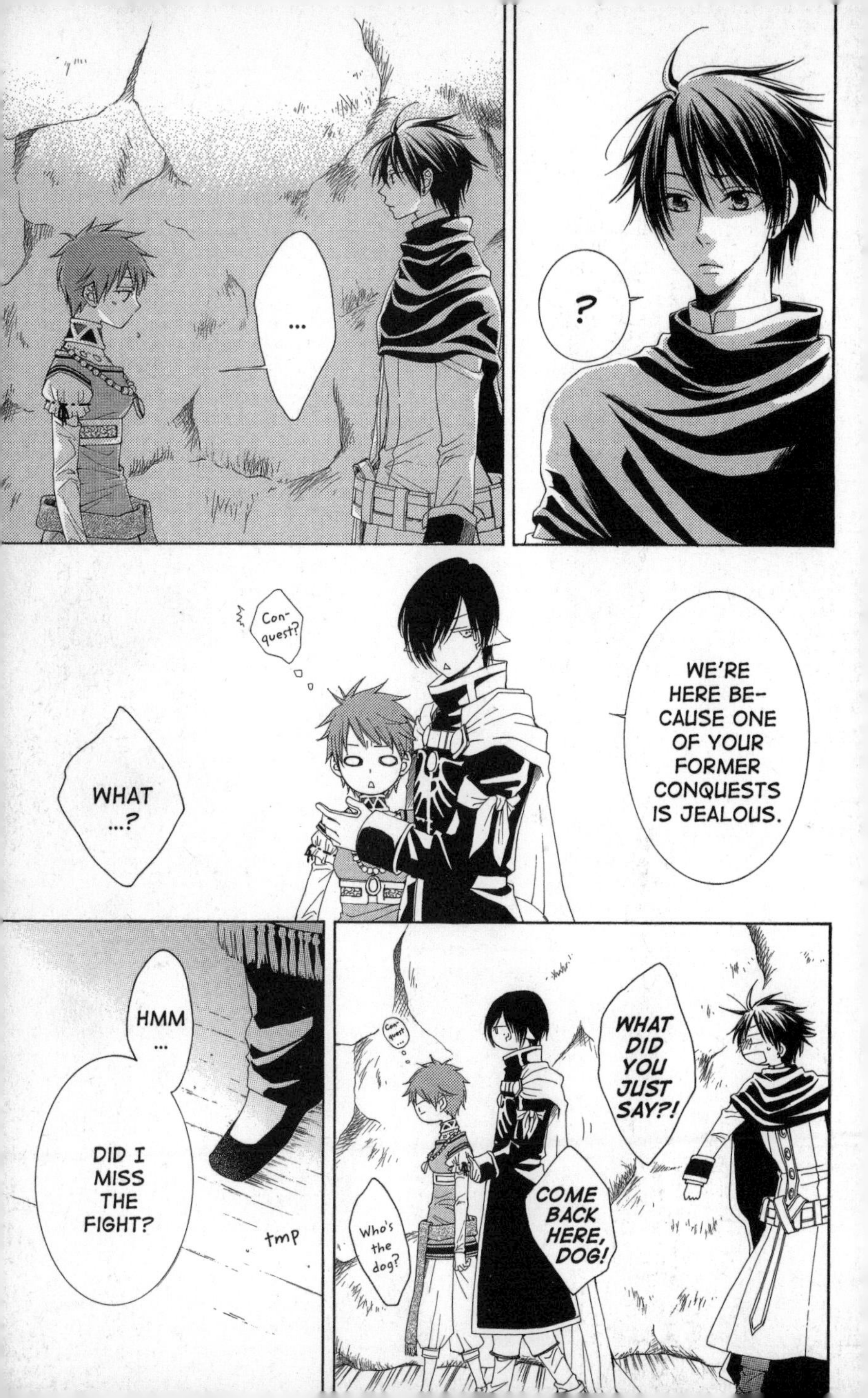
?
...
WE'RE HERE BE-CAUSE ONE OF YOUR FORMER CONQUESTS IS JEALOUS.
Con-quest?
WHAT ...?
WHAT DID YOU JUST SAY?!
COME BACK HERE, DOG!
Con-quest ...
Who's the dog?
HMM ...
DID I MISS THE FIGHT?
tmp

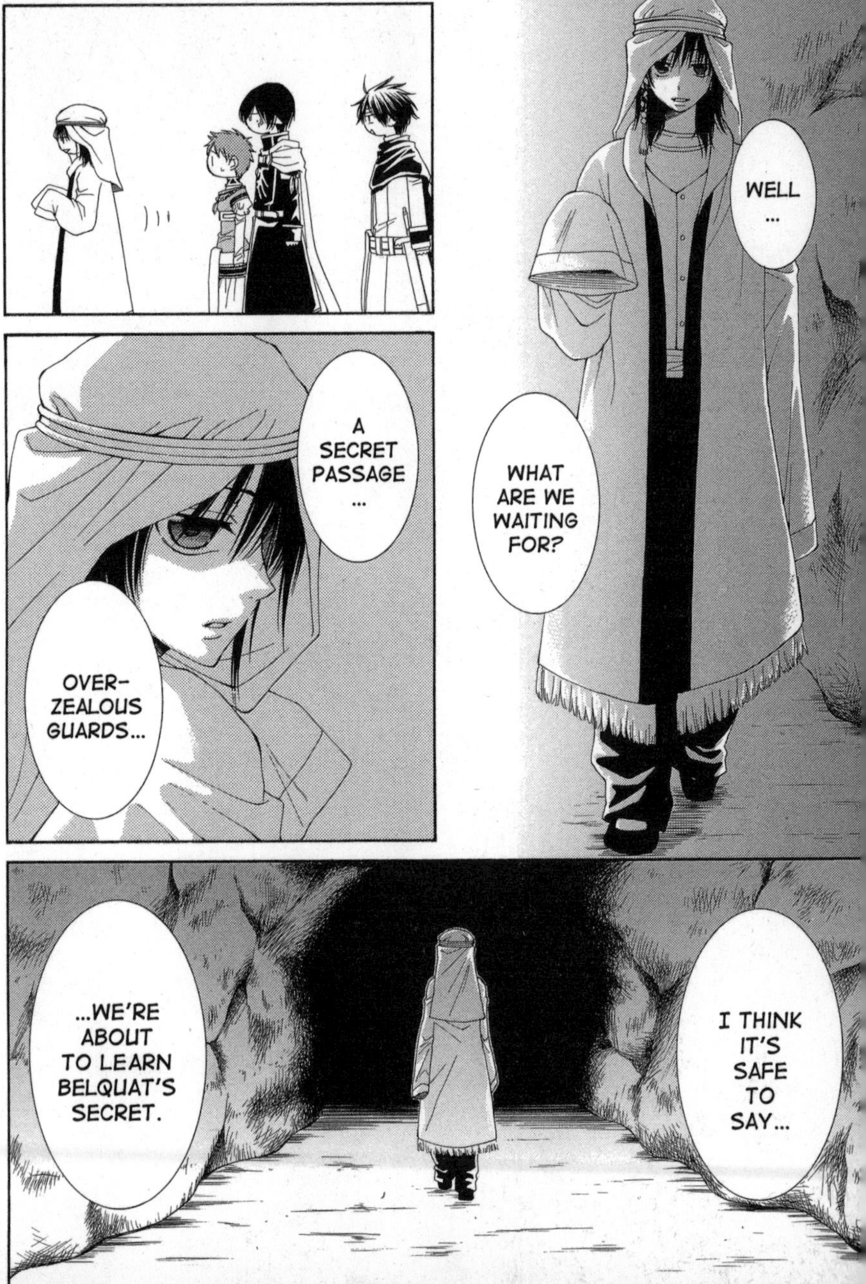
WELL ...
WHAT ARE WE WAITING FOR?
A SECRET PASSAGE ...
OVER-ZEALOUS GUARDS...
I THINK IT'S SAFE TO SAY...
...WE'RE ABOUT TO LEARN BELQUAT'S SECRET.

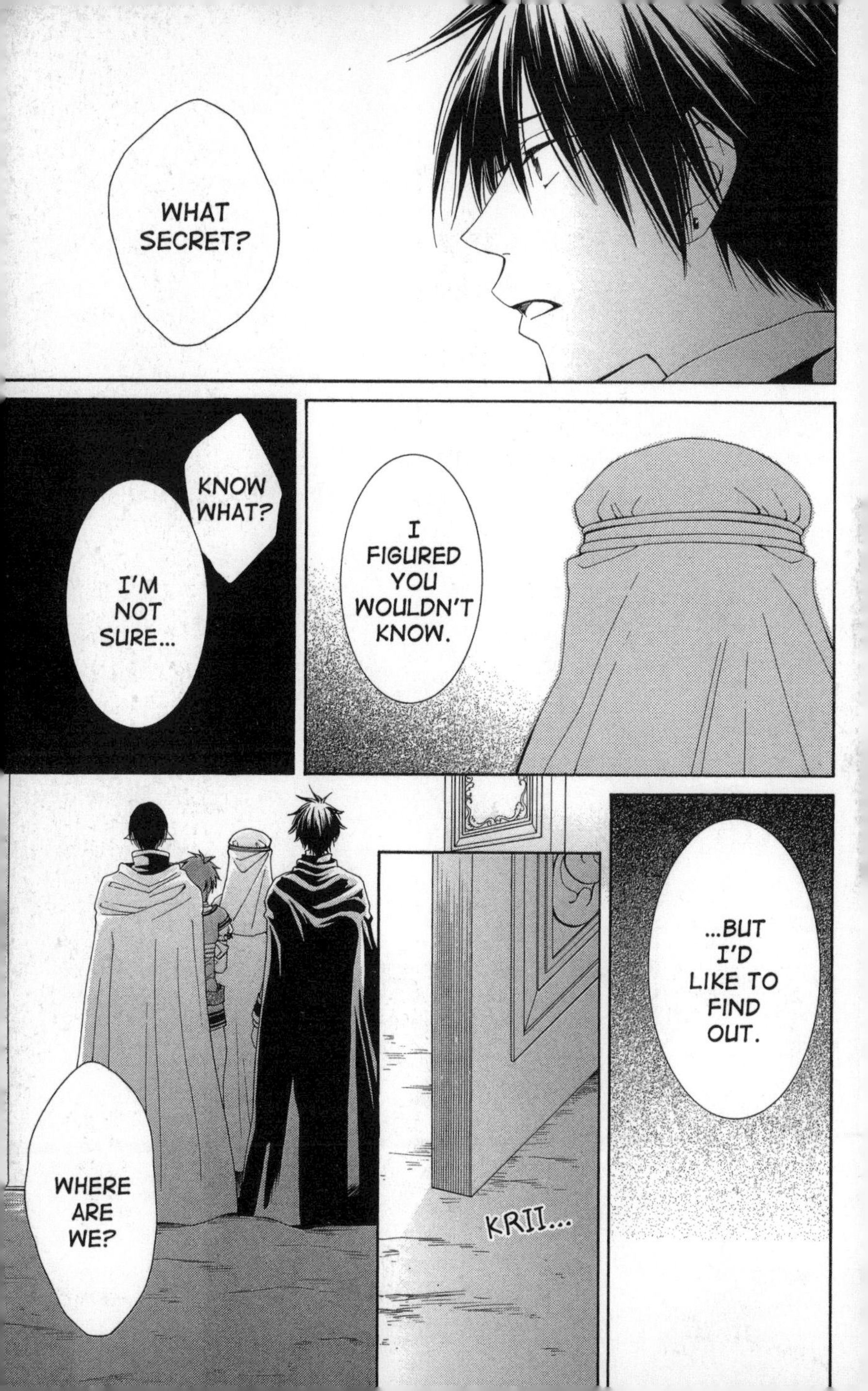
WHAT SECRET?
I FIGURED YOU WOULDN'T KNOW.
KNOW WHAT?
I'M NOT SURE...
...BUT I'D LIKE TO FIND OUT.
KRII...
WHERE ARE WE?

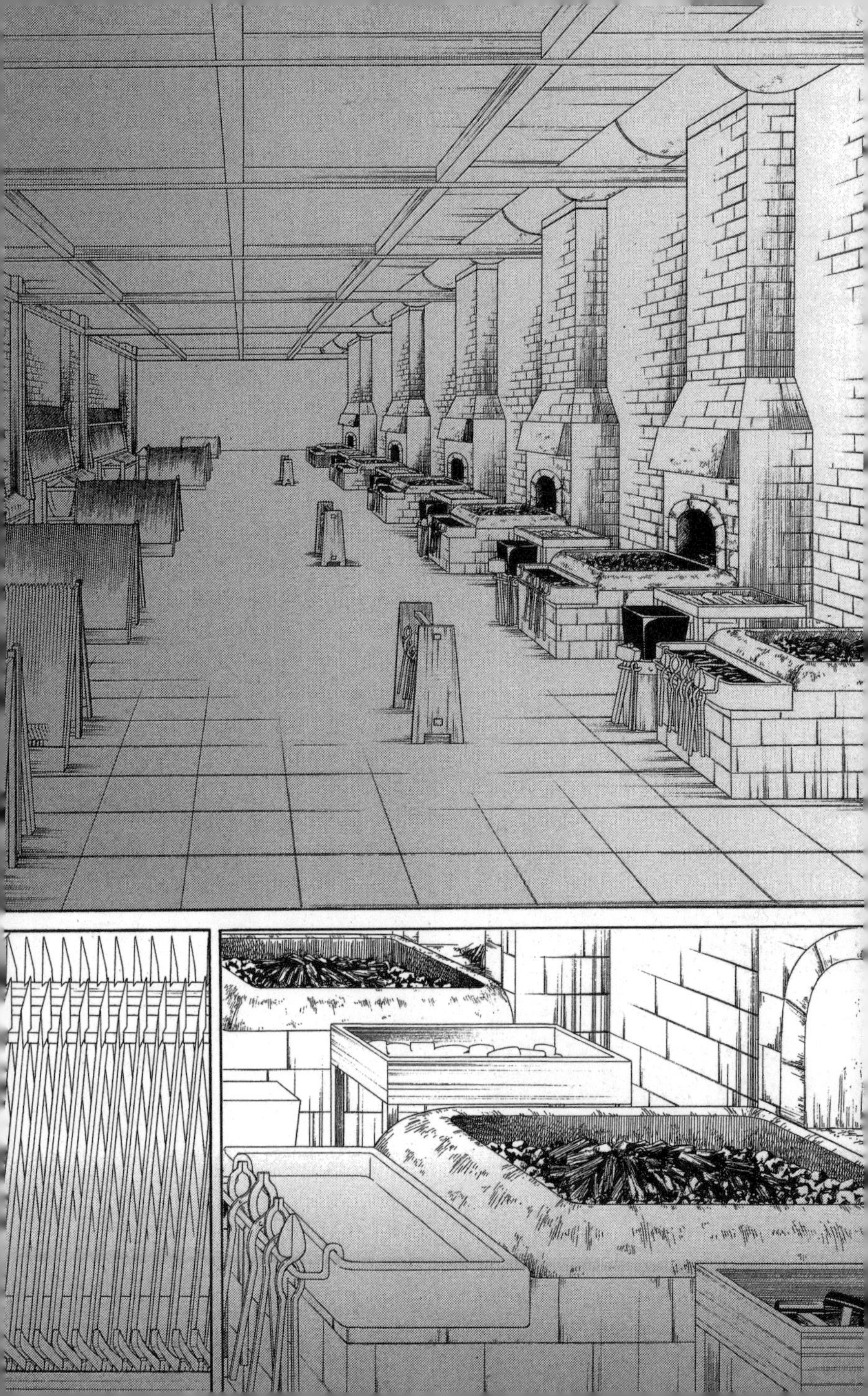

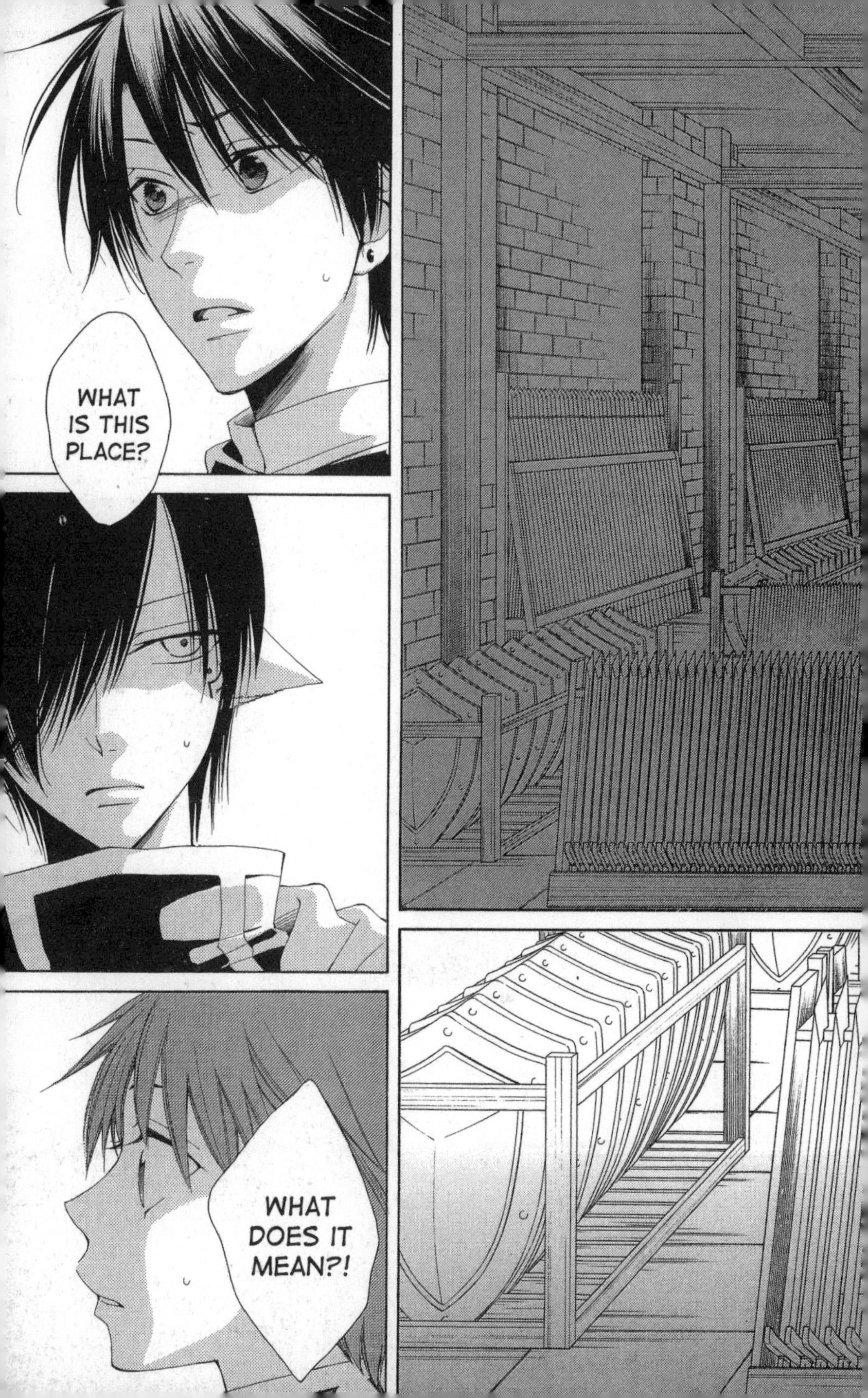
WHAT IS THIS PLACE?
WHAT DOES IT MEAN?!

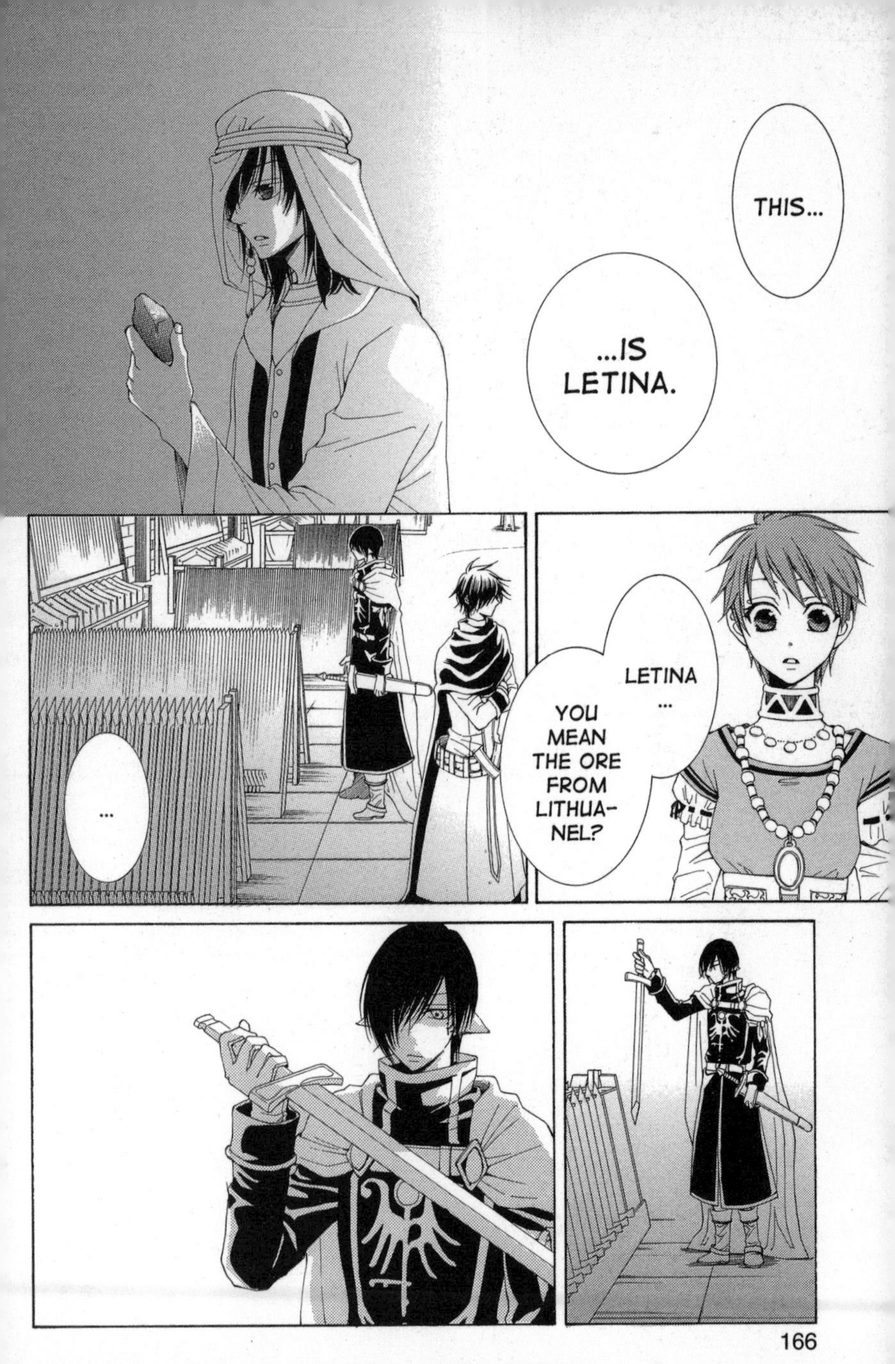
THIS...
...IS LETINA.
LETINA...
YOU MEAN THE ORE FROM LITHUA-NEL?
...

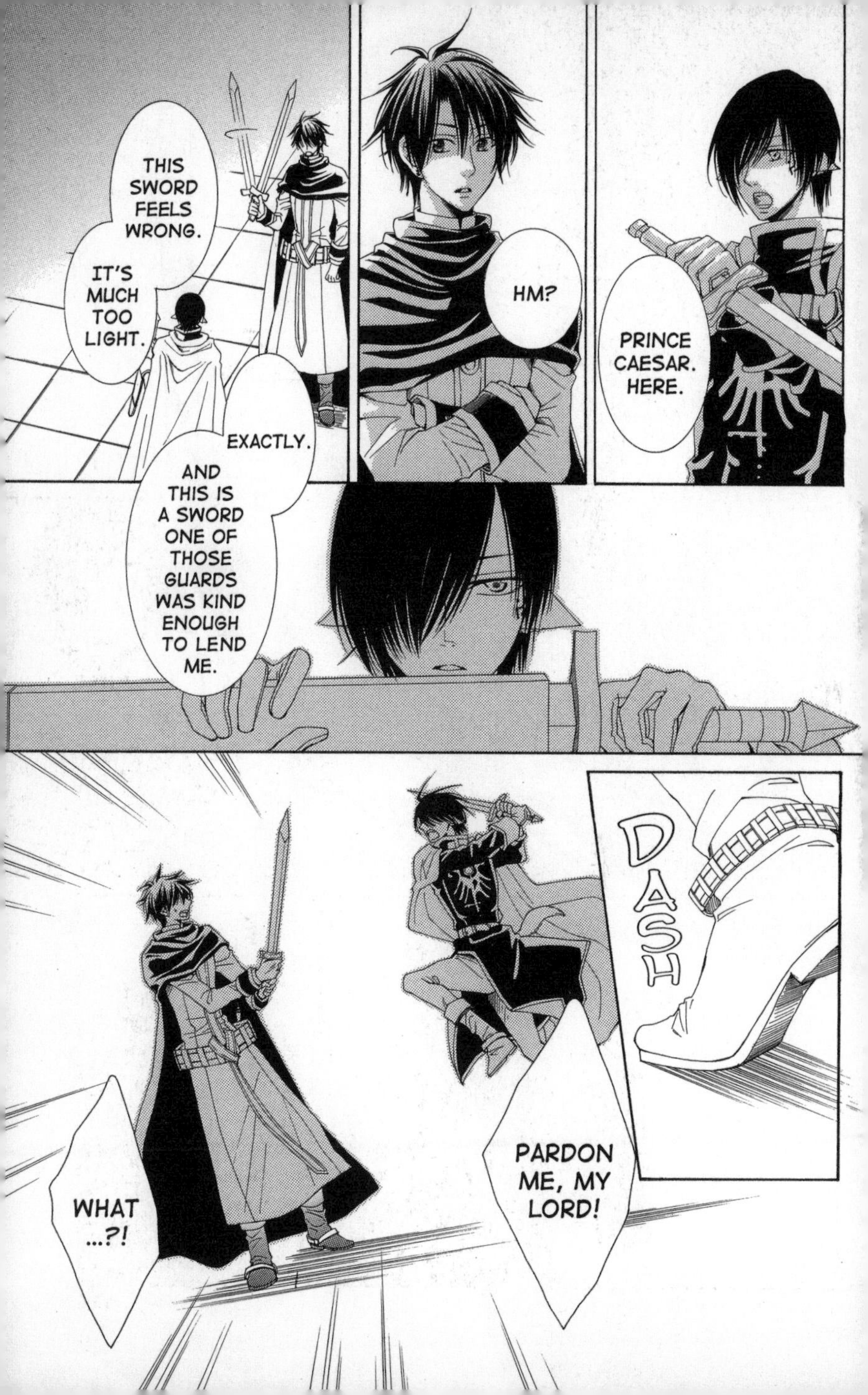
PRINCE CAESAR. HERE.
HM?
THIS SWORD FEELS WRONG.
IT'S MUCH TOO LIGHT.
EXACTLY.
AND THIS IS A SWORD ONE OF THOSE GUARDS WAS KIND ENOUGH TO LEND ME.
DASH
PARDON ME, MY LORD!
WHAT ...?!

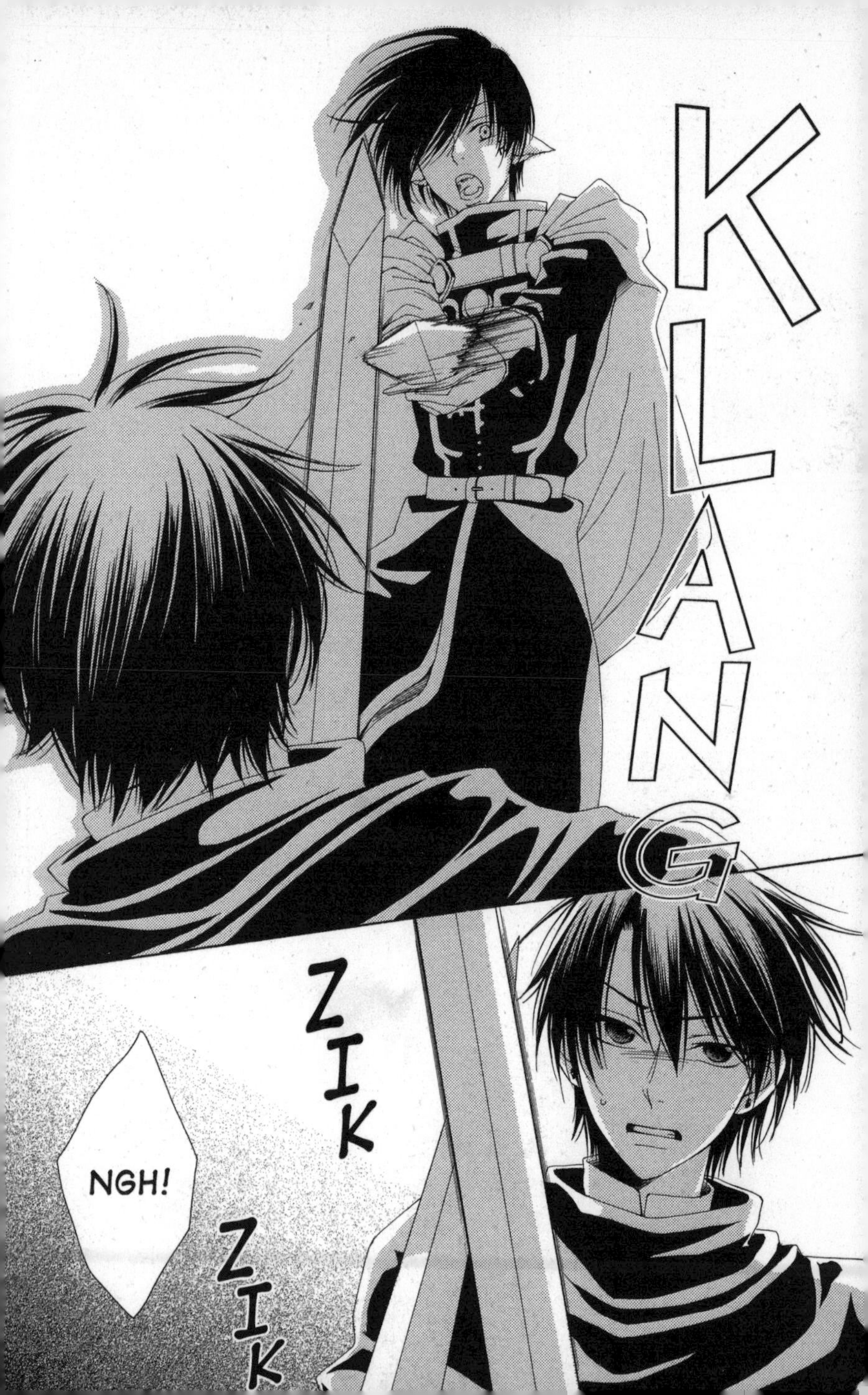
KLANG
ZIK
ZIK
NGH!

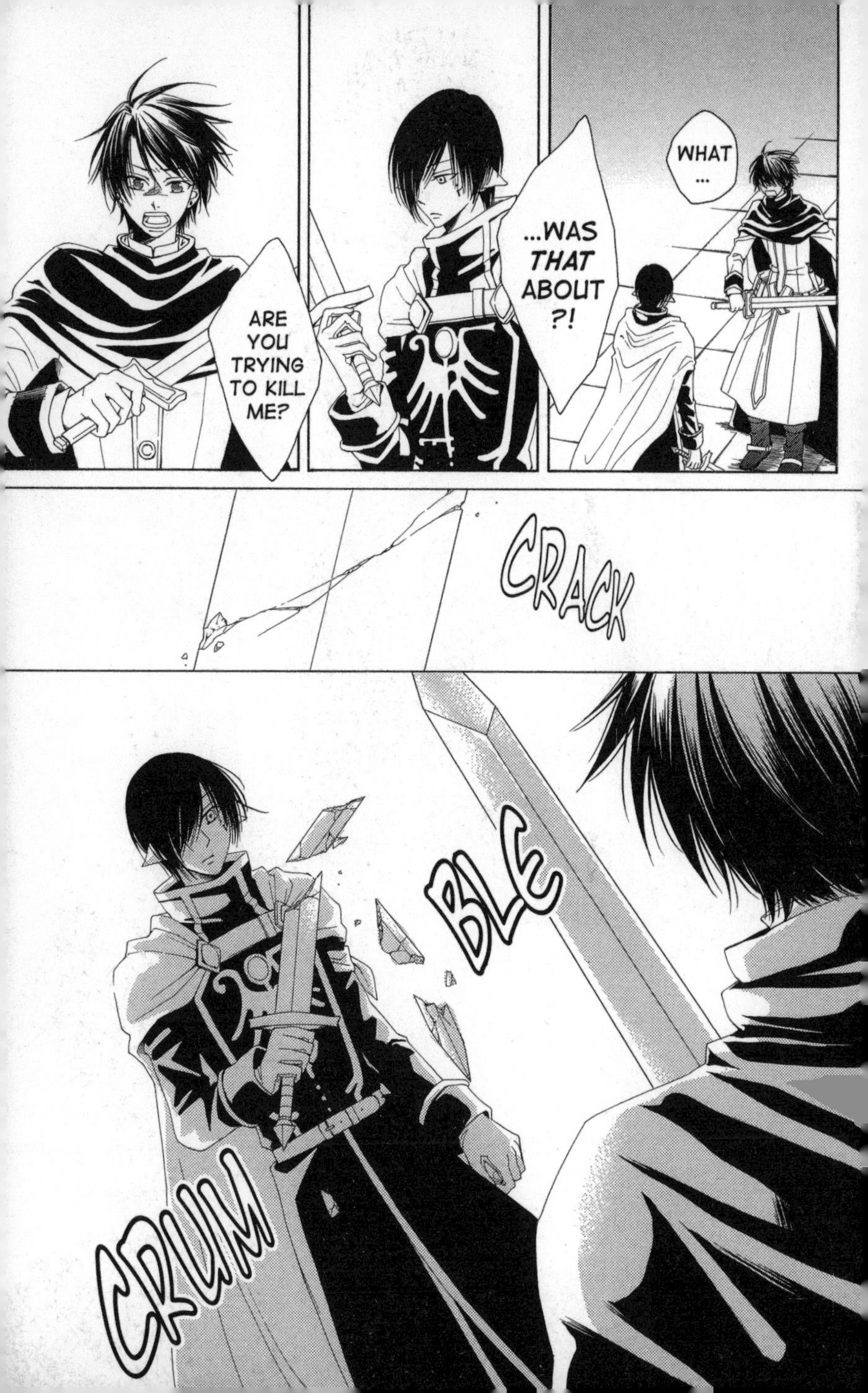

WHAT ...
...WAS *THAT* ABOUT?!
ARE YOU TRYING TO KILL ME?
CRACK
CRUM
BLE

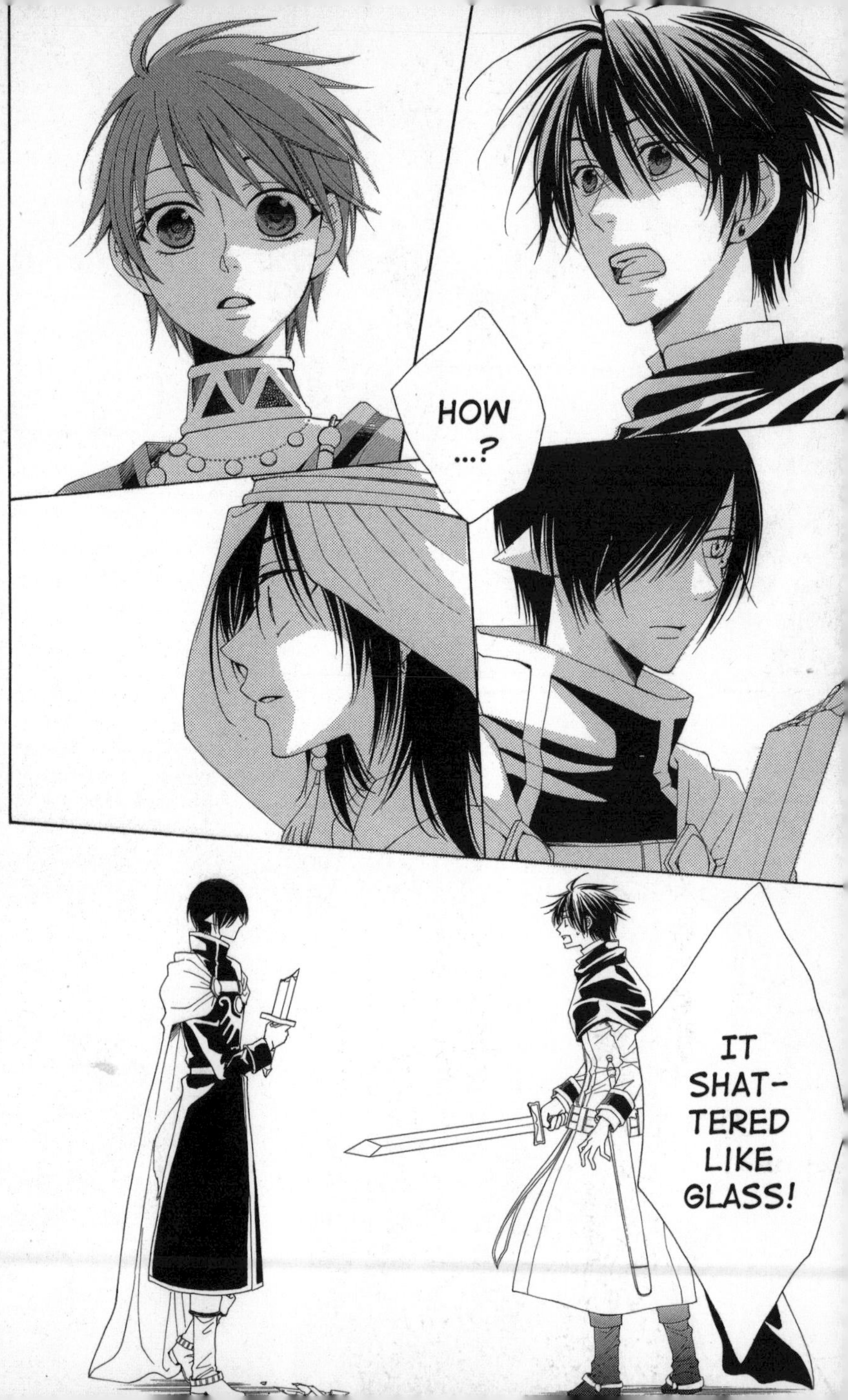
HOW ...?
IT SHAT-TERED LIKE GLASS!

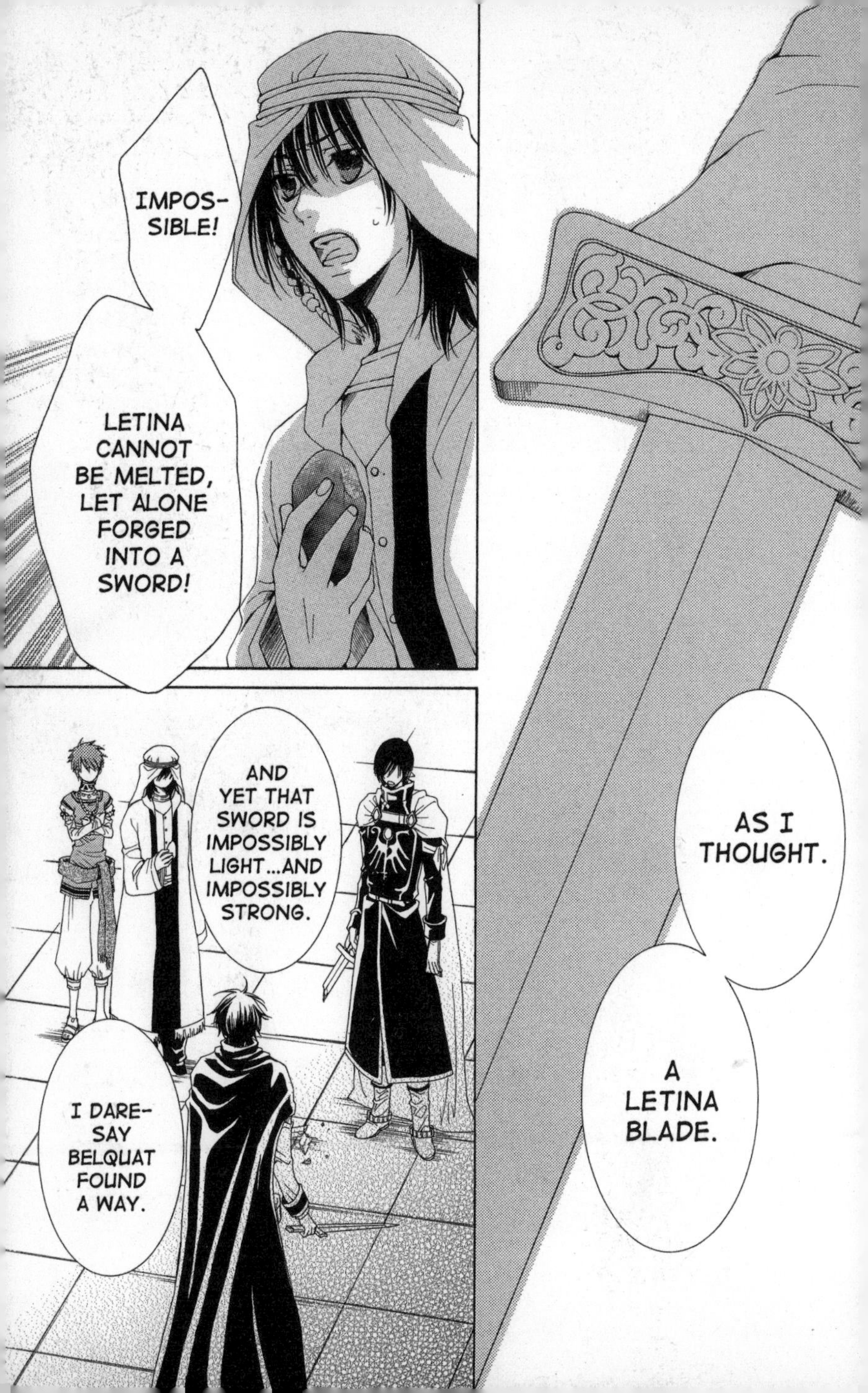
AS I THOUGHT.
A LETINA BLADE.
IMPOS-SIBLE!
LETINA CANNOT BE MELTED, LET ALONE FORGED INTO A SWORD!
AND YET THAT SWORD IS IMPOSSIBLY LIGHT...AND IMPOSSIBLY STRONG.
I DARE-SAY BELQUAT FOUND A WAY.

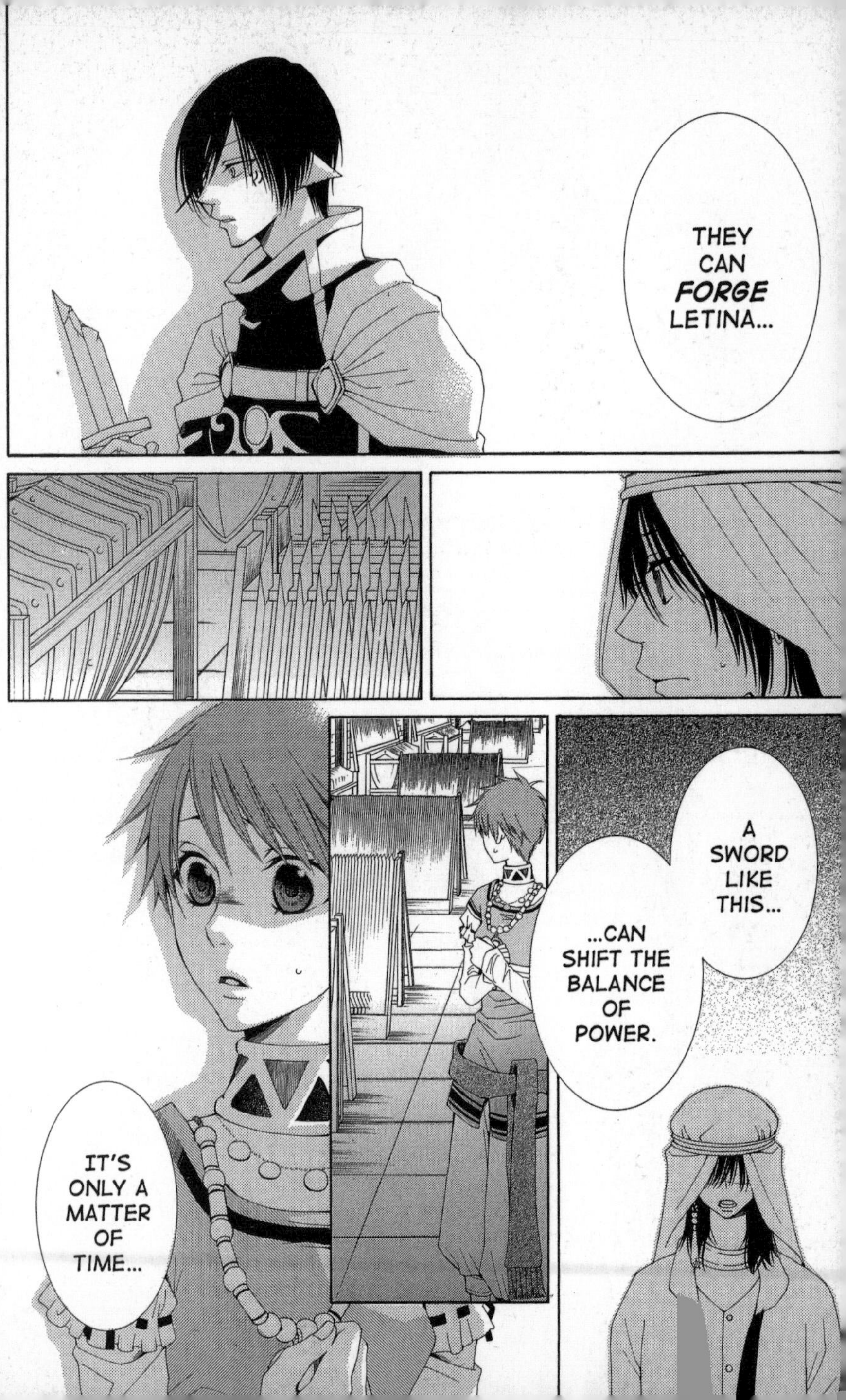
THEY CAN *FORGE* LETINA...
A SWORD LIKE THIS...
...CAN SHIFT THE BALANCE OF POWER.
IT'S ONLY A MATTER OF TIME...

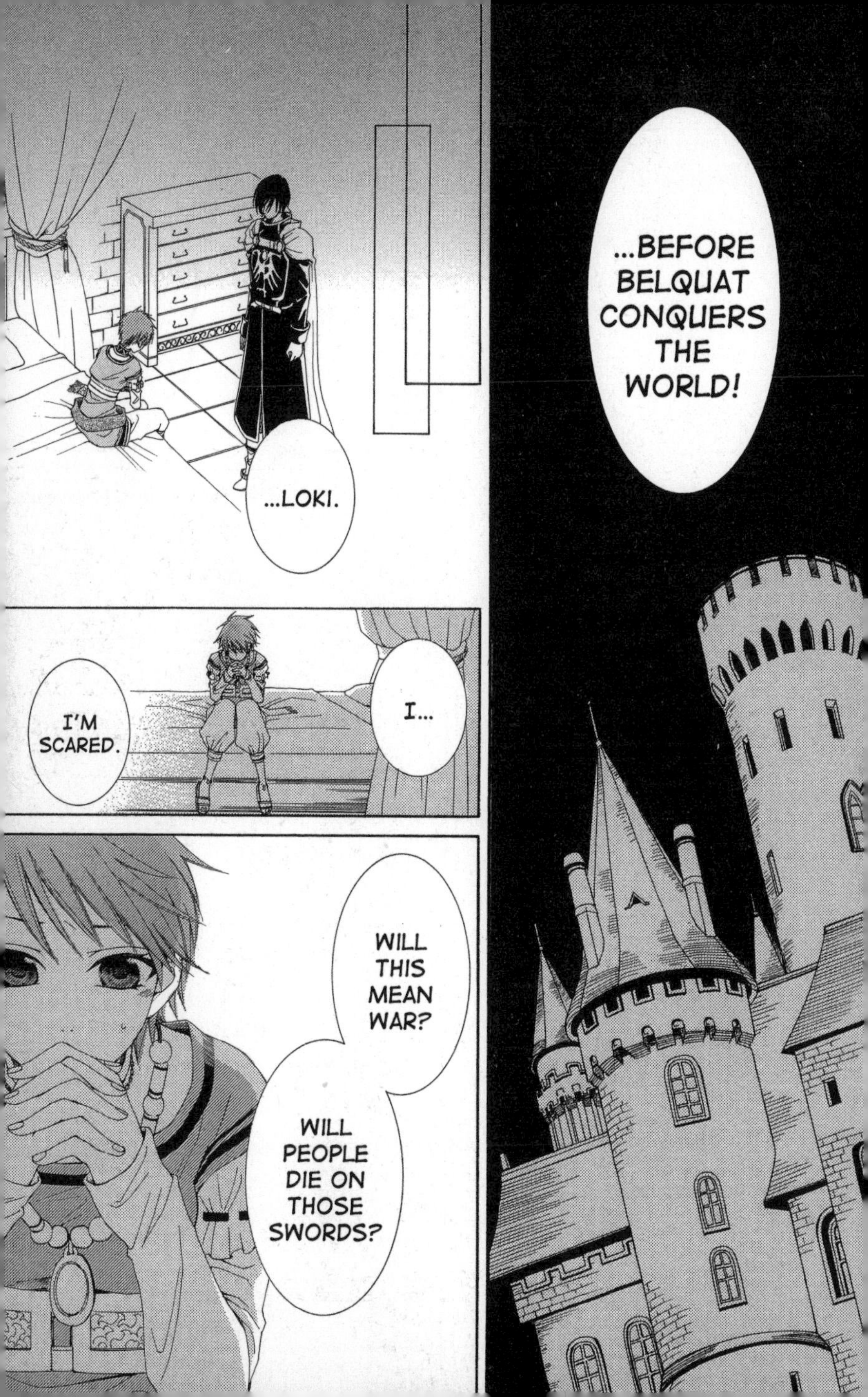
...BEFORE BELQUAT CONQUERS THE WORLD!
...LOKI.
I...
I'M SCARED.
WILL THIS MEAN WAR?
WILL PEOPLE DIE ON THOSE SWORDS?

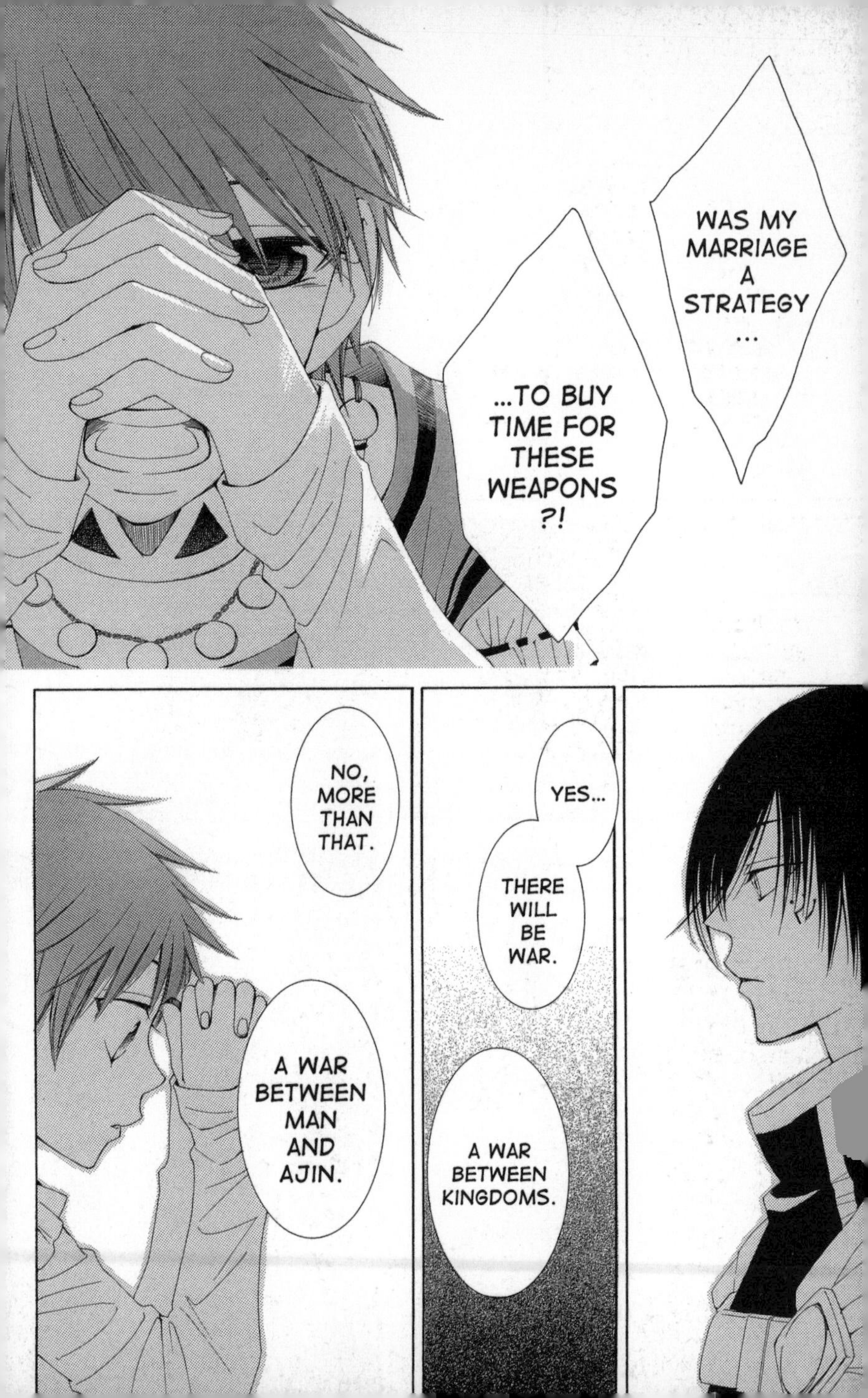
WAS MY MARRIAGE A STRATEGY...
...TO BUY TIME FOR THESE WEAPONS?!
YES...
THERE WILL BE WAR.
A WAR BETWEEN KINGDOMS.
NO, MORE THAN THAT.
A WAR BETWEEN MAN AND AJIN.

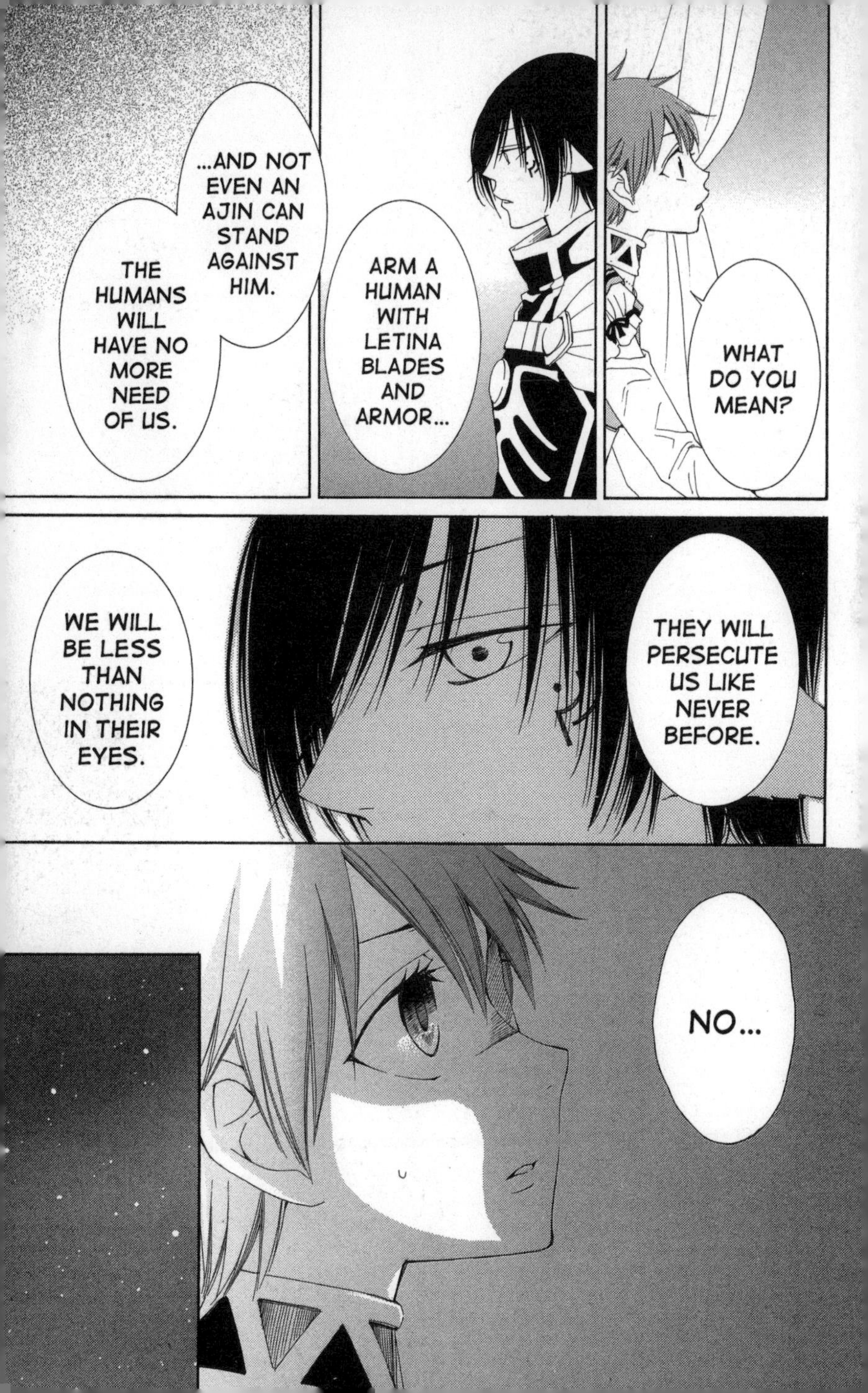
WHAT DO YOU MEAN?
ARM A HUMAN WITH LETINA BLADES AND ARMOR...
...AND NOT EVEN AN AJIN CAN STAND AGAINST HIM.
THE HUMANS WILL HAVE NO MORE NEED OF US.
THEY WILL PERSECUTE US LIKE NEVER BEFORE.
WE WILL BE LESS THAN NOTHING IN THEIR EYES.
NO...

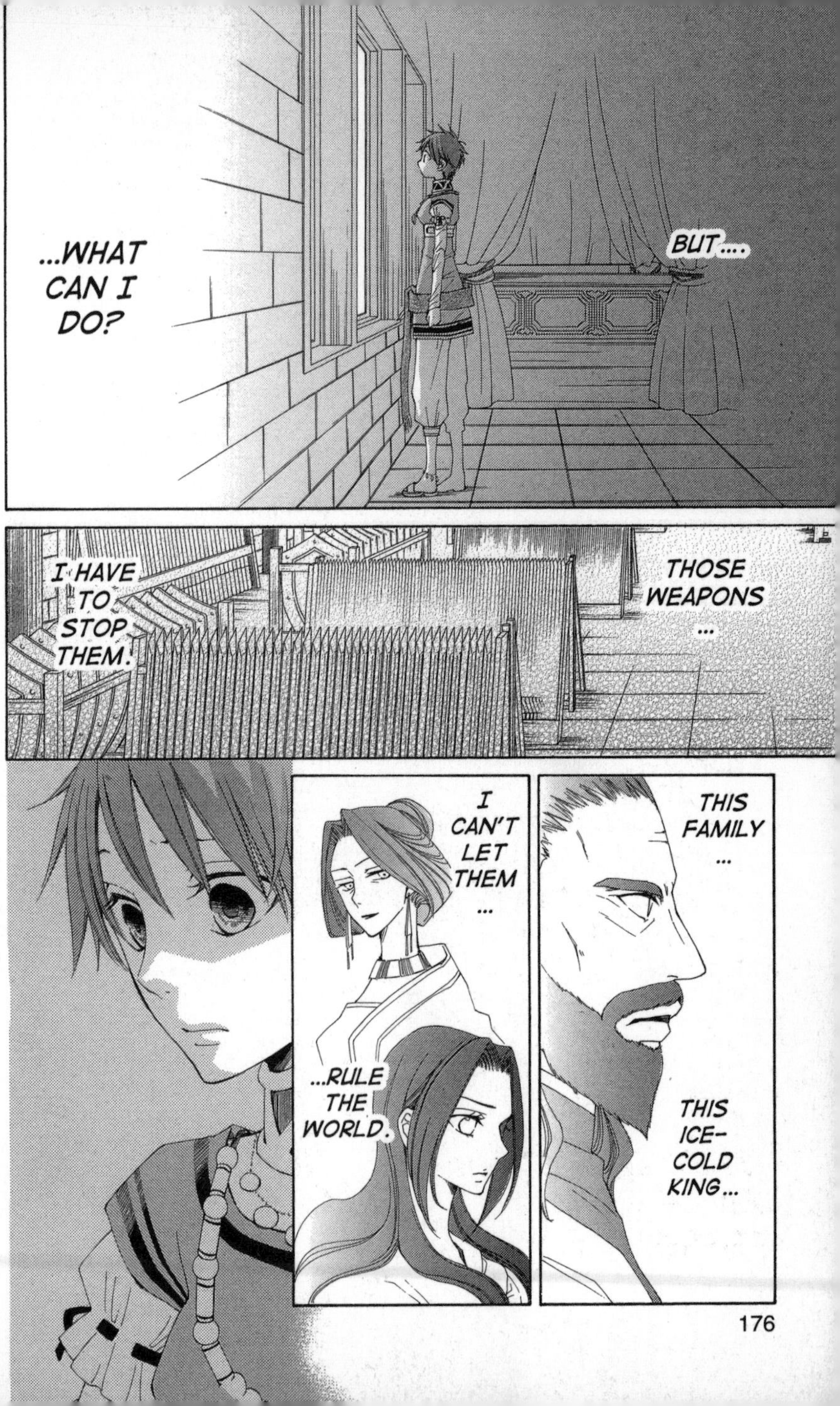
BUT....
...WHAT CAN I DO?
THOSE WEAPONS ...
I HAVE TO STOP THEM.
THIS FAMILY ...
THIS ICE-COLD KING...
I CAN'T LET THEM ...
...RULE THE WORLD.

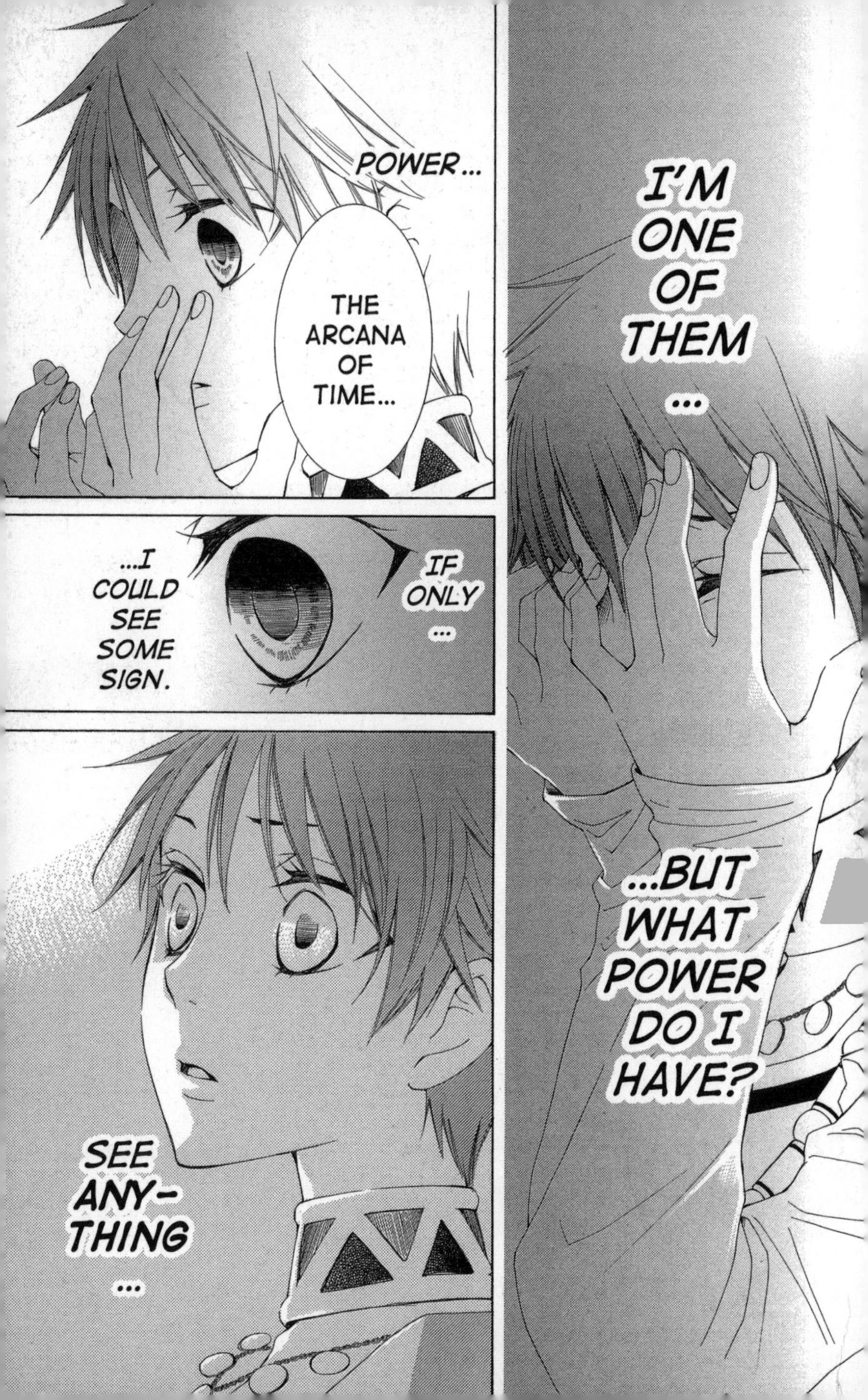
I'M ONE OF THEM ...
...BUT WHAT POWER DO I HAVE?
POWER...
THE ARCANA OF TIME...
IF ONLY ...
...I COULD SEE SOME SIGN.
SEE ANY-THING ...

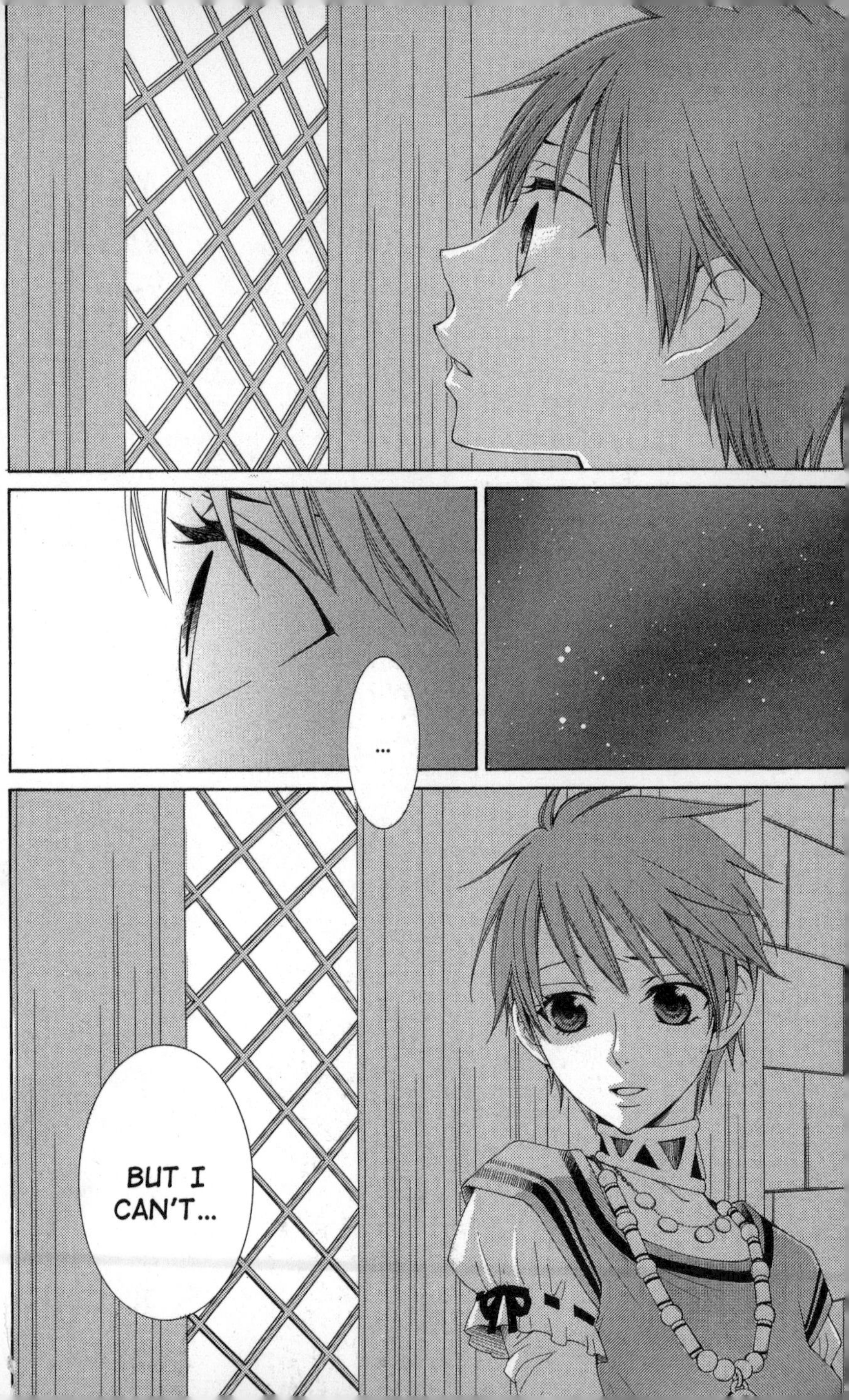
...
BUT I CAN'T...

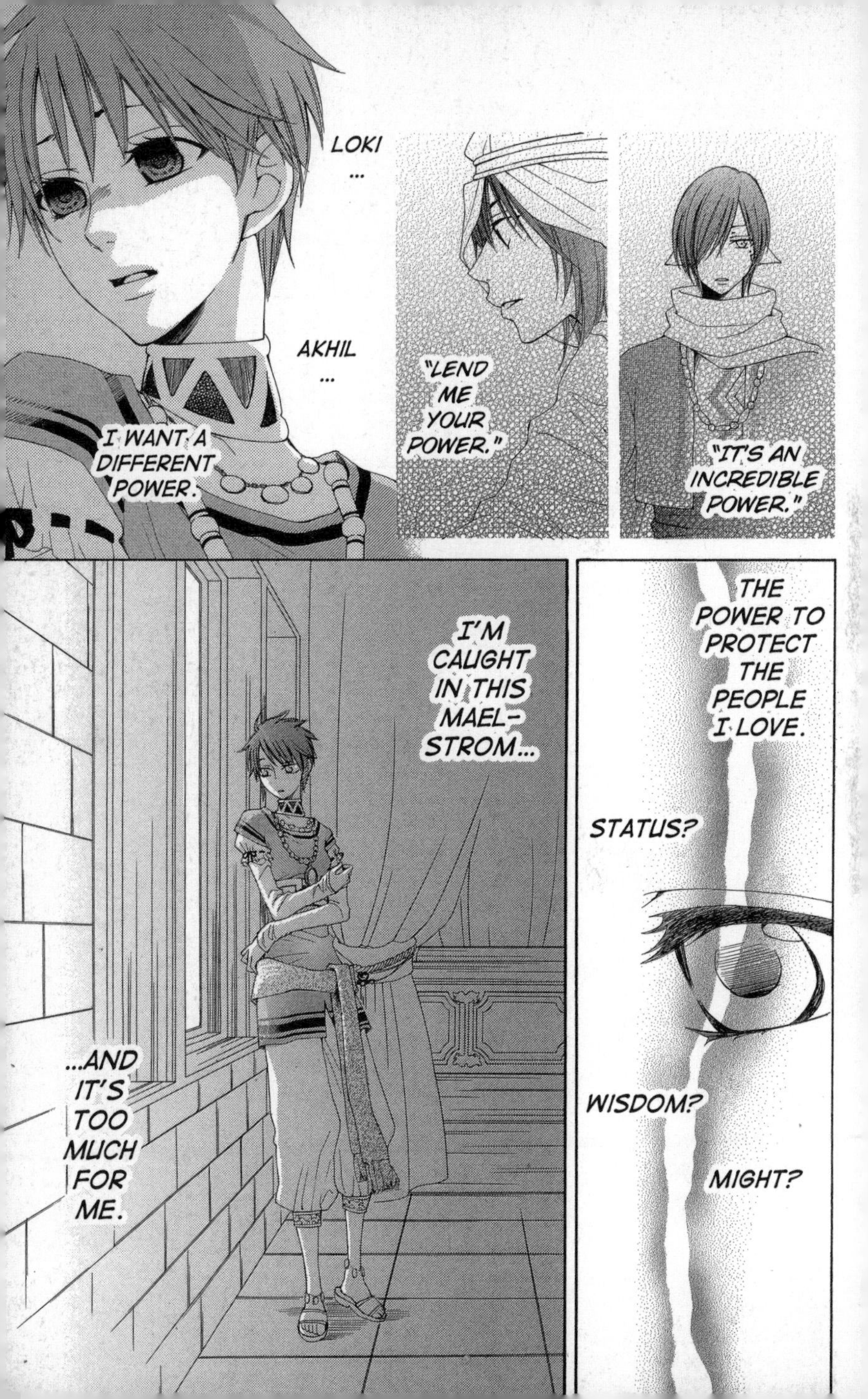
"IT'S AN INCREDIBLE POWER."
"LEND ME YOUR POWER."
LOKI ...
AKHIL ...
I WANT A DIFFERENT POWER.
THE POWER TO PROTECT THE PEOPLE I LOVE.
STATUS?
WISDOM?
MIGHT?
I'M CAUGHT IN THIS MAEL-STROM...
...AND IT'S TOO MUCH FOR ME.

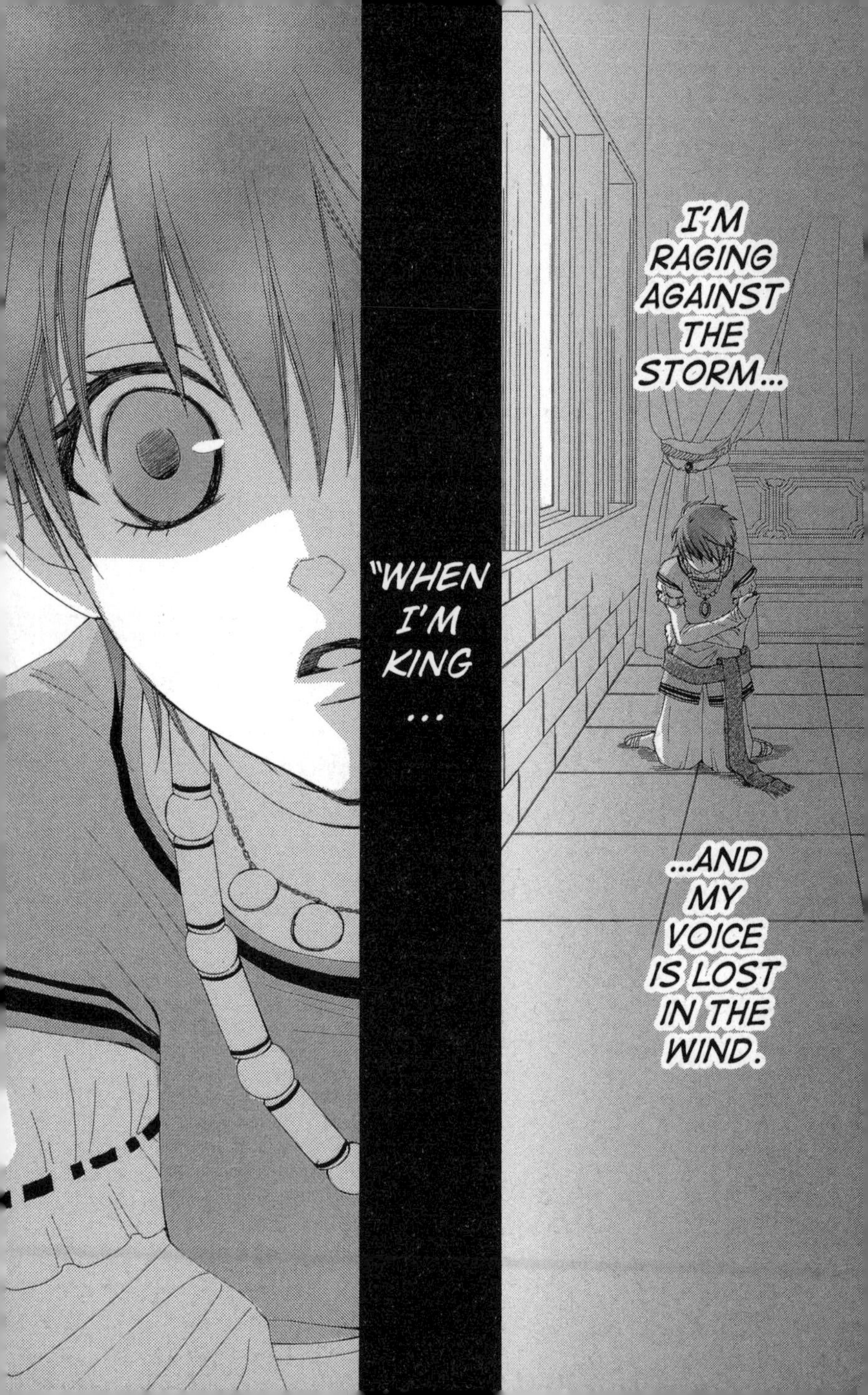
I'M RAGING AGAINST THE STORM...
...AND MY VOICE IS LOST IN THE WIND.
"WHEN I'M KING ...

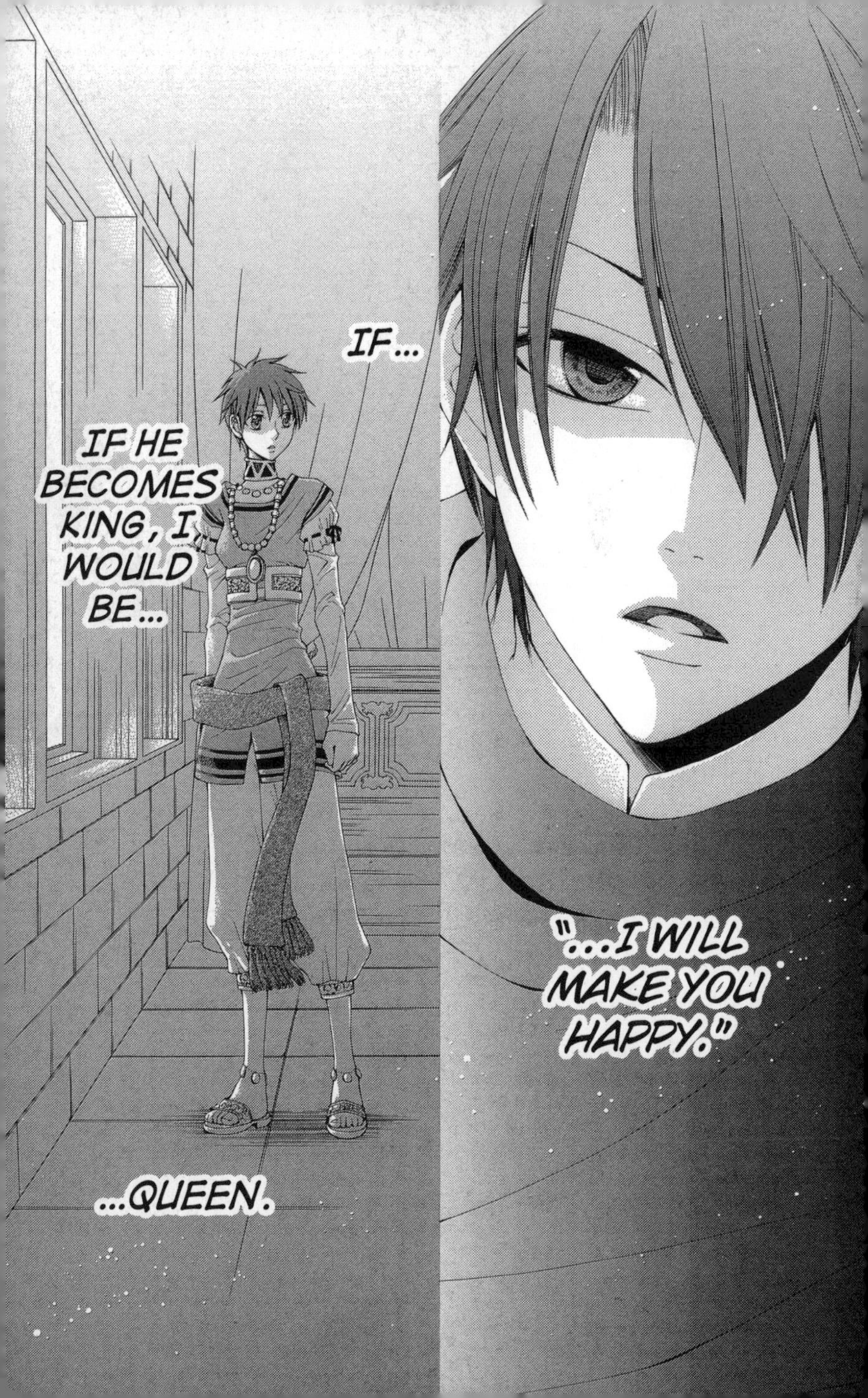
"...I WILL MAKE YOU HAPPY."
IF...
IF HE BECOMES KING, I WOULD BE...
...QUEEN.

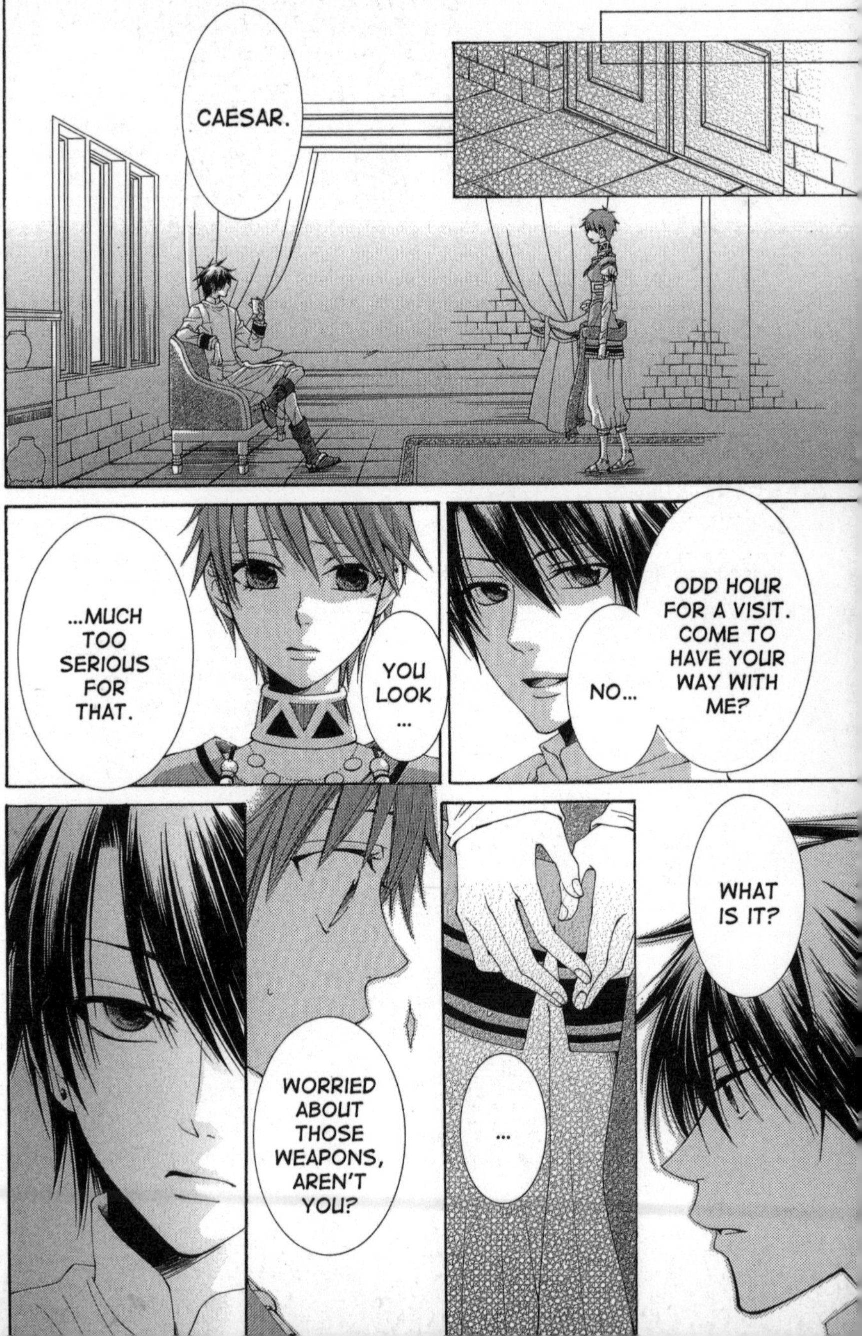
CAESAR.
ODD HOUR FOR A VISIT. COME TO HAVE YOUR WAY WITH ME?
NO...
YOU LOOK ...
...MUCH TOO SERIOUS FOR THAT.
WHAT IS IT?
...
WORRIED ABOUT THOSE WEAPONS, AREN'T YOU?

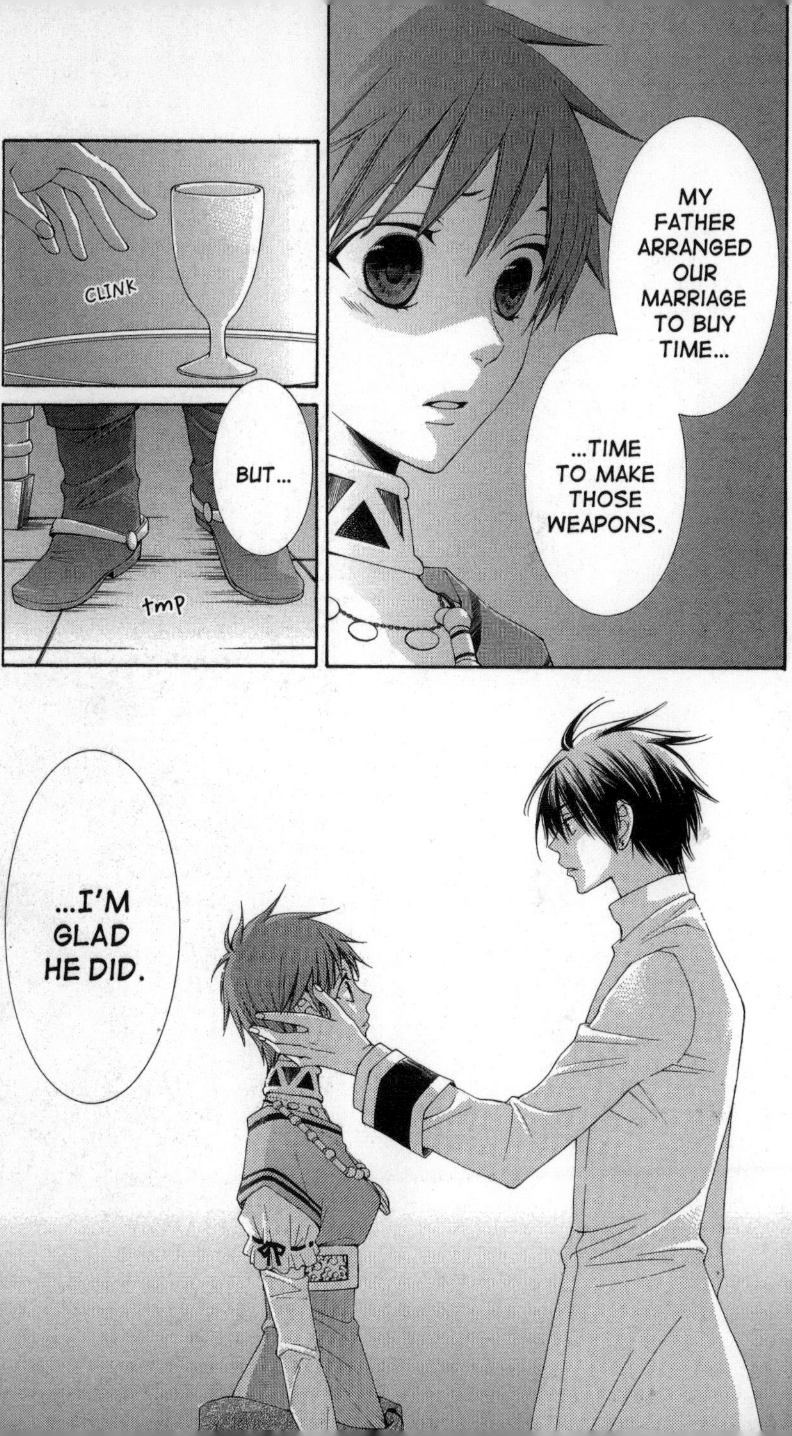
MY FATHER ARRANGED OUR MARRIAGE TO BUY TIME...
...TIME TO MAKE THOSE WEAPONS.
CLINK
BUT...
tmp
...I'M GLAD HE DID.

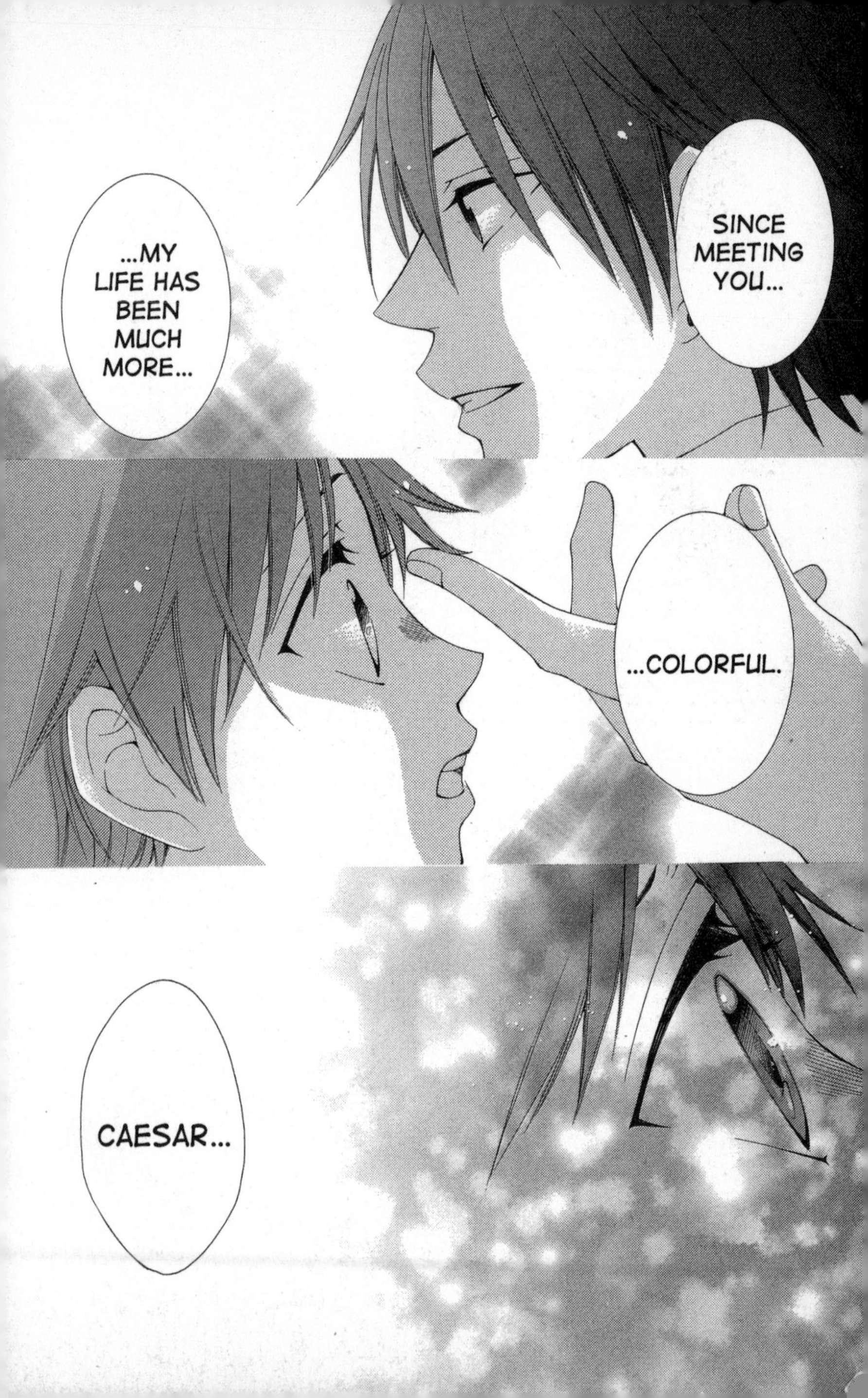
SINCE MEETING YOU...
...MY LIFE HAS BEEN MUCH MORE...
...COLORFUL.
CAESAR...

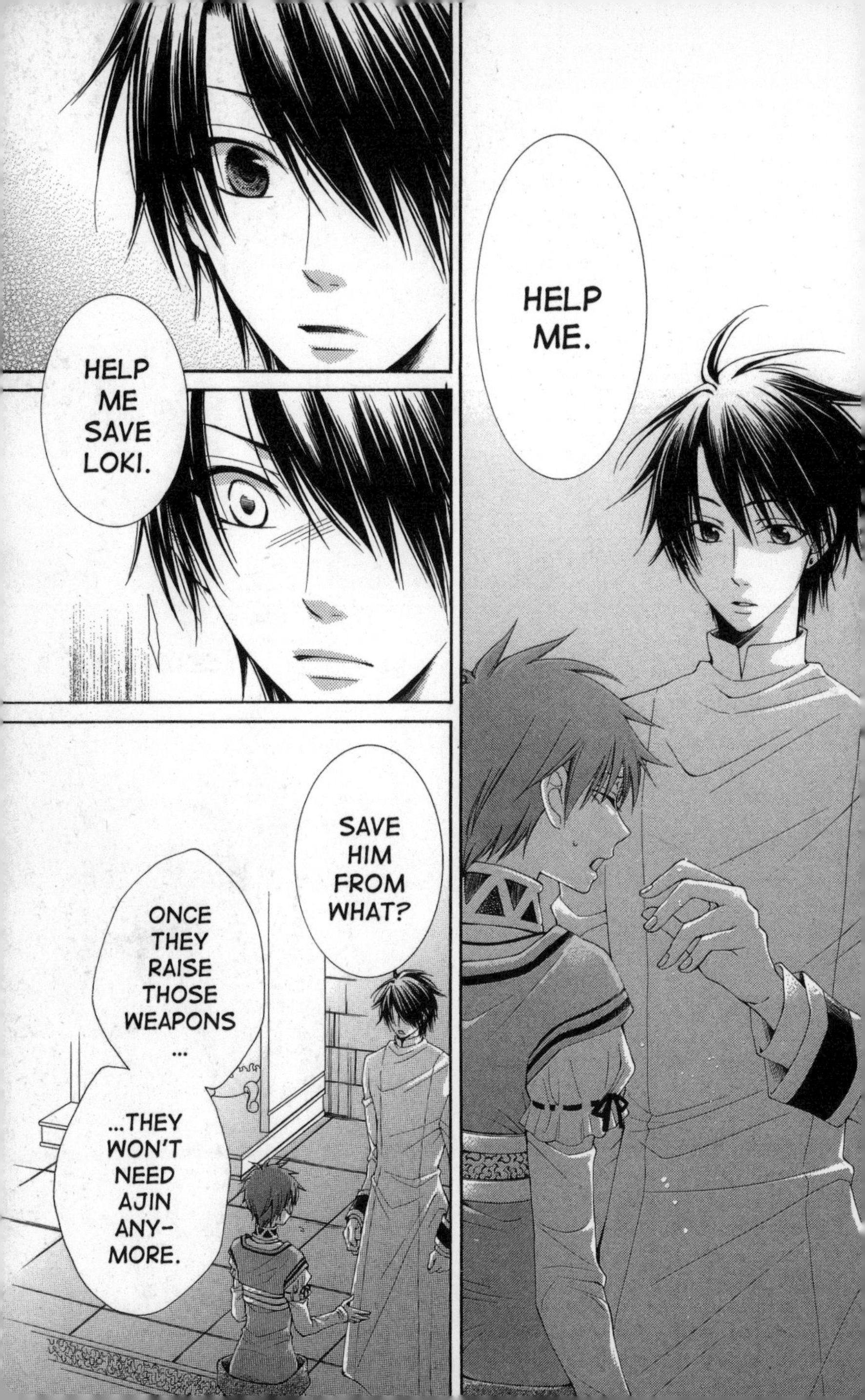
HELP ME.
HELP ME SAVE LOKI.
SAVE HIM FROM WHAT?
ONCE THEY RAISE THOSE WEAPONS ...
...THEY WON'T NEED AJIN ANY-MORE.

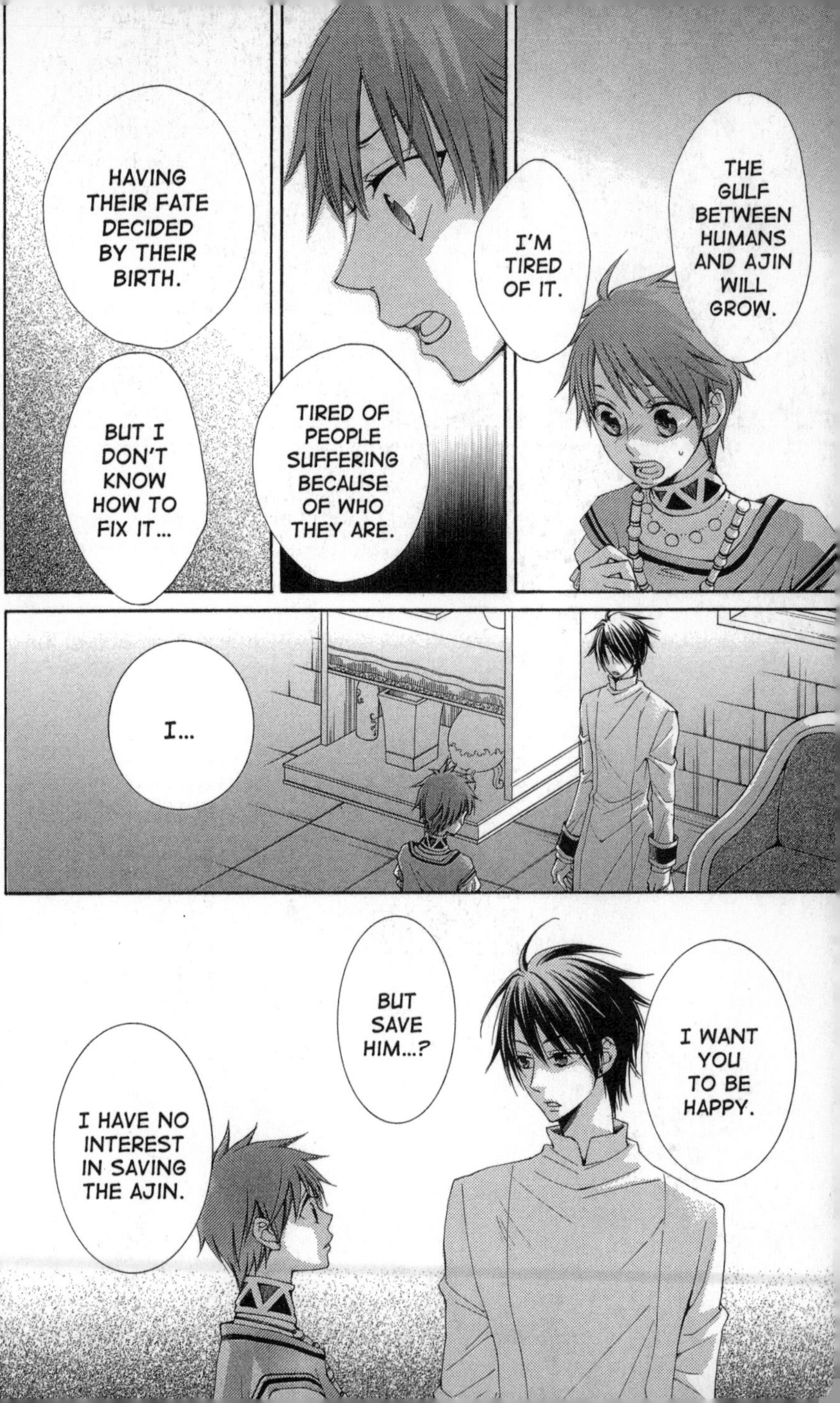
THE GULF BETWEEN HUMANS AND AJIN WILL GROW.
I'M TIRED OF IT.
TIRED OF PEOPLE SUFFERING BECAUSE OF WHO THEY ARE.
HAVING THEIR FATE DECIDED BY THEIR BIRTH.
BUT I DON'T KNOW HOW TO FIX IT...
I...
I WANT YOU TO BE HAPPY.
BUT SAVE HIM...?
I HAVE NO INTEREST IN SAVING THE AJIN.

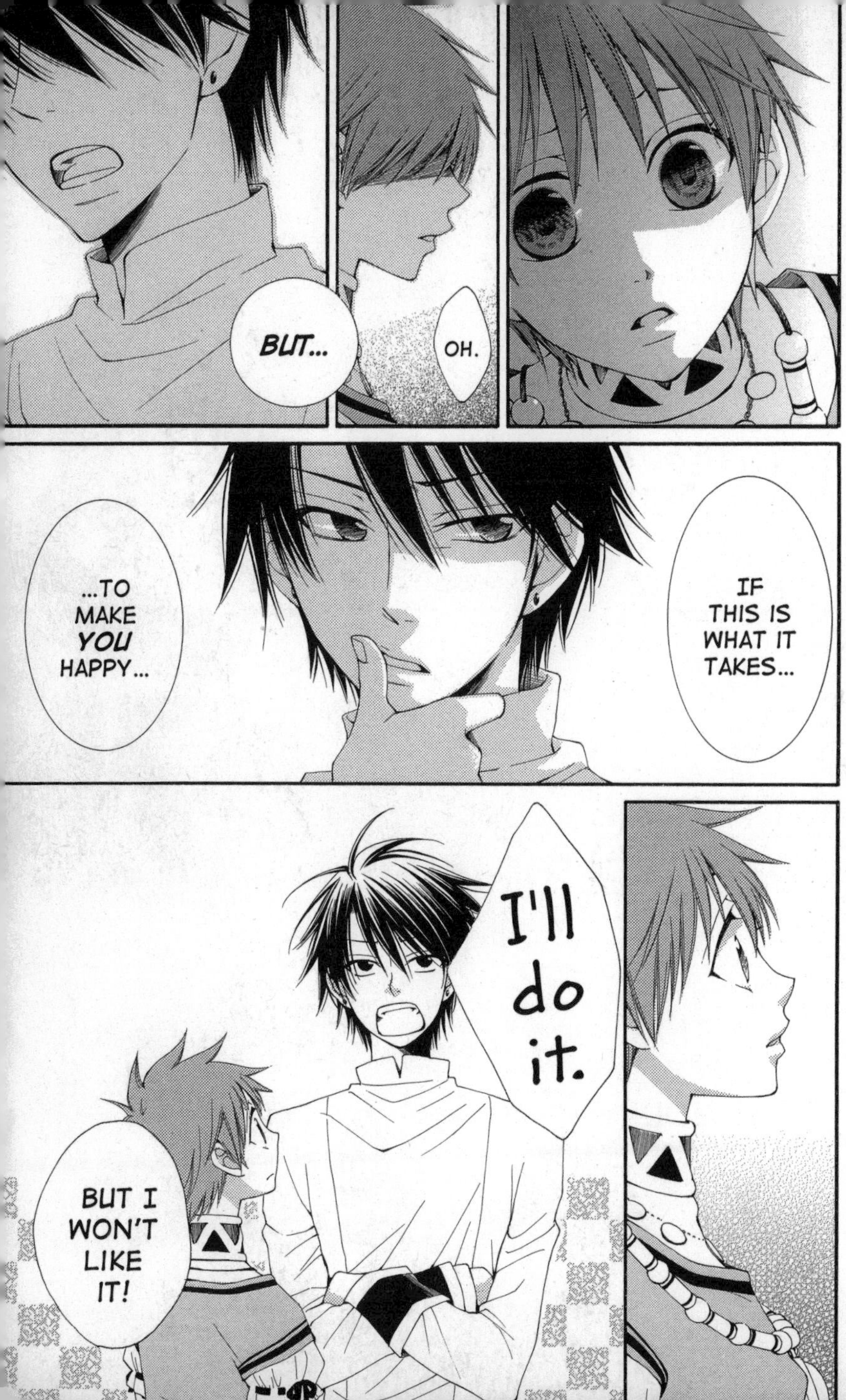
OH.
BUT...
IF THIS IS WHAT IT TAKES...
...TO MAKE YOU HAPPY...
I'll do it.
BUT I WON'T LIKE IT!

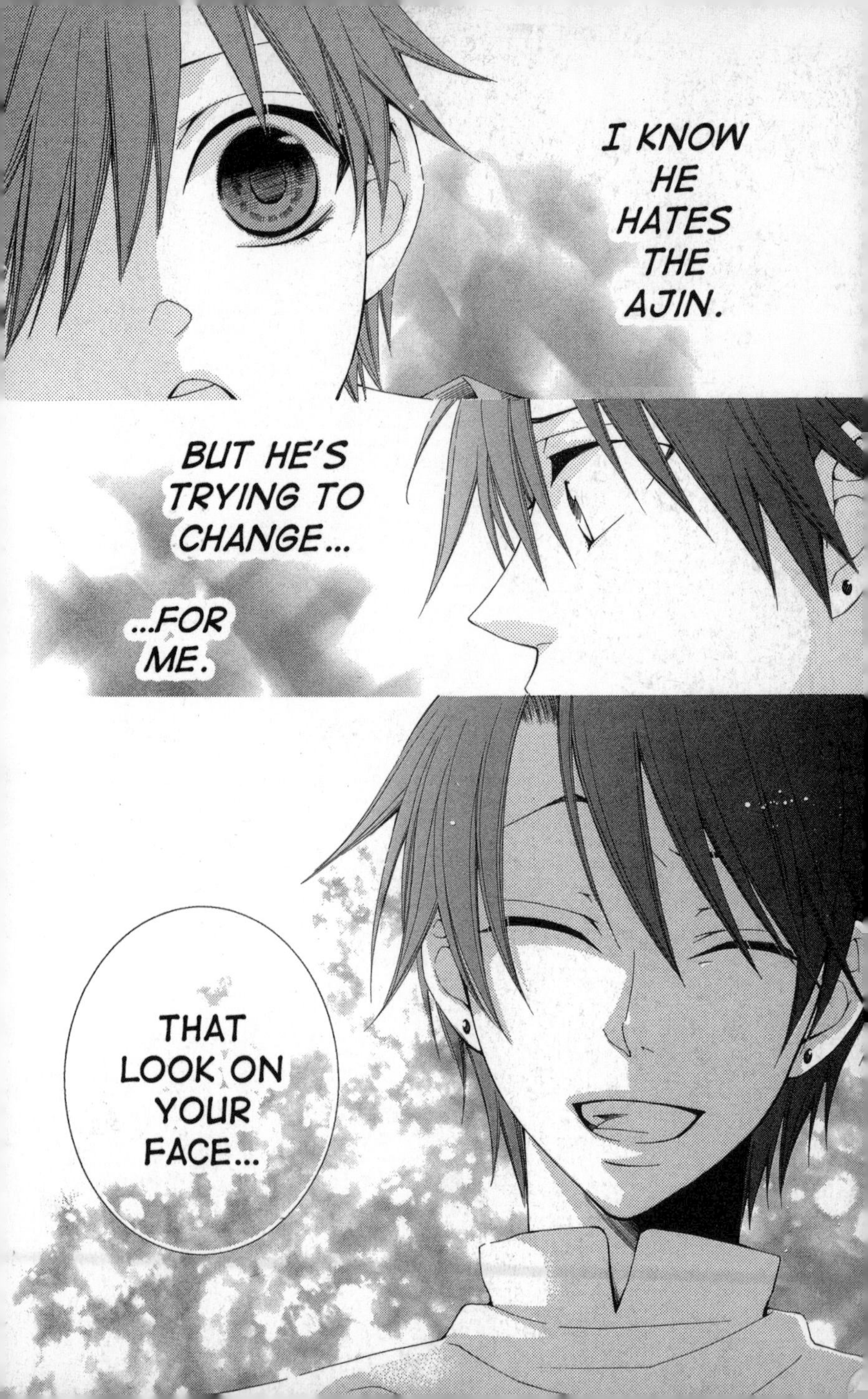
I KNOW HE HATES THE AJIN.
BUT HE'S TRYING TO CHANGE...
...FOR ME.
THAT LOOK ON YOUR FACE...

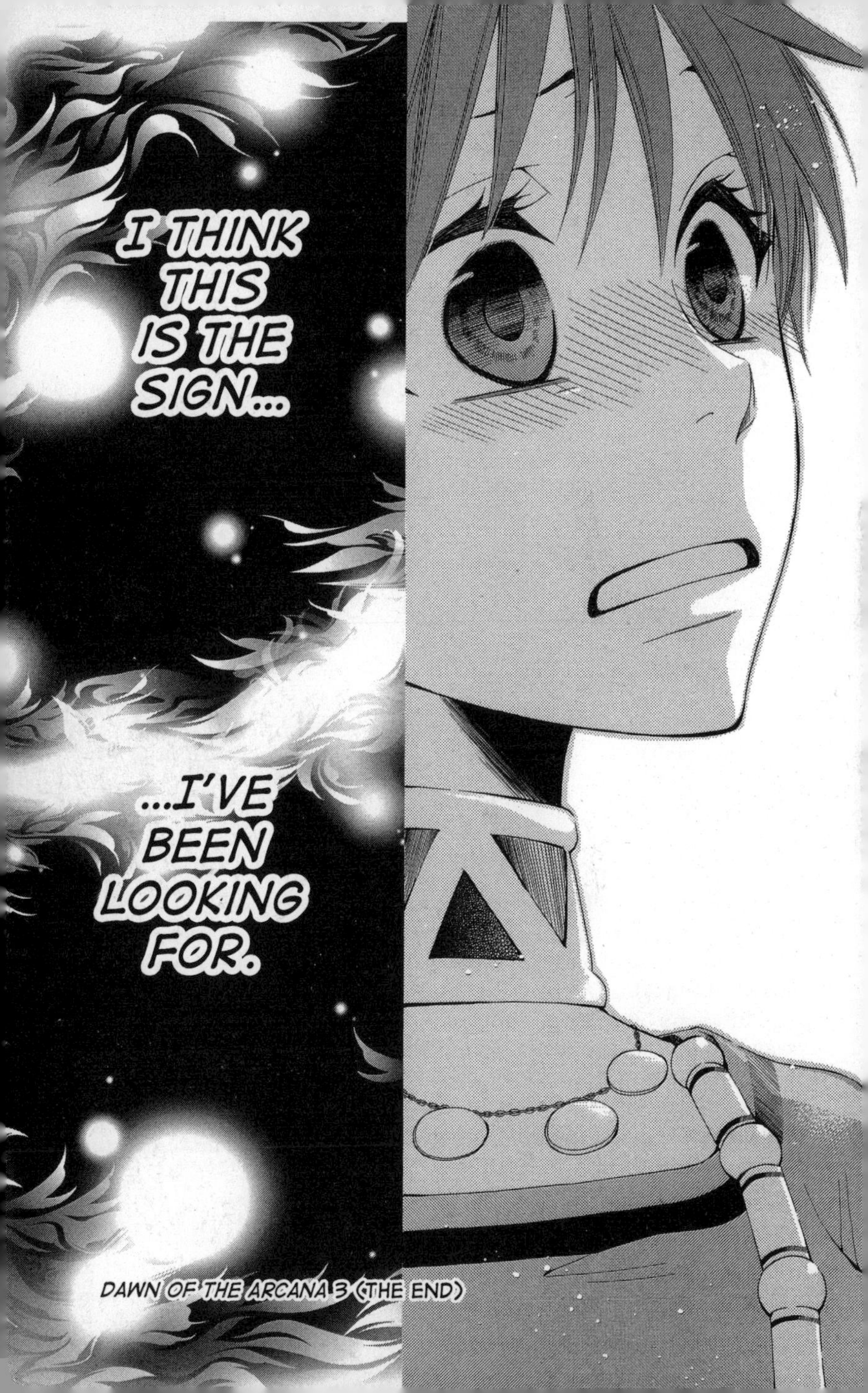
I THINK THIS IS THE SIGN...
...I'VE BEEN LOOKING FOR.
DAWN OF THE ARCANA 3 (THE END)

I forgot to update this little doodle for volume 2.
Sorry! (*laugh*)

–Rei Toma

Rei Toma has been drawing since childhood, but she only began drawing manga because of her graduation project in design school. When she drew a short-story manga, *Help Me, Dentist,* for the first time, it attracted a publisher's attention and she made her debut right away. Her magnificent art style became popular, and after she debuted as a manga artist, she became known as an illustrator for novels and video game character designs. Her current manga series, *Dawn of the Arcana,* is her first long-running manga series, and it has been a hit in Japan, selling over a million copies.

DAWN OF THE ARCANA
VOLUME 3
Shojo Beat Edition

STORY AND ART BY
REI TOMA

© 2009 Rei TOMA/Shogakukan
All rights reserved.
Original Japanese edition "REIMEI NO ARCANA"
published by SHOGAKUKAN Inc.

Translation & Adaptation/Kajiya Productions
Touch-up Art & Lettering/Freeman Wong
Design/Yukiko Whitley
Editor/Amy Yu

Printed in the U.S.A.

Published by VIZ Media, LLC
P.O. Box 77010
San Francisco, CA 94107

10 9 8 7 6 5 4 3 2 1
First printing, April 2012

www.viz.com   www.shojobeat.com

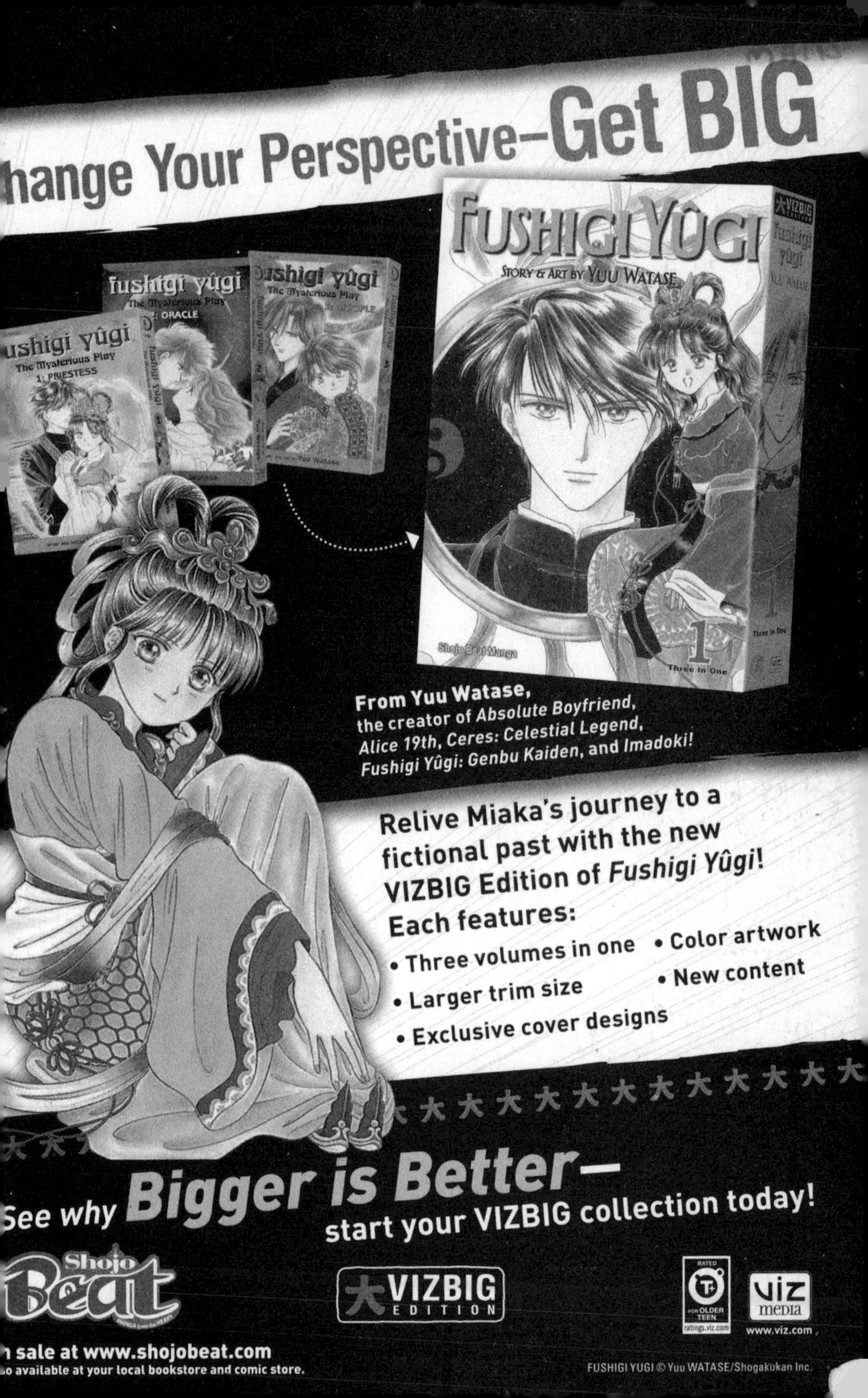
hange Your Perspective–Get BIG
FUSHIGI YÛGI
STORY & ART BY YUU WATASE
Shojo Beat Manga
1
Three in One
fushigi yûgi
The Mysterious Play
1: PRIESTESS
2: ORACLE
From Yuu Watase,
the creator of Absolute Boyfriend,
Alice 19th, Ceres: Celestial Legend,
Fushigi Yûgi: Genbu Kaiden, and Imadoki!
Relive Miaka's journey to a fictional past with the new VIZBIG Edition of Fushigi Yûgi!
Each features:
• Three volumes in one
• Larger trim size
• Exclusive cover designs
• Color artwork
• New content
See why Bigger is Better—
start your VIZBIG collection today!
Shojo Beat
VIZBIG EDITION
RATED T+ FOR OLDER TEEN ratings.viz.com
viz media
www.viz.com
n sale at www.shojobeat.com
o available at your local bookstore and comic store.
FUSHIGI YUGI © Yuu WATASE/Shogakukan Inc.